W9-DHV-561

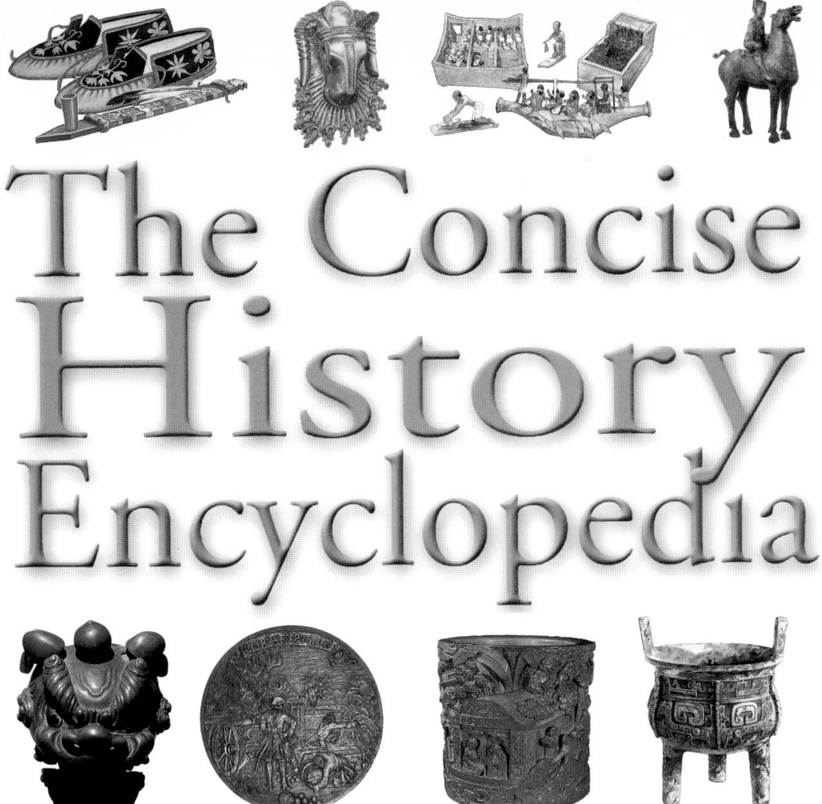

The Concise History Encyclopedia

KINGFISHER
Larousse Kingfisher Chambers Inc.
80 Maiden Lane
New York, New York 10038
www.kingfisherpub.com

First published as *The Kingfisher History Encyclopedia*
by Kingfisher Publications Plc in 1999
Reprinted in a revised format by Kingfisher Publications Plc 2001

2 4 6 8 10 9 7 5 3 1
ITR/0701/SF/UNV(RNB)/157MA

LIBRARY OF CONGRESS CATALOGING-IN-PUBLICATION DATA
has been applied for.

ISBN 0-7534-5417-3

Printed in China

PROJECT TEAM
Project Director and Art Editor Julian Holland
Editorial team Julian Holland, Norman Brooke
Designers Julian Holland, Nigel White/RWS Studio
Picture Research Anne-Marie Ehrlich, Josie Bradbury
Maps Jeffrey Farrow

FOR KINGFISHER
Managing Editor Miranda Smith
Senior Editor Aimee Johnson
Editor Dileri Johnston
Art Director Mike Davis
DTP Coordinator Nicky Studdart
DTP Operator Primrose Burton
Artwork Research Katie Puckett
Production Manager Oonagh Phelan

CONTRIBUTORS
Teresa Chris, Neil Grant, Ken Hills, Julian Holland, Palden Jenkins,
Elizabeth Longley, Fiona Macdonald, Hazel Martell,
Mike McGuire, Theodore Rowland-Entwhistle

This edition produced in 2001 by PAGE*One*

The Concise History Encyclopedia

KINGfISHER
NEW YORK

CONTENTS

INTRODUCTION

Often, fact is stranger than fiction. *The Concise History Encyclopedia* is packed full of fascinating facts and real-life stories about the people, places, and events of the past that have shaped the colorful, but still turbulent world that we know today. The causes and effects of the actions and events are explained in full, giving a vivid picture of how leaders, tyrants, artists, and scientists who lived hundreds of years ago have left a legacy that still impinges on people's lives at the beginning of the twenty-first century.

Use *The Concise History Encyclopedia* to discover past events and find out how people have lived their lives over the last 40,000 years—from Stone Age cave dwellers to the Anglo-Saxons, from the Aztecs and Incas of Mesoamerica to the Manchus in China, and from the American Revolution to United Nations peacekeeping.

This user-friendly encyclopedia contains many features to help you look things up easily, or just have fun browsing. The in-depth coverage of each historical period also makes the encyclopedia perfect for all your school projects and homework assignments.

The clear, informative text is accompanied by key date boxes, colorful photographs, and superb illustrations and maps. At-a-glance world maps at the beginning of each chapter highlight the major events that happened during a particular time period. These are arranged according to continent or area of the world.

Whether you use *The Concise History Encyclopedia* for homework, or just dip into it at random, it will add considerably to your understanding of the past, and will stimulate you to explore the lives of our ancestors further.

◀ Man-made structures tell us a great deal about the past. One of the largest and most famous is the Great Wall of China. Its construction was ordered by the first Qin emperor, Shi Huangdi, around 221 B.C., to keep out invaders from the north. Stretching for 4,000 mi. (6,400km), the wall was built by joining together shorter walls that had been built earlier. The wall has been rebuilt many times. Most of the wall that can be seen today was constructed during the Ming dynasty (1368–1644).

The Ancient World

40,000–500 B.C.

This is the earliest history of humanity, as it evolved from cave dwellers to village-dwelling farmers to populations in towns, up to and including the first advanced civilizations. It was around 40,000 B.C. that humans first built their own homes, made music, and painted pictures on the walls of caves. It was not until around 8000 B.C. that the first farming and trading villages were built, and another 5,000 years—250 generations—passed before important civilizations appeared in Egypt and Mesopotamia.

▲ The first peoples lived in caves and made fire by using a bow to spin a stick against another piece of wood to create sparks.

◀ The ancient Egyptians believed in life after death. They worshiped many gods, including Osiris, the god of the dead, whose image is seen here in a painting on the tomb of Horemheb.

THE WORLD AT A GLANCE 40,000–500 B.C

Though there is fossil evidence that the earliest humans evolved at least 130,000 years ago on the continent of Africa, their lives were extremely simple compared to ours. By 40,000 B.C., humans had learned how to use fire to keep themselves warm, cook food, and scare away wild animals. From being hunters and gatherers of wild fruit, berries, and seeds, they slowly found out how to grow crops and keep domestic animals. Around 8000 B.C., life became more complex as farming villages developed in the Middle East. It was much later that other parts of the world developed in this way. During the next 3,000 years, important basic activities such as building, tilling the land, pottery, copperworking, sewing, and animal breeding were introduced.

It was not until 3000 B.C. that the first towns were built, beside rivers in Egypt, Mesopotamia, and China. By 2600 B.C., large constructions such as the pyramids in Egypt, the stone circles in eastern Europe, and the first temples in Peru were built. Around the same time, the people in the kingdom of Kush in East Africa were learning to work metal, and Chinese astronomers first observed an eclipse of the sun. Civilization had come into being.

NORTH AMERICA

MESOAMERICA AND SOUTH AMERICA

NORTH AMERICA

In ancient times, North Americans hunted animals and foraged for food on a vast continent with no civilizations. Although these peoples lived off the land, they still had their beliefs, medicines, tools, and simple homes. The first steps toward civilization were made about 700 B.C. by the Adena people in the woodlands of what is now Ohio. They built temple mounds, lived in villages, and worked with copper.

MESOAMERICA AND SOUTH AMERICA

Farming was established in Mexico (Mesoamerica) by 3000 B.C., and by 2000 B.C., the Peruvians of the Andes had also developed farming communities. The growing population lived in permanent villages and over hundreds of years these gradually grew larger and became towns. By 2600 B.C., large temples had been built on the coast of Peru—around the same time as the earliest stone circles in eastern Europe and the pyramids in Egypt began to appear. At the same time, the Olmec civilization emerged in Mexico. By 500 B.C., the Maya in Mexico were also building pyramids.

EUROPE

Farming communities sprang up in southeast Europe around 6000 B.C., though it was not until 4000 B.C. that they were established in the northwest. On the Atlantic seaboard, an advanced culture started building mounds and stone circles from around 4000 B.C. The oldest of these are in Ireland, and there are many impressive examples in England, Scotland, and Brittany in France. Later, in the period leading up to 500 B.C., the Celts dominated Europe though the most advanced town-building civilizations were those of the Mycenae in Greece and the Etruscans in Italy.

ASIA

There were four centers of development in Asia. In the Indus Valley (now Pakistan), an advanced civilization developed from around 2600 B.C. Although farming communities flourished in northern China from 4000 B.C., Chinese tradition has it that civilization was started there by the Yellow Emperor around 2700 B.C. The others centers were the Mekong Delta of southeast Asia, where rice-growing had developed, and New Guinea.

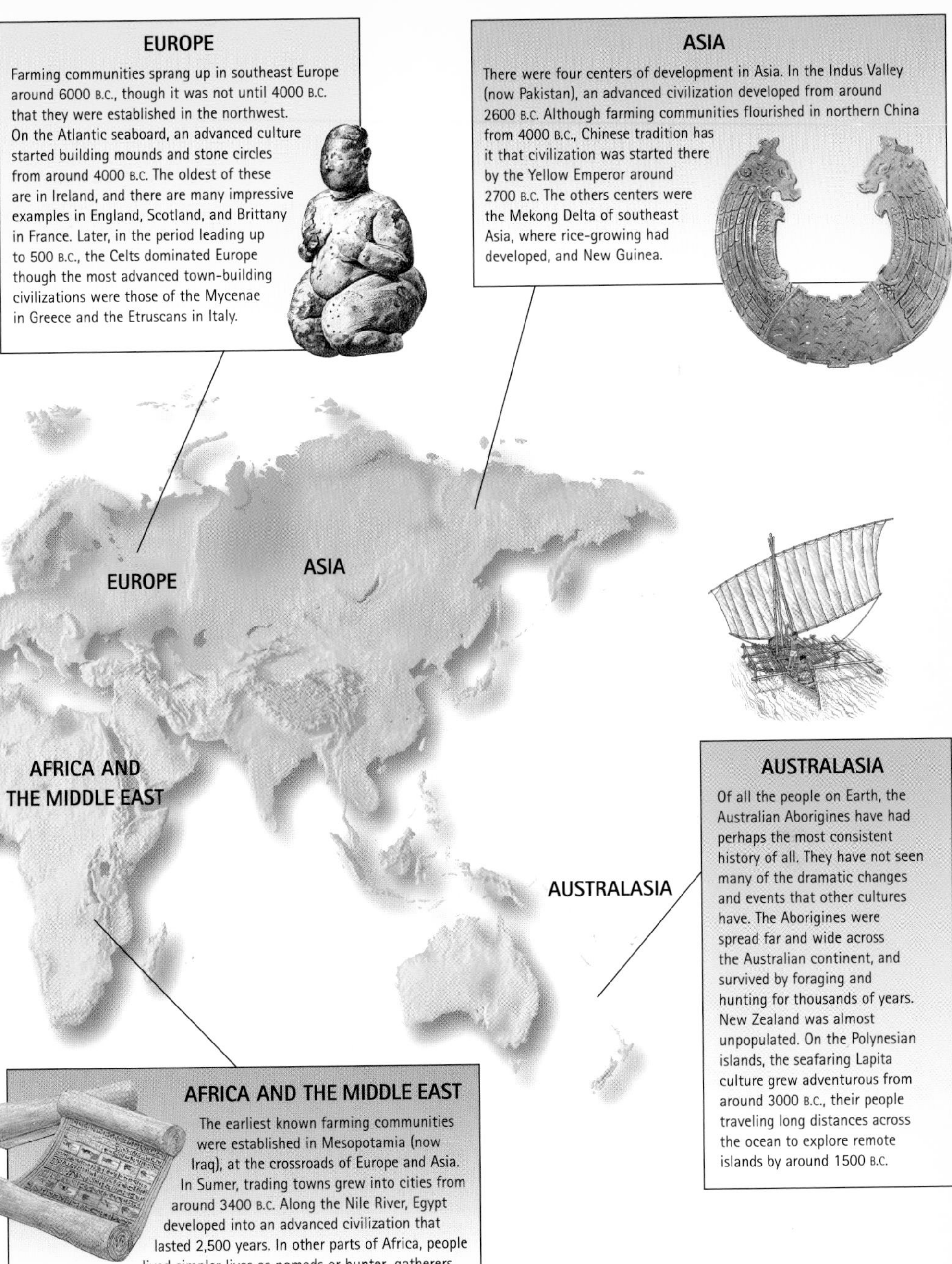

AUSTRALASIA

Of all the people on Earth, the Australian Aborigines have had perhaps the most consistent history of all. They have not seen many of the dramatic changes and events that other cultures have. The Aborigines were spread far and wide across the Australian continent, and survived by foraging and hunting for thousands of years. New Zealand was almost unpopulated. On the Polynesian islands, the seafaring Lapita culture grew adventurous from around 3000 B.C., their people traveling long distances across the ocean to explore remote islands by around 1500 B.C.

AFRICA AND THE MIDDLE EAST

The earliest known farming communities were established in Mesopotamia (now Iraq), at the crossroads of Europe and Asia. In Sumer, trading towns grew into cities from around 3400 B.C. Along the Nile River, Egypt developed into an advanced civilization that lasted 2,500 years. In other parts of Africa, people lived simpler lives as nomads or hunter–gatherers.

THE FIRST HUMANS 40,000 – 10,000 B.C.

The earliest humanlike creatures evolved over a period of several million years. Our closest true human ancestors have developed only within the last 50,000 years.

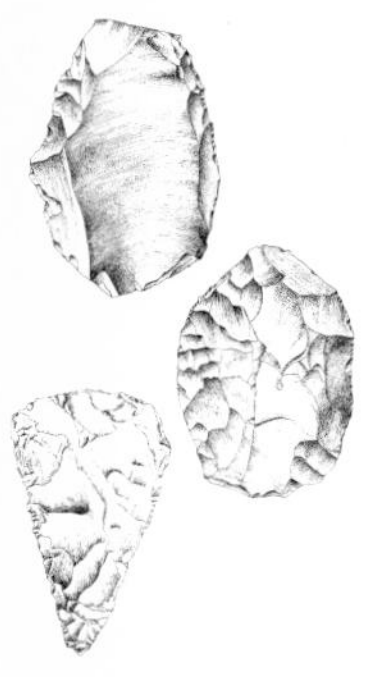

Early peoples used flints of different shapes for making scrapers, knives, arrowheads, and borers.

The earliest hominids (humanlike creatures) were the *Australopithecines.* Many of their bones have been found in East Africa. They walked upright and made simple tools from pebbles. They were probably not true humans because their brains were very small in comparison.

PROTOHUMANS

Homo habilis (handy human) appeared about two million years ago. This hominid had more skills, and lived alongside the last of the Australopithecines. The most advanced early human was *Homo erectus* (upright human), and remains have been found in Africa and Asia. By learning to use fire to cook and keep warm, *Homo erectus* was able to move from place to place.

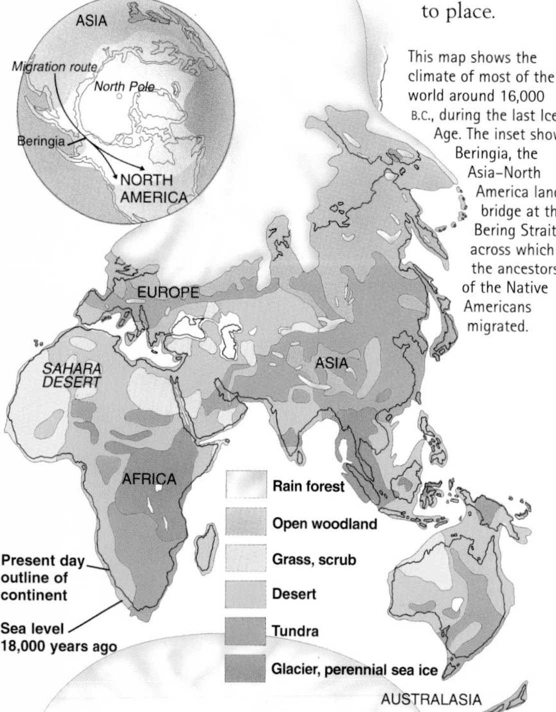

This map shows the climate of most of the world around 16,000 B.C., during the last Ice Age. The inset shows Beringia, the Asia–North America land bridge at the Bering Strait, across which the ancestors of the Native Americans migrated.

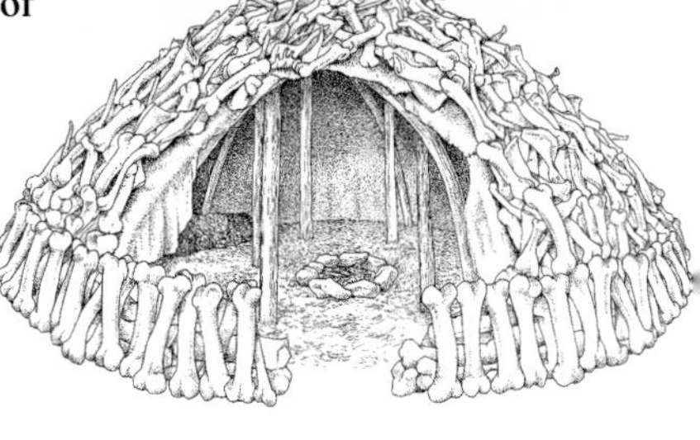

This shelter, discovered in the Ukraine, was made of wood covered with animal skins weighed down with mammoth bones. It was built to survive harsh winters and fierce winds.

NEANDERTHALS

About 200,000 years ago *Homo sapiens* (wise human) developed from *Homo erectus*. At the same time another human type, the *Neanderthal,* adapted to the colder climates of the last Ice Age, spreading through the continent of Europe and the Middle East. The Neanderthals developed many different simple stone tools, though their language was limited. They did not survive into modern times—the last known Neanderthals died out in Spain around 28,000 years ago.

THE ICE AGE

The last Ice Age, at its height around 16,000 B.C., had a major influence on how early people developed. It was the most recent of several ice ages that have occurred over the last 2.3 million years. With much water trapped in ice, the sea level was about 300 ft. (90m) lower than today. As a result there was dry land between Siberia and Alaska, between Australia and New Guinea, and between Britain and Europe, that allowed people to migrate.

In places such as Lascaux in southwest France, Ice Age people made cave paintings, possibly to honor the spirits of the animals they hunted for food and clothing.

CRO-MAGNONS

The humans of today are probably descended from the Cro-Magnons, a group of hunter-gatherers who seem to have entered Europe from the Middle East and eventually replaced the Neanderthals. These people gathered fruits, berries, and roots and hunted wild animals. They lived in simple caves and shelters. Around 40,000 years ago, they had developed mentally to become more like modern humans, with more ideas and a larger vocabulary. They began creating artworks, including cave paintings in France, Spain, and the Sahara. They made jewelry, figurines, clothes, shelters, tools, and hunting weapons.

▲ This is a tented encampment in eastern Europe about 25,000 years ago. Using this camp as their base, the hunters gathered their food, using skins for clothes and shelter, and bones for tools and ornaments. This way of life demanded teamwork and cooperation among the community.

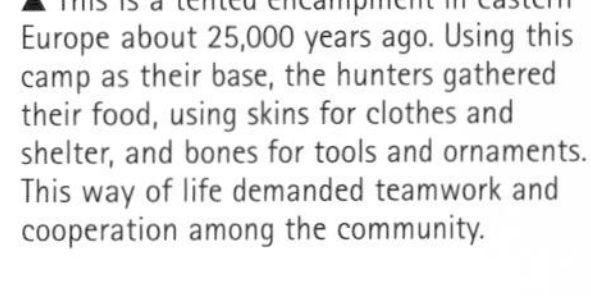

◀ Using a bow to spin a stick against a piece of wood, heat was built up by friction to create fire. This could take 10–20 minutes.

The Cro-Magnons made jewelry from stones, bones, ivory, shells, and teeth. It was often buried in graves.

Cave-dwelling hunters tackled very large animals, such as mammoths, but they also brought back a variety of smaller animals, including hares and deer.

ANCIENT EGYPT 4000–1800 B.C.

Ancient Egypt was surrounded by deserts, but it was green and fertile because of the Nile River. It flooded every year, depositing rich, silty soil along its banks.

The Egyptians loved to wear lucky charms. Their favorites were carved stone scarabs. The scarab beetle was sacred to the sun god, Ra.

The Egyptians used the Nile for transportation and cultivated the land alongside it. They grew wheat and barley for bread and beer, and flax for linen; they raised cattle as beasts of burden. Egyptians had a highly developed religion and advanced medical, astronomical, and engineering knowledge.

THE PHARAOHS

For most of their history, Egyptians were united in one kingdom. Administrators and priests ran everyday affairs, but the head of society was the pharaoh—a living god. People believed that ceremonies he performed kept the good will of the gods, kept the Nile flowing, and kept society in order. When the pharaoh died, his body was mummified and placed inside a stone sarcophagus in an imposing tomb, along with jewelry, clothing, furniture, and food—everything he would need for eternity. Sacred writings on the tomb walls were meant to protect him in the afterlife.

Papyrus is a stiff paper made from papyrus reeds. The Egyptians glued sheets of it together to make scrolls. Administrative and religious texts were written in hieroglyphs.

Egyptian civilization hugged the Nile River. The flood plains of the delta were rich and highly populated, though cities stretched a long way up the Nile. Riverboat transportation was important to traders.

EGYPTIAN SOCIETY

Most people in Egypt were farmers. They gave part of their produce to the local temple as taxes. Very few people could read and write, and schooling was only for boys. Those who could write were called scribes. It was they who went on to become the priests and administrators who ran the country for the pharaoh. But at the heart of Egyptian life was communication with the gods.

PYRAMIDS

From around 2630 B.C., Egyptians built many pyramids, the most famous being the Great Pyramid at Giza. No one knows exactly why the shape was chosen, but the scale and dimensions suggest astronomical, mathematical, and spiritual purposes. By building such great monuments, the pharaohs sought to please the gods and to leave a significant, permanent mark on history. Some of the long stone blocks above the king's Chamber weighed 60 tons, and around 2.3 million of them were used.

The Great Pyramid, the first of three pyramids at Giza and the tomb of the pharaoh Khufu, had many passageways and chambers.

King's chamber
Grand gallery
Queen's chamber
Entrance
New passage
Underground chamber

Pyramid-building involved immense skill. The largest, the Great Pyramid at Giza, may have taken over 30 years to build.

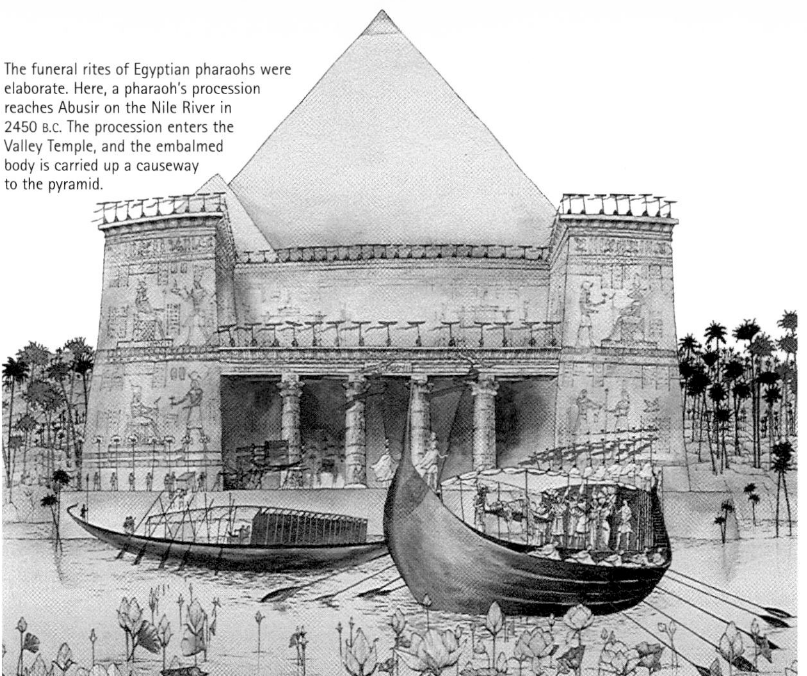

The funeral rites of Egyptian pharaohs were elaborate. Here, a pharaoh's procession reaches Abusir on the Nile River in 2450 B.C. The procession enters the Valley Temple, and the embalmed body is carried up a causeway to the pyramid.

Toward this end the Egyptians created remarkable works of stone carving. They built enormous pyramids and temples. Tall obelisks were cut from one block of stone. No effort or expense was spared to honor the gods—or the pharaoh, who was their living link with humanity. The Egyptians developed a way to preserve the body of their god-king, and many building projects were undertaken to provide him with a tomb for his eternal protection. In time, everyone who could afford it would have their preserved bodies placed in tombs, with treasures for the afterlife and sacred scrolls to guide them to it.

RETURN TO GREATNESS

After the time of the first pharaohs and the pyramid builders, there was a decline that lasted for over 100 years. With no strong ruler, the people felt the gods had abandoned them. Then, around 2040, Mentuhotep became pharaoh, brought order, and restored Egypt's greatness. This period was called the Middle Kingdom.

The pharaohs reorganized the country and again built pyramids, although not as large as those at Giza. Some of Egypt's finest art and literature was produced during the Middle Kingdom.

Egypt had been isolated from the rest of the world at this time. Ancient Egyptians were not great travelers, sailors, or conquerors, but great Middle Kingdom rulers such as Amenemhat I and Senwosret III expanded Egypt's boundaries. They built forts to protect the country, and created a strong army. They invaded countries such as Nubia to take control of gold reserves.

KEY DATES

3300 Growth of towns in lower Nile valley and development of hieroglyphics
3000 Upper and Lower Egypt united
2920 The first pharaohs
2575 Old Kingdom, capital Memphis—high point of Egyptian civilization
2550 The Great Pyramid is completed
2040 Middle Kingdom—expansion and development
1550 New Kingdom—Egypt at its largest and wealthiest

EGYPTIAN GODS

Horus was the sky-god, and his spirit entered the living pharaoh. His eyes were the sun and the moon.

Ptah, the creator-god, invented the arts. He was the local god of the capital, Memphis.

Hathor, the goddess of love and beauty, once raised the sun up to heaven on her horns.

Isis, sister and wife of Osiris, was the mother of Horus. She had great magical powers.

Re-Horakhty, the sun-god and Horus joined together, is shown with the sun on a hawk's head.

Osiris was the god of the dead. In his realm, souls were judged for their worthiness.

THE INDUS VALLEY 4000–1800 B.C.

The early peoples of the Indian subcontinent lived on the banks of the Ganges and Indus rivers. The first civilization sprang up in the Indus Valley, now in Pakistan.

The two largest cities in the Indus Valley around 2000 B.C. were Mohenjo-Daro and Harappa, each with around 40,000 people. They were among the world's largest cities at the time. At the center of each lay an artificial mound which served as a citadel (stronghold). On this mound stood a large granary which, to the population, served as a kind of central bank. These forgotten cities were only discovered in the 1920s.

Indus seals like this were attached to bales of merchandise. They have been found not only in Mohenjo-Daro, but also as far away as Sumer. This is evidence of a wide trade network.

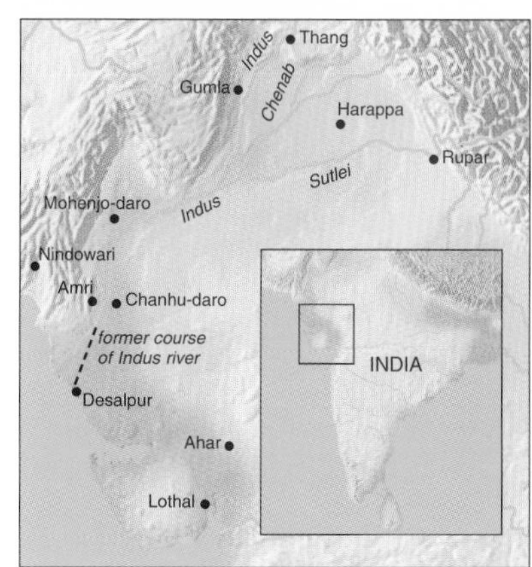

The climate was wetter in the Indus Valley than today. The rivers were used not only for trade and transportation, but also for irrigation of the flat lands of the valley.

CITY LAYOUT

Around the citadel the city buildings were arranged in a grid pattern—administration buildings, markets, storage areas, workshops, houses, and temples. Each house was built around a courtyard, and had rooms, a toilet, and a well. Buildings were made from mud bricks baked in wood-fired ovens. The citadel at Mohenjo-Daro had a bathhouse, as well as private and public baths and meeting places.

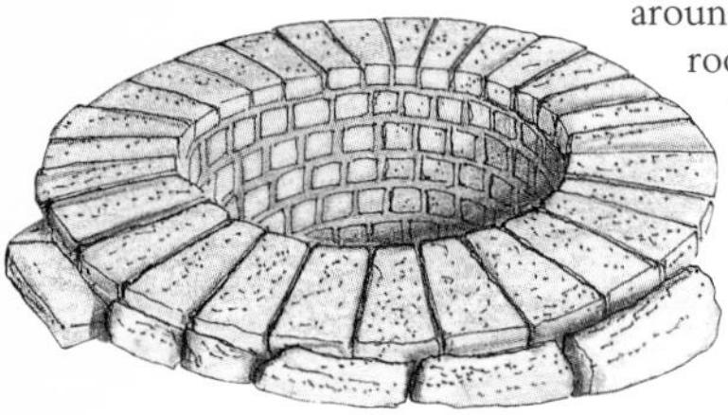

Brick-lined shafts like this are found in the courtyards of Mohenjo-Daro. They may have been wells or used for cool storage of grains and oil.

These ruins are all that remain of the 4,000-year-old city of Mohenjo-Daro.

FARMERS AND CRAFTWORKERS

Among other crops, the farmers of the Indus Valley grew barley, wheat, cotton, melons, and dates. Elephants and water buffalo were tamed to work in the fields. The area had many skilled potters who used wheels for throwing pots—a new technology at the time. Harappans used stone tools and made knives, weapons, bowls, and figures in bronze. They had an advanced system of waste-disposal that included the building of covered drains and the installation of garbage chutes.

These are the excavated remains of the Great Bath at Mohenjo-Daro. The people appear to have placed great importance on hygiene and access to water. They may also have used the baths for sports and ceremonies.

THE END OF A CIVILIZATION

No one knows who the people of the Indus Valley were or where they came from. We do not understand their writing, either. The area had similarities to Sumer, but also major differences. The city dwellers traded with the cities of Sumer; they also traded with the tribespeople of India and central Asia. The Indus Valley civilization lasted 800 years, but came to an end about 3,700 years ago. No one knows why it ended, but there are various possible causes: floods; disease; a breakdown in trade, the economy, or civil order; or immigration and takeover by the Aryans who moved into India from central Asia. All trace of the cities lay buried under sand until they were rediscovered in the 1920s.

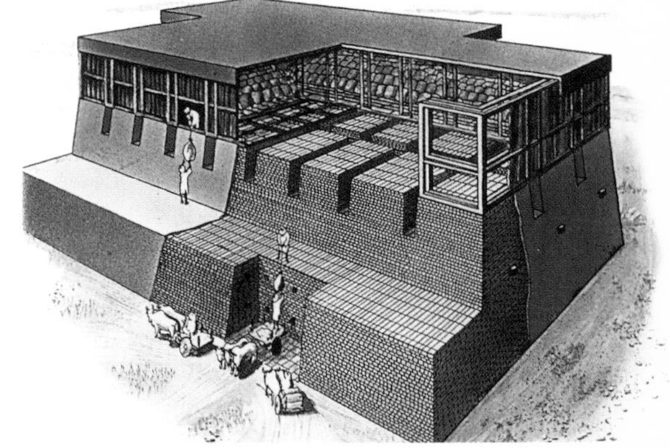

▲ The storehouses at the center of the cities were very valuable to the inhabitants—they could have had religious as well as practical significance, since grain may have been regarded as sacred.

◀ An artist's impression shows Mohenjo-Daro at the height of its prosperity. Unlike Sumerian cities, it was built in a grid pattern, suggesting orderly government and planning. The bathhouse had its own indoor well, and what seems to have been a granary had a sophisticated storage and ventilation system.

ANCIENT CRETE 3000–1450 B.C.

The earliest European civilization began on the island of Crete about 4,500 years ago. It is called the Minoan civilization after the legendary King Minos.

Stories say that Minos built a labyrinth (maze) in which he kept a Minotaur, a creature with the head of a bull and the body of a man. The Minoan civilization was at its height from 2200 to 1450 B.C. The Minoans owed their prosperity to their abilities as seafarers and traders.

This figure was found at Knossos. It combines the snake cult of Crete and worship of the mother-goddess. The figure itself wears the typical clothing of a Minoan woman.

Crete was well placed for trading with and influencing other areas. In the end, this was the Minoans' undoing, since the Mycenaeans envied their civilization and eventually invaded.

MINOAN CITIES

The Minoans built several large cities connected by paved roads, each of them a small city-state. At the heart of each city was a palace with a water supply, decorations, windows, and stone seats. Minoan craftsmen were renowned as potters and builders. They also made beautiful silver and gold jewelry. The capital, Knossos, had the grandest palace. It had splendid royal apartments, rooms for religious ceremonies, workshops, and a school.

Minoans were expert shipbuilders. They traveled around the Aegean Sea and to Egypt in boats like this, carrying their pottery and other craftworks far and wide.

The massive royal palace at Knossos, 500 ft. sq. (150m sq.), was several stories high and built from wood, stone, and clay. A large courtyard, was in the center. Royal apartments were on the east of the court, on the first floor.

The internal walls of the palace were plastered and decorated with large, magnificently painted pictures.

DOWNFALL OF A CIVILIZATION

Advanced Minoan civilization came to a sudden and mysterious end in about 1450 B.C. A volcanic eruption on the nearby island of Thera had already been a major disaster, overwhelming much of Crete. The end came when Knossos was invaded by the Mycenaeans who greatly admired the Minoans and took their ideas to the European mainland. In Crete lay the roots of the later Greek classical civilization.

The walls of the state rooms at Knossos were elaborately decorated. The wall painting shows the sport of bull leaping. The bull was a sacred symbol of power, and the ability to vault over its horns symbolized the mastering of its strength.

THE MYCENEANS 2000–1200 B.C.

Mycenae was a city on the southern peninsula of Greece. It was the center of the first Greek civilization, which developed after that of the Minoans in Crete.

This gold mask was found in a grave in Mycenae by archaeologist Heinrich Schliemann. He thought it was Agamemnon's mask—modern scholars think it belonged to a man who lived 300 years earlier.

This beautiful gold goblet from Mycenae clearly demonstrates the skill of the local craftsworkers. It shows men hunting bulls, a common theme at that time.

The Mycenaeans (known as Achaeans) migrated to Greece from the Balkans around 2000 B.C. Mycenaean civilization began as a series of hillside villages occupied by people speaking an ancient form of the Greek language. By about 1650 B.C., many villages had grown into fortified towns, with rich palaces and luxurious goods that rivaled those made by the highly skilled Minoans. Mycenae consisted of about 20 city-states.

MYCENAEAN TOMBS

Before they built fortresses and cities the Mycenaeans buried their leaders in elaborate "beehive tombs." These were built of large stone blocks, shaped to form a great dome. One tomb at Mycenae, the Treasury of Atreus, has a doorway nearly 20 ft. (6m) high, that opens into a chamber 43 ft. (13m) high and 46 ft. (14m) wide. It was once lined with bronze plates. The richness of these tombs shows that a great deal of money and effort was spent on royalty and the aristocracy. One king had as many as 400 bronzesmiths and hundreds of slaves. Wealthy Mycenaeans treasured the gold that they imported from Egypt. Skilled craftworkers made gold cups, masks, flowers, and jewelry; even their swords and armor were inlaid with gold.

The ruins of the Lion Gate at Mycenae, the main entrance to the city, built around 1300BC. It was one of the few ways through the walls, which were built with huge stones and were easy to defend.

EXPANSION AND DOWNFALL

Around 1450 B.C., the Mycenaeans conquered Crete and established colonies around the Aegean Sea and on the islands of Rhodes and Cyprus. They traded throughout the Mediterranean, particularly with Phoenicia, Egypt, and Italy. However, around 1200 B.C., Mycenae fell to invading wandering raiders called the Sea Peoples. Many Mycenaeans were forced to flee to other countries.

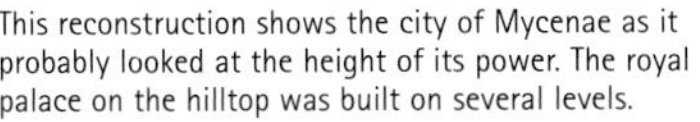

This reconstruction shows the city of Mycenae as it probably looked at the height of its power. The royal palace on the hilltop was built on several levels.

SHANG DYNASTY 1766–1122 B.C.

The earliest civilizations in China from around 3200 B.C. grew up on the banks of the three largest rivers: the Huang He, Chang Jiang, and Xi Jiang.

Like the people of Sumer, Egypt, and the Indus Valley, Chinese farmers relied on the country's rivers for transportation and water to grow their crops—paddy fields needed floods in springtime to help the rice grow. But the Chinese also faced two dangers: major floods and devastating raids by tribes from the north and west.

A piece of bronze Shang money, cast in the shape of a spade. This may have been made to slot into a case or sheath where several coins would be kept.

EARLY CULTURES

The first small towns appeared around 3000 B.C., during the Longshan period, around the Huang He (Yellow River) in the north. According to tradition, Huangdi, the Yellow Emperor, was the first emperor from around 2700 B.C. The first dynasty was that of the Xia (Hsia), who ruled for four centuries from 2200 B.C. Yu, its founder, is credited with taming the rivers by building dikes to stop floods, and also irrigation channels.

TANG AND THE SHANG

The earliest dynasty we have evidence for was the Shang, founded by Emperor Tang. The Shang ruled north China for more than 600 years. They lived in a string of cities along the Huang He, with the capital at Anyang. The city had many large palaces and temples, built mainly of carved wood. The Zhou dynasty replaced the Shang in 1122 B.C.

This is an oracle bone from the 1300s B.C. Large numbers of these have been found, engraved with early Chinese pictograms (picture writing). Diviners used these to interpret the future.

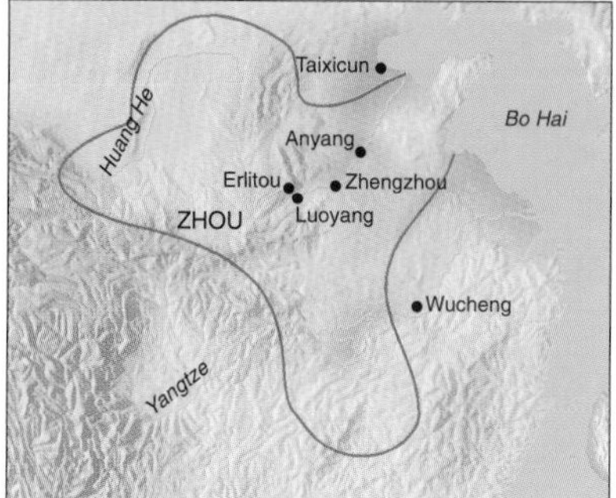

Shang civilization was based around the Huang He River in the north, though it also influenced central China. Later, the Zhou dynasty extended control over a larger area.

The Shang people grew millet, wheat, and rice, and also mulberries for feeding silkworms, from which they produced silk. They kept cattle, pigs, sheep, dogs, and chickens, and hunted deer and wild boar. The Shang used horses to draw plows, carriages, and chariots. Early in their history, they used cowrie shells as money, later switching to bronze. They were skilled in working bronze and jade, and made highly decorated practical and religious objects.

▼ Tradition says that silk was discovered by Empress Xiling Ji around 2690 B.C. She was the wife of the legendary Yellow Emperor, Huangdi, who was reputed to have brought civilization, medicine, and writing to China. The empress found that silkworms fed on mulberry leaves, so she had mulberry groves planted. Silk was spun into a fine textile that was so valued it was even used as a form of money. Silk manufacture remained a closely kept secret by the Chinese for about 3,000 years.

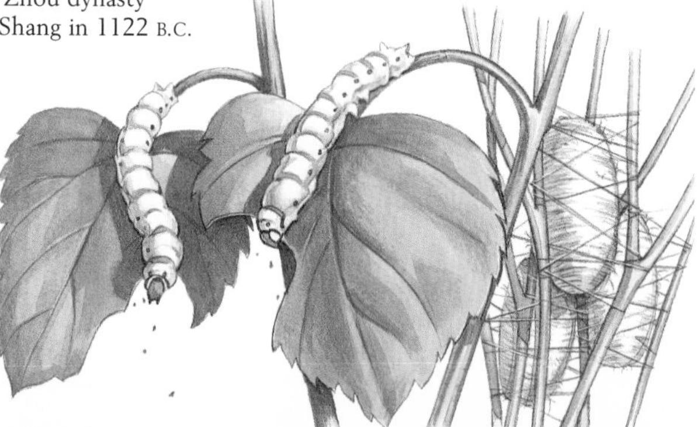

KEY DATES

- 3000 The first Chinese towns appear, during the Longshan culture
- 2700 Huangdi, the "Yellow Emperor," becomes emperor
- 2200 Period of Xia dynasty—Yu is the emperor
- 1766 Foundation of the Shang dynasty by Emperor Tang
- 1400 Peak of the Shang period
- 1122 Zhou dynasty displaces the Shang

CHINESE WRITING

Around 1600 B.C., the Shang developed the earliest forms of Chinese calligraphy—a pictorial writing in which each letter represents a whole word. The Chinese script we know today evolved from Shang writing. The Shang worshiped their ancestors, who were seen as wise guides for their way of life, and they used oracles to help them make decisions.

Shang warriors fought in cumbersome armor made of bamboo and wood, padded with cloth. Early Chinese were warlike, and tribes used to fight long feuds. Centralized states such as the Shang developed to stop the feuding between warlords.

BRONZE

Bronze is a mixture of copper and tin, which, when polished, looks like gold. The Shang became strong through their bronze-working, since it was a hard metal with many uses in tools, household items, and weapons. Bronze was also used for adornments, artistic, and religious items. It was cast in clay molds carved with patterns. Across the world, bronze represented a technological breakthrough.

▼ When found in 1970, this bronze vessel held well over 300 pieces of jade. It was designed during the Shang period as a vessel for storing large amounts of wine and was known as a *pou*. The high quality and intricate design show that by this time bronze casting was a highly developed art. Other bronze vessels, called *jue*, with three legs and a long spout, were used for pouring wine during ceremonies.

▲ The ancient Chinese cooked sacrificial food in large bronze decorated vessels like this one. It had long legs so that it could stand over a coal fire.

THE HITTITES 1600–1200 B.C.

Around 1650 B.C., a number of small city-states were united, through warfare. The result was the rich and powerful Hittite kingdom.

The Hittites consisted of several tribes and they spoke as many as six languages among them. One was the language of the Hatti, the original occupants of Anatolia. The Hittites were the first use iron—a metal that replaced the softer bronze.

This Hittite stela (carved standing stone) from Anatolia (Turkey) shows a woman doing her spinning, while she speaks to a scribe who holds a clay tablet and pen.

THE HITTITE EMPIRE

The Hittites were a warlike people. They controlled the supply of iron, and they used chariots, which gave them a great military advantage. They worshiped around 1,000 gods, chief of which was a storm-god. Early on, in 1595 B.C., they sacked Babylonia, plummeting it into a dark age. Gradually they conquered Anatolia, Syria, and the Levant (Lebanon), challenging the hold that the Assyrians and Egyptians had on the area.

The Hittites carved many works of art on boulders, shaping only part of the rock and leaving the rest in its natural form. This sphinxlike gateway once guarded a Hittite settlement located at Alaca, in what is now modern Turkey.

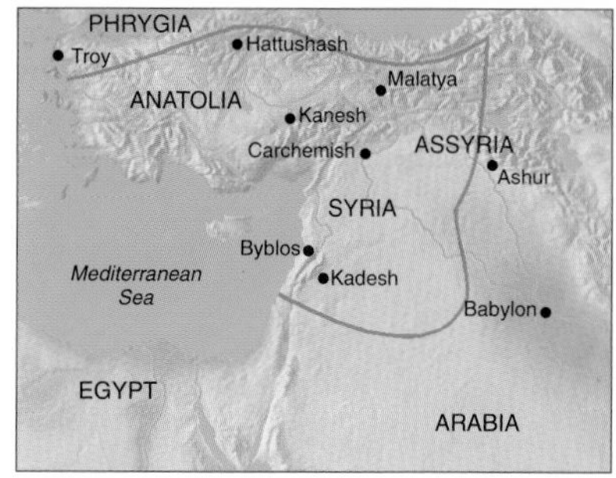

The Hittite territories at their peak, around 1300 B.C. They fought with the Egyptians, Assyrians, and Phrygians, and their empire disappeared in less than a century.

The Hittites adopted civilized ways, such as writing, from other peoples. They also introduced the horse into the Middle East from China. Men were dominant in society, and they were rich and well traveled. The Hittites reached their peak around 1300 B.C. The Hittites survived many threats until they fell to the Sea Peoples. Finally, they were destroyed and occupied by the Phrygians, who came from the Balkans, to the north. The Hittites were never heard of again, but they had had a strong influence on their neighbors.

This Hittite rock-carved relief at Yazilikaya shows the protector-god Sharruma with the goddess Ishtar in the background. The relief was carved around 1250 B.C.

BABYLON 1900–700 B.C.

Ur's domination of Mesopotamia was followed by many invasions. Around 1894 B.C. the Babylonians replaced their rulers with a dynasty that lasted 300 years.

A local boundary stone from Babylon is carved with prayers that ask the gods to protect the owner's land.

The Babylonians began to dominate southern Mesopotamia under their sixth ruler, Hammurabi the Great (1780–50 B.C.). He was a highly efficient ruler, famous for the code of laws that he laid down, and he gave the region stability after turbulent times.

Babylon became the central power of Mesopotamia. The armies of Babylonia were well-disciplined, and they conquered the city-states of Isin, Elam, and Uruk, and the strong kingdom of Mari. But Mesopotamia had no clear boundaries, making it vulnerable to attack. Trade and culture thrived for 150 years, but then the Hittites sacked Babylon in 1595 B.C.

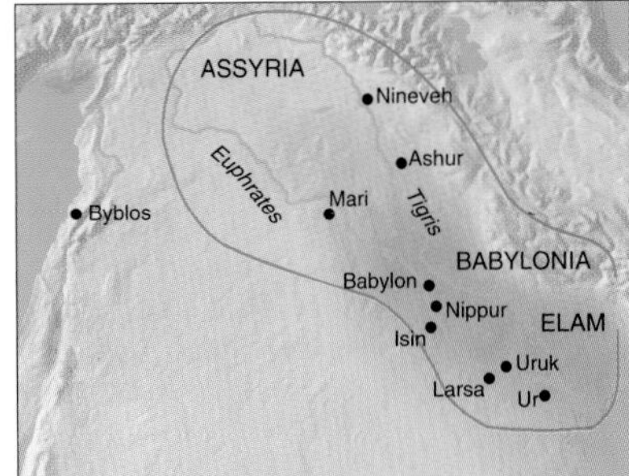

Under Hammurabi and his successors, Babylon controlled the whole of Mesopotamia. However, it became vulnerable to invasion from the north and west.

Its cities continued for 100 years under different foreign rulers. Then, for 500 years, Babylon was overshadowed by Assyria before its next rise to greatness.

EARLY SCIENCE

The mathematicians of Babylonia devised a system of counting based on the number 60, from which we get the number of minutes in an hour and the degrees (60 x 6) in a circle. Babylonian scholars developed early sciences and astrology from the knowledge they gained from the Sumerians.

Hammurabi was famous for his detailed code of laws. Well known to us today is "An eye for an eye, and a tooth for a tooth," prescribing punishments for personal crimes. The laws brought all of Babylon under a uniform legal system. They protected the weak from the strong, and regulated business and land ownership.

This stela shows Shamash, the god of justice, giving Hammurabi the instruction to formulate a code of laws. Underneath are inscribed the laws that Hammurabi codified, for all to see. In this way, people were shown that the laws were given to Hammurabi by the gods.

Skilled archers helped Babylon to defend itself against the Assyrians and many other invaders—Kassites, Aramaeans, Elamites, and Hittites. Its wealth, and its location at the meeting place of roads from Asia to the Mediterranean, was envied by jealous neighbors.

THE ASSYRIANS 1900–612 B.C.

While Babylonia ruled southern Mesopotamia, the warlike Assyrians dominated the north. Their kingdom lay in the valley of the upper Tigris River.

Ashurbanipal was the last great ruler of Assyria. A ruthless soldier, he was also a patron of the arts, building the great library at Nineveh and vast gardens stocked with plants from all over the known world.

King Adadnirari I, the country's first powerful ruler (1770–50 B.C.), enlarged the Assyrian lands and took the boastful title "King of Everything." He and his successors were fierce dictators, who did not allow individual states to be independent. Assyria grew rich through the activities of its trading families, who sold textiles and metals far and wide.

COLLAPSE AND REBIRTH

As Assyria grew in size, rebellions by its conquered subjects increased. Eventually, Assyria fell to the Hurrians (relatives of the Hittites). The Hurrians dominated Assyria for over 250 years. As their overlordship dwindled, Assyria grew in strength again. Its next period of greatness lasted for 300 years. It reached its height under Tiglathpileser I (1115–1093 B.C.), who led many campaigns against neighboring lands. Assyria eventually dominated the whole region, including Babylon.

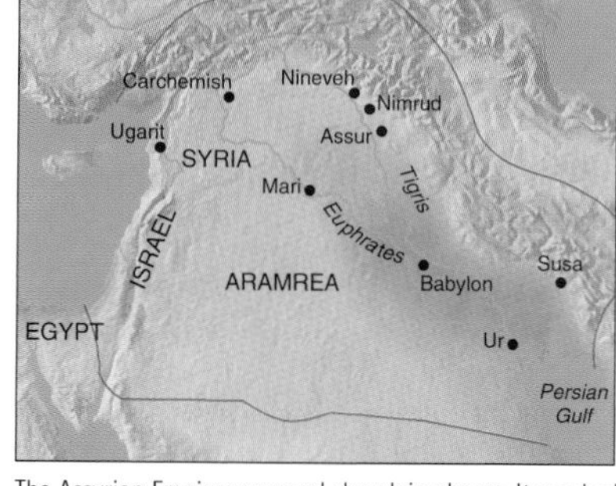

The Assyrian Empire grew and shrank in phases. It reached its greatest extent at the end, around 650, covering the whole of the Fertile Crescent. When Ashurbanipal died, Egypt and Babylon broke away and the empire collapsed.

The Assyrian king meets his courtiers and administrators.

ASHURBANIPAL'S PALACE

The Assyrian king was an absolute ruler with very active involvement in all matters of state. In his magnificent palace, Ashurbanipal, surrounded by his advisors, heard the cases presented by the people. The palace was large, with extensive gardens. As a patron of learning, the king ordered many historic records from Babylon and Sumer to be written down, and texts on mathematics, chemistry, and astronomy were produced. Literary texts such as the *Epic of Gilgamesh* and the story of the Flood, from Akkadian times, were also recorded. All of these were destroyed by invaders after Ashurbanipal's death, though many records survived.

The Assyrians believed that the winged lion from Ashurbanipal's palace could ward off evil.

Here, Assyrian workers bring in materials for the building of a new palace, supervised by their king. Oarsmen in hide-covered boats tow a raft along the Tigris.

ASSYRIA FLOURISHES

From about 1076 B.C., Assyria and Babylonia were overrun by Aramaean tribes from Syria. But 150 years later, Ashurdan II and his successors reconquered the Assyrian Empire. The capital was moved to Nineveh, and buildings were erected and irrigation schemes undertaken. Assyrian kings expanded their lands to control all trade routes and suppress troublesome neighbors. The Assyrian Empire was at its greatest extent under Tiglathpileser III (745–727 B.C.), when it included the lands of Babylon, Syria, Palestine, Cyprus, northern Arabia, and Egypt.

ASSYRIAN LIFE

The Assyrians were great builders and erected magnificent cities, temples, and palaces. The men wore long coatlike garments and were bearded. Women wore a sleeved tunic and a shawl over their shoulders. It was not unknown for men to sell their wives and children into slavery to pay off debts.

The Assyrians were experts at siege warfare. Their battering-rams knocked holes in city walls; then scaling ladders and mobile towers helped the men climb over. The soldiers protected themselves with large shields.

KEY DATES

2500	Assyrians settle the upper Tigris valley
1900	Growth of Old Assyria
1680	Assyria falls to the Hurrians (until 1400)
1300–1200	Assyrian expansion
1076	Assyria falls to the Aramaeans (until 934)
730–630	Assyrian expansion at its greatest
612	Fall of Assyria to the Babylonians and Medes

THE FINAL CHAPTER

The last and greatest ruler of Assyria was King Ashurbanipal. He was a scholarly king and during his reign he created a huge library in Nineveh, his capital. The ancient records of Sumer and Akkad were preserved on clay tablets, together with literature and histories, mathematics, and astronomy from ancient times. When Ashurbanipal died in 627 B.C. the Assyrian empire fell to the Babylonians and Medes.

Ishtar was the goddess of war to the Assyrians. To the Babylonians she was the mother-goddess.

THE HEBREWS 1800–587 B.C.

The Hebrews first settled in Palestine about 4,000 years ago. They came to Palestine from Ur, although no one knows exactly where they came from before then.

Their name meant "the people from the other side" of the Euphrates River. Their story is told in the Bible. According to the Old Testament, the leader of the first Hebrews was Abraham, a shepherd who lived in Ur. Abraham traveled with his family first to Syria and then to Canaan (now Palestine), where they finally settled.

Solomon (965–928 B.C.) was one of the wiser kings of history and he carried out his royal duties fairly. His rule brought order and peace and Jerusalem became one of the richest cities of the period.

EARLY YEARS

Abraham's grandson, Jacob (also called Israel), had twelve sons. He is said to have started the twelve tribes of Israel, which were named after his sons. When famine struck Canaan, Jacob led his people to safety in Egypt. Later, they became slaves of the Egyptians until Moses led them out of Egypt and took them back to Canaan, probably around 1200 B.C. There, led by Joshua, they fought the Philistines (Palestinians) for the right to settle and establish the land of Israel. Tradition has it that they used the sound of trumpets to bring down the walls of the city of Jericho.

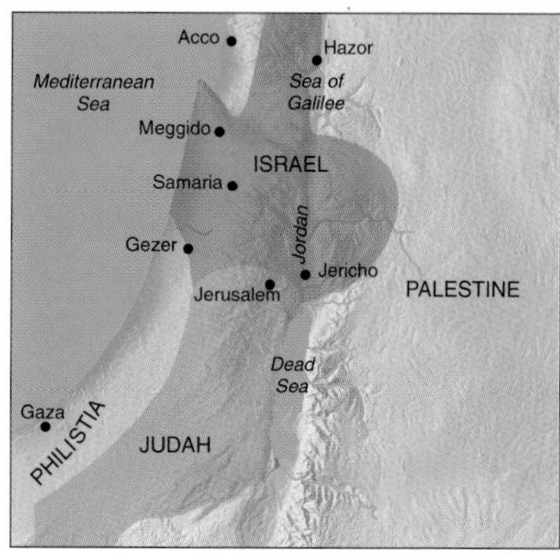

After Solomon's death, Israel split into two different states, Israel and Judah—this weakened them against outside attack and led to their downfall.

THE FIRST STATE OF ISRAEL

Around 1020 B.C., the Philistines began to threaten the Hebrews. To defend themselves, the Hebrews banded together and appointed Saul their first king. His successor, David, united all the tribes, made Jerusalem the new nation's capital, and added a number of other territories. As defensive measures, his son Solomon built several new cities and a wall around the capital. The great temple at Jerusalem was his most famous work. He was a peace-loving and wise king.

SOLOMON'S TEMPLE

Solomon built an impressive temple in Jerusalem, at great expense, to house the Israelites' holy treasure, the Ark of the Covenant, which contained Moses' Ten Commandments. The Temple became the focus of Jewish culture. It is said that Solomon's temple had walls inlaid with precious jewels, and that it was designed in accordance with mathematical principles learned from the Egyptians.

The Judaean desert, often mentioned in the Bible, is a landscape of astounding beauty. It was probably greener in ancient times because of a milder climate.

According to the Bible, Solomon was a wise king. It is said that two women came before him with a child, each claiming to be its mother. Solomon suggested that he cut the child in two, so each mother could have half. One woman broke down and gave up her claim. Solomon recognized her as the true mother, and gave her the child. His reign marked the peak of Israel's history. After he died, his people argued and divided into two nations: Israel and Judah.

This copy of a wall-painting from Beni Hasan in Middle Egypt shows a group of Semitic, or Asiatic, people, very possibly Hebrew, entering Egypt to trade.

TROUBLES AND DISPERSION

After a rebellion by the Israelites, the Assyrians captured Israel in 721 B.C., and then Judah in 683. The Jews scattered in various directions, and many were carried away to Assyria as slaves. Nebuchadnezzar of Babylon crushed a Jewish rebellion in 597 and most of the Jews were taken to Babylon. During that exile, much of the Old Testament of the Bible was written down. This was the beginning of the *diaspora*, the dispersion of the Jews, which lasted into the 1900s.

KEY DATES

- c.1800 Abraham and the Hebrews move to Canaan
- c.1200 Moses and Joshua take the Jews to Canaan
- c.1020 Saul becomes king of the Hebrews
- c.1000 David becomes king of the Hebrews
- 965–928 Solomon, king of Israel, reigns
- 721 Assyrians invade Israel, dispersing many Jews
- 587 Babylonians destroy Jerusalem and deport most of the Jews to Babylon

A Jewish man blows on a *shofar*, a ram's horn fitted with a reed to amplify the sound it makes. It is possible these were used to bring down the walls of Jericho—or at least to frighten the inhabitants into opening the gates. The shofar is one of the world's oldest musical instruments, and it is blown on Jewish holy days. The woven prayer-shawl is called a *tallith*.

AFRICA 6000–200 B.C.

Although the earliest human remains have been found in Africa, not much was known until recently of the continent's history before 1500 B.C., except for Egypt.

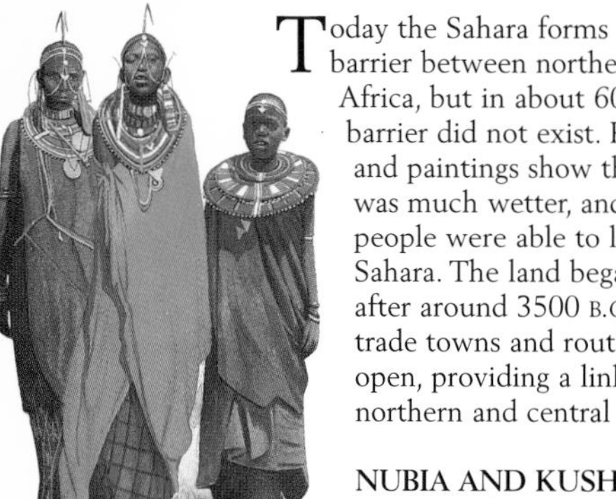

These are Masai women of recent times, from what is now Kenya. They are dressed in traditional ceremonial clothes.

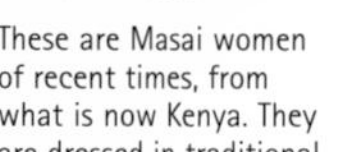

Today the Sahara forms a great desert barrier between northern and central Africa, but in about 6000 B.C. that barrier did not exist. Rock drawings and paintings show that the climate was much wetter, and that more people were able to live in the Sahara. The land began to dry up after around 3500 B.C., but desert trade towns and routes remained open, providing a link between northern and central Africa.

NUBIA AND KUSH

Egyptian culture spread up the Nile to Nubia (now Sudan). The kingdom of Kush grew out of Nubia from 2000 B.C. onward. Kush was valuable to Egypt as a trading partner and a source of gold. Egypt conquered Kush in 1500 B.C., to secure gold deposits there but in 750 B.C. was itself conquered by the Kushites, who founded the 25th dynasty of pharaohs. Kush never had a Bronze Age, but went straight from using stone to using iron. The capital was moved from Napata, its religious center, to Meroë, because Meroë was surrounded by rich iron ore deposits.

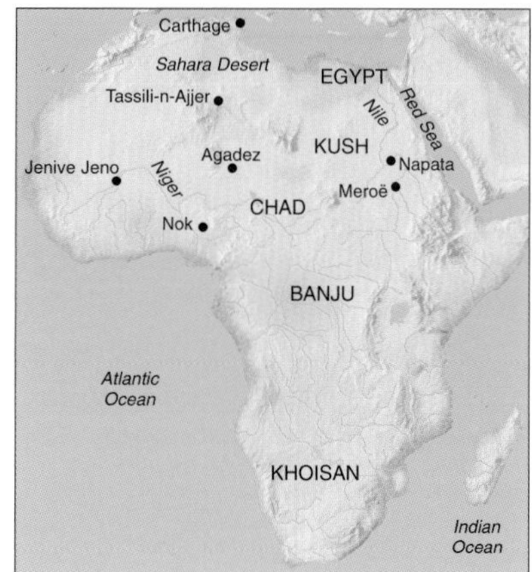

Africa, a vast continent, has many different environments in which many diverse cultures have grown up. North Africa was dominated by Egyptian and Mediterranean cultures. South of the Sahara Desert people lived without being affected directly by them.

This meant that Kush became an important center of ironworking, supplying Egypt, Babylon, Arabia, and Ethiopia. Meroë imitated Egypt, and it preserved many Egyptian traditions for the future at a time when Egypt itself was going through cultural changes. Ethiopia was also an important, though self-contained, area of culture with religious traditions of its own.

These ancient rock paintings of warriors from Oum Echna in the Sahara, date from before 3500 B.C. when the Sahara was habitable grassland.

These ruined pyramids are at Meroë, east of today's Khartoum. The kingdom of Meroë developed from Nubia, a kingdom once influenced by Egypt.

CENTRAL AND SOUTHERN AFRICA

Around the Niger River lived farming tribes, with a few trading towns. Downstream, the Nok nation of Nigeria became ironworking and village-dwelling craftspeople. To the east there were the nomadic shepherds and village-dwelling people of Chad. Across central Africa, Bantu peoples were moving south from Nigeria, taking ironworking and farming with them. Southern Africa was occupied by shepherds as well as hunter-gatherers known as the Khoisan.

KEY DATES
3000 Desertification of the Sahara begins
2750 Farming begins in West Africa
700 Nubian kingdom of Kush flourishes
600 Growth of Nok culture, Nigeria, and Meroë
200 Jenne-jeno, the first African city, is established

▲ A wall painting in the tomb of Sobekhotep shows foreigners bringing tribute to the pharaoh. Here, a group of African peoples bring gifts prized by the Egyptians: from Nubia, gold in large rings; from farther south, logs of ebony and fly whisks made from giraffe's tails, and fruit and a small monkey, and, finally, a baboon.

▶ Rock paintings and relief carvings are found across much of the Sahara. This cattle-herding scene was painted on rock in the Tasili area in the central Sahara. The artist has even recorded the color patterns of the individual cows.

AMERICA 1500–350 B.C.

The first Americans arrived in North America overland from Asia in the Ice Age when the sea level was lower. Over thousands of years they populated South America.

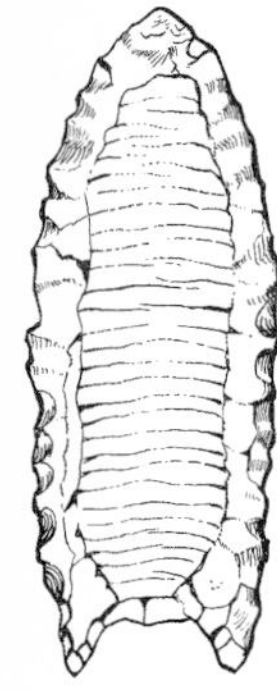

A Folsom point, a type of arrowhead found at Folsom in North America, dating from 9000 B.C.

Many early Americans remained hunters, fishers, and food gatherers, but in two separate areas, new civilizations developed—Mesoamerica (Mexico), and Equador and Peru.

THE OLMECS OF MEXICO

In Mesoamerica, some 9,000 years ago, the Native Americans settled and grew crops of Indian corn, beans, and pumpkins. Small villages sprang up in which the people made pottery and wove cloth. Out of this culture, around 1500 B.C., the first American civilization was born. The city-dwelling Olmecs built their capital at La Venta, on the Gulf of Mexico. The Olmecs built large earth and stone pyramids as centers for religious worship, and they produced huge sculptures and fine jade carvings. Many of their sculptures mix human and jaguar-like features. The Olmecs also had their own kind of writing and a sophisticated calendar system. Their neighbors, the Zapotecs and Maya, also developed advanced city civilizations.

This fine stone bowl is a magnificent example of the Chavín people's skill in stone carving. It was the work of a sculptor living in Peru 2,500 years ago.

CIVILIZATION IN THE ANDES

The first fishing and farming villages in South America were in northern Peru. About 2,800 years ago a more advanced culture appeared, called the Chavín. The Chavín people made pottery, wove cloth on looms, built in stone, and made elaborate carvings. The largest building in their capital was three stories high. Inside was a maze of rooms, corridors, and stairs.

KEY DATES	
2600	Ceremonial centers built in Peru
2200	Farming villages founded in Mexico
1200	Olmec towns and ceremonial centers built
850	Chavín culture grows
600	Earliest Maya temple-pyramids built
350	Decline of the Olmecs

▲ This is one of eight enormous heads carved from basalt by the Olmecs; some are almost 10 ft. (3m) tall. They may represent early rulers, and each wears a distinctly different head covering.

▶ Dating from around 1200 B.C., this Olmec "altar" was probably a throne. The figure of an Olmec ruler sits in the niche underneath.

ARYAN INDIA 1500–500 B.C.

About 3,500 years ago the Aryans, a band of tough warriors and shepherds, fled south across the Hindu Kush mountains to settle in the subcontinent of India.

Gautama Siddhartha (c.563–483 B.C.) was a prince. He saw the suffering of the people and left his family to search for truth. He later attained enlightenment, becoming known as Buddha. He taught a kinder faith that respected all living beings.

A natural disaster, maybe drought or disease, or a civil war, made the Aryans flee from their homelands in southern Russia. They spread out to Anatolia and Persia as well as India. They lived in tribal villages, probably in wooden houses, unlike the brick cities of the Indus Valley people.

THE ARYANS IN INDIA

Aryans counted their wealth in cattle and sheep. They were not as advanced as the Indian peoples, but they were tougher. They were warriors and gamblers, beef-eaters and wine drinkers, and loved music, dancing, and chariot racing. Gradually, they settled down and adopted many of the ways of the native Indians, becoming crop growers and ironworkers. Among the crops was rice, unknown to the Aryans but already grown in the Indus Valley.

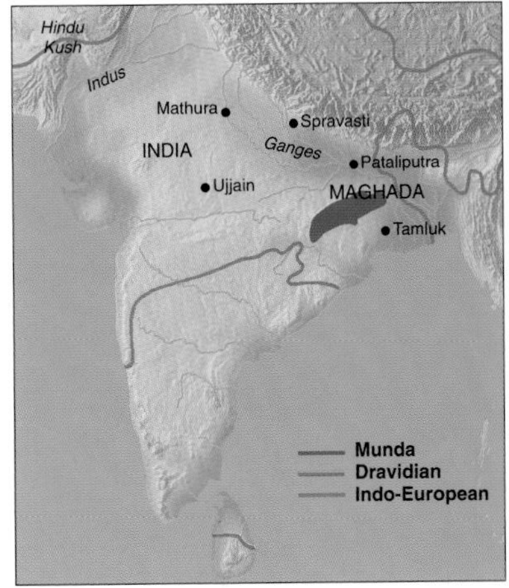

After the Aryans invaded northern India, many of the native people, the Dravidians and the Munda, moved to the southern and eastern parts of India.

HINDU CULTURE

The use of the plow and irrigation systems enabled the Aryans to grow enough crops to support large towns. By 500 B.C. there were 16 major kingdoms in northern India, the most prominent being Maghada. Maghada was the birthplace of the Mauryan Empire and of two new religions—Jainism and Buddhism.

The Aryans had no form of writing. Like many ancient peoples, they passed on their history and religious beliefs by word of mouth. These traditions, called the *Vedas*—the Books of Knowledge—were written down much later. The oldest of these is the *Rig-Veda*, a collection of more than 1,000 hymns, composed in their language, Sanskrit. Most of what we know about the Aryans' daily lives in ancient times comes from the *Vedas*, the ancient "old testament" of the Hindus. Unlike other faiths, Hinduism was not started by one teacher—its beliefs accumulated gradually over time.

▲ The Aryans introduced the caste system, headed by the educated Brahmin priests who ruled the country. The Kshatriyas were warriors, and the Vaisyas were traders and farmers. The darker skinned native Dravidians were servants and workers. It was impossible to change caste or marry outside it.

◀ One of the chief Hindu deities is Shiva, the transformer, who is both a creator and destroyer, the lord of change. He is depicted dancing in a halo of flames.

THE FOUNDING OF ROME 753–510 B.C.

According to tradition, the city of Rome was founded in 753 B.C. by local tribespeople who had established their camps on Rome's seven hills.

Legends say that early Rome was ruled by local kings, of whom Romulus was the first. The citizens were Sabines and Latins, who united to form one town, thinking of themselves as Romans. They were influenced by their neighbors to the north, the Etruscans, and traders from Greece and Carthage, who brought in new ideas about culture and society.

According to legend, Rome was founded by twin brothers, Romulus and Remus, grandsons of King Numitor. The king's wicked brother Amulius put the babies in a basket to float down the Tiber River to their deaths. However, they were rescued and suckled by a she-wolf. They founded Rome, but quarreled, and Remus was killed. Romulus became the first king of Rome.

ETRUSCANS

The Etruscans, whose kingdom was called Etruria, lived in a group of city-states which emerged around 800 B.C. They were farmers, metalworkers, seafarers, and traders and liked music, games, and gambling. They were greatly influenced by the Greeks, adopting the Greek alphabet, wearing himaton (robes), and believing in Greek gods. Many of their ways were passed to the Romans, who eventually took Greek-style culture to its ultimate expression.

In its early days, Rome was surrounded by Etruscans, Samnites, and others. Greeks and Phoenicians also had colonies in and around Italy. As Rome expanded, it had to overcome these older societies.

Legend has it that seven successive kings ruled Rome for 240 years. Kings did not have complete power—they had to contend with an assembly of nobles, who grew more influential as time passed.

KINGS OF ROME

The kings of Rome wore togas with purple borders. In processions, the kings were preceded by standard-bearers who carried a *fasces* (a bundle of rods and an ax blade), a symbol of power representing the king's right to rule over everyone else.

This terracotta sarcophagus of an Etruscan husband and wife was made around 510 B.C. Women had more status in Etruscan society than they did among Greeks or Latins, where they were kept in the background.

An assembly had a say in electing the king and what he could do, especially in war. The kings formed armies to defend Rome. There were arguments between the kings and the patricians (the leading families). The kings represented the old ways, and urban Rome was changing. The new elite of patricians eventually overthrew the monarchy in 509 B.C., and declared Rome a republic. It was the first republic in the history of the world. The Romans did not plan to become a great imperial power—at first they wanted only to protect themselves and fight off their interfering neighbors. However, within 500 years, Rome was to become the center of the Western world, taking over from the Greeks.

KEY DATES	
800	The Etruscan civilization emerges
753	Traditional date for the founding of Rome
509	Foundation of the Roman Republic
400	Decline of Etruria

▲ The Etruscans left little writing, but their paintings were vivid. This one from a tomb shows lyre and flute players.

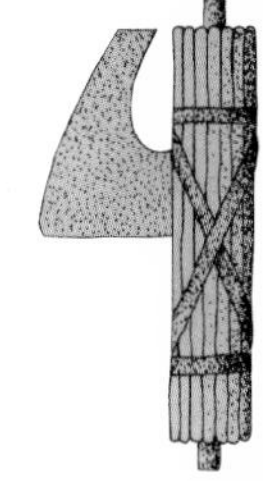

▲ A *fasces* was a symbol of power in Rome. The wooden rods symbolized punishment, and the ax represented life and death.

◄ Greek art and dress greatly influenced the Etruscans. The figures in the tomb of the Augurs—diviners or soothsayers—at Tarquinia, painted around 500 B.C., clearly show Greek touches.

Babylon Revived 626–539 B.C.

Tribespeople from the west, called Chaldeans, migrated into Assyria and Babylonia from about 1100 B.C. Several Chaldeans served as kings under their Assyrian overlords.

Nebuchadnezzar reigned for 43 years and his reign was marked by many military campaigns. Twice he subdued revolts in Judah, and when Phoenicia rebelled he besieged its chief port, Tyre, for thirteen years.

In 626 B.C., a Chaldean king called Nabopolassar took power, declared Babylonia independent, and threw off the Assyrian yoke. Nabopolassar then crushed the Assyrians in 612 B.C. His son Nebuchadnezzar drove the Egyptians back into Egypt and took Syria.

NEBUCHADNEZZAR

Nebuchadnezzar was one of the most famous kings of Babylonia. He came to power in about 605 B.C. His story is told in the Bible, in the Book of Daniel. He invaded many of the former Assyrian lands and the deserts west of Babylon. Among other conquests, Nebuchadnezzar captured Jerusalem and forced thousands of Jews to live in Babylon as prisoners because they had been rebellious. He made Babylon the master of all the lands within the Fertile Crescent.

▲ Flanked by lions and owls, the goddess Ishtar wears a crown of lunar horns. Ishtar was the chief goddess of the Babylonians.

BABYLON

Nebuchadnezzar devoted most of his time to making Babylon still more beautiful, a capital of the world. He had huge walls built around the city, and he named the main gate after the goddess Ishtar. He also built the Hanging Gardens—stepped gardens overlooking the city. He built a large bridge over the Euphrates River, and an enormous ziggurat, the Temple of Marduk or Bel (the "tower of Babel"). Nebuchadnezzar built himself a fine palace and he also improved the other cities. He encouraged the worship of the old god Marduk, seeking to revive Babylon's and Sumer's former greatness. Nebuchadnezzar ruled for more than 40 years, but in his later years he suffered from spells of madness.

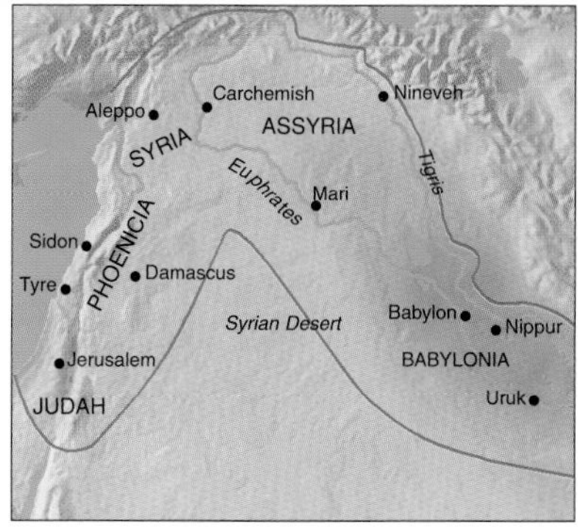

The map shows Nebuchadnezzar's Babylonian Empire at its fullest extent, controlling all of the lands known as the Fertile Crescent.

▶ Babylon was a seafaring nation, situated on the Euphrates River. Great reed boats were built that traveled as far as India and East Africa. It was also the focus of land routes from Asia to the West.

THE CITY OF BABYLON

The Greek historian, Herodotus, described Babylon as the most splendid city in the world. It was already ancient when Nebuchadnezzar rebuilt it with new temples, palaces, roads, walls, gates, and a bridge across the Euphrates. The Temple of Marduk, or Bel, a Sumerian-style ziggurat, was very tall and became known as the Tower of Babel. The Greeks regarded the Hanging Gardens as one of the wonders of the world. Babylon was a metropolis with markets and workshops selling and making everything imaginable. It supplied Greeks, Indians, Persians, and Egyptians with all kinds of goods.

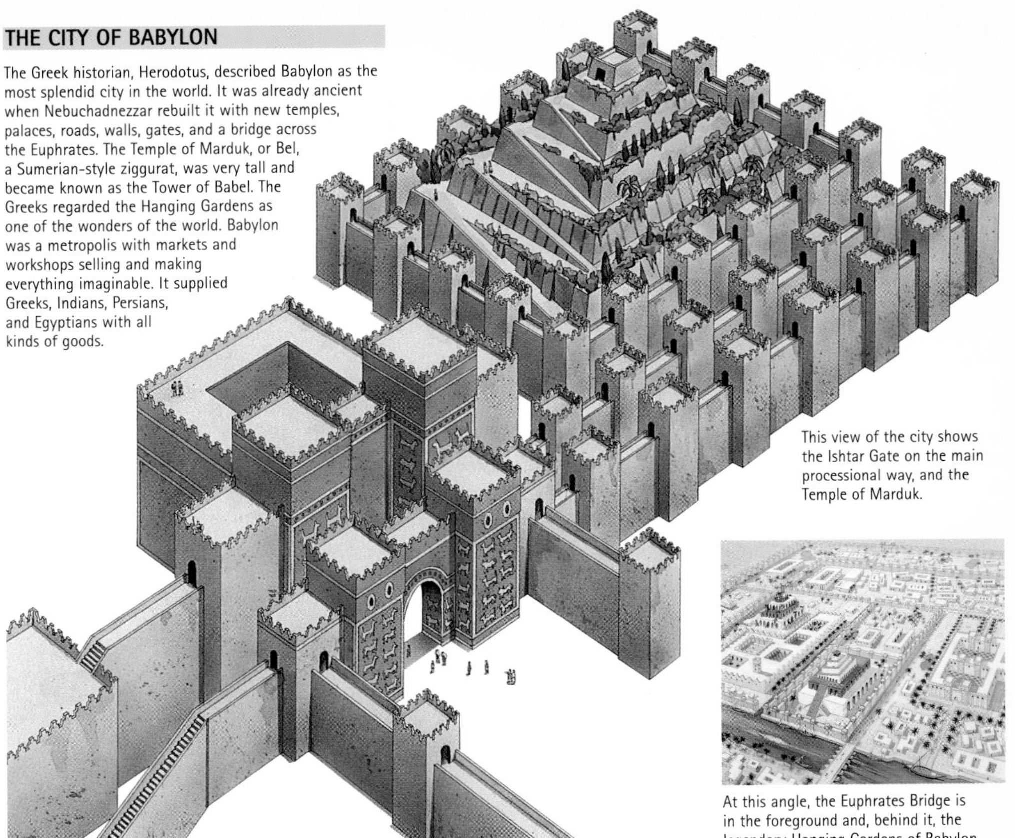

This view of the city shows the Ishtar Gate on the main processional way, and the Temple of Marduk.

At this angle, the Euphrates Bridge is in the foreground and, behind it, the legendary Hanging Gardens of Babylon.

DECLINE AND FALL

The Babylonian Empire survived for only six years after Nebuchadnezzar died. His son, Awil-Marduk (given the name of "Evil Merodach" in the Bible), reigned for three years before being assassinated. Two other kings, one of them a child, reigned for just three more years.

A Syrian prince, Nabu-Na'id, then seized power in Babylon, and tried to persuade the people to worship his own god, Sin, rather than Marduk. He made Belsharusur (Belshazzar) co-ruler.

Meanwhile, in Persia, a new young king, Cyrus II, had risen to power after taking the throne in 557 B.C. He had ambitions to take over Mesopotamia and found a Persian empire. In pursuit of this goal, he invaded Babylonia and captured the city of Babylon in 539 B.C. Nabu-Na'id was deposed and his son killed by the invading forces. Cyrus the Great, as he became known, freed the rebellious Jews who had been made captive in 586 B.C. by the young Nebuchadnezzar.

Babylonia was then ruled by the Persians for more than two relatively peaceful and stable centuries, until the time of another youthful king, Alexander the Great, who defeated the Persians and captured Babylon in 331 B.C., making it his capital.

KEY DATES	
853	Assyria takes control of Babylon
626	Babylonians rebel against the Assyrians
612	Nineveh (Assyria) sacked by the Babylonians and the Medes
604	Nebuchadnezzar becomes king—Babylon's peak
539	Babylon conquered by Cyrus the Great of Persia

THE PERSIAN EMPIRE 559–331 B.C.

Iran used to be known as Persia. Its people comprised two groups, the Medes and the Persians, who migrated to Persia from central Asia about 2,800 years ago.

Darius I (548–486 B.C.) was a great general who extended the empire east and west, reorganizing it into 20 provinces. He built good roads as well as a new royal capital at Persepolis. From Lydia in Anatolia, he introduced gold and silver money to Persia. Darius called himself *Shahanshah*, king of kings.

At first the Medes were very powerful. Then, nearly 2,550 years ago, Cyrus, the ruler of the Persians, rebelled against the Medes and seized control. Cyrus the Great made Persia the center of a mighty new empire. His capital was at Ecbatana on the Silk Road, now buried under the modern city of Hamadan.

CONQUERING KINGS

Cyrus commanded a mighty army of cavalry and skilled archers. Taking advantage of the weaknesses of his neighbors, he conquered an empire extending from the Mediterranean to Afghanistan. His son Cambyses invaded Egypt. The Persians gained the support of their subjects by ruling fairly. Darius I eventually extended the empire into India and Greece. He also reorganized it, appointing *satraps* (governors) to each province. They paid him taxes in cereals, silver, and agricultural produce.

This frieze was carved in low relief on a thin stone at the Palace of Apadana, Persepolis. These works of art covered the walls and stairways of the palace.

UNITING THE ANCIENT WORLD

Darius built roads and market towns to reach all parts of his huge empire, and encouraged trade by introducing a standard coinage. The Persians controlled the western end of the Silk Road from China, and all trade from India to the Mediterranean. This wealthy, cosmopolitan empire linked most of the ancient civilizations of the time. However, it relied on the strength of its rulers. Eventually, the Greeks brought the empire down and took it over.

▶ The tomb of Darius was built at Pasargadae in Iran. After his death, the high point of the Persian Empire had passed and it went into a steady decline, and the great Persian monuments fell to ruins. This tomb now sits alone in a vast field.

This is a Persian infantryman. The Persian army was successful because of its clever use of strategy. It covered tremendous distances during its campaigns.

RELIGIOUS TEACHING

In religion, the Persians followed the teachings of a Persian prophet named Zarathustra (in Greek, Zoroaster). Zoroaster had adapted the ancient Persian tribal religion, which the Persians had brought with them from central Asia. They worshiped one god, Ahura Mazda, who they believed was locked in divine battle with Ahriman (representing sleep) and Satan (representing evil).

Although Zoroastrianism did not become a world religion, it later influenced many other faiths including Christianity. This influence can be clearly seen in the biblical Book of Revelations.

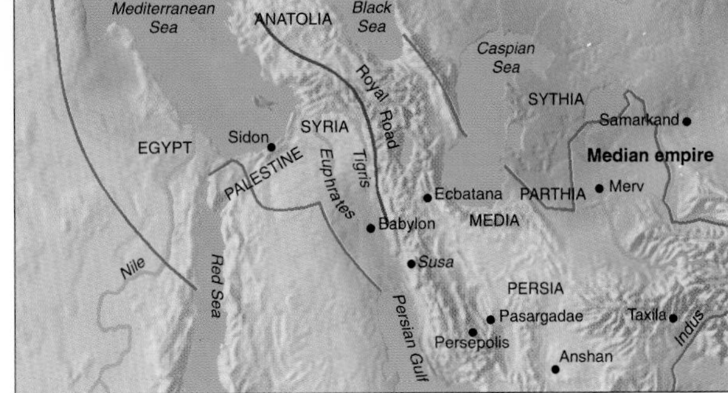

This map shows the Persian Empire at its greatest extent under Darius. Susa became its administrative center and Persepolis was its center of state. The Royal Road was built to speed communications.

KEY DATES

c.850–750 The Medes and Persians migrate into Iran
c.600 Zoroaster reforms the ancient Persian religion
559–525 Cyrus the Great creates the Persian Empire
521–486 Darius expands empire to its high point
480 Greeks halt Persian expansion at Salamis
331 Fall of Persia to Alexander the Great

An impression from a cylinder seal, with cuneiform writing on the left, shows Darius I hunting a lion from a chariot with a bow and arrow. The winged figure overhead is an image of Ahura Mazda, main god of the Persians.

Darius built himself a grand palace in his new capital city of Persepolis. The staircase of the palace was carved with this procession of dignitaries in ceremonial attire.

THE CLASSICAL WORLD

499 B.C.–A.D. 500

This was the great age of ancient Greece and Rome. These two extraordinary civilizations were responsible for shaping much of the world we live in today. By about 100 B.C., the ancient world was dominated by four empires. The Roman Empire was the most powerful, stretching from Europe to North Africa. In the Far East, the Han dynasty controlled almost all of what is now China, and the Middle East was ruled by the Sassanids. In India, the Gupta family held power. But, by about A.D. 450, these four empires had collapsed.

▲ Sages and philosophers traditionally influenced Chinese society, but they came under attack during the modernizing Qin period.

◀ The Temple of Olympian Zeus in Athens, Greece, was begun in the 500s B.C., but not completed until the 100s B.C.

THE WORLD AT A GLANCE 499 B.C.–A.D. 50

The classical civilizations that thrived during this period set many trends and patterns for later times. Discoveries by the Greeks form the foundation of the modern knowledge of biology, mathematics, physics, literature, philosophy, and politics. Alexander the Great spread Greek ideas into much of Asia. Later, by A.D. 100, the Romans took Greek culture farther afield into Europe and North Africa. Farther east, the Han dynasty controlled large areas of China, and the Guptas spread classical Hindu culture throughout much of India.

In these empires, life was mainly secure and peaceful, with strong governments and armies. But they soon came under attack from tribes of nomads called barbarians, and the cost of fighting these was high. By about A.D. 450 the great empires had collapsed.

At about the same time, the city of Teotihuacán in Mesoamerica was at its height. Its neighbors, the Maya, built great cities and roads, and dominated Mesoamerica until the 1400s.

NORTH AMERICA

North American tribes were spread thinly across the continent. They led simple lives—hunting, gathering, and farming in a variety of environments. In the Ohio area, the Hopewell culture built towns and ceremonial mounds, marking the first civilization north of Mexico. About A.D. 500, the Anasazi culture began to develop in Utah, Arizona, and New Mexico.

NORTH AMERICA

MESOAMERICA AND SOUTH AMERICA

MESOAMERICA AND SOUTH AMERICA

In Mexico and in Peru, a number of civilizations grew. They had their greatest periods between A.D. 1 and A.D. 600. In Mexico, the great trading city of Teotihuacán, with its pyramids and palaces led the way. The Maya were beginning a civilization that would develop writing and astronomy. Quite separately, in Peru, the city of Tiahuanaco grew, high in the Andes. On the Peruvian coast, the Chavin, Nazca, and Moche cultures also began to establish themselves.

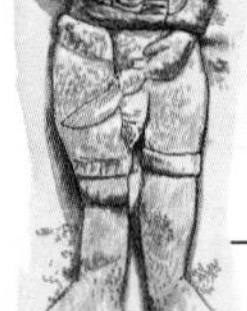

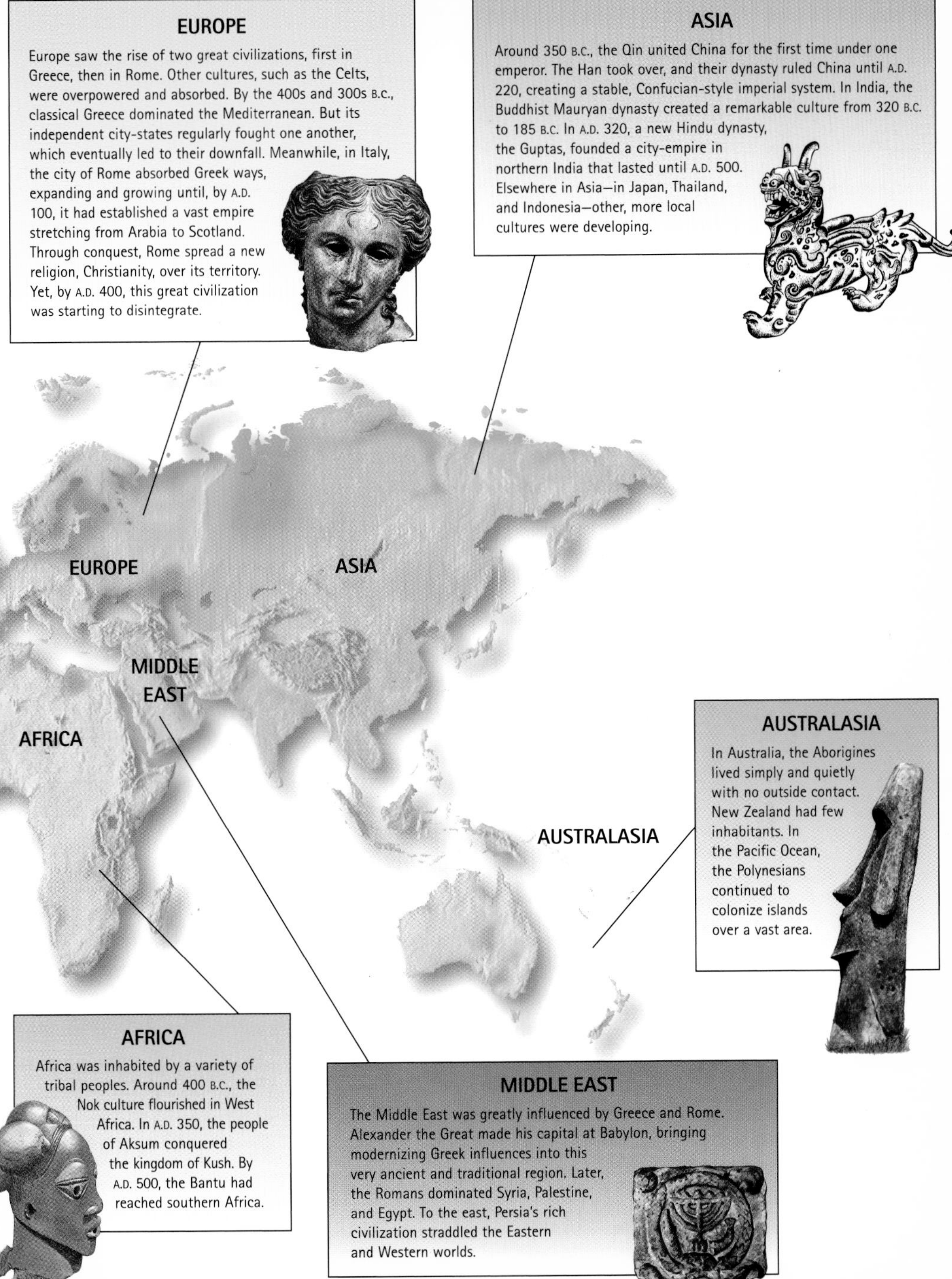

EUROPE

Europe saw the rise of two great civilizations, first in Greece, then in Rome. Other cultures, such as the Celts, were overpowered and absorbed. By the 400s and 300s B.C., classical Greece dominated the Mediterranean. But its independent city-states regularly fought one another, which eventually led to their downfall. Meanwhile, in Italy, the city of Rome absorbed Greek ways, expanding and growing until, by A.D. 100, it had established a vast empire stretching from Arabia to Scotland. Through conquest, Rome spread a new religion, Christianity, over its territory. Yet, by A.D. 400, this great civilization was starting to disintegrate.

ASIA

Around 350 B.C., the Qin united China for the first time under one emperor. The Han took over, and their dynasty ruled China until A.D. 220, creating a stable, Confucian-style imperial system. In India, the Buddhist Mauryan dynasty created a remarkable culture from 320 B.C. to 185 B.C. In A.D. 320, a new Hindu dynasty, the Guptas, founded a city-empire in northern India that lasted until A.D. 500. Elsewhere in Asia—in Japan, Thailand, and Indonesia—other, more local cultures were developing.

AUSTRALASIA

In Australia, the Aborigines lived simply and quietly with no outside contact. New Zealand had few inhabitants. In the Pacific Ocean, the Polynesians continued to colonize islands over a vast area.

AFRICA

Africa was inhabited by a variety of tribal peoples. Around 400 B.C., the Nok culture flourished in West Africa. In A.D. 350, the people of Aksum conquered the kingdom of Kush. By A.D. 500, the Bantu had reached southern Africa.

MIDDLE EAST

The Middle East was greatly influenced by Greece and Rome. Alexander the Great made his capital at Babylon, bringing modernizing Greek influences into this very ancient and traditional region. Later, the Romans dominated Syria, Palestine, and Egypt. To the east, Persia's rich civilization straddled the Eastern and Western worlds.

CLASSICAL GREECE 600–337 B.C.

Ancient Greece was made up of independent city-states, each with its own laws and customs. Here, the Greeks created a new society with new ideas.

Athens led the way in the development of richly painted pottery.

Each city-state or *polis* grew up on the plains, and the mountains around them provided natural limits and defenses. Citizens built high, strong walls around their cities, and an *acropolis* (fort) was erected on a high place inside the walls. At the heart of each city was the *agora*, a large open space used for meetings and markets.

CITIES AND COLONIES

The two most important city-states were Athens and Sparta. There were many other cities, such as Corinth, Chalcis, Miletos, Smyrna, and Eretria, each with its own way of life, customs, and forms of government. The city-states expanded to build colonies northward on the Black Sea, in Cyrenaica on the coast of north Africa (Libya), Sicily, southern Italy, and even as far away as the southern coasts of France and Spain. Greek city-states were very competitive with each other.

The Aegean Sea was well placed for the founding of a maritime civilization, with cities dotted along both coastlines, and easy access to the Mediterranean Sea.

GREEK CULTURE

The Greeks created a new society with new ideas. They fought hard for their freedom, especially against the Persians who threatened Greece. Being traders, sailors, and adventurers, the Greeks influenced many faraway cultures. Philosophers, doctors, and scientists taught a new way of thinking, based on observation and discussion. Old rural traditions died off as the cities grew to dominate the countryside. New art, architecture, and sciences were created.

Here, the traders of a Greek colonizing expedition, around 500 B.C., draw their ships up onto the beach to start business. The newly built walled city would contain a marketplace, temples, law courts, and government offices as well as houses, workshops, and defenses.

◀ At the battle of Salamis, c. 480 B.C., 380 Greek ships, called *triremes*, faced a Persian force of 1,200 ships. The more mobile triremes drove the Persians into a confused huddle. Persian defeats on land and at sea led them to withdraw from Greece.

EDUCATION

The sons of freemen were sent to school, and girls were taught weaving and household skills by their mothers. Starting at the age of six or seven, the boys learned reading, writing, dancing, music, and athletics. They wrote on wax tablets, using a stick called a *stylus*.

◀ Here, Greek children study a number of subjects with their tutors.

▼ This painting shows a schoolboy being tested by one of his tutors.

DISUNITY BETWEEN CITY-STATES

Athens, Sparta, and other city-states united to fight off Persian invasions for 60 years, and triumphed at the battles of Marathon and Salamis around 480 B.C. However, from 431 B.C. they spent more than 25 years fighting each other in the Peloponnesian War because Sparta feared the growth of Athenian power. The independent Greek cities, therefore, never united as one country. This disunity eventually resulted in an invasion around 330 B.C. by Philip II of Macedon, father of Alexander the Great.

KEY DATES

800s	The first city-states founded in Greece
594	Reform of the Athenian constitution
540s	Persians conquer Ionia (eastern Aegean)
480	Persian invasion ends
431–404	Peloponnesian Wars: Athens against Sparta
404	Athens falls to Sparta
371	Sparta declines—Thebes now main city-state
337	Philip of Macedon invades Greece

A silver four-drachma "owl" piece was the most common coin in the ancient Greek world. Issued in Athens, one side carried a picture of Athena, goddess of wisdom and patron and protector of Athens. The other side carried a picture of an owl, Athena's symbol, carrying an olive branch.

Greek philosophers have had a great impact on history, and their works are still studied today. The freethinking atmosphere in Athens stimulated questioning and discussion on many different subjects. Herodotus and Thucydides were famous Greek historians, and Plato, Socrates, and Aristotle were philosophers and scientists.

CHINA: THE QIN DYNASTY 221–206 B.C.

The warlike Qin tribes of western China conquered their neighbors from 350 B.C. onward. By 221 B.C. they had built the empire from which China takes its name.

King Zheng of Qin (pronounced "*Chin*") united most of China in just ten years, ending the Warring States period. He changed his name to Shi Huangdi (meaning "First Emperor") and founded the first imperial dynasty of China.

The ancient Chinese were great inventors. They invented the wheelbarrow, which they used to carry both goods and people in the 2nd century B.C.—Europe only adopted it 1,000 years later.

IMPERIAL CHINA

Shi Huangdi reorganized the government, bringing everything under central control. He standardized all weights and measures, Chinese writing, and even the width of wagon wheels; he made laws and institutions in the Qin tradition, and introduced a single currency. He was a ruthless modernizer, abolishing the powers of the feudal aristocracy and sending out administrators to run the regions. He built roads and canals, and improved farming with irrigation and drainage schemes. To protect China from barbarians, construction began on the Great Wall, much of which still exists today. He established imperial traditions that remained consistent through different dynastic periods over 2,000 years. In 221 B.C., Shi Huangdi destroyed many traditional literary works, including those of Confucius, and even executed 400 scholars, to ensure modernization.

Sages and philosophers traditionally influenced Chinese society and government and also played a religious role. As preservers of knowledge, they came under attack during the modernizing Qin period.

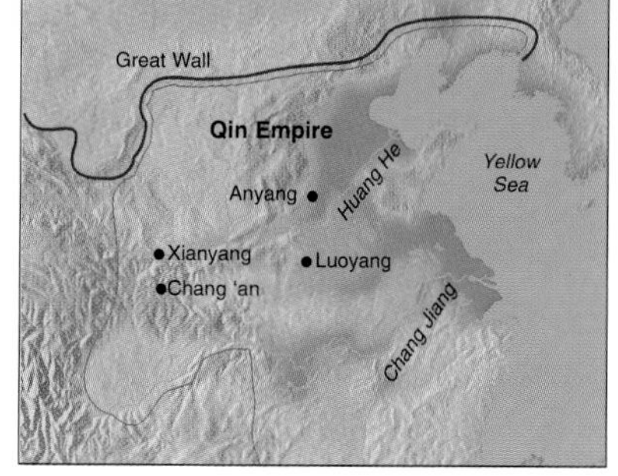

For the first time, China was united. The Qin built the Great Wall to protect it from tribes from the north. The Qin capital was Xianyang on the upper Yellow River, the area where the Qin originated.

THE MANDATE OF HEAVEN

Shi Huangdi was a warrior who used cavalry rather than chariots. He was used to being obeyed, and some of his actions made him very unpopular. Yet he commanded respect and achieved results, and he used his power to make changes quickly and to unite China. He also had principles. He believed that the emperor had been given the "mandate of heaven" by the gods, and that he must earn the support of the gods by governing well. This principle meant that the emperor could also be deposed if he misgoverned the country.

Life was bustling in a typical Qin town of a few thousand people, with its market, buildings, and defenses.

KEY DATES

350s	Qin becomes a militaristic state
315	Qin becomes the leading state in China
256	Qin annexes the state of Zhou (Luoyang)
230	King Qin Zheng begins to unify China by force
221	Qin dynasty unites the country for the first time in one empire
214	To protect China from Hun raids, construction of the Great Wall begins
212	Shi Hunagdi burns all historical documents, books are banned, and Chinese script standardized
209–202	Civil war between competing warlords
202	Founding of the Han dynasty by Liu Bang

This bronze statue is a fantastic fire-breathing, winged animal from Chinese mythology. The Chinese also made creatures like this in jade.

THE QIN LEGACY

Shi Huangdi died in 210 B.C., and four years later the Qin dynasty was overthrown because the changes and laws they made were too harsh. A civil war broke out. The idea of a united empire, however, had become fixed in the minds of the people. An ordinary man, named Liu Bang, who had become a Qin official, founded a new dynasty and, as a result, gained popular support. The Han dynasty was to rule for 400 years, on the basis that Shi Huangdi had established.

Shi Huangdi's tomb housed his body and possessions for use in the afterlife. It also contained 7,000 larger-than-life terracotta soldiers. Each face was realistic and may have represented the actual faces of a specific soldier.

THE GREAT WALL OF CHINA

The Qin used large numbers of forced laborers to build much of the Great Wall. It was 1,400 mi. (2,250km) long and built from packed earth and rubble. Stone, bricks, and mortar were added later. The scale of this operation shows how important it was to the Chinese to keep the raiding tribes of the north out. These tribes preyed on Chinese security and prosperity, and China suffered greatly before the wall was built and the raiders beaten off.

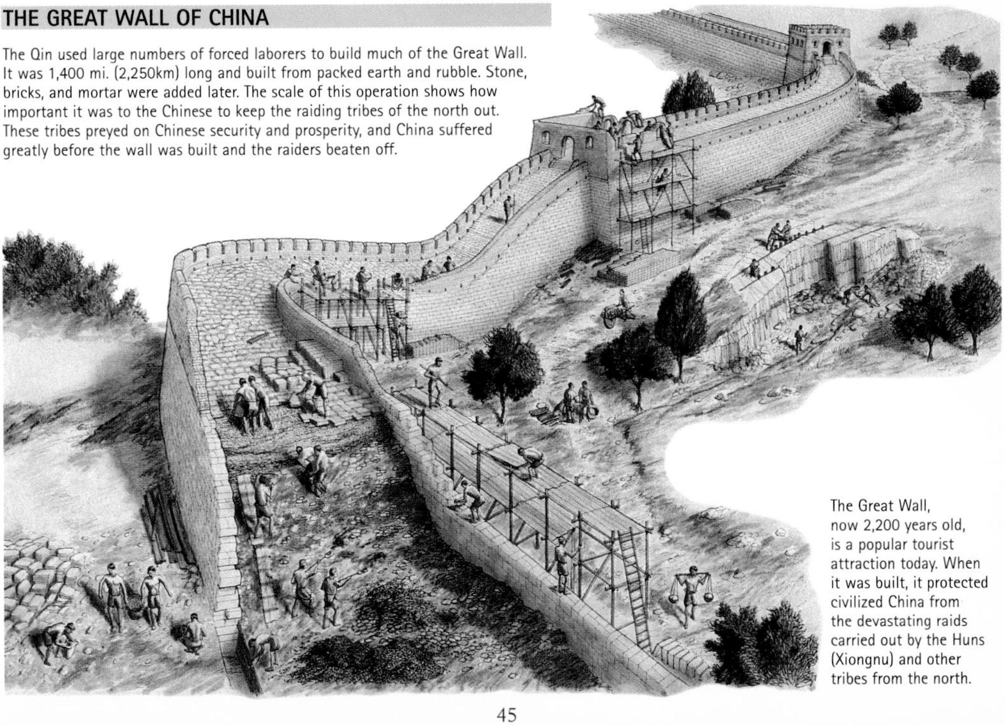

The Great Wall, now 2,200 years old, is a popular tourist attraction today. When it was built, it protected civilized China from the devastating raids carried out by the Huns (Xiongnu) and other tribes from the north.

AFRICA 500 B.C.–A.D. 500

Most of Africa was unaffected by outside influences. In West Africa, new nations were being formed, and migration was changing southern Africa.

This terracotta head from Nok is a fine example of sculpture that flourished from 400 B.C. to A.D. 200.

The introduction of the camel to the Sahara brought major changes around 100 B.C. Caravans were able to cross the desert carrying gold, ivory, gums, spices, and slaves. Trading towns became established in West Africa: Jenne-jeno, Niani, Yelwa, and Nok were on rivers or at the edges of deserts and rain forests. These towns were the capitals of the first budding African states. North–south trade passed through Meroë and Aksum, bypassing the Sahara into the regions now known as Chad, Rwanda, and Kenya.

AKSUM

Meroë collapsed in 350 B.C., and Aksum, on the Red Sea coast of Ethiopia, grew rich exporting ivory, precious stones, and perfumes to Arabia, Greece, and Rome, reaching its peak in A.D. 350. Around that time its king, Ezana, adopted Christianity. Cities and great monoliths were built. Aksum thrived until A.D. 1000.

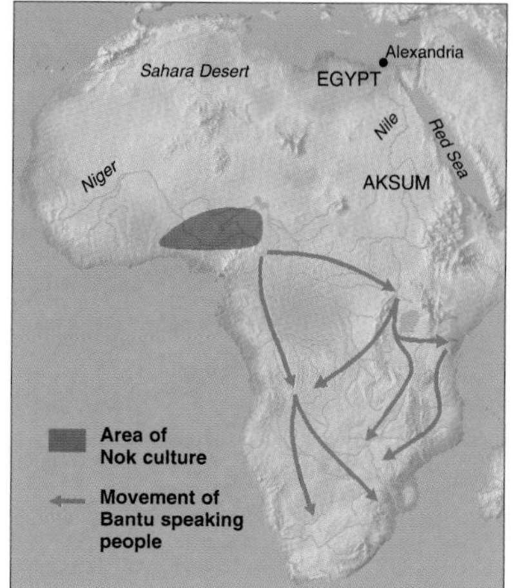

Africa had four main centers of cultural growth: Aksum (Ethiopia), the Berber north African coast, negro West Africa, and the developing Bantu areas farther south.

BANTU EXPANSION

Farming, Bantu-speaking people from Nigeria gradually migrated south and east, and by A.D. 500 they had occupied central and southern Africa, leaving the rain forests to the pygmies and the Kalahari Desert to the Khoisan bushmen. On Africa's east coast the Bantu had started to trade with Greeks and Romans.

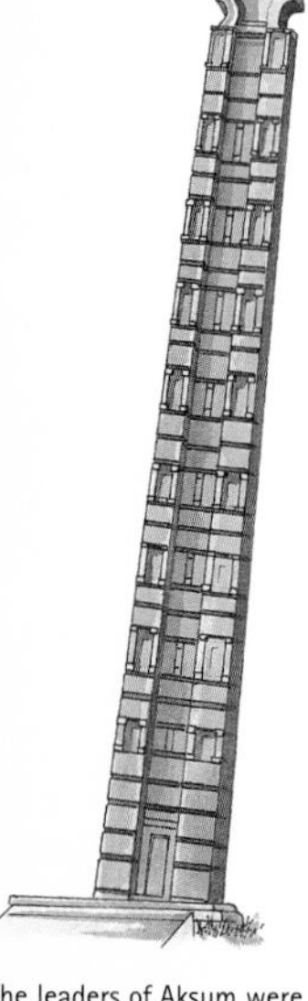

The leaders of Aksum were very religious. They built tall monoliths like this at places of importance, such as over royal tombs.

To smelt iron, iron ore was put into an earthen furnace. Bellows were then used to raise its temperature to extract metal from the ore.

Greek trading missions on the east African coast bought medicinal herbs, aromatic gums, jewels, and gold from the Bantu-speaking tribespeople of the hinterlands.

JUDEA 600 B.C.–A.D. 135

Since their 60-year exile in Babylon, from 597 B.C., the Jews, with their different religious beliefs, had grown further apart from their Near-Eastern neighbors.

The Western Wall in Jerusalem is at the site of the Temple that was destroyed by the Romans in A.D. 70.

The Jews worshiped one god, Yahweh, built synagogues, and observed strict religious laws. On returning from exile in Babylon in 538 B.C., they emphasized Jewish law and beliefs, and set themselves apart from non-Jews, or Gentiles. Palestine was under Greek rule and many Jews fought to stop their influence destroying Jewish traditions.

ROMAN PALESTINE

After Greek rule, Judea was independent for nearly 80 years before being conquered by Rome. The Romans appointed Herod as king of Judea in 37 B.C. Jewish people were free to travel and trade, and many left to settle elsewhere. When Pontius Pilate became Judea's Roman governor in A.D. 26, life became hard for the Jews. They loathed the Romans and their taxes. After much rebelliousness, the Romans forced the Jews to leave Judea in A.D. 135.

The *menorah*, a Jewish ceremonial candlestick, was shaped by Moses to signify the seven days of Creation. One stood in the Temple at Jerusalem.

The ancient fortress of Masada is where besieged Jewish rebels committed suicide in A.D. 132 rather than surrender to the Romans.

THE ROMAN REPUBLIC 509–27 B.C.

Rome was by now run by patricians (the ruling class). They sought to expand Rome's interests, first in Italy and later throughout the Mediterranean.

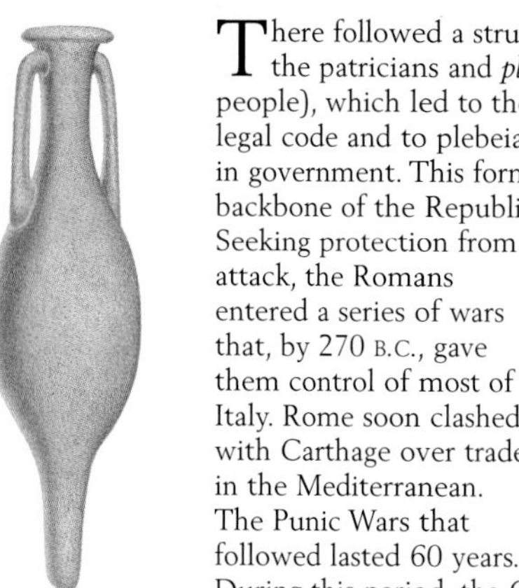

Jars like this *amphora* were used to store and transport olive oil and wine throughout the Roman Empire.

There followed a struggle between the patricians and *plebeians* (ordinary people), which led to the writing of a legal code and to plebeian influence in government. This formed the backbone of the Republic. Seeking protection from attack, the Romans entered a series of wars that, by 270 B.C., gave them control of most of Italy. Rome soon clashed with Carthage over trade in the Mediterranean. The Punic Wars that followed lasted 60 years. During this period, the Carthaginian emperor, Hannibal, led his army across the Alps to invade Italy. After a series of victories by Hannibal, the brilliant Roman general, Scipio, set off to Africa to attack Carthage. This forced Hannibal back to Carthage, where he was finally defeated by Scipio. The Romans soon established new cities, building order and prosperity and giving conquered peoples a form of Roman citizenship if they cooperated. By 44 B.C. the Romans ruled Spain, France, Europe south of the Danube, Anatolia, and northern Africa, dominating the Mediterranean. In less than 200 years, the Romans had become the controlling force in the West.

The central square or *forum* of a Roman town was where people met each other, announcements were made, markets were held, and where the town hall, treasury, and law courts were located.

The Colosseum in Rome, an enormous stadium, was used for gladiatorial contests, sports, and the gory killing of animals, captured enemies, and slaves.

Vital to the growing empire was the system of roads built to speed up trade, mail delivery, and troop movements. On the right, a water-carrying aqueduct is being built over a road.

THE END OF THE REPUBLIC

In 100 B.C., friction grew between the patricians and plebeians. The army was opened up to landless citizens, who were rewarded for their services with land and status in the colonies. Power struggles between generals ended in civil war, and, in 44 B.C., Julius Caesar became dictator for life. Alarmed Republicans assassinated him, and the Republic soon ended.

THE PUNIC WARS

Expanding their influence, the Romans came up against the Phoenicians in Carthage. The Punic Wars (264–241 and 218–202 B.C.) began over a fight for Sicily, but grew to threaten the great cities of Rome and Carthage. The Carthaginian general, Hannibal, nearly won, after invading Italy from the Alps. The Roman general, Scipio Africanus, avoided a head-on battle, instead attacking Spain in 206 and then Carthage itself in 202 B.C. The Phoenicians lost everything, and the Romans then dominated the Mediterranean Sea and its trade.

Hannibal's route
The Alps
Rome
CORSICA
SARDINIA
Mediterranean Sea
Carthage
SICILY
AFRICA
Zama

Hannibal's army marched from Spain, over the Alps, and into Italy. It was so formidable that the Romans avoided confronting it. They attacked Carthage instead, and forced Hannibal to rush back to defend it.

The Carthaginians used African elephants to frighten the Roman troops. When they crossed the Alps, most of the elephants died.

Hannibal was a brilliant strategist and a modest man who carried out maneuvers no one believed could work. The Romans beat him only by outwitting his strategy.

THE ROMAN EMPIRE 27 B.C.–A.D. 475

After Julius Caesar's death in 44 B.C., Romans preferred dictatorship to chaos. Octavian, his successor, gradually took control. He became the first emperor.

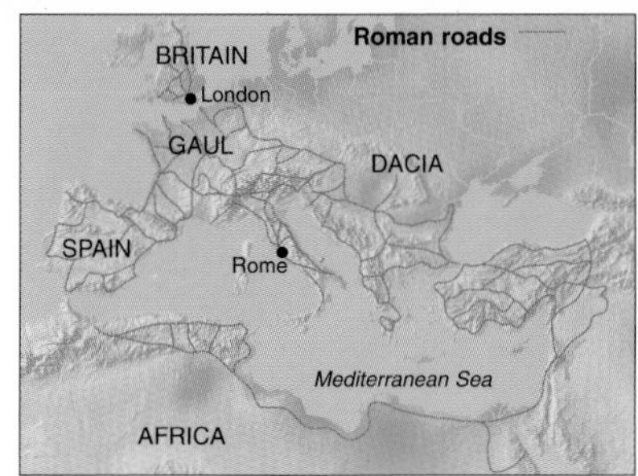

The Roman Empire dominated most of the Western world, uniting it into one economic system, under one goverment.

Octavian was Caesar's nephew. He was an able politician, getting himself elected as Consul (president) year after year. He called himself *princeps* ("first citizen"), not king. Renamed Augustus ("imposing one"), he reorganized the government and empire and imposed peace. Under him, trade extended as far as East Africa, India, and China, and the empire's towns, roads, and territories grew ever larger.

Julius Caesar was a ruthless and ambitious general and politician who conquered the Celts of Gaul and later became Rome's first dictator for life—an appointment that angered Republicans and led to Caesar's murder.

ROMAN EMPERORS

Emperors relied more on the army than on the Roman people for support. Patricians no longer had great power. Many had moved to rich country estates and the far provinces. Most of the Roman emperors chose their successors; some unpopular or controversial ones were deposed by soldiers. In A.D. 68–69, four emperors were deposed in one year. From A.D. 100, Rome was ruled by strong emperors—Trajan, Hadrian, Antoninus, and Marcus Aurelius—most of whom were not actually Roman. By A.D. 117 the empire had grown too large and Rome's soldiers could no longer be paid with booty, slaves, and land taken in conquest. The burden on Rome grew.

Heavily armed Roman legionnaires: a *centurion* (officer) with a *ballista* (catapult), a legionary (soldier), and a standard-bearer.

When attacking a fortress, legionnaires would form a protective shield like this—a *testudo* (tortoise), that advanced slowly under fire from stones and arrows.

THE ROMAN ARMY

Soldiers joined the army to gain rewards of promotion, land, or power—especially if they were not Roman. This meant that soldiers dominated the empire and its colonies, becoming landowners and the ruling class. The army was very international, often hiring barbarians as mercenaries. Legions fought in such faraway places as Scotland, Morocco, and Arabia. Roads, forts, and border walls were built to maintain security.

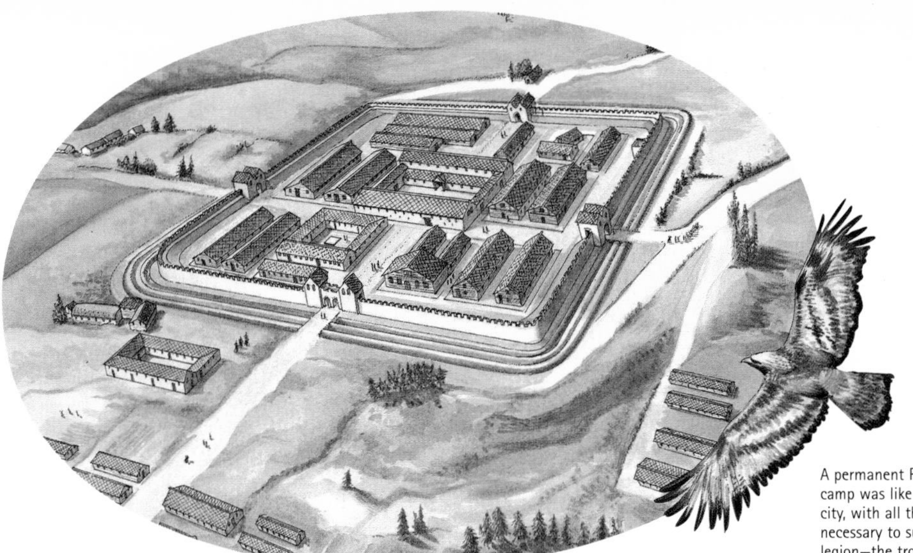

A permanent Roman army camp was like a miniature city, with all the services necessary to support a legion—the troops were, after all, far from their homes in other parts of the empire. These military bases were located in the areas that were most in need of permanent protection.

THE ROMAN EMPIRE

The final conquests, in the century following Augustus, had been in Britain, Syria, Palestine, and Egypt. The Jews and British had been difficult to beat, and the Parthians impossible. However, most of the conquered peoples adapted. People in Gaul, North Africa, Syria, Britain, and Hungary adopted Roman ways and thought of themselves as Roman citizens. Running a huge empire was difficult, and it was united by business, not religious or ethnic ties. Provincial peoples were allowed to get on with their lives, as long as they obeyed the rules set by the Romans.

The Appian Way, a major road from Rome to the southeast coast, was built in 312 B.C. Soldiers, traders, and travelers could now travel along it very quickly.

KEY DATES	
509 B.C.	Roman republic founded
496	Romans defeat Latins at Battle of Lake Regillus
493	Roman-Latin alliance forms the Latin League, which fights the Etruscans
390	Rome sacked by Celts
306	Romans defeat Etruscans
300s	Romans expand to dominate Italy
264–202	Punic Wars and the fall of Carthage
146	Rome takes Greece
50s	Caesar conquers France
49–31	Civil War between competing generals
27 B.C.	Octavian: end of republic, growth of empire
A.D. 160	Plague and crisis cut population and trade
212	Roman citizenship granted to all inhabitants of the empire
286	Diocletian divides and reorganizes the empire
324	Founding of Constantinople
370	Barbarian attacks on the empire
410	The Visigoths sack Rome—rapid decline of the city results
476	Fall of the last emperor, Romulus Augustus

THE CELTS 500 B.C.–A.D. 43

The Celts were a loose grouping of tribes living in southern Germany from around 1500 B.C. By Roman times, the Celts dominated much of Europe.

This Celtic bronze shield was made around A.D. 100. Set with precious stones, it was more likely to have been made for ceremonial use than for use in battle.

Around 500 B.C., the Celts were the dominant European power. They had expanded from a heartland in what is now southern Germany. They were not a nation, but more a confederation of individual tribes with a shared culture. Their influence eventually stretched from Spain to Britain, Germany, and northern Italy, and as far as central Anatolia.

CELTIC LIFE

The Celts were tribal farmers who gathered around their chiefs' *oppidae* or strongholds. These were often hill forts, and some of them later became villages or towns. Most Celts were homesteaders and small farmers, living in a variety of tribes. Sometimes these tribes divided, with one group moving to another place, so that certain tribes might be spread through different areas. The Celts were bound together by the Druids, who were learned priests, lawmakers, bards, and wise men. They also had gifted musicians, artists, and metalworkers. Their jewelry, pottery, weapons, and drinking vessels were often decorated with intricate designs and geometric shapes. The Celts traded with Rome, Greece, and other countries, but they were not much influenced by these civilizations.

Vertcingetorix was a Gaulish chief who organized a successful rebellion against Julius Caesar's invasion of Gaul in 52 B.C., but he was later forced to surrender.

This bull's head appeared on a huge bronze ceremonial cauldron found at Gundestrup in Denmark. Animal figures, like this, and geometric designs were a popular feature on pieces of elegant Celtic metalwork.

POWER AND LAW

Each Celt was a free person with individual rights. Druidic justice was famous, and bonds of loyalty within each tribe were strong. The chiefs were elected by tribespeople, and the high kings by the chiefs. Both could be deposed if they did not do a good job.

A Celtic chief and members of his tribe feast in their timbered hall while listening to the poetic songs of a bard. Laws, history, stories, news, and religious teachings were communicated by the druidic bard.

Celtic roundhouses were made of timber and thatch, with wattle-and-daub (or sometimes stone) walls. Smoke floated out through the thatched roof, but rain was unable to seep in. Sleeping space was around the inside of the wall, and cooking and washing were done around the central fire.

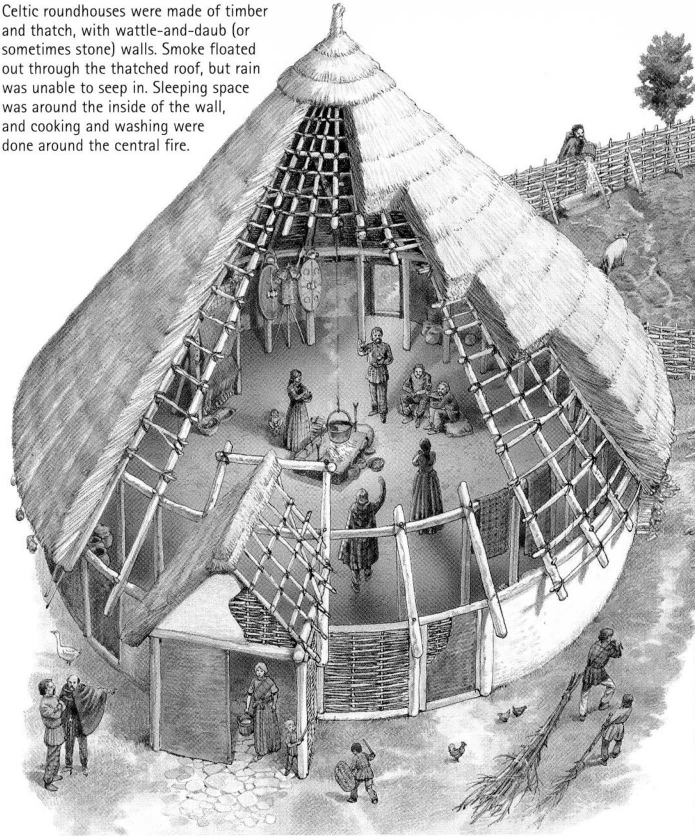

▼ The Celtic stag-god Cernunnos or Hurn was hammered and chiseled into the side of this large bronze cauldron around 1,900 years ago.

CELTIC WARRIORS

Known as fierce warriors (the women also fought), the Celts used iron to make their weapons and tools. In 390 B.C., they sacked Rome, and in 280 B.C. they raided Greece and Anatolia, seeking booty. Sometimes they even fought among themselves. The Romans exploited this when conquering Gaul (France) and Britain. The British Celtic leader, Caradoc (Caractacus), was betrayed by other Celts. Disunited, the British warriors lost their independence in A.D. 43–80. The Celts came to accept Roman rule and later fought with the Romans against Germanic barbarians. The Celts were also the first European Christians. After the fall of Rome, Celtic ways in Europe survived only in Ireland, Cornwall, Brittany, and parts of Scotland and Wales.

Boudicca was the queen of the Iceni of the East of England. She headed a rebellion against the occupying Romans in Britain in A.D. 60 in which seventy thousand Romans were killed. However, the rebellion was eventually crushed, and Boudicca committed suicide.

CHINA: THE HAN DYNASTY 202 B.C.–A.D 220

The Han was the first long-lasting dynasty of united imperial China. Han China enjoyed stability and greatness and was a fine example of civilization.

▲ A ceramic horse and rider made in Han China around 80 B.C. Stirrups were not introduced into China until around A.D. 300.

For 400 years from 202 B.C. to A.D. 220, China was ruled by emperors of the Han dynasty. They were more lenient and stable than the Qin, and practiced fair Confucian principles of law and administration.

THE EARLY HAN

The dynasty was founded by Liu Bang, a commoner who was popular because he relaxed the harsh laws, cut taxes, and favored the people. The capital was Chang'an, which, after 100 years, became the world's largest city. It was at the end of the Silk Road along which China traded with Persia and Rome. Han China saw itself as the "Middle Kingdom," the center of the world. There was a great flowering of culture, wealth, and learning. At this time, Han China was as large and developed as the extensive Roman Empire. The Han developed a system of administration by highly educated officials called mandarins. People who wanted to work as public officials had to take an examination on the writings of Confucius.

This bronze model of a prosperous man in his carriage was found in the tomb of the Han general, Wuwei. It was probably made around A.D. 100.

THE MARTIAL EMPEROR

Wu Di, the "Martial Emperor," reigned for 55 years from 141 B.C. He added part of central Asia, Korea, and much of southern China to his empire. At great expense, he beat back the Xiongnu (Huns) of Mongolia, who often raided China. He improved the mandarin administration, built schools, canals, cities, and buildings, and encouraged foreign contact. Buddhism was introduced to China during this high point in the country's long history.

▼ Here, Chinese soldiers of the Han period engage in battle. Lacking stirrups, the horsemen on both sides were easily knocked to the ground during fighting at close quarters.

The emperor's many representatives were always treated with great respect. The speedy transportation of officials from one place to another was helped by stations where fresh horses were provided.

◀ Emperor Kuang-Wu declared himself ruler and ruled from A.D. 25–57.

WANG MANG

During the following century, the Han grew weak, while the nobles grew ever stronger. A courtier, Wang Mang, rebelled, took power, and ruled from A.D. 9–23. He introduced many changes and reforms, favoring the people against landowners and nobles, and reforming land rights and the judicial system. Eventually the nobles overthrew Wang Mang, and the Han dynasty was restored.

THE LATER HAN

The Han produced exquisite objects of wood, lacquer, and silk. They also replaced many of the writings that had been destroyed by the Qin. Chinese inventors were far ahead of the rest of the world. Their invention of paper took centuries to reach the West. Many of the cities they built were large and elegant. However, the population had grown, and rebellions among landless and poor peasants became frequent. Barbarians again attacked the borders, and warlords took over the army. The last Han emperor gave up his throne in A.D. 220 and the empire fell apart.

City streets in Han China were crowded. The muddy roads were full of carts, chariots, and traders. Craftsmen, letter writers, storytellers, and astrologers also plied their trade noisily in the open air.

CHRISTIANITY A.D. 30–400

Around the time that Jesus of Nazareth was born there were many faiths and sects in the Roman Empire. Within 400 years, Christianity became dominant.

The Chi-Rho symbol, or labarum, was adopted by early Christians. Its P and X are the first two letters in the Greek spelling of Christ. The symbol Chi-Rho itself is a short form of the word *chreston*, or "good omen."

The Jewish people believed that a Messiah (savior) would be born to lead them. At the time that Jesus of Nazareth was born, Judea was suffering under Roman rule. At about the age of 30, Jesus began publicly teaching, and it is said that he performed many miracles, such as healing. The Jewish authorities accused him of blasphemy and he was tried before the Roman governor, Pontius Pilate. He was crucified, but his followers reported seeing him alive after his death.

A CHURCH IS BORN

This "resurrection" formed the basis of a new faith, breaking with old Jewish traditions and founded by Jesus' closest disciples, the apostles. It gradually spread among both exiled Jews and non-Jews throughout the Roman world. Early followers—especially Paul—taught that Christianity was open to anyone who chose to be baptized. By A.D. 300, it had spread to Egypt, Aksum, Syria, Armenia, Anatolia, Greece, Rome, France, Britain, and India.

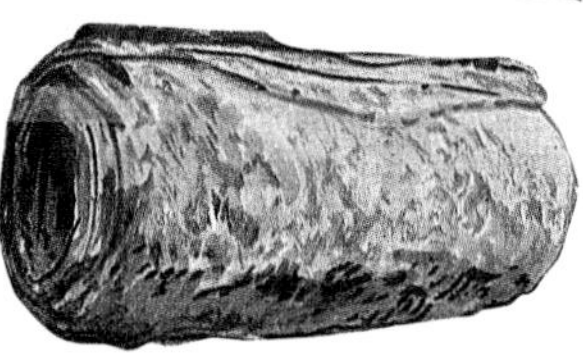

The Essenes were a Jewish sect. Their abandoned scrolls, found in a cave at Qumran near the Dead Sea, in 1947, included one which deals with the Messiah and what was to happen after he appeared.

Christians kept their faith quietly, because the Roman authorities often persecuted them, and caused many of them to go into hiding. Many died a painful death in the arena. In Egypt, a group of Christians withdrew to the desert to live as hermits. They were the first Christian monks.

A painting of Jesus as he was portrayed in the first centuries after his death.

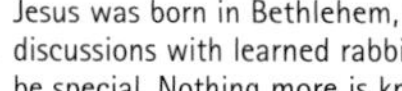

JESUS OF NAZARETH

Jesus was born in Bethlehem, in Judea. Around the age of 12, in discussions with learned rabbis at the temple, Jesus showed himself to be special. Nothing more is known about his life until he was around 30 years of age. He then began a public life of teaching. Jesus attracted large crowds. He used parables—stories that taught lessons by example. Love and respect for others was at the heart of his teaching. Three years after he began his mission, the Romans put him to death.

KEY DATES

3 B.C.	Probable year of the birth of Jesus of Nazareth, in Bethlehem
30	Approximate date of the crucifixion of Jesus Christ
45–64	The missions of Paul to Greece, Anatolia, and Rome
65–100	The Christian Gospels are written
180	Foundation of early Church institutions
249–311	Periodic persecutions of Christians in the Roman Empire
269	St. Anthony establishes Christian monasticism in Egypt
313	Emperor Constantine recognizes the Christian church
325	Church doctrine formalized
337	Constantine is baptized on his deathbed

In the A.D. 300s , an Egyptian Christian, Anthony, traveled to the Sinai desert and began the monastic tradition. St. Catherine's monastery, at the base of Mt. Sinai, is one of the oldest monasteries in the area.

STATE RELIGION

Religious persecution in the Roman Empire was halted when Emperor Constantine recognized Christianity in A.D. 313. Later it became the official state religion. Constantine called the first council of all bishops, at Nicaea, urging them to resolve their differences and write down one doctrine—the Nicene Creed. Politically, he saw the Church as a way of bringing new life to his empire. His actions defined Christianity, greatly affecting Europe and, eventually, most of the rest of the world. It also meant that the ideas of some teachers were outlawed as "heresies," and this led to the disappearance of many aspects of the faith. It also led to death or exile for those who disagreed with the doctrine. The Gnostic (Egyptian), Celtic, and Nestorian churches were examples of branches that eventually died out—although the Nestorians journeyed to Persia and as far as China to prevent this.

Constantine changed the church from a sect into a powerful institution. Legend has it that he adopted the Christian symbol after being told in a dream to paint it on his soldiers' shields before a crucial battle outside Rome in A.D. 312—a battle he won.

THE GUPTA DYNASTY A.D. 320–510

The Guptas became emperors of northern India in A.D. 320 and remained in power for 200 years. The stage was set for them by a people called the Kushans.

Krishna ("the first wise man") is one of the ten incarnations of the god Vishnu. He is associated with love and wisdom, and is featured in the *Mahabharata* and *Bhagavad Gita*, two great Hindu holy books.

The Kushans were Greek-influenced Asian nomads in Bactria (now northern Afghanistan). They founded a kingdom there in A.D. 25, then moved north into Turkestan and farther south into Afghanistan and India, dominating the area by 100. Their greatest king was Kanishka (100-130), a Buddhist who supported social tolerance and the arts. Controlling most land trade across Asia, the wealthy Kushans gave stability to Asian trade. Around 240, however, Shapur of Persia took much of their land, and they never recovered.

The Guptas were minor princes in Maghada. Chandragupta I married a Maghada princess and became king in 320. He started the Gupta tradition of aiding the arts and religions and helped develop Indian society.

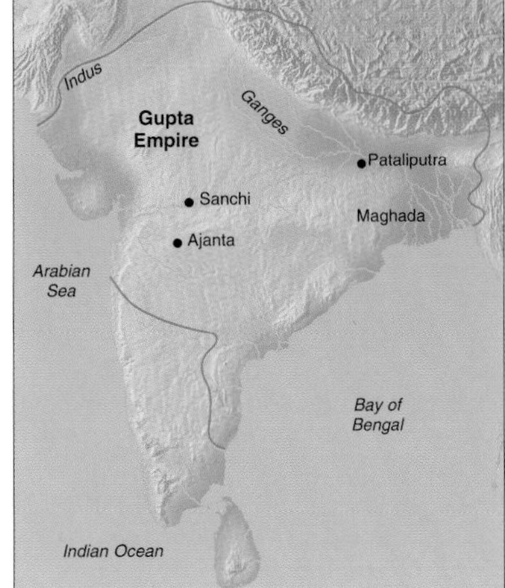

The Guptas ruled most of India and were responsible for its golden age. Their capital, Pataliputra, was one of the largest cities in the world at that time.

THE GUPTA MAHARAJAHS

Chandragupta's son Samudragupta continued in his father's footsteps. Ruling from 335 for 45 years, he expanded Gupta rule by force and diplomacy across northern India and into southeastern India. His own son Chandragupta II (380-414) took Gupta India to its high point, one of the greatest times of Indian history. Skandagupta (455-467) beat off an invasion of India by Huns from central Asia. However, the Gupta Empire had been ruled through a loose arrangement of local *rajahs* (kings) under the Gupta *maharajah* (emperor), and after Skandagupta died, many local kingdoms broke away. By 510, the Guptas had been beaten by another wave of Hun invaders, and India broke up into *rajputs* (small kingdoms). An alliance of these rajputs beat off the Huns again in 528. India remained divided for 650 years, except for a period when Sri Harsha, a religious rajah of Kanauj (606-647), succeeded in uniting northern India for 40 years.

These large seated stone Buddhas are in Cave 17 of the vast complex at Ajanta. Each of the images is shown with different *mudras*, the symbolic hand gestures still used in Indian dancing.

AJANTA CAVES

The Ajanta caves were rediscovered by a group of British officers on a tiger hunt in 1819. The 29 caves near Bombay were created by Buddhist monks between 200 B.C. and A.D. 650, using hammers and chisels. They were built as a monastic retreat, and the walls were covered with fine paintings that depict stories from the life of the Buddha. There were also many sculptures. The caves mark the peak of the religious culture of India, in which yoga and meditation were fully developed. Not far away, at Ellora, other caves contain art from the Hindu, Buddhist, and Jain religious traditions which, during the tolerant Gupta period, thrived happily alongside one another.

▲ The elaborately carved Chaitya Hall in the Ajanta caves complex was used as a temple and a hall for meditation and philosophical debates.

◀ A wall painting from Ajanta shows musicians and dancers entertaining the royal household. Actors, magicians, acrobats, and wrestlers would also have taken part in this entertainment.

GUPTA CULTURE

The Gupta maharajahs succeeded one another as good and strong rulers. Copying Asoka, they set up monuments inscribed with religious texts all over India. They built new villages and towns, putting Hindu brahmins (priests) in charge. Agriculture and trade flourished. Indians migrated as far as Indonesia, and Buddhism spread to China. Both Hindu and Buddhist cultures developed. The Hindu sacred epics, the *Mahabarata* and the *Ramayana*, were written at this time. Kalidasa, India's great poet and dramatist, wrote about love, adventure, and the beauty of nature. The Buddhist university at Nalanda had an impressive 30,000 students. This was India's golden age, its classical era of music, dance, sculpture, art, and literature.

The Buddhist Wheel of Life. The eight main spokes represent the eight different states of being that Buddhists identify in the cycle of reincarnation of souls—only one of which is waking daily life.

KEY DATES

A.D. 75–100 The Kushan invasion of India
100–130 Kanishka—the peak of the Kushan period
320–335 Rule by Chandragupta I (founder of the Gupta Empire)
335–380 Rule by Samudragupta (conquers northern and eastern India)
380–414 Rule by Chandragupta II (Gupta Empire at its peak)
470s Decline of the Gupta Empire
505 Gupta Empire ends

THE DECLINE OF ROME A.D. 200–476

In 165, a plague swept through the Roman Empire and dramatically reduced the population. Rome's subsequent decline lasted three hundred years.

The plague lasted for two years and was followed from 180 by the rule of the mad emperor Commodus, uprisings in Africa and Britain, and a succession of quickly toppled and inadequate emperors. The government at home was falling apart, and Rome was in chaos.

PROVINCIAL CHANGES

Power shifted to the provinces where the people wanted to keep their Roman status. The Parthians in the east and the British in the north created trouble, and a new force was appearing: the barbarians. Marcomanni, Goths, Franks, Alemanni, and Vandals were pressing in, and in 260–272 the Romans had to abandon Hungary and Bavaria to them. Parts of the empire such as Gaul, Britain, and Syria, were becoming separate and the Roman economy was also declining.

The emperor Diocletian created a *tetrarchy* (rule of four) to administer the two halves of the empire. The tetrarchy consisted of two emperors helped by two lieutenants.

From 250–550 the Romans were constantly battling with Germanic and Asiatic barbarians, who sought to join the empire, to raid it for booty, or to bring it down.

THE EMPIRE DIVIDES

In 284, the emperor Diocletian decided that the empire was too large for one man to rule and divided it into two, the Greek-speaking East and the Latin-speaking West. He appointed a co-emperor called Maximilian to rule the western half. The army was reorganized and enlarged to 500,000 men, and taxes were changed to pay for it. Provinces were reorganized to make them more governable. Romanitas was promoted by emphasizing the emperor's divine authority.

Hadrian's Wall
York
London
Rhine
Paris
Barbarians
Bordeaux
Danube
Huns
Milan
Marseille
Ravenna
Black Sea
Caspian Sea
Sassanians
Lisbon
Saragossa
Rome
Constantinople
Cordoba
Hippo
Antioch
Carthage
Mediterranean Sea
Jerusalem
Alexandria
Eastern Roman Empire
Western Roman Empire

The vast empire grew too large and complex to rule, so Diocletian divided it. This meant that the rich East was not inclined to help the embattled West, so the West ground to a halt. High taxation levels meant that many Romans cared little—it was cheaper to live without the empire.

Constantine ruled as emperor from 312 to 337.

CONSTANTINE

Constantine saw himself as the savior of the Roman Empire. He decided to use the growing strength of Christianity to build a new culture in the empire. Calling bishops to a number of councils, he made them settle church doctrine and become organized. He favored the Christians, whom he considered to be less corrupt and self-seeking than the Romans. However, he was not a Christian himself until he converted on his deathbed. He was the last strong emperor of the Roman Empire. By moving the capital to Constantinople and founding the Byzantine Empire, however, he also weakened the West and hastened Rome's eventual downfall. The Roman Catholic church continued to be a cultural and religious force in the West long after Rome fell.

▲ Constantine's arch in Rome was built to bring back a spirit of victory and supremacy to Rome, after a century of many disappointments. However, Rome's real achievements at the time were not as great as the arch was meant to suggest.

◀ A detail from the arch of Constantine shows Roman soldiers besieging the town of Verona in 312. This battle was part of Constantine's war against his coemperor Maxentius. The arch was dedicated in 315.

THE END OF THE EMPIRE

Emperor Constantine tried to revive the empire. He favored and promoted Christians, built churches, and held church councils, making Christianity a state religion. In 330 he moved the capital to Byzantium, calling it Constantinople. This city became as grand as Rome, and the west grew weaker and poorer. The western half of the empire, under attack by the barbarians, collapsed after Rome was sacked in 410 and 455. The last emperor was deposed by the Goths in 476. Following this, the western empire was replaced by a number of Germanic kingdoms. The empire in the East, known as the Byzantine Empire, lasted until 1453. Though many Roman ways were adopted by the barbarians, the Roman Empire was at an end.

KEY DATES

165–167 Plague sweeps through the Roman Empire
167–180 The Marcomanni Wars against the first barbarians
250 Emperor worship made compulsory under Decius
250–270 Barbarians attack the empire from the north
276 Emperor Tacitus killed by his troops
286 Diocletian divides the empire in two and rules eastern empire; Maximilian rules western
324 Constantinople founded as the new imperial capital
370 Arrival of Huns in Europe: Germans seek refuge in empire
378–415 The Visigoths rebel and ravage the empire
406 Roman withdrawal from Britain, Gaul, and Iberia
410 The Visigoths sack Rome
441 The Huns defeat the Romans
476 Death of the last Roman emperor

Emperor Justinian continued the fight against the barbarians. This gold coin was minted in 535 to celebrate his general Belisarius' defeat of the Vandals.

THE BARBARIANS A.D. 1–450

The term barbarian means "outsider"—and Romans thought them to be uncivilized. They lived in small farming communities and were ferocious warriors.

An ornate bronze brooch, commonly used by barbarians to fasten their cloaks, is an example of the fine craftsmanship of these people. This piece of jewelry was made around 400 in a style that was fashionable in Denmark and later in Saxon England.

The Germans living in southern Sweden and northern Germany moved south and pushed the Celts west. The Romans tried to control the Germans and were seriously beaten by them in A.D. 9. The Romans traded with some friendly German tribes, and recruited some into the Roman army. Some tribes, such as the Franks, Alemanni, and Goths raided the empire in 260–270, and the Romans had to make peace and settle them.

THE HUNS

The Huns (Xiongnu) had been evicted from Mongolia by the Chinese. They swept into Europe, settling in Hungary around 370. The German tribes panicked, pushing into the empire for safety. The Romans settled many of them, though the Vandals in Greece rebelled, and by 410 they sacked Rome itself. From 440–450, the Huns ravaged Greece, Germany, and Gaul, destroying everything. An alliance of Romans and Germans defeated them, but the empire was then in decline. After Attila the Hun attacked northern Italy, the western empire finally broke down.

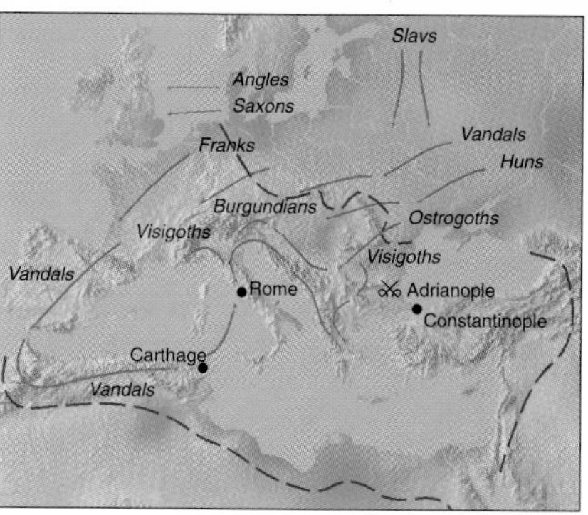

A map showing the complex movements of the main barbarian tribes around 370–450, as they occupied different parts of the western Roman Empire.

THE NEW EUROPEANS

As Rome collapsed, barbarians settled in Germany, Italy, Spain, Britain, and France, gradually adopting many Roman customs. By 800, the Frankish king Charlemagne ruled an empire spanning Germany and France. The Visigoths settled in Spain, and the Vandals took Carthage. The Huns retreated to Romania and the Ukraine. The Lombards settled in Italy and founded a strong kingdom under King Odoacer. The Burgundians settled in eastern France, and the Saxons and Jutes took England.

A scene based on a Roman tomb carving from around 200 shows Roman soldiers in a fierce battle with German barbarians.

This relief from the obelisk of Theodosius was erected in Constantinople in 390. The stone carvings show the emperor receiving the submission of the barbarian peoples. Theodosius was the last emperor of a united Roman Empire (379–395), and an enthusiastic Christian. He was of barbarian blood, born of Germans who had joined the Roman Empire.

▼ This painting shows Attila the Hun marching on Paris during his army's invasion of Gaul in 452.

ATTILA THE HUN

Attila became king of the Huns (Xiongnu) in 433. He set up a new Hun homeland in Hungary after they had massacred, looted, and taken slaves throughout eastern Europe (433–441). The Huns then devastated the Balkans and Greece (447–450), forcing the Romans to pay gold to save Constantinople. The Huns later invaded Gaul and northern Italy, but they were beaten by a combined Roman and Visigoth army. In 453, Attila took a German wife and died suddenly in bed, possibly from poisoning. Attila was a military genius and a great Hun leader. When he died, the Huns migrated eastward to the Ukraine and caused no more trouble in the West.

◀ Attila the Hun was highly respected, mainly because no one could beat him and his soldiers. When he died, the Huns fell.

KEY DATES

70 B.C.	Germans migrate to Gaul, beating the Celts
56	Julius Caesar sends the Germans out of Gaul
A.D. 9	German rebellion against the Romans
200	Germans form a confederation
260	Barbarians move into the Roman Empire
367	Scots, Picts, and Saxons attack Roman Britain
451–454	Huns devastate Gaul and northern Italy

JAPAN 300 B.C.–A.D. 800

Japan is one of the oldest nations in the world. People have been living there from around 30,000 B.C. Classical Japan took shape from around 300 B.C.

In ancient times, Japan was occupied by the Ainu people. The Ainu were unique, and not related to any other tribe. Today's Japanese people moved onto the islands in prehistoric times, from Korea and Manchuria on the mainland. They forced the Ainu onto the northernmost island, Hokkaido.

The Ainu, or Ezo, did not look like modern-day Japanese—they had lighter complexions and much more hair, like these two tribal elders. The Ainu had no written language, and, because they were looked down on by the Japanese, there are few records of their history.

THE YAYOI

Around 300 B.C., the Yayoi were beginning the rise that would make them Japan's predominant tribe. They introduced bronze and iron and also rice and barley from Korea and China. They shaped Japanese culture and the Shinto religion, in which nature spirits (*kami*) and tribal ancestors were worshiped. Tradition says that Jimmu, the legendary first emperor (*tenno*), great-grandson of Ameratsu, "Goddess of the Sun," appeared in 660 B.C. In fact, if he existed at all, it was probably several hundred years after this.

A painted scroll from the A.D. 300s shows a Yamato court lady being dressed by her servant. The boxes are for cosmetics.

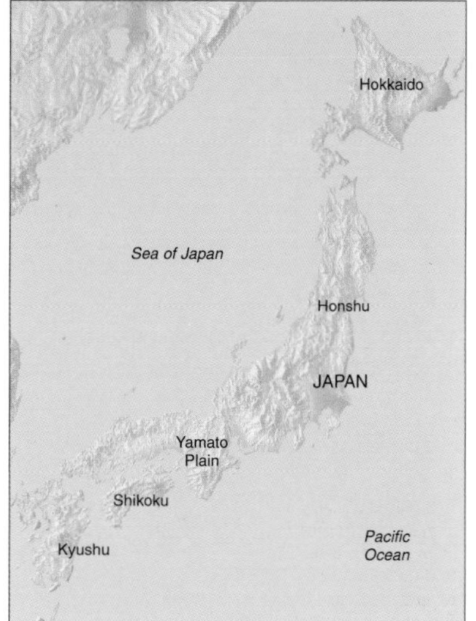

Japan is made up of four main islands, and the biggest, Honshu, has always been the dominant one. In early times, the indigenous Ainu people were squeezed out of Honshu and north onto the island of Hokkaido.

THE YAMATO

Around A.D. 167, an elderly priestess called Himiko of the Yamato tribe became ruler. She used her religious influence to unite about 30 of the Japanese tribes. Himiko sent ambassadors to China, and from that time Chinese culture and, later, Buddhism, influenced the Japanese. The Yamato increased in power during the A.D. 200s. Today's Japanese emperors can trace their ancestry to the Yamato, who claimed descent from the sun goddess. During this period, until 646, much of Japan was united as one state, and it invaded southern Korea. With the establishment of Buddhism during the 500s, Shinto was threatened. Around 600, Prince Shotoku reformed the Yamato state, centralizing it in the Chinese style and reducing the power of the tribal lords. Temples and towns were built, and there was great cultural development. The 700s saw Japan's golden age. Rivalry between Shinto and Buddhism was also resolved by merging both into a common Japanese religious culture.

THE SHINTO RELIGION

Shinto is the ancient nature religion of Japan. Its mythology was written down in the 700s, in the *Kojiki* and the *Nihongi*. Shinto worshipers believed in the power of natural energies and spirits, or kami. Shinto priests sought to please the spirits, attracting their support and protection. In Shinto, it is believed that all life began in a cosmic egg that formed in the primordial chaos. The egg separated and became the gods (kamis), and the union of two kamis brought the Earth into being, with Japan as their special home. The sun goddess also came from this marriage, and the emperor was thought to descend from her. Many influences entered Shinto from Buddhism, and both religions coexisted throughout Japanese history, although there were periods of rivalry.

▲ Shinto priests were originally tribal shamans. In later times, their traditions, dress, and temples became more formal, in response to the challenge from Buddhism.

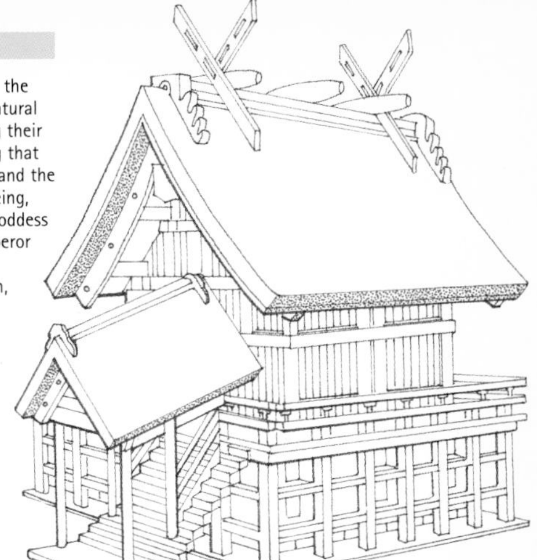

▶ This is a reconstruction of a Shinto shrine at Izumo, an area known for its places of Shinto worship. The priests held ceremonies of renewal and purification there at special times of the year to appeal to the kami to send them bumper crops and give the people good health and fertility.

▶ This is the main gate of the Shinto Kasuga shrine at Heian. These gates not only served the usual purpose, they also marked the energy lines along which the spirits traveled to reach the temple, which was carefully placed in a special location.

THE NARA PERIOD

A permanent capital was established at Nara around 710. Gradually, the emperor became a ceremonial figure, serving as the representative of the gods. Government was controlled by officials and monks and there were greater political struggles. In 794, the emperor moved the capital to Heian (Kyoto), where a new phase of Japanese history began. Japan had developed from a tribal land to become a strong state. Little has been recorded about the life of ordinary people, because records were only kept about the imperial court and temples.

KEY DATES

300 B.C.	Beginning of the Yayoi culture
A.D. 239	Queen Himiko sends an embassy to China
300	The Yamato period—farming, towns, ironworking
366	The Japanese invade southern Korea (until 562)
552	Full introduction of Buddhism
593-622	Prince Shotoku creates a Chinese-style centralized state
646	Yamato period ends
710	Nara becomes permanent capital (the Nara period)
794	Emperor Kammu moves his court to Heian (Kyoto)

In Shinto, small clay figures were used as totems to bring good fortune to places or to the souls of the dead in the afterlife.

THE MAYA 300 B.C.–A.D. 800

The Maya lived in what is now southern Mexico and Guatemala. They created a civilization that was at its peak while the Roman Empire was crumbling.

The engraved figures found in Mayan ruins often show richly dressed people, such as this priest with his ornate headdress. He appears to be holding a knife in his left hand.

The Maya existed as far back as 2000 B.C. Over the centuries, by draining marshy land and building irrigation systems, they became successful farmers, able to support a large population. In the early phase, from 300 B.C. to A.D. 300, they built many cities in Guatemala, Belize, and southern Yucatán, each with its own character and artistic style. Their cities had temple pyramids, a fortified palace, marketplaces, workshops, and living quarters.

MAYAN CLASS SYSTEM

The Maya had a class system: the nobles, priests, rulers, officials, and their servants lived in the cities while ordinary people lived on the land, going into the cities for markets and religious festivals. There was an alphabet of 800 hieroglyphs, and the Maya studied advanced mathematics, astronomy, and calendar systems. As in ancient Greece, each city was an independent city-state, and there was feuding between them, usually to demand tribute and take prisoners. Around A.D. 230, a violent volcanic eruption blew apart Mount Ilopango in the south, and covered a large area with ash. The southern cities had to be abandoned, and this marked the end of the "pre-classic" period of Mayan civilization.

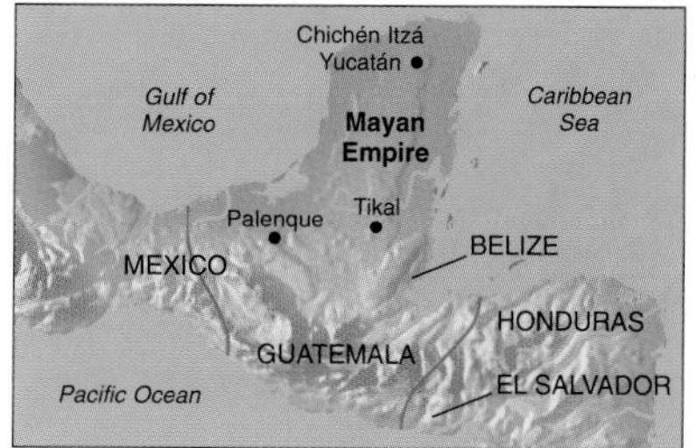

The Mayan heartland moved from the south in early times to the center around Tikal. After A.D. 800 the Maya lived in the north of Yucatán.

THE CLASSIC PERIOD

Between 300 and 800, Mayan civilization reached its peak. Many new cities were built in Yucatán. The dominant city was Tikal, although Palenque, Yaxchilán, Copán, and Calakmul were also important.

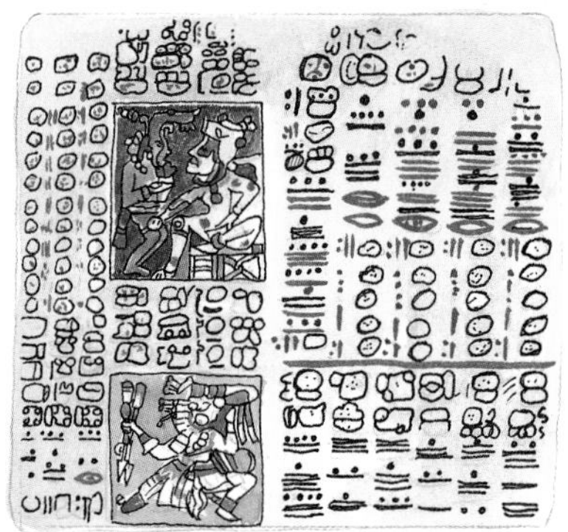

The Maya wrote in hieroglyphs (picture writing), which are found carved on huge stone monuments and written in books made of bark paper.

The Maya played a ball game which may have had religious importance to them as a kind of oracle. In vast courts they bounced a solid rubber ball back and forth using their hips, thighs, and elbows, aiming for a hoop in the side wall. The ball probably represented the sun.

The Maya were skilled craftspeople, making stone sculptures, jade carvings, decorated pottery, paintings, advanced tools, and gold and copper objects. They built roads and shipping lanes to encourage trade. Their mathematical system counted in 20s, and used three symbols: a bar for "five," a dot for "one," and a shell for "zero."

HUMAN SACRIFICE

The Maya practiced blood sacrifice. They viewed this life and the afterlife as equal worlds, and killing people for religious purposes, to please the gods and ancestors and to bring fertility and prosperity, was an acceptable thing to do. In later times, ambitious building projects meant that peasants had to supply ever more food and labor, and hostage-taking wars to capture sacrificial victims drastically cut the population. The agricultural system collapsed, and with it the cities. By 950, most central Mayan cities lay in ruins—though a later phase followed. The Maya still live in the uplands of Central America.

These were the four kinds of people at the top of the Mayan social pyramid: an official, a warrior, a noble, and a priest.

MAYAN CITIES

In the early days of Mayan city building, the largest city was El Mirador, founded in 150 B.C., and had a population of 80,000 people by A.D. 100. It was abandoned around A.D. 150. Tikal, ruled by its king Stormy Sky, later became the largest city, with some 100,000 people around 450. Most cities were impressive and planned in grids. They were built around the ceremonial centers, and often oriented to astronomical events such as the rising and setting points of the sun. The religious basis of Mayan cities and their use of pyramids resembled that of the ancient Egyptians 2,000 years earlier.

Mayan cities were carefully laid out, with numerous sacred shrines and temples covering many acres of land, and large open spaces, platforms, and meeting places.

EARLY MIDDLE AGES

501–1100

This period used to be called the Dark Ages because historians thought that civilization ended when the Roman Empire fell. Many people now call these years the Early Middle Ages because they mark the start of the period that separates ancient and modern history. The former Roman Empire split into two: the western part peopled by farmers, skilled metalworkers, and shipbuilders; the eastern part became the Byzantine Empire. The Chinese and Arabs still led the way in science and technology. Buddhist and Christian religions were spread through trade, while Islam was spread through military conquest.

▲ The Carolingian Renaissance inspired this ivory carving, from the 800s, of St. Gregory and other scholars at work.

◀ This Mayan stone carving from the 900s was found in the ruins of the city of Chichén-Itzá on the Yucatán Peninsula of Mexico.

THE WORLD AT A GLANCE 501–1100

After the fall of the Roman Empire, new countries and peoples emerged in Europe. The lives of these people were governed by the Christian Church and a rigid social system, later called feudalism.

Between Europe and the Far East, there was a huge area containing many different people who all shared the same religion, Islam. Farther north, Slavic countries such as Russia and Bulgaria were also forming.

China was still culturally and scientifically far ahead of the rest of the world. Its influence spread all over Asia, and to Japan, where the arts flourished.

In North America, the first towns were being built, and the Toltec civilization developed in Mexico. In South America, huge independent empires, such as the Huari Empire, were forming.

Contact between the civilizations of the world was very limited. Only a few countries traded with each other. But Islam was gradually spreading over the whole of northern Africa through conquest and trade.

NORTH AMERICA

In about 700, two separate town cultures began to develop in North America. One was the Temple Mound culture around the Mississippi area—a culture that traded far across the continent in copper and goods. Another was the Anasazi *pueblo* (village) culture in the Southwest, where people lived in stone pueblos connected by roads. The Anasazi had an advanced religion. Elsewhere, many Native American tribes grew bigger and stronger, though they were still mainly farming and hunting peoples, living either in permanent villages or as nomads. Far to the northeast, in Newfoundland, the first white men arrived—the Vikings settled there for a short time around the year 1000.

MESOAMERICA AND SOUTH AMERICA

Around 600–700, the great Mexican city of Teotihuacán was at its greatest. Decline began around 750, both there and among the Maya farther south. But the Mayan Empire of city-states survived this whole period. From 900 to 1100, the warlike Toltecs flourished in Mexico. In Peru, in South America, the city-states of Tiahuanaco in the Andes and the Huari near the coast grew larger and more developed. Tiahuanaco preceded the Inca Empire. By 1000, the Huari Empire was replaced by the Chimú Empire, which was developing around Chan Chan in northern Peru.

EUROPE

Europe was busy finding its feet during the period known as the Dark Ages. The Byzantine Empire acted as a stable focus for Christendom, though its fortunes rose and fell. In the 700s, the Muslims invaded Spain, setting up an advanced culture there that lasted 700 years. At the same time, farther north, the Carolingians created the first European empire, though it declined in the 800s after Charlemagne's death. In the rest of Europe, nations were slowly taking shape, overseen by the Catholic Church in Rome. This process was accelerated by threats from the Magyars and Vikings, and by the Muslims in Spain and Anatolia. By 1100, some European nations were growing strong, stable, and prosperous. Universities were founded, churchbuilding flourished, and towns grew in size and importance. Medieval leaders started overseas military adventures and conquests—for example, the European Crusades to win land in Palestine.

ASIA

In India, the Gupta Empire collapsed in 535 and the country was disunited. Both Hindu and Buddhist influences expanded into Southeast Asia. Around 775, the kingdom of Srivijaya in Sumatra conquered the Malayan peninsula, and in Cambodia, the Khmer dynasty established the kingdom of Angkor in 802. In China, one of its greatest dynasties, the Tang, lasted for 300 years, producing some of the finest works of art in Chinese history. From 960, it was replaced by the Song dynasty for a further 300 years. Elsewhere, a strong Tibetan kingdom rose and fell, and rich states grew up in Thailand, Vietnam, Japan, and Indonesia. In Central Asia, Turkic and Mongol nomads were growing in strength.

EUROPE

ASIA

MIDDLE EAST

AFRICA

AUSTRALASIA

AUSTRALASIA

Polynesians occupied new Pacific islands, moving to New Zealand around 900. In Australia, the Aborigines were untouched by outside influences.

AFRICA

By 700, the whole of northern Africa was part of the Islamic Empire. In West Africa, gold-rich Ghana grew wealthy and strong, and other trading kingdoms such as Mali and Kanem-Bornu began to develop on the fertile southern edge of the Sahara Desert.

MIDDLE EAST

The Sassanid Empire reached its greatest extent in 579. On the death of Muhammad in 632, the Islamic Empire began to expand. In 634, the Arabs conquered Persia and overthrew the Sassanid Empire. But by 756, the Islamic Empire started to break up. At the end of the 1000s, Jerusalem was captured by crusaders.

THE BYZANTINE EMPIRE 476–1453

Byzantium inherited the eastern half of the Roman Empire, surviving nearly a thousand years until, finally, it was taken over by the Ottoman Turks.

Justinian ruled Byzantium for 38 years with his wife Theodora. They were lawmakers and reformers, and they restored the empire's power and lands. They gave shape to the sophisticated culture of Byzantium, building great churches and acting as patrons of art and literature.

Constantinople, the eastern Roman capital, had been built by Emperor Constantine on the site of the ancient Greek port of Byzantium. When the Roman Empire collapsed in 476, the city became the capital of the new Byzantine Empire. The edges of the Roman Empire's territories had been captured by barbarians, so the early emperors of Byzantium, Anastasius (491–518) and Justinian (527–565), fought to reclaim Rome's former territories. During Justinian's long reign, he sent able generals—Belisarius, Narses, and Liberius—to add North Africa, much of Italy, and southern Spain to its list of reclaimed territories. However, many of these gains were soon lost under his successors.

A revival followed when Emperor Heraclius (610–641) reorganized the empire and brought state and church closer together. He beat back the Sassanid Persians, who had occupied Syria, Palestine, and Egypt. Under his rule, Constantinople became a rich center of learning, high culture, and religion. The city was well placed for controlling trade between Asia and Europe. The empire produced gold, grain, olives, silk, and wine, which were traded for spices, precious stones, furs, and ivory from Asia and Africa.

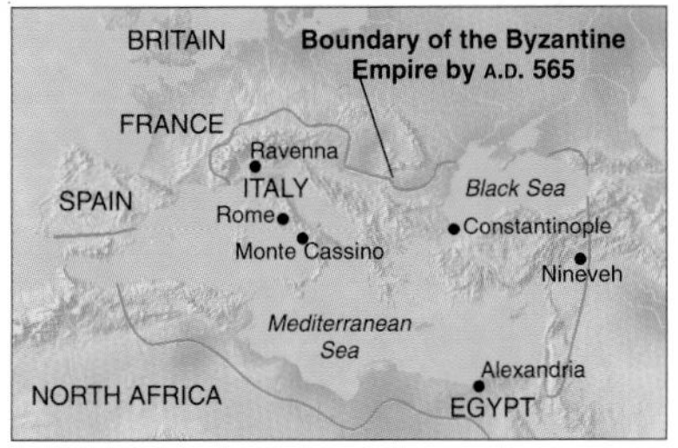

Centered on the strategic city of Constantinople, Byzantium controlled east–west trade and for long periods dominated the Mediterranean Sea and the Black Sea.

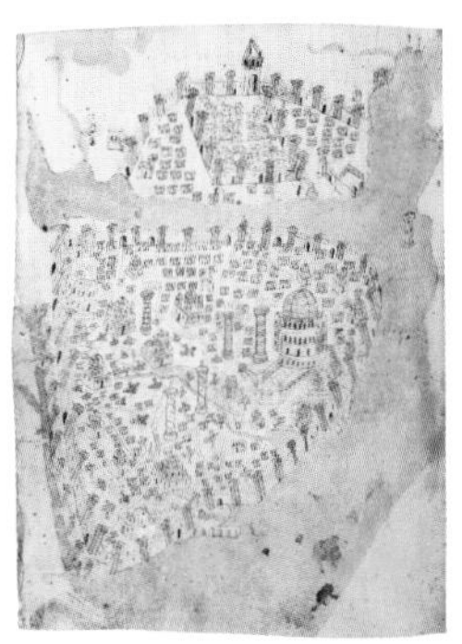

▲ This pictorial map shows Constantinople in 1422, not long before it fell to the Ottomans. It became a Muslim city, and was renamed Istanbul in 1453. The city stood on a promontory called the Golden Horn.

▼ Byzantium was often under attack. Its navy had a secret weapon invented by Kallinikos in 677 called "Greek Fire," a mixture that burst into flames when it touched water. It was made from lime, sulfur, and petroleum.

This classic Byzantine Orthodox mosaic is on the inside of a church dome in Ravenna, Italy. It shows Jesus being baptized by John the Baptist. The presence of the god of the Jordan River identifies the place of the baptism.

The Byzantines made elaborate crosses, icons, caskets, and other sacred relics. These became an important part of life in the Orthodox Church.

▼ Saint Sophia, the Church of the Holy Wisdom, was built in Constantinople for Justinian around 530. It took 10,000 people to build it. Later it became a mosque, and it is now a museum.

KEY DATES

476 Fall of the last Roman emperor
491–518 Emperor Anastasius in Constantinople
527–565 Emperor Justinian's generals reconquer former territories
610–641 Emperor Heraclius expands Byzantium
633–640 Arabs take Syria, Egypt, and North Africa
679 Bulgars overrun Balkan territories
976–1026 Basil II rebuilds the empire
107 Seljuk Turks take Anatolia
1204–61 Norman Crusaders capture Constantinople
1453 Fall of Byzantium to the Ottoman Turks

The Byzantine basilica of St. Apollinare was built near Ravenna in Italy during the 500s. In this period, Byzantine architecture was gradually steering away from the old Roman styles.

The Byzantine Empire declined during the 700s—the Arabs twice tried to take Constantinople itself. However, under Basil II (976–1025), the empire flourished again. Then, soon after Basil died, Anatolia was lost to the Turks, and the empire again declined. It was taken over by the Crusaders for 50 years during the 1200s, but it was reclaimed again by Michael VIII in 1261. Finally, the city of Constantinople was taken by the Ottoman Turks in 1453. The sophisticated Byzantine culture had been the most lively and creative in Europe, and the Orthodox faith had spread as far as Russia and eastern Europe.

SUI AND TANG CHINA 589–907

The Sui dynasty reunited China after 370 years of division, but it lasted only 30 years. It was followed by the Tang dynasty, which lasted nearly 300 years.

The Tang people believed that dragons symbolized the energies of the Earth and that all things should be in harmony with one another. These beliefs even influenced their thinking about building practices.

From the fall of the Han to the rise of the Sui, China was divided into three kingdoms—Wei in the north, Shu in the west, and Wu in the south. There was constant warfare, as well as nomad invasions from Mongolia and Tibet. Many towns were ruined, and the population fell. Devastation in the north led to migrations southward, making the south more politically important. During this time, Buddhism became more widespread in China, bringing in many foreign ideas. Finally, in 581, Yang Jian, a general from Wei, overthrew his rulers and founded the Sui dynasty. By 589 he had unified China.

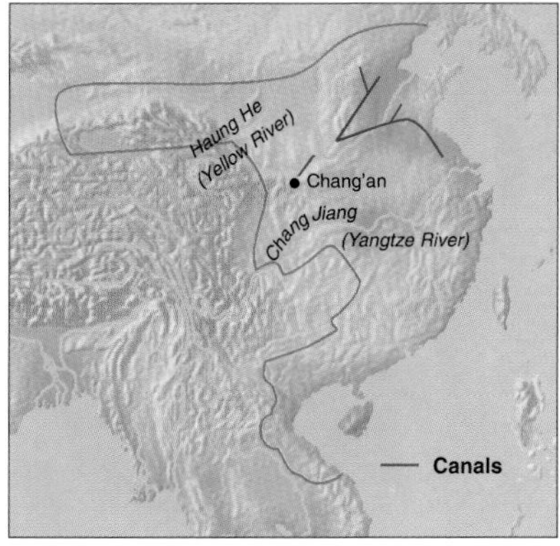

China grew in size during the Tang period. It expanded into central Asia, and many large projects were started, such as the canal system and irrigation schemes.

SUI DYNASTY

Yang Jian renamed himself Emperor Wen. Before he came to power, taxes were high and people were drafted into the army for long periods of time. As emperor, he cut taxes and abolished compulsory military service, governing firmly from his capital, Chang'an. He also encouraged the development of agriculture by setting up irrigation schemes and redistributing land. All these things helped make the country wealthy.

The second Sui emperor was Yang Di. Under Yang Di's rule, China's Grand Canal was rebuilt so that it linked the main rivers of China. He also had palaces and pleasure parks built. The money for them was raised by ordering people to pay ten years' tax in advance. The peasants rebelled and, in 618,Yang Di was killed.

TANG DYNASTY

The second Tang emperor, Taizong (626–649), reorganized government, cut taxes, and redistributed land. The reorganization of this united empire was far in advance of anything found

Rice paddies need controlled watering and large-scale drainage works. The Tang dynasty created conditions in which such large-scale projects became possible.

This wall painting from a tomb shows the Tang princess Yung Tai, who was forced to commit suicide at the age of 17 for criticizing her grandmother, Empress Yu. In China, obeying and submitting to one's parents and elders was considered to be very important.

THE GRAND CANAL

Started by the Sui and completed by the Tang, the Grand Canal was an enormous undertaking. It stretched over 500 mi. (800km) from the Huangho River to the Yangtze, and linked the major cities and capitals of the north with the rice-growing and craft-producing areas of the south. Road travel from north to south was difficult, and sea travel was hampered by typhoons and pirates. The canal allowed safe, long-distance, freight-carrying transportation, to bind China's northern and central regions closer together.

in other parts of the world. This stable period marked the beginning of nearly 300 years which promoted Chinese excellence in the arts, science, and technology. Between 640 and 660, Tang China expanded into central Asia, seeking to keep troublesome nomads from controlling the Silk Road. The Chinese went as far as modern-day Korea, Afghanistan, and Thailand. After Taizong's time, a rebellion by An Lushan in Beijing in 755 challenged Tang rule, and the Tang never fully recovered. Imperial rule became a formality, and power shifted to regional governors and courtiers. The Tibetans also defeated the Chinese in central Asia and there were more rebellions during the 800s. By 907 the Tang dynasty had collapsed and there followed a period of civil wars that lasted until 960.

KEY DATES

589 Yang Jian unites China, founding Sui dynasty
602–610 Military actions in Taiwan, Vietnam, Korea, and central Asia
618 Tang dynasty founded by Li Yuan
626–649 Emperor Taizong—expansion of Tang China
640–660 Chinese expansion in central Asia and Korea
755–763 An Lushan's rebellion—Tang power declines
870s Major peasant rebellions throughout China
907 Tang dynasty collapses

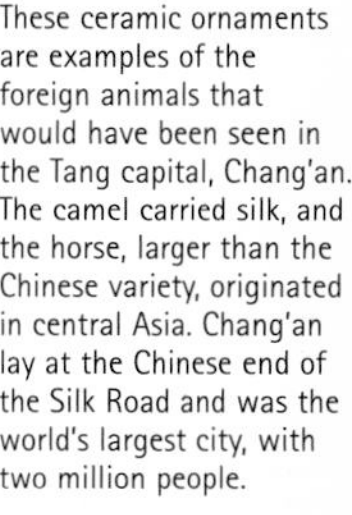

These ceramic ornaments are examples of the foreign animals that would have been seen in the Tang capital, Chang'an. The camel carried silk, and the horse, larger than the Chinese variety, originated in central Asia. Chang'an lay at the Chinese end of the Silk Road and was the world's largest city, with two million people.

ISLAM 622–750

Islam established itself very quickly and influenced many other civilizations. Within 150 years it had grown into a huge empire guided by religious principles.

This is a Muslim portrayal of the Archangel Gabriel (Jizreel). Gabriel is recognized by Muslims as the messenger of Allah to the prophet Muhammad.

The prophet Muhammad, who founded the religion called Islam, was born in Mecca in 570. At the time, the Arab peoples worshiped many different gods. Muhammad became a successful, widely-traveled trader, and was influenced by the Judeo-Christian belief in just one God. When he was 40 years old, his life changed: he saw the Archangel Gabriel in a series of visions. Muhammad then wrote down the *Koran*, the Muslim holy book, under dictation from Gabriel. He was instructed to teach about prayer, purification, and *Allah*, the one God. The word *Islam* means "surrender to Allah."

When Muhammad started teaching, the rulers of Mecca felt threatened by his ideas. Muhammad and his followers had to flee to Medina in 622 and the Muslim calendar counts its dates from this flight—the *Hegira*. In Medina, Muhammad organized a Muslim society, building a mosque. His following grew quickly—many Arabs were poor and Islam preached a fairer society. In 630, Muhammad recaptured Mecca and became its ruler. He kept nonbelievers out and banned idol-worship. Muhammad died in 632.

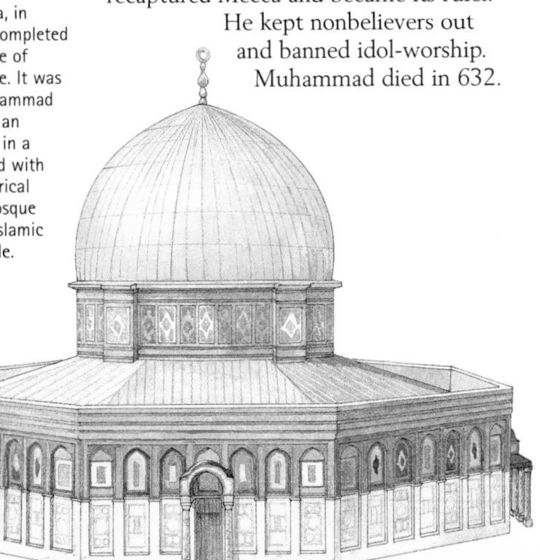

The Dome of the Rock, the important Muslim shrine known as al Aqsa, in Jerusalem, was completed in 691 on the site of Solomon's Temple. It was built where Muhammad had experienced an important vision in a dream. Decorated with complex geometrical patterns, this mosque shows an early Islamic architectural style.

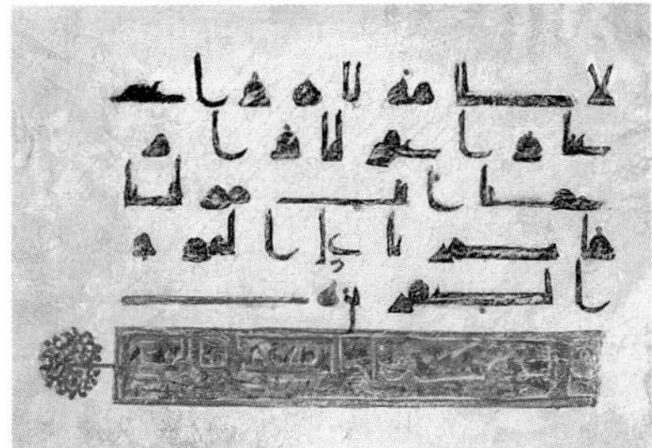

This page from the *Koran* was written in early Arabic lettering style during the 800s. One aspect of the new Islamic culture was its artistic and cultural creativity.

ISLAMIC EXPANSION

The new Muslim *caliph* (leader), called for a *jihad*, or holy war. Within ten years, under Caliph Umar, the Arabs conquered Syria and Palestine (defeating the Byzantines), Mesopotamia and Persia (bringing down the Sassanids), as well as Egypt and Libya. After the death of Caliph Uthman, there were disputes between his successor, Muawiya, and Ali, Muhammad's son-in-law. Ali's murder in 661 led Muslims to split permanently into two factions—the Sunnis, and the Shiites, who were followers of Ali.

Muslims traveled widely, as explorers and traders, and carried ideas about Islam with them. Their faith decreed that they should make at least one pilgrimage to Mecca.

◀ At the battle of Yarmuk, in Syria, in 636, Muslim forces defeated a Byzantine army twice their size. This was a major loss for Byzantium, and the Muslims captured Syria and Palestine, the most prosperous part of the Byzantine Empire. They took Jerusalem and established the beginnings of a large empire.

THE UMAYYAD DYNASTY

In 661, the Arabs established a capital at Damascus, and Muawiya became the first Umayyad caliph. Territorial expansion followed—Muslim armies invaded central Asia, Afghanistan, Armenia, northern Africa, and even Spain. They twice attacked Constantinople, without success. When they invaded Europe, they were defeated by the Franks in France in 732 and had to retreat. The Umayyads organized their empire in the Byzantine style. They were tolerant and did not force conversion to Islam. Many people converted because Muslims were seen as genuine liberators, bringing an end to the old order, establishing clear laws, and increasing trade. Arabic became a universal language across Islam, except in Persia which was mainly Shiite and retained its distinct culture. This common language helped ideas and knowledge to spread quickly from one place to another.

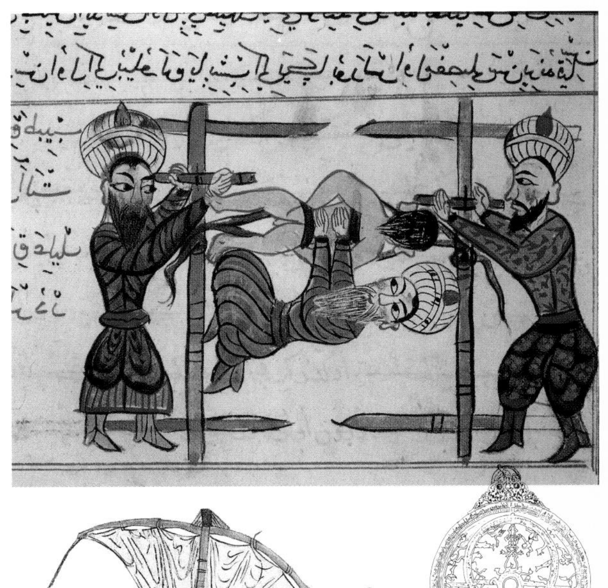

▼ Arabic knowledge of medicine, healing, and surgical technique was well advanced for this time. This picture shows doctors setting a broken limb.

KEY DATES

- **610** Muhammad experiences his first vision
- **622** The *Hegira*—the flight from Mecca to Medina—takes place
- **630** Muhammed takes Mecca and forms an Islamic state
- **636–642** Muslims take Palestine, Syria, Persia, and Egypt
- **656–661** Caliphate of Ali—dispute between factions
- **661–680** Founding of Umayyad dynasty
- **711** Arabs invade Spain
- **732** Franks defeat the Arabs at Poitiers, France
- **750** Umayyad dynasty overthrown by the Abbasids

Arabs were good astronomers. The astrolabe allowed them to navigate at sea—and in the desert.

The Arabs sailed in *dhows*. These wooden boats had large triangular sails and carried cargo and passengers.

BULGARS AND SLAVS 600–1453

Bulgaria and Kiev had a significant influence on eastern Europe. Their adoption of Orthodox Christianity affected both their peoples and the Orthodox church.

The Bulgars were the descendants of the Huns, who settled beside the Volga River in Russia, and reached the height of their power around 650. Then the Khazars from lower down the Volga destroyed their kingdom. As a result, many Bulgars migrated to the Danube area, dominating the local Slavs and founding a Bulgar state. Byzantium took action against them, especially when the Bulgars killed their emperor in battle in 811. In the 860s, two missionaries, Cyril and Methodius, were sent to convert the Bulgars and draw them into Byzantium's influence. This helped, but the quarrels did not end until the Bulgars were beaten in 1014. To punish them, Basil II had 14,000 Bulgars blinded, and the Bulgar khan died of shock.

Vladimir, Grand Prince of Kiev (c.956–1015), interviewed Catholic and Orthodox Christians, Muslims, and Jews, and opted for the Orthodox faith, probably for political as much as religious advantages. Vladimir was the youngest son of Grand Prince Svyatoslav, who brought down the Khazars. Vladimir conducted campaigns to secure Kiev's territories.

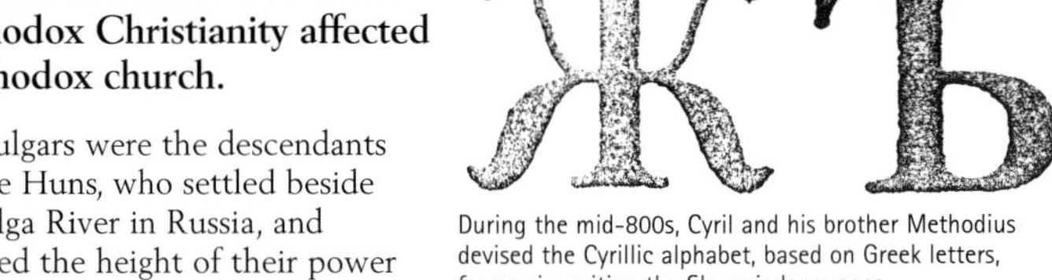

During the mid-800s, Cyril and his brother Methodius devised the Cyrillic alphabet, based on Greek letters, for use in writing the Slavonic languages.

ORTHODOX DIPLOMACY

In Byzantium, the state and the church were closely linked. Religious and diplomatic missions were sent out and, in this way, Byzantium converted the Bulgars to Christianity. Catholic Rome and Orthodox Constantinople competed for influence in eastern Europe. Kiev adopted the Orthodox beliefs, and a Russian Orthodox culture was born there. Cyrillic lettering, still used today by Russians and Bulgarians, was invented by Cyril the missionary and his brother Methodius. By the time Byzantium fell in 1453, Russia had become the home of Orthodoxy.

When the Bulgars killed the Byzantine emperor Nicephorus in 811, they made his skull into a goblet to take to their khan, Krum. The Byzantine emperors called the Bulgar khans *czars*—a name that was adopted later by Russian rulers.

The Church of Intercession, an example of early Orthodox church construction in Russia, was built at Bogolyubovo in 1165.

A central theme of Orthodox culture was the icon, or holy image, which was believed to have spiritual and healing powers. Icon painting spread from Byzantium, through Kiev, into later Russian culture.

THE RISE AND FALL OF KIEV

The Slavs came from what is now Belarus. The first states in Russia were Slavic, and led by Swedish Viking traders (*Ros*, or "oarsmen"). The greatest Ros leader was Rurik, who founded Novgorod, Smolensk, and Kiev. The Vikings traded with Baghdad and Constantinople, and Kiev grew rich as a trading city. The Vikings considered themselves a superior class, mixing only gradually with the Slavs. In 988, the Kievan prince Vladimir converted to Christianity, marrying a Byzantine princess. He then made the nobility and people adopt Christianity. This brought Kiev new trade, culture, and respectability abroad. Under Jaroslav the Wise (1019–54) Kiev was a center of splendor and influence that rivaled Constantinople, with diplomatic connections across Europe. Churches were built, and the first Russian laws were written, as well as the first works of Russian art and literature. Kiev was on the steppes (plains) of the Ukraine, and vulnerable to nomadic warriors such as the Pechenegi who threatened, and the Polovtsy who sacked, the city. After Jaroslav died, the state of Kiev broke up, and the Russians retreated into safer northern areas. Here a new Russia was being established, centered around the growing city of Moscow.

This helmet from the 1200s belonged to the prince of a small principality called Suzdal, once part of Kievan Russia.

THE CAROLINGIANS 751–843

The Carolingian dynasty established Europe's first rich and powerful empire. These people were the former Germanic "barbarians" known as the Franks.

This gold image of Charlemagne, inset with precious stones and known as a reliquary, was made in Germany around 1350, to hold parts of Charlemagne's skull.

The Franks had settled in what is now Belgium and northern France. Their leader, Clovis (481–511), of the Merovingian dynasty, established a capital at Paris. Clovis became a Christian and earned Rome's support. He united the Frankish tribes, defeated the Gauls, the Alemanni (a confederation of Germans), and the Visigoths, and created a kingdom resembling today's France. His sons consolidated this, but quarrels broke out. Power fell to Charles Martel, who led the Franks against the invading Muslims at Poitiers in 732. Charles founded the Carolingian dynasty, and in 751, under his son Pepin, the Carolingians replaced the Merovingians as Frankish rulers. In 768, Pepin's sons, Carloman and Charlemagne, inherited his kingdom. Carloman died in 771, and Charlemagne took full control. He first conquered the rest of France, and then what is now Germany, Italy, and the Netherlands, creating an enormous European empire. In central Europe he quelled the Saxons and the Avars, forcing them both to accept Christianity.

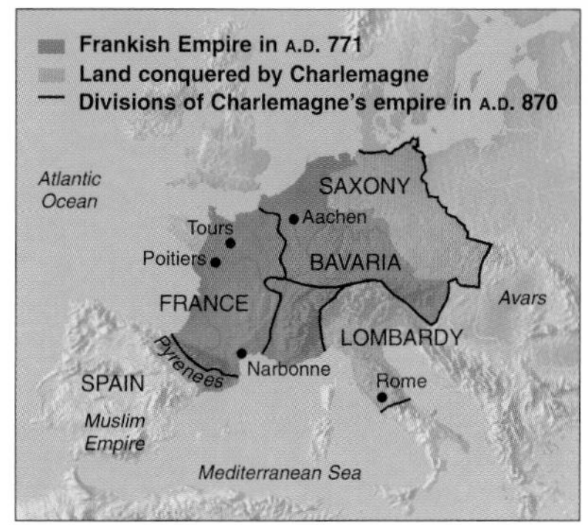

Charlemagne's empire unified most of western Europe. Its capital, Aachen, lay not far from the capital of today's European Union in Brussels.

CHARLEMAGNE'S CORONATION

Obtaining the blessing of the Church gave a nation greater respectability. For the pope, Charlemagne's grand coronation in 800 was a political move against Constantinople—there was now a Christian empire in the West as well as in the East. Charlemagne offered to marry the Byzantine empress Irene, but this was unacceptable to many people. Missions were sent to Charlemagne from Persia and the Baghdad Caliphate, as well as from the rulers of Europe. Had Charlemagne's empire remained intact, European history might have been very different.

Pope Leo III crowned Charlemagne Holy Roman emperor in 800.

Holy Roman emperors were crowned in the Palatine Chapel, Aachen.

THE CAROLINGIAN RENAISSANCE

Charlemagne supported the Roman church, favoring its influence in his kingdom. In return, in 800, the pope crowned Charlemagne as the first Holy Roman emperor. Charlemagne was a lawmaker and founded schools, cathedrals, and monasteries run by Irish, British, and Italian monks. He also invited scholars, scribes, architects, and philosophers to his court. His capital at Aachen became the chief center of learning in western Christendom. Charlemagne died in 814. His successor Louis the Pious ruled successfully but, on his death in 843, the empire was divided between his three sons. The empire later became two countries: Germany and France. The Carolingians ruled Germany until 911 and France until 987.

Charlemagne was a great military leader who, once he had invaded lands, tried to improve conditions and encourage the poor to improve their standard of living.

Beatissimo papae damaso hieronimus

▲ The Carolingian Renaissance inspired this ivory carving of St. Gregory and other scholars at work, in 850–875. The Aachen scholars created a new script called *minuscule*, with clear, rounded letters, but Charlemagne never learned to write.

KEY DATES	
486–510	France united by Merovingian king, Clovis
732	Charles Martel beats the Arabs at Poitiers
751	Pepin, the first Carolingian king
768	Charlemagne becomes Carolingian king
782	Charlemagne defeats the Saxons
790s	Charlemagne defeats the Avars in Austria
800	Pope crowns Charlemagne
814	Charlemagne dies
843	Carolingian Empire divided into three

THE ABBASID DYNASTY 750–1258

During the 500 years of rule by the Abbasid dynasty, the Islamic Empire was unified, its culture flourished, and Baghdad became one of the world's greatest cities.

When Harun al-Rashid became caliph in 786, he ended a decade of uncertainty and rivalry in the Islamic Empire.

In 750, there were disagreements between the Arabs as well as dissent among the invaded peoples. The Umayyads were overthrown by the Abbasid family who then ruled the Islamic world for 500 years. The Abbasids were descended from Muhammad's uncle, al-Abbas. Under al-Mansur, their first caliph, they moved their capital to the new city of Baghdad in 762, and adopted many Persian and Greek traditions. Their most famous ruler was Harun al-Rashid (786–809), the fifth caliph. From 791 until 806, he fought a long war with the Byzantine Empire, which he eventually won. Parts of the empire sought independence, but Harun al-Rashid managed to suppress them. In spite of these wars he found time to encourage learning and the arts, bringing together Persian, Greek, Arab, and Indian influences. Baghdad became a world center for astronomy, mathematics, geography, medicine, law, and philosophy. The court in Baghdad was the setting for much of *The Thousand and One Nights*, a book still enjoyed today. Under later caliphs, various provinces became independent, but they still followed Islam, its law, and culture. The Abbasid caliphs increasingly lost power and became spiritual figureheads. The Muslim empire separated into emirates, whose fortunes rose and fell at different times. Yet the Muslim world acted as one civilization with many different centers.

The stories for *The Thousand and One Nights* came from many different countries, including India, Syria, and Egypt. The stories feature Ali Baba, Sinbad the Sailor, and Aladdin.

This elaborately decorated tile, made in Persia during the 1100s, shows that Islamic art in the Abbasid period which was very rich and sophisticated.

People came to the Abbasid court in Baghdad from all over the empire, even from as far away as central Asia and Spain.

This decorated Persian bowl was made during the Abbasid dynasty. It shows how Muslim artists created new styles with intricate designs.

GHANA 700–1240

Ghana was the first truly African state. Most Africans still lived in tribal village societies, but Ghana, a center of the gold trade, opened up new possibilities.

Prester John was a legendary king who was said to rule over a Christian empire in the heart of Africa.

The medieval kingdom of Ghana lay farther north, inland from today's nation of Ghana. Its roots lay in the 300s, when the African Soninke tribes were ruled by the Maga, a Berber clan from Morocco. The Berbers had mastered transsaharan camel travel, and traded salt for gold from the Soninke. When the Arabic Muslims invaded northern Africa there was an upsurge in the gold trade, and by 700, Ghana was rich and important as a trading center. In 770, the Soninke ousted the Maga, and built a nation under Kaya Maghan Sisse, who became Soninke king around 790. Ghana's capital was the city of Koumbi Saleh, where Africans and Berbers met and traded. During the 800s, Arab traders described Ghana as "the land of gold." The gold came from Ashanti and Senegal to the south and west, and trade routes led north and east to Morocco, Libya, and Aksum, and so on to Europe and Asia.

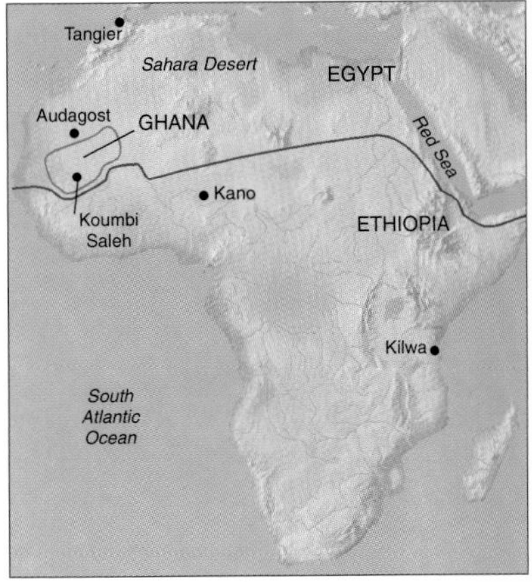

Ghana grew rich on gold, making it the first African nation. Its capital, Koumbi Saleh, was very cosmopolitan. Gold was transported north to Morocco, Tunisia, the Nile, and Arabia.

Ghana reached its peak during the 900s, controlling both the gold and salt trades. Other goods that passed through Ghana included woolen cloth and luxury items from Europe, and leather goods and slaves from the south. In 990, Ghana took over the neighboring Berber kingdom of Audagost—making Ghana 500 mi. (800km) across. In 1076, however, it fell to the Almoravids, a puritanical Berber Muslim sect. The Almoravids ruled Morocco and Spain, but they fell in 1147, and power returned to Ghana until, in 1240, the country became part of a new African nation, Mali.

Berber and Arab traders transported goods hundreds of miles across the Sahara Desert with camel caravans. Without traders, Ghana and its successors, Mali and Songhai, would not have become rich nations.

ANGLO-SAXON BRITAIN c.600–1066

The arrival of the Angles, Saxons, and Jutes in Britain during the 400s and 500s created a new people, the English, who were to dominate Britain.

The Angles buried their kings, with their possessions, in ships, to take them to the afterlife. This gold clasp comes from a famous burial ship of the early 600s, discovered at Sutton Hoo, in eastern England.

The Romans left Britain around 410. There was a brief revival of power for the now romanized British. In 446, the British high king, Vortigern, invited German Saxons from the Rhineland to enter Britain as mercenaries to support in his struggle with the Picts. The Saxons gained a foothold in the southeast, but were held off between 500 and 539, by the now legendary British leader Arthur. After a battle in 552, the Saxons started taking over southern and central England. Many Britons were killed or lost their lands; many emigrated to Wales, Cornwall, Ireland, Scotland, Brittany, and northwest Spain.

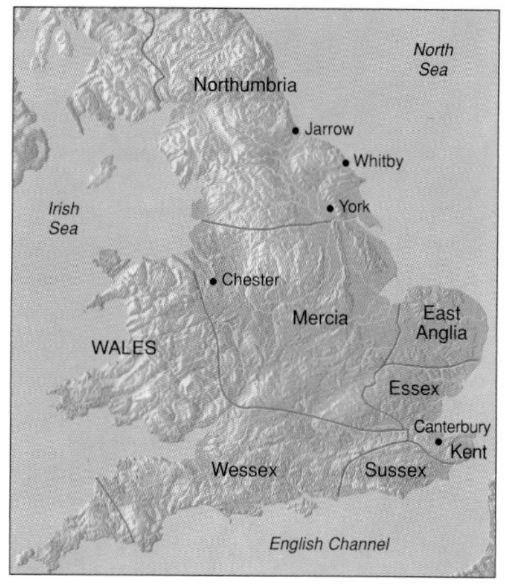

England was divided into seven kingdoms. From 878 Northumbria, East Anglia, and much of Mercia came under Viking control and formed the Danelaw.

THE BIRTH OF ENGLAND

In the wake of the German invaders, many of their countrymen emigrated to England. During the 500s and 600s, they slowly populated the country. British towns, villages, and farms were abandoned, and the Celtic Christian church retreated with them. The Germans brought new farming and ownership patterns, and their pagan tribal groupings gradually took the shape of kingdoms. Seven kingdoms were eventually formed: East Anglia, Mercia, and Northumbria (ruled by the Angles); Essex, Sussex, and Wessex (ruled by the Saxons); and Kent (ruled by the Jutes).

In 597, the pope sent Augustine to convert the English. These converts coexisted with the pagans, but there were disputes with Celtic Christians. These were settled at the Synod of Whitby in 664, where the Celts agreed to submit to papal authority. The seven kingdoms often fought to claim the title "Bretwalda" (lord of Britain). In the 600s, the Northumbrian kings Edwin, Oswald, and Oswy, and in the 700s, the Mercian kings Ethelbald and Offa, gained supremacy. Egbert of Wessex was the first king of a united England, in 829.

Vortigern, the British high king, hired German mercenaries, but failed to pay them. In revenge, they set out to conquer Britain. Settlers soon followed, beaching their boats and wading ashore with cattle and sheep.

▼ This statue of King Alfred the Great stands at Wantage, his birthplace. Alfred was one of England's great leaders. He created laws based on justice and encouraged education.

STRUGGLES FOR POWER

In 789, the first Vikings appeared in England, and by the middle of the 800s they had started to settle. When Alfred the Great was king of Wessex in 871, the Vikings were threatening to overrun his kingdom. Alfred fought nine battles against them in one year alone. He finally defeated them in 878 and made them sign the Treaty of Wedmore. which divided England in two—the Saxon west and Danelaw in the east. Alfred was a lawmaker, a scholar, and a just king. In his time, texts were translated into early English, and *The Anglo-Saxon Chronicle*, an important history book, was begun. By 940, Danelaw had been won back from the Danes. England was reunified under Edgar (959–75), but in 1013 the Danes returned, and England was ruled until 1035 by the Danish king, Canute the Great. There was better cooperation between the Danes and Saxons under Edward the Confessor but, in 1066, his son Harold, having just fought invading Norwegians in Yorkshire, was beaten by invading Normans, under Duke William.

▲ The Ruthwell Cross, carved in a Celtic style by Saxon monks during the 700s, was richly decorated with scenes from the Gospels.

KEY DATES

446 Arrival of Jutish mercenaries led by Hengist and Horsa
560 onward Large-scale immigration of English Saxons
597 Augustine arrives to convert the English Saxons
793 The first Viking raid, on Lindisfarne monastery
870 onward Immigration of the Danes into Danelaw
871-99 Alfred the Great crowned king of Wessex
1013 The Danes conquer all of England
1066 The Normans, led by Duke William, conquer England

▼ English Saxon society had three classes—thanes or nobles, churls or freemen, and serfs or slaves. In this picture, serfs are harvesting barley.

THE HOLY ROMAN EMPIRE 962–1440

Otto I became king of Germany in 936. He wanted to revive the old Roman Empire and was crowned as the first Holy Roman emperor by the pope in 962.

Otto I was on the throne of Germany for 37 years. He made the Holy Roman Empire a great and lasting institution by uniting his country's regional rulers and making them cooperate with him.

The Holy Roman Empire was neither particularly holy, nor Roman. Founded by Charlemagne in 800, it was concerned with the power of kings and it was German. After Charlemagne's death the Carolingian Empire gradually broke up, and France and Germany were separated. In Germany, a high king was elected as an overlord so that he could bind together the many independently ruling dukes, counts, and bishops. The first of these overlords was Conrad I of Franconia, elected in 911. Later, the ambitious Otto I (936–973) wanted to revive the Roman Empire. Otto brought stability by uniting all of the rulers who owed him allegiance and by defeating the Magyars.

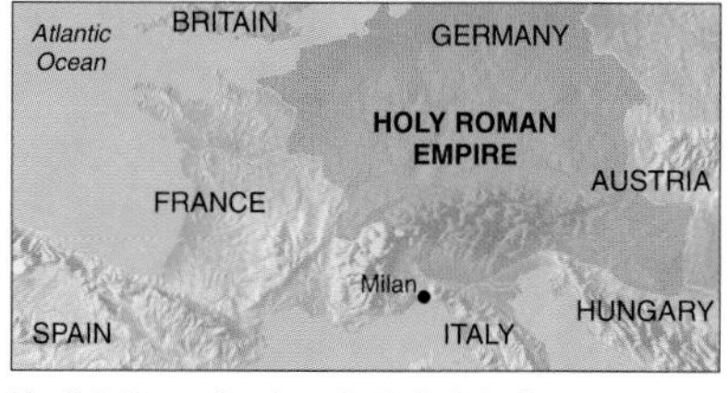

The Holy Roman Empire united all of the German-speaking peoples and extended its power into Italy, both to protect and to try to control the popes.

Otto conquered Bohemia, Austria, and northern Italy. After 25 years, he had the pope crown him Emperor Augustus, founding an imperial tradition that lasted 850 years until 1806. His empire became a revived Holy Roman Empire.

The Holy Roman emperor had the right to be crowned by the pope in Rome. Many popes and emperors disagreed over questions of power and authority, and this led to problems because each side wanted to interfere in the other's affairs.

Henry IV went to see the pope at Canossa, in January 1077, to settle a dispute over power. Pope Gregory VII kept him waiting outside in a snowstorm for three days before forgiving him and removing the ban of excommunication.

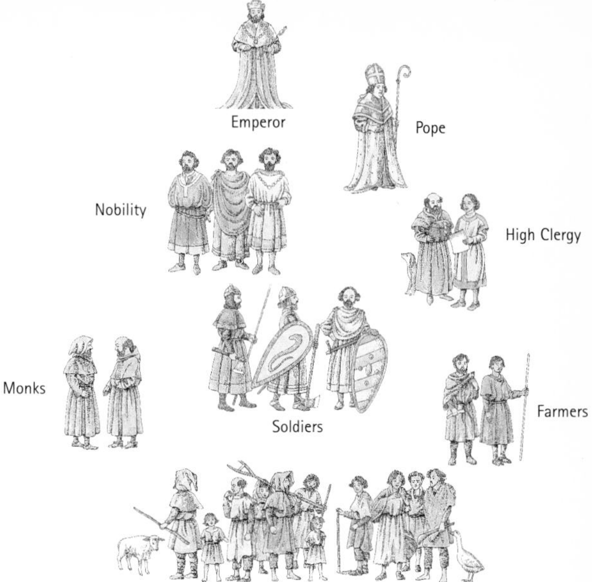

▲ Noblemen usually supported the emperor against the pope, but sometimes they rebelled. Soldiers usually supported the nobles, who gave them land; and peasant laborers were employed by soldiers and nobles. Similarly, monks supported clerics, who supported the pope. These were "feudal" relationships, where a person gave allegiance and taxes in return for protection, land, or rights. Everyone was bound into feudal relationships throughout society.

POPES AND EMPERORS

Several popes wanted help in ruling Christian Europe but often came into conflict with the emperors. Catholics had to obey the pope, so he was powerful. Popes wanted to choose emperors, and emperors wanted to choose popes and control Church affairs. Finally, Emperor Henry IV and Pope Gregory VII clashed—in 1075, Gregory said Henry had no right to choose bishops. In revenge, Henry said that Gregory was no longer pope. Gregory excommunicated him, which meant that Henry was no longer recognized by the Christian Church and his subjects did not have to obey him. In 1077, Henry asked to be forgiven. The quarrel over choosing bishops was finally settled in 1122, but there were more disputes, which led to a gradual separation of church and state.

KEY DATES

911	Conrad I of Franconia is elected German king
936–973	Otto I strengthens the Holy Roman Empire
955	Otto I defeats the Magyars
1056–1106	Henry IV in conflict with the pope
1122	Concordat of Worms: an agreement between emperor and pope
1200	Peak of the political power of the Roman Catholic Church
1300	Popes lose political power
1440	Holy Roman Empire passes to the Austrian Hapsburg dynasty

In 1100, the pope and the Holy Roman emperor signed an agreement at St. Peter's Cathedral, in Worms, in southwestern Germany. The agreement ended a long-running dispute over who was responsible for the appointment of bishops.

THE AMERICAS 500–1200

In Mesoamerica, the Toltecs came into prominence following the destruction of Teotihuacán. Meanwhile, in South America two new civilizations were developing.

The Toltecs were very militaristic. Their temples were guarded by stone statues of warriors such as this one from Tula.

By 600, Teotihuacán was in decline, and around 750 it was burned to the ground, possibly by tribes from the north. Various peoples tried to assume control, and around 900, the Toltecs established a capital at Tula. It became the center of a military state and trading network that reached from Colorado to Colombia. In 1000, far away in Yucatán, a faction of the Toltecs invaded the Mayan Empire, expanding the northern Mayan city of Chichén Itzá. The Toltec Empire came to an end in 1168, when it was overrun, and Tula was destroyed. Soon afterward, the Aztecs moved into the area.

THE LATER MAYA

Many Mayan cities were abandoned around 800, although some still flourished in northern Yucatán from 900 onward. Around 1000, Yucatán was invaded by Toltecs, who stayed there until 1221, building a copy of Tula at Chichén Itzá. Warrior chiefs took power from the priests, and caused crafts such as pottery, art, and literature to decline in quality.

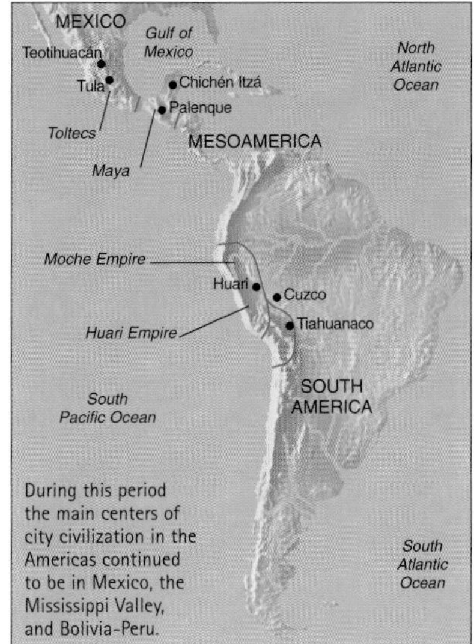

During this period the main centers of city civilization in the Americas continued to be in Mexico, the Mississippi Valley, and Bolivia-Peru.

The Toltecs were beaten by the Maya from Mayapán, whose Cocom dynasty dominated Yucatán for 200 years until civil war broke out in 1480. The Spanish arrived during the 1500s, but the last Maya city-state, Tayasal, did not fall until 1697.

THE PYRAMIDS OF ETOWAH

Etowah was one of the towns of the Mississippian culture in North America. This city culture spread far beyond the Mississippi valley—Etowah was near today's Atlanta, and famous as a source of mica, a transparent form of rock which could be split into fine sheets, like glass. The Etowans used tools of copper and stone, and built earthen pyramids with temples or the palaces of their chiefs on top. Their cities often had 10,000–20,000 inhabitants. They traded with Mexico and the Great Lakes area, and they made items to trade with the village-dwelling tribes of North America.

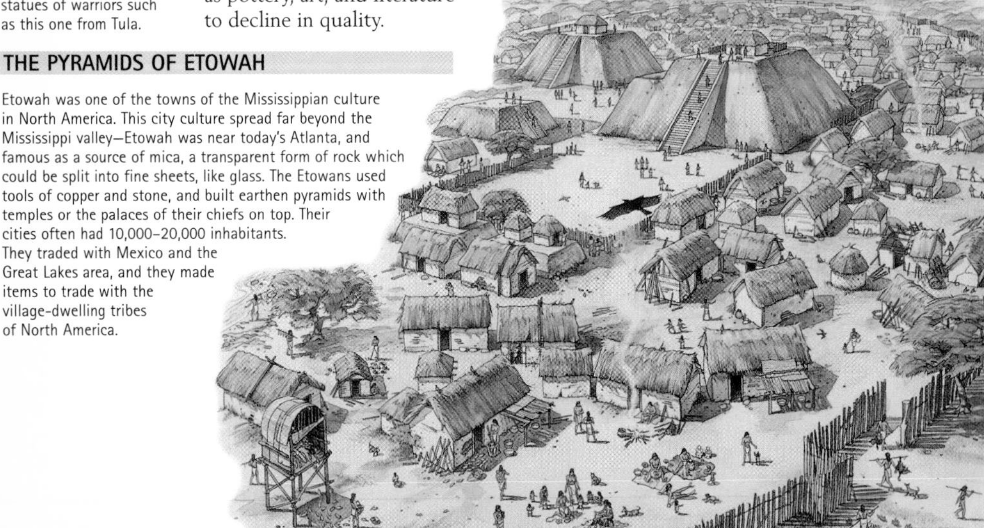

TIAHUANACO AND HUARI

Civilization in South America was based in two places. One was at Tiahuanaco, a large temple-city 12,000 ft. (3660m) above sea level near Lake Titicaca in Bolivia. Between 600 and 1000, it had a population of 100,000. The people of Tiahuanaco made distinctive pottery and jewelry, massive stone dry-stack walls, and enormous temple-stones. They created a string of towns stretching to the coast and into the Brazilian rain forests. The other civilization was Huari, which included remnants of several earlier local cultures such as Nazca and Moche. This was a powerful military empire, covering over half of modern Peru. Huari and Tiahuanaco may have followed the same religion, but Huari was militaristic and Tiahuanaco was peaceful. The two empires prospered until about 1000, when they were both abandoned, possibly because of drought.

KEY DATES	
600	Teotihuacán is sacked and burned
800	Toltec migration into central Mexico
900	Toltecs establish a city-state at Tula
1000	Tiahuanaco and Huari abandoned
1168	Tula destroyed
1200	Building of the Mississippian temple-cities
1200	Rise of the Aztecs and the Incas

▲ This is one of the many massive carved stone figures of Tiahuanaco, erected around 700. Tiahuanaco, near the southern edge of Lake Titicaca, was ruled by a priesthood according to religious principles. The city had several large temples.

This pottery image of a god from Huari, decorated with corn, was probably honored by farmers to help grow their crops.

This bowl from the Mimbres people of the southwest had a hole made in it to "kill" the bowl. It was then buried with its owner.

▲ This earring from Huari is made of stone inlaid with bone and shell. The Huari people also made beautiful jewelry and small objects out of gold.

◀ The sun god Viracocha was carved on the Gateway of the Sun at Tiahuanaco around 600. This giant gateway opened into the Kalasasaya, the largest of the city's building areas and the main temple.

THE VIKINGS c.600–1000

The Vikings have a reputation as raiders and violent warriors. But they were also traders and settlers, whose impact on European history has been great and lasting.

During the 700s, the Vikings began to venture from their homelands in Norway, Denmark, and Sweden in search of adventure, treasure, and better farmland. They made excellent wooden ships that could sail on rough seas and up rivers, and landed easily on beaches. At first they raided rich monasteries and coastal towns, and later they sailed up the Rhine, Seine, and Loire rivers to attack inland cities. Local rulers bought them off with silver and gold. Not all Vikings were raiders. Many were farmers looking for new land or traders seeking business. They were first-class sailors and traders, and ventured as far as Constantinople and Baghdad in search of conquest or trade.

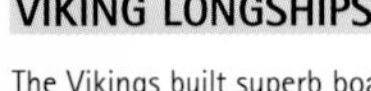

Viking coins minted in the 800s were made of real silver or gold, so the coins themselves were actually worth the value they represented.

Viking men and women wore everyday clothes that were both practical and fashionable. Their gold and silver jewelry was sometimes broken up and used as money.

VIKING LONGSHIPS

The Vikings built superb boats, with sturdy keels acting as frames, which made the ships faster and more seaworthy. The boats were capable of being sailed or rowed. They could also be hauled by teams of men across land when necessary—even being dragged long distances overland in Russia, to get from one river to another. They could be beached easily without the need for a harbor. A dragon's head on the bow was intended to scare off evil spirits, sea monsters, and enemies.

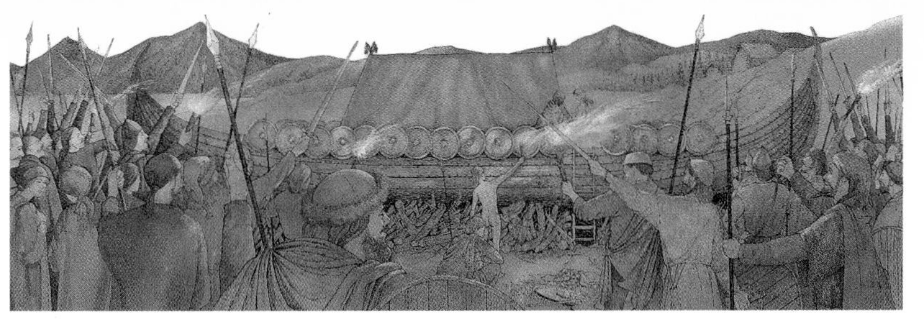

For the cremation of a Viking headman, the dead body was placed on a ship with his belongings, for use in the next life, and a slave girl was often sacrificed. The ship was set alight by a close relative, naked to symbolize how we enter and leave life naked.

VIKING TRADERS AND SETTLERS

In Britain, the Vikings settled mainly in northern and eastern England, northern Scotland, the Isle of Man, and Ireland. In Ireland they destroyed many monasteries and founded the first towns. In France, the Vikings settled in Normandy, which had been given to them by the French king in 911 to discourage their raiding. In 1066, as Normans, they invaded England, and in the early 1070s, southern Italy, and Sicily. Vikings also settled in Iceland, and some sailed on to Greenland and North America. Others entered the Mediterranean, raiding southern France, Spain, and Byzantium. Beaten back by the Byzantines, Vikings sold them their services as traders and warriors instead. Swedish Vikings took over the Baltic Sea, and built trading towns such as Visby, Novgorod, and Kiev. Sailing down Russia's rivers, they met Bulgar, Khazar, Byzantine, and Arab traders. By 1000 the Vikings had settled down, and their Nordic homelands became Christian nations. They had an enormous effect on the future of northern Europe: they established trading routes and towns; founded Russia, greatly influenced Holland, Poland, Britain, France, and Ireland; and weakened the Carolingian Empire. Their descendants, the Normans, were influential in Europe and led the Crusades. Because of the Viking raiders, people had to rely on local feudal lords, and exchanged work, produce, and fighting men for protection. Gradually, Europe became more disunited, fighting grew frequent, and gaps grew between the rich and poor.

▲ The Vikings were skilled metalworkers. This is a die, used for stamping a pattern onto hot metal. It shows two shamans with weapons, poised for ritual animal sacrifice.

▼ The Viking town in Denmark called Hedeby, was well known for its craftworkers and traders. Hedeby was one of the ports from which the Vikings sailed far and wide.

THE NORMANS c.800–c.1200

The Normans invaded England in 1066 and soon ruled the Saxon and Viking English, the Welsh, and the Irish. They also wielded influence farther afield.

William the Conqueror, Duke of Normandy, was king of England from 1066 to 1087.

The Normans were Danish overlords who lived in Normandy from 900 onward. They had absorbed Carolingian and Christian ideas. There were not many of them, but they were tough warrior lords. William the Conqueror was crowned on Christmas Day 1066—in France he had been only a duke, but now he was also the English king.

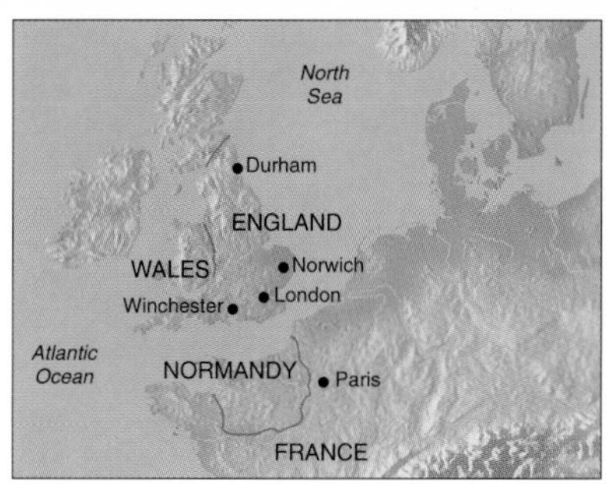

The Norman invasion of England took five years, and it raised the Normans from provincial French vassals to being the wealthy rulers of a whole country.

NORMAN RULE

After the Norman invasion of 1066 many of the English protested. William put down rebellions brutally, taking English land and giving it to his Norman nobles, for them to rule the local areas. He gave land to the Church in order to gain its support, replacing English with French bishops, and he encouraged French traders and craftworkers to settle in England. The Normans built large castles, churches, monasteries, and great cathedrals, and many towns grew up around them. The nobility spoke French, and the ordinary people spoke early English. A central administration and tax system was established, and a tax assessment of England's land and wealth, the *Domesday Book,* was made. Norman rule was harsh. They were mainly interested in wealth and power, and used England as a base for foreign adventures that the English had to finance. However, England developed economically, and within 100 years the Normans began the invasion of Wales, Ireland, and Scotland. England was changing—its landscape, towns, and culture were all influenced by the Normans. By 1140 there was a disagreement over who should rule the country. This weakened the king and strengthened the nobles' power. A new Norman dynasty, the Plantagenet was founded in 1154, and its first king, Henry II, ruled England and half of France. During this time, the English class system, dominated by nobles, began to develop.

▲ William the Conqueror was succeeded by two of his sons. William II ruled from 1087–1100, Henry from 1100–1135. They established firm Norman rule, but it collapsed under the next king, Stephen, who died in 1154.

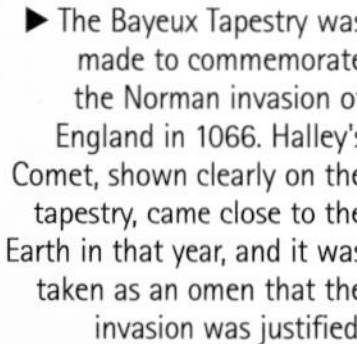

▶ The Bayeux Tapestry was made to commemorate the Norman invasion of England in 1066. Halley's Comet, shown clearly on the tapestry, came close to the Earth in that year, and it was taken as an omen that the invasion was justified.

THE NORMANS IN EUROPE

The Normans were also busy elsewhere in Europe. Around 1060, Norman soldiers under Robert Guiscard invaded Sicily and southern Italy, to support the pope against the Byzantines and Arabs. As a result, they were favored by the pope and often protected him. In the 1200s, they became leaders of the Crusades. Through political marriages, and by serving as knights, papal agents, bishops, and royal courtiers, Norman lords formed a feudal network which became very influential across Europe in the 1200s. In these feudal relationships, a noble who pledged allegiance and gave military support to a king was rewarded with lands and titles. These nobles then ruled estates and provinces, demanding loyalty of their followers and in exchange rewarding them with lands and positions of power. And so feudalism that started in France became established throughout Europe.

To honor ancient traditions, local law courts were often held outdoors. The lord of the manor was the judge. This court, or assize, held in 1072, met to decide whether some lands belonged to the Bishop of Bayeux, in Normandy, or to Canterbury Cathedral.

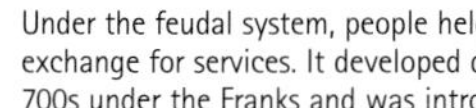

THE FEUDAL SYSTEM

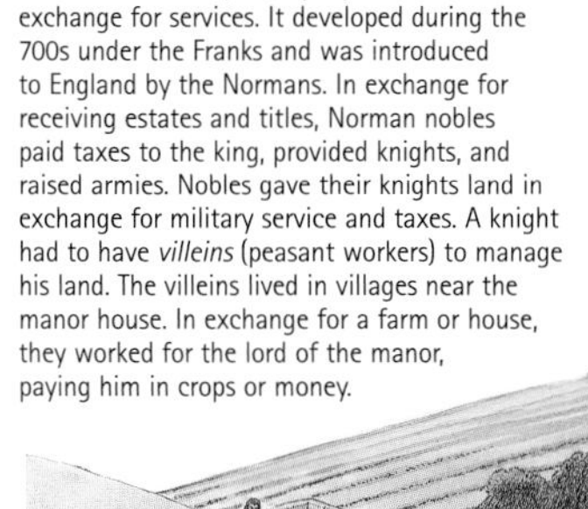

Under the feudal system, people held land in exchange for services. It developed during the 700s under the Franks and was introduced to England by the Normans. In exchange for receiving estates and titles, Norman nobles paid taxes to the king, provided knights, and raised armies. Nobles gave their knights land in exchange for military service and taxes. A knight had to have *villeins* (peasant workers) to manage his land. The villeins lived in villages near the manor house. In exchange for a farm or house, they worked for the lord of the manor, paying him in crops or money.

Stories about heroic knights and courtly love between lords and ladies were very popular in Norman England.

THE SELJUK TURKS 1037–1243

The Seljuks invaded the Middle East from 1037 onward, ending Arabian domination of the Islamic world and opening the way for the Ottomans.

This minaret at the Jami mosque in Simnan, Iran, shows typical Seljuk patterns in its elaborate brickwork. The Seljuks became Muslims around 970, and considered themselves defenders of the Islamic faith.

The Turks were originally a family of tribes living in Turkestan, central Asia. They split up during the 500s, and spread to Russia, China, India, and Persia. Some Turks abandoned the nomad life to become administrators and mercenary warriors. They served the Abbasids, Fatimids, and others, and sometimes rose to high office. Turks such as the Seljuks, Ottomans, Mamluks, Bulgars, and Khazars soon began to have great influence. They also joined forces with the Mongols. The Turkish cities of Samarkand and Bokhara grew wealthy and cultured in Islamic times.

SELJUK EXPANSION

To the east of the Caspian Sea lived a Turkic group called the Ghuzz, or Turkomans. The Seljuk broke away from the Ghuzz in 950, moving south and west. The Abbasid caliph in Baghdad was having difficulties, and he asked the Seljuks for their help. Led by Tughril Beg, the Seljuks invaded Persia and occupied Baghdad by 1055. The Abbasid caliph appointed Tughril as sultan under him—in effect, he gave the Abbasid Empire to the Seljuks. In this way, the Seljuks rose from being a simple nomadic tribe to rulers of the Islamic world.

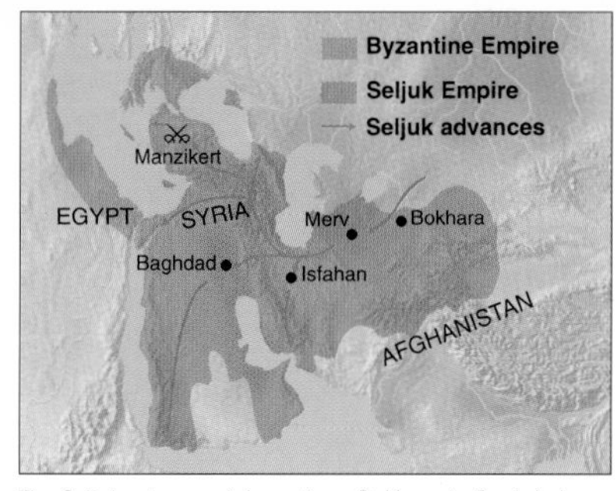

The Seljuks streamed down from Bokhara to Baghdad, and later, westward into Anatolia, almost as far as Constantinople. Anatolia (Turkey) then became Muslim.

Alp Arslan, Tughril's nephew, became sultan in 1063. He took Syria and Armenia and raided Anatolia. In 1071, the Byzantine emperor fought back. Alp Arslan hired Norman and Turkish mercenaries and marched into Armenia. The armies met at Manzikert. The Seljuks won because they pretended to be defeated and ran away. When the Byzantines pursued them, they turned around and badly defeated the Byzantine army. The Seljuks captured the Byzantine emperor and held him for ransom. This victory laid the foundation of what later became the Ottoman Empire. Alp Arslan was a compassionate leader and ruled the empire well. With his blessing, many Turkomans and Seljuks moved into Anatolia.

Like most nomads from the Asian steppes, the Seljuks were great horsemen. Using the new invention of stirrups, they could stay on horseback and fire arrows accurately in battle. This picture shows them defeating the Byzantines at the battle of Manzikert.

MALIK SHAH

The Seljuk Empire reached its greatest power under the rule of Alp Arslan's son, Malik Shah (1072–92). He was a patron of the sciences and the arts and built fine mosques in his capital, Isfahan. His minister, Nizam al-Mulk, was respected as a statesman. During this time, Seljuks took over Anatolia (Turkey) completely, and founded the Sultanate of Rum right next to Constantinople. On Malik Shah's death, the Seljuk Empire broke up into small states, and a variety of Seljuk, Mamluk, and Kurdish sultanates continued through the 1300s, all under the eye of the Abbasid caliph in Baghdad. Then, in 1220, the Mongols overran the area, finally occupying Baghdad in 1258.

▲The Tomeh or Friday mosque was built in Isfahan, Persia, in the Seljuk style. The Seljuks were great patrons of learning, architecture, and culture.

KEY DATES

950	The Seljuks break away from the Ghuzz Turks
1038	Seljuks conquer Khorasan (Afghanistan)
1055	Seljuks conquer Baghdad
1071	Seljuks defeat the Byzantines at Manzikert
1072	Peak of the Seljuk Empire
1081	Founding of the Seljuk sultanate of Rum
1092	Death of Malik Shah—Seljuk Empire breaks up
1243	Mongol invasions: Seljuks become Mongol vassals
1258	Mongols destroy the Abbasid caliphate

▲This is a tiled detail from the tomb of the Seljuk sultan Kaykavus I at Sivas in Turkey. The Seljuks produced beautiful and intricate patterns that were used to adorn their religious buildings.

◀Though the Seljuks brought new life to the Abbasid Empire, life in the Muslim world went on very much as before. This scene shows what a souk, or indoor trading hall,in Baghdad, would have looked like during the 1100s.

CHINA: THE SONG DYNASTY 960–1279

The Song (or Sung) dynasty created the third united Chinese Empire. This was a time of great innovation and took China into a long period of cultural eminence.

This Song temple painting from the 1100s shows disciples of the Buddha feeding the poor.

After the Tang dynasty fell in 907, China became fragmented. In the Huang He Valley, five emperors tried to start new dynasties over 53 years. None succeeded until Song Taizu took power in 960, founding the Song dynasty. He brought the many warlords and armies under control, and by both military and diplomatic means began to reunify China. This took 16 years and was completed by his brother, Song Taizong, the second Song emperor, in 979.

THE NORTHERN SONG PERIOD

Now surrounded by other states, China under the Song was smaller than in Tang times. In the northwest was Xixia, which was Tibetan; in the northeast was Liao, ruled by Mongol Khitans; in the southeast was Nan Chao, a Thai state; and in the south was Annam, a Vietnamese kingdom. The Song emperors worked hard to make peace with all of them.

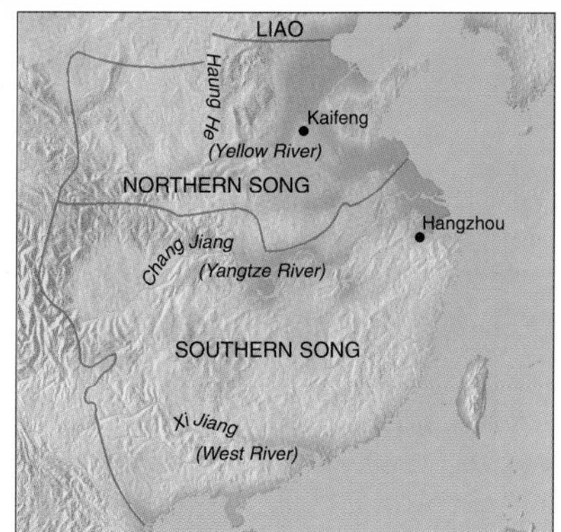

Until the Jin invaded the north in 1127, the Song ruled all of China. They were then forced to move south where they prospered for another 150 years until the Mongols invaded.

Agriculture expanded and the population grew—especially in the south, which was now wealthy and important. By the end of the Song period there were probably around 100 million people living in China.

▼ Song artists often painted landscapes with small central features in them. This example of landscape painting from the Song period is called "Fisherman."

This vase with a butterfly and leaf-and-flower design is typical of the porcelain of the Song period. Europe didn't master porcelain-making techniques for many centuries.

"A Buddhist Temple in the Mountains" was painted by Li Cheng during the 900s.

THE SOUTHERN SONG PERIOD

In 1068, the prime minister, Wang Anshi, reformed the government. He simplified the tax system and reduced the size of the huge army. Although these cuts saved money, they also made invasion easier. In 1127, northern China was attacked by the Jin, and the Song capital, Kaifeng, was lost. The Song withdrew to Hangzhou, south of the Yangtze, and the north was then ruled by the Jin until Kublai Khan's Mongols took over in 1234. Hangzhou became a large, beautiful city, with canals, parks, and fine buildings. The Southern Song lasted until 1279, when southern China was overrun by the Mongols.

The Song period saw great prosperity and advancement in new technologies, arts, and literature. They invented gunpowder rockets, clocks, movable-type printing, paddle-wheel boats, magnetic compasses, and waterpowered machinery. Landscape painting, fine porcelain, poetry, and theater flourished. Banking and trade became important, towns grew large, and new crops were introduced. Song China could have become even greater, had it not been brought down by the Mongol invaders.

KEY DATES

907	Fall of the Tang dynasty
960	Song Taizu founds the Song dynasty
979	Song Taizong completes unification of China
1000	Culture and the economy thrive in China
1068-86	Wang Anshi's reforms
1127	The Jin take northern China: the Song retreat to Hangzhou
1234	The Mongols conquer northern China, ousting the Jin
1279	The Mongols conquer southern China: Song period ends

CHINESE PORCELAIN

Throughout the world, pottery had been made of clay that produced a chunky and rough finish. Around 900, the Song dynasty Chinese invented porcelain, which was made from kaolin, a fine white clay. Their craftworkers made smooth and delicate porcelain which, when used with special glazes and painting styles, could be beautifully decorated—making each piece a work of art. During this period, Chinese emperors even had factories built to make porcelain specially for their palaces. Porcelain production soon became an enormous industry in China.

Song emperors had ceramic factories built to supply fine porcelain.

This porcelain wine vessel stands in another vessel used for warming.

THE MIDDLE AGES

1101–1460

During the Middle Ages, empires rose and fell around the world. Many wars were undertaken in the name of religion. In Europe, alliances were made and quickly broken and a sense of nationalism began to grow. European traders ventured as far afield as China, camel caravans trudged across the Sahara and Venetian ships sailed the Mediterranean Sea with their goods. These were times of faith and fortune, of war and torture, famine and wealth. By the end of the Middle Ages, learning had become a possibility for everyone who could read.

▲ The Krak des Chevaliers, in what is now Syria, was the largest and strongest castle built by the crusaders. It was garrisoned by 2,000 men, but finally fell to the Saracens in 1271.

◀ The French king, Saint Louis IX, embarks in Aigues Mortes in 1248 for the seventh Crusade to the Holy Land.

THE WORLD AT A GLANCE 1101–1460

During this period, trade increased people's knowledge of many parts of the world, but it also helped spread the Black Death, a disease carried by the fleas that lived on rats found on ships. In Europe, the Black Death killed a fourth of the population.

Information about Africa was spread by Arab traders who sailed down the east coast of the continent. They brought with them stories of vast inland empires, rich with gold, and centered on large stone cities. In West Africa, the kingdom of Mali flourished.

In the Far East, the Khmer Empire of Cambodia was at its height. In Japan, military rulers called shoguns were supported by samurai warriors, and were virtual dictators of their country.

The Mongols conquered much of Asia and Europe to form the largest empire of all time—although it was to be short-lived. Their success was based on brilliant military tactics and superb horsemanship.

In the Americas, the Aztecs built their capital city of Tenochtitlan in the center of Lake Texcoco in Mexico, while in South America, the Inca Empire was expanding by conquering neighboring tribes.

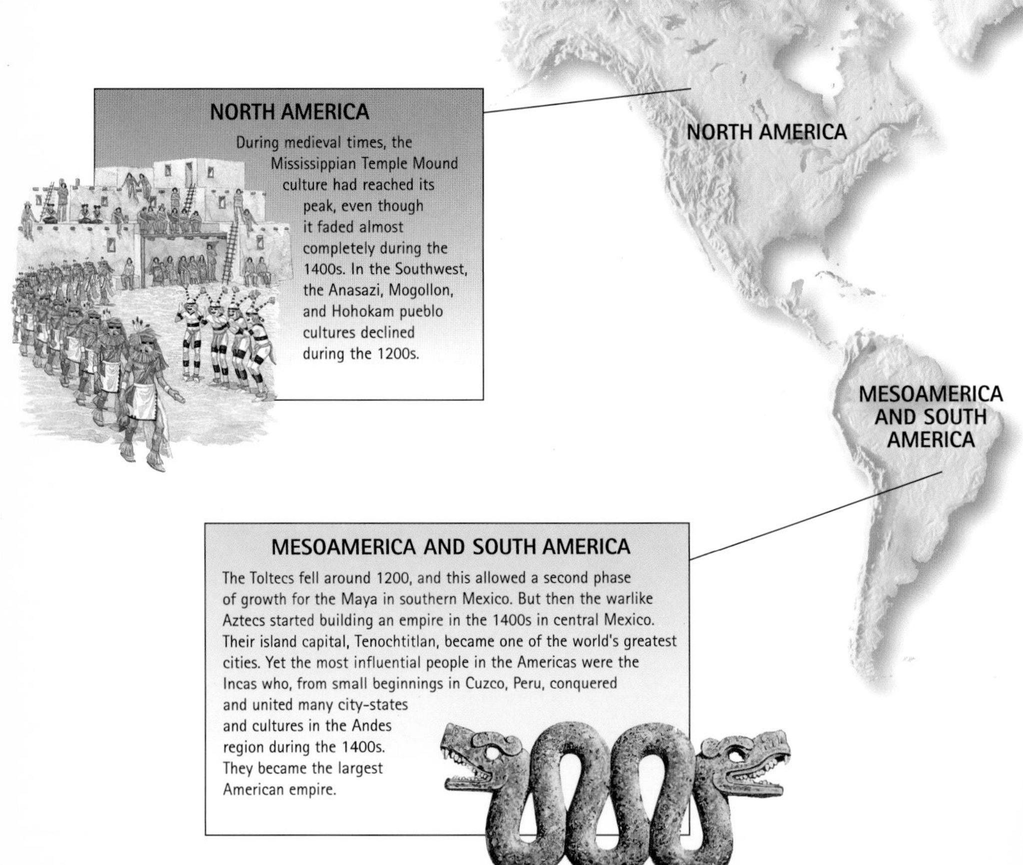

NORTH AMERICA

During medieval times, the Mississippian Temple Mound culture had reached its peak, even though it faded almost completely during the 1400s. In the Southwest, the Anasazi, Mogollon, and Hohokam pueblo cultures declined during the 1200s.

MESOAMERICA AND SOUTH AMERICA

The Toltecs fell around 1200, and this allowed a second phase of growth for the Maya in southern Mexico. But then the warlike Aztecs started building an empire in the 1400s in central Mexico. Their island capital, Tenochtitlan, became one of the world's greatest cities. Yet the most influential people in the Americas were the Incas who, from small beginnings in Cuzco, Peru, conquered and united many city-states and cultures in the Andes region during the 1400s. They became the largest American empire.

EUROPE

In the Middle Ages, European nation-states grew more stable and established. Much depended on the ruling classes, the nobility, and the clergy, though in later centuries the merchant classes grew in wealth and power by becoming their financiers. There was a violent elimination of freethinkers—so-called "heretics" were persecuted and killed for their beliefs. The Crusades against Muslims had a major effect both on Europe and the Middle East. Then came the shock of the Black Death, which swept through Europe in the 1340s, ruthlessly killing one third of the population. This was a major turning point. It led to new political and social developments that in time would put Europe in a position to dominate the world.

ASIA

The Mongols dominated Asia for 100 years during the 1200s, creating the world's largest-ever empire, embracing China, Persia, and central Asia. Later, Asiatic Turkic peoples played an important role in India and the Middle East, becoming overlords in many areas. In 1271, the explorer Marco Polo set out for China from Venice. In China, the Ming dynasty gained control in 1368 after the fall of the Mongols, and Muslim rule overcame Hindu culture in north India. Islam spread as far as the East Indies and into central Asia.

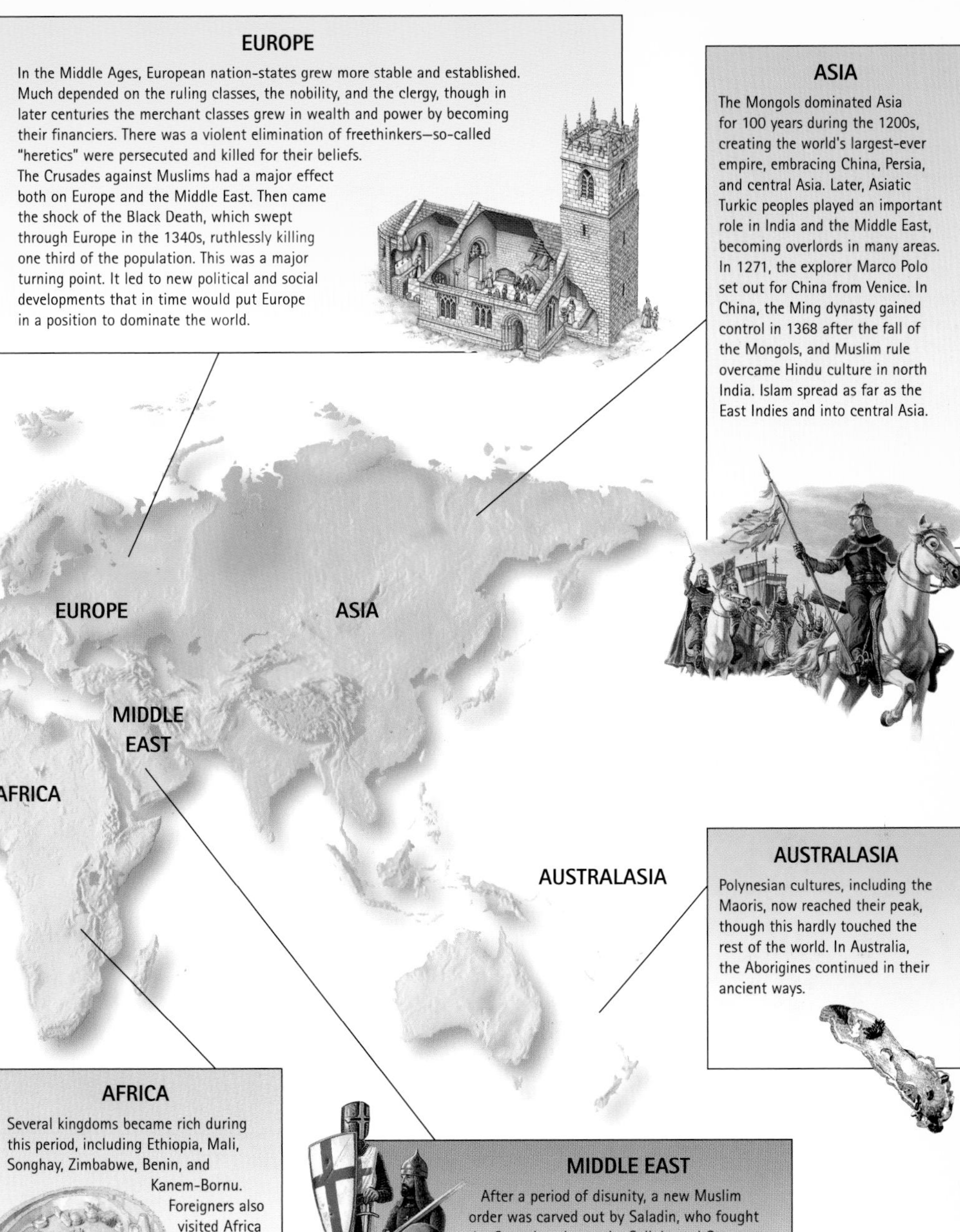

AUSTRALASIA

Polynesian cultures, including the Maoris, now reached their peak, though this hardly touched the rest of the world. In Australia, the Aborigines continued in their ancient ways.

AFRICA

Several kingdoms became rich during this period, including Ethiopia, Mali, Songhay, Zimbabwe, Benin, and Kanem-Bornu. Foreigners also visited Africa from Europe, China, and Arabia.

MIDDLE EAST

After a period of disunity, a new Muslim order was carved out by Saladin, who fought the Crusaders. Later, the Seljuks and Ottoman Turks become powerful. The Ottomans took over Byzantium and also took control of the Middle East and southeast Europe—their empire survived until 1917.

THE CRUSADES 1095–1291

Palestine became the center of a struggle for political and religious power when the pope called for a crusade to free the Holy Land from Muslim control.

To Christians and Muslims, Palestine was the Holy Land, a place of pilgrimage for hundreds of years. After the Arabs conquered Palestine in 637, Christian pilgrims were still able to visit Jerusalem safely, but this changed with the arrival of the Seljuk Turks. In 1095, Pope Urban II called on Christians to free Palestine from Muslim rule. Knights and ordinary people set out, led by Peter the Hermit and Walter the Penniless. Most of them never reached Palestine, and the rest became a wild, hungry mob. In 1099, a well-disciplined Crusader army recaptured Jerusalem, massacring its inhabitants.

They established four so-called Latin States, or kingdoms in Palestine and Syria. At first the Saracens, as the Crusaders called the Seljuk Turks, left the Crusader kingdoms alone.

The Crusaders wore heavy armor and rode large stallions, and the Muslims, called Saracens, wore light armor and rode mares. Both armies were formidable looking, but the Saracens were more mobile.

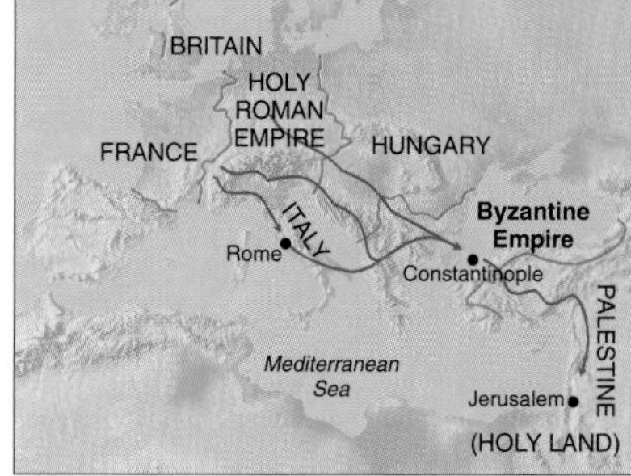

At first the Crusaders traveled overland from France and Italy to Palestine, but, to avoid having to fight the Seljuk Turks in Anatolia, they started to go by sea from Venice.

Some of the heads of the Christian kingdoms behaved badly toward the Muslims. In 1187, Saladin defeated the Christians at Hattin and recovered Jerusalem. In 1191, England's Richard I ("the Lionheart") led an army to the Holy Land. He took Cyprus and the city of Acre, which had been under siege by Christian forces, but he was unable to recapture Jerusalem. He and Saladin signed a treaty sharing the Holy Land, including Jerusalem—the Christians founded a "Second Kingdom" of the holy city with its heart at Acre.

The Crusaders built Norman-style castles in Palestine and Syria. The Krak des Chevaliers in Syria, built by the Knights Hospitallers, was besieged by the Muslims in 1271. They eventually starved the Crusaders into surrender.

Saladin (c.1137–1193), a pious leader, led his people in a *jihad* or holy war against the Crusaders.

Richard I of England (1157–1199), known as the Lionheart (on the right), led an army of knights to the Holy Land in 1191, on the third Crusade. They failed to recapture Jerusalem, but Richard was able to secure a five-year peace treaty with Saladin. This allowed European pilgrims to visit the holy places again. On his return to England, in 1192, he was captured by Leopold of Austria and then Henry VI, the Holy Roman emperor, who held Richard for ransom for about a year. He finally reached England in 1194.

The fourth Crusade began in 1202, but the Crusaders were unable to pay Venice for transportation. So, in exchange for transportation, they agreed to loot Constantinople on Venice's behalf. In 1212, up to 50,000 children from France and Germany set off for Palestine, but most of them died of hunger or became slaves—this is known as the Children's Crusade. The fifth Crusade to Egypt failed; the last three crusades (1218–1272) were also unsuccessful. In 1291, Palestine was finally conquered by the sultan of Egypt.

Louis IX, of France (1226–1270), was deeply religious. He led the seventh Crusade (1248) and was captured. He also led the eighth, but died of plague.

KEY DATES

1096–99	First Crusade takes Palestine and Syria
1187	Saladin wins back Jerusalem
1189–92	Third Crusade
1202–04	Fourth Crusade loots Constantinople
1212	Children's Crusade—a tragic failure
1218–21	Fifth Crusade—a failure
1228–29	Sixth Crusade—partly successful
1291	Acre is lost—the last Crusades

▼ At the decisive battle of Hattin in 1187, Saladin tricked the Crusaders onto a hill on a hot day. While the Crusaders roasted in their metal armor, he surrounded and defeated them. Saladin then went on to win back Jerusalem.

HENRY OF ANJOU 1154–1189

Henry of Anjou became Henry II, the first Plantagenet king of England, in 1154. With his lands in France he became one of the most powerful rulers in Europe.

Henry II (1133–89) was a man of great humor but he also had a violent temper. Through his strong rule, he brought a period of peace and prosperity to both England and France.

Henry of Anjou was William the Conqueror's great-grandson. His mother, Matilda, was the widow of the Holy Roman emperor Henry V, who had died in 1125. She was the daughter of Henry I of England, who named her his heir after his sons had died. Henry I also wanted to strengthen his hold on Normandy, so, in 1128, he had Matilda marry Count Geoffrey of Anjou in France. In 1127, Henry had forced the English nobles to accept a woman as heir to the thrones of England and Normandy, but they were now furious that Matilda had married into a French royal house. When Henry died in 1135, the Church and the nobility split, and most threw their support behind Matilda's cousin Stephen as king. Civil war broke out in 1139, but in the end, Stephen remained king. He was later forced to make Matilda and Geoffrey's son, Henry of Anjou, his heir.

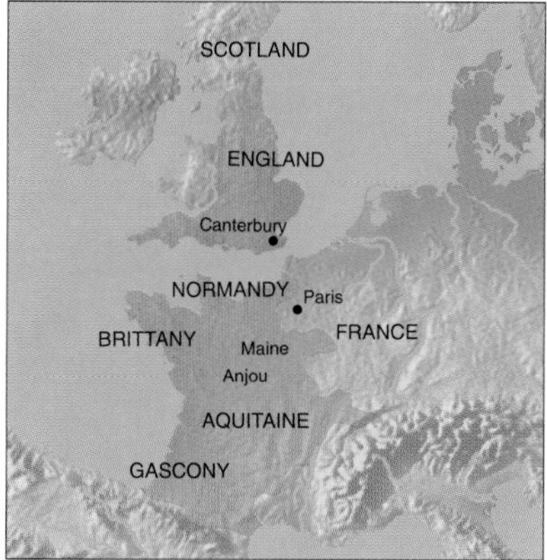

Henry ruled over a greater area of France than the French king, Louis VII. He also ruled England, and eventually spread his influence to Wales, Scotland, and Ireland.

When Henry of Anjou became Henry II of England at the age of 21, he inherited the French provinces of Anjou, Maine, and Touraine from his father, and Normandy and Brittany from his mother. In 1152, he married Eleanor, the abandoned wife of the French king Louis VII, thus gaining Aquitaine. As a result of this, he ruled England and two thirds of France.

Eleanor of Aquitaine (c. 1122–1204), wife of Louis VII of France, had no children, so the marriage was annulled. She then married England's Henry II.

▲▶ Thomas à Becket (c.1118–70), Henry's chancellor, became Archbishop of Canterbury in 1162. He frequently opposed the king, and in 1170, was murdered in Canterbury Cathedral (right). This was a mistake that Henry much regretted.

HENRY AND BECKET

Henry was an energetic ruler and traveled widely throughout his kingdom. He was well educated and cultured, and his court at Chinon in France was attended by many erudite scholars and troubadours (minstrels). Henry brought his nobles firmly under control, improved the laws of England, and forced the Scots and Welsh to obey him. When Norman nobles took control in Ireland, he subdued them and made himself king of Ireland in 1172. Henry chose capable ministers, among them Thomas à Becket, who became his chancellor. When Henry made him Archbishop of Canterbury, Becket began to assert the rights of the Church. After years of quarrels, Henry is said to have exclaimed, "Who will rid me of this turbulent priest?" Four knights took him at his word and killed Becket. Henry later did penance for this crime.

Eleanor of Aquitaine died in 1204. Her tomb in the abbey church at Frontrevault, in western France, lies next to that of one of her sons, Richard I. Her husband, Henry II, who died in 1189, lies nearby.

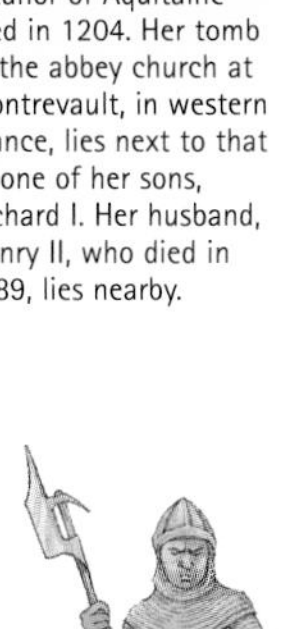

After the murder of Becket, the pope demanded that Henry do penance and be flogged. This was done, and Henry expressed his regrets. He was later pardoned.

Henry's empire was a family possession, not a country, and he planned to divide it among his four sons. They squabbled over this and then revolted against him. Two of them died, leaving Richard (the Lionheart) and John. Richard became king of England in 1189, and was followed after his death in 1199 by John. Henry had been a great and creative king, who had set up English common law, but he died in 1189, feeling that his life had been a failure. After his death, his sons lost most of his French lands, and the new order that Henry had built in England soon disintegrated.

KEY DATES

1122	Eleanor of Aquitaine is born
1133	Henry of Anjou born
1139	Eleanor of Aquitaine marries Louis VII of France; marriage later annulled
1152	Henry marries Eleanor of Aquitaine
1154	Henry becomes king of England
1157	Submission of the king of Scotland
1162	Thomas à Becket becomes Archbishop of Canterbury
1166–76	Legal reforms in England
1170	Murder of Thomas à Becket
1171	Henry becomes king of Ireland
1173	Thomas à Becket made a saint
1174	Rebellions by Henry's sons
1189	Henry dies in France

LIFE IN A CASTLE

Castles were large buildings that were cold and drafty to live in. They were military fortresses that also housed the lord's soldiers and servants. Towns soon grew outside the castle walls. In the lord's dwellings, the lady's servants lived in the top room, where linen and clothes were stored. Under this was the master bedroom, where the lord and lady slept. Below this was the *solar*, the lord's private living room, and on the ground floor were the great hall and a secure storeroom for the master's weapons and valuables.

IRELAND 700–1350

This period of Irish history saw increasingly permanent domination by foreigners, following invasions first by the Vikings and then by the English.

▲ Strongbow, or Richard de Clare (c. 1130–1176) invaded Ireland from Pembroke, in Wales. He became king of Leinster.

▼ MacMurrough Kavanagh, king of Leinster, rides to make peace with the Earl of Gloucester during the Norman invasions.

Ireland was inhabited mainly by Gaelic Celts who lived in about 150 *tuath* or tribes. They frequently feuded and warred, which became a hindrance to Ireland's prosperity. Then, in 432, a man arrived who changed the course of Irish history—St. Patrick. He traveled around Ireland converting Irish chiefs to Christianity and preaching peace. By 600, Ireland had become Europe's main Christian center, and Irish monks preached all across Europe. In 795, the Vikings invaded the island, and for the next 40 years raided and destroyed monasteries. By 840, they began to settle, founding towns such as Dublin, Waterford, Cork, and Limerick. From these, they traded and mixed with the Irish people, adopting many of their customs.

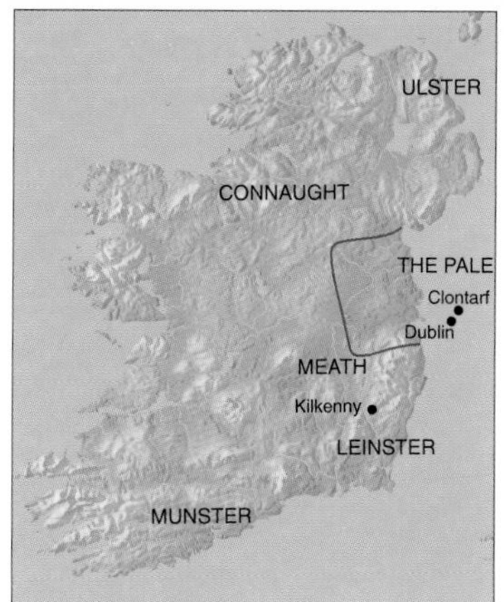

In medieval times, there were five kingdoms in Ireland. All that was left of direct Norman rule was a small area around Dublin called the Pale.

The rest of Ireland was still traditionally Irish. By now, the five largest kingdoms were Ulster, Leinster, Munster, Connaught, and Meath. In 976, Brian Boru, king of Munster, set about invading his neighbors. By 1011, he dominated Ireland, but on his death other local kings fought to be high king. The last strong high king was Turlough O'Connor of Connaught. After he died in 1156, two kings became rivals. One of these, Dermot MacMurrough of Leinster, asked for help from the Normans in England.

THE COMING OF THE ENGLISH

The Earl of Pembroke, or "Strongbow," supported Dermot MacMurrough in return for marrying his daughter and inheriting Leinster. In 1170, Strongbow and other Norman nobles invaded, seizing Irish lands for themselves. This alarmed the king of England, Henry II, who proclaimed himself overlord of Ireland. Many Irish, fearing chaos, supported him and the Norman nobles submitted. Like the Vikings before them, many Normans soon adopted the customs of the Irish. However, in 1366, Lionel, Edward III's son and governor of Ireland, ordered the Irish-Norman families to stop speaking Gaelic and marrying Irish women. This demand was not accepted, and the Irish-Normans now looked upon the English as interfering foreigners. By the late 1400s English rule existed only in the Dublin area, called "the English Pale."

During the unsuccessful English campaigns in Ireland, between 1367 and 1400, ships had to carry provisions across the Irish Sea to the English troops.

KEY DATES	
432	St. Patrick introduces Christianity to Ireland
795	The start of Viking raids—destruction of Irish monasteries
840	Vikings settle, establishing coastal trading towns
1014	Brian Boru, king of Munster, defeats Vikings at the Battle of Clontarf
1148	Richard de Clare becomes Earl of Pembroke
1166	Rory O'Connor becomes first king of Ireland since 1014
1170	Norman invasion of Ireland led by Richard de Clare
1171	Richard de Clare becomes king of Leinster; Henry II annexes Ireland
1366	Irish-Normans revolt against English orders banning Gaelic and mixed marriages
1530s	Henry VIII reimposes English control

▼ On the Rock of Cashel, in County Tipperary, site of royal fortifications since the 300s, stand the ruins of St. Patrick's Cathedral. Given to the Church in 1101, the cross (far left) is where the kings of Munster were traditionally crowned.

Shoguns and Samurai 1200–1500

The shoguns were generals who acted as governmental dictators, and the samurai were Japanese knights. They both dominated Japan for almost 700 years.

A samurai's main weapons were a bow made of boxwood or bamboo and one or two single-edged swords. Samurai were strictly trained from childhood, following a code called *bushido*—the warrior's way.

The Fujiwara family had held power in Japan for 300 years since the 800s. However, their influence broke down when local dissent spread and when they ran out of daughters, the traditional brides of the emperor. For a time, some of the former emperors ruled. Then the Taira clan took over briefly until a rival clan, the Minamoto, rallied under Minamoto Yoritomo and seized power. Yoritomo assumed the title *sei-i tai shogun*, which means "barbarian-conquering great general." In 1192, he set up the Kamakura shogunate, through which he ruled Japan from his estate, Kamakura, near Edo (Tokyo). His powers were unlimited. From that time on, shoguns ruled Japan as military dictators until 1868. When Yoritomo died in 1199, the Hojo family, a branch of the Taira clan, became regents to the shoguns, and held power in an unofficial capacity until the Kamakura shogunate ended in 1333.

Minamoto Yoritomo (1147–1199) was an ambitious nobleman who saw his chance in the chaos that followed the breakdown of the power of the Fujiwara. Yoritomo ruthlessly crushed his enemies, including many of his own family. He set up the shogunate, a rigid feudal system that affected the whole country with him—the first shogun—as its head.

Japanese government was complicated. The emperor was a ceremonial figure to whom everyone bowed down, but the shogun had the real power. The regents to the emperors and shoguns also had influence, as did the *daimyos* or lords, who jostled for position at court and frequently battled over land. As a result, a class of warriors, or *samurai*, developed, who fought for the daimyos.

Samurai had elaborate decorated armor and many rituals. They were not only warriors who followed the code of *bushido*—the observance of very rigid rules that affected everything they did—but also had to be trained in the arts and religion.

▶ During the 1100s, Zen, a branch of Buddhism, spread from China to Japan. It had simple but strict rules, which the samurai followed. Buddhist shrines, like this gateway, were also built in the Chinese style.

As with European knights and Muslim warriors, religion and war were very closely connected for a samurai. He took a long time dressing and arming himself for battle, with strict rules of cleanliness and ritual.

KNIGHTS OF JAPAN

The samurai were knights who were prepared to fight to the death for their daimyos, to whom they swore undying loyalty. Like the European knight, a samurai believed in truth and honor, and had a strict code of conduct called *bushido*. Before combat, a samurai would shout his name and those of his ancestors, and boast of his heroic deeds. In battle he fought hand to hand, often using two swords at once. If defeated or captured by his enemy, he had to commit ritual suicide (*hara-kiri*) in order to save face. At times, rivalry between samurai was destructive.

In 1333, the Ashikaga clan overthrew the Kamakura shogunate and the emperor, putting a new emperor in power. He appointed them as shoguns, this time in Kyoto. However, there was frequent samurai fighting between daimyos. This increased until the Onin civil war broke out, lasting from 1467–77, and Japan split into nearly 400 clan-states. The Kyoto emperors became powerless and impoverished. Despite this, trade and culture grew in Japan, centered on the daimyo estates. For ordinary people, the daimyo wars brought high taxes, insecurity, and disruption to their lives.

THE SAMURAI IN BATTLE

Samurai battles were very ritualistic. They involved prayer and posturing (making oneself look strong) beforehand, with shouting and noisemaking using rattles and gongs to frighten the enemy. Individual samurai would undertake duels and contests. Often, battles were like a dance or a ceremonial game of chess. However, samurai warfare was deadly once they joined in full battle. During the Ashikaga period (1338–1573), much of the fighting deteriorated into meaningless squabbles for honor and plots of land.

EUROPEAN TRADE 1100–1450

Trade and industry rapidly grew to provide services for rising populations. Merchants and bankers thrived and found new influence from meeting society's needs.

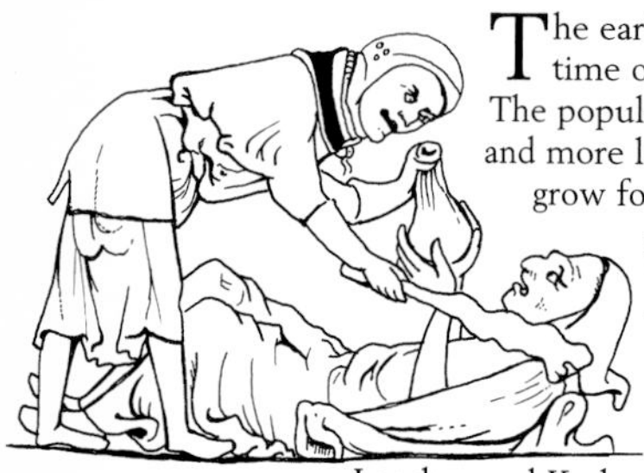

The perils of travel in medieval times are shown in this drawing of a highwayman stealing a traveler's money. Highwaymen often lay in wait for their victims at roadsides.

The early Middle Ages was a time of growth for Europe. The population was increasing, and more land was cultivated to grow food. This led to surplus produce for trading. Towns grew larger, with regular trade fairs at places like Troyes, Lyons, Antwerp, Kiev, Frankfurt, Leipzig, London, and Krakow. River links and shipping routes were busier. Instead of exchanging goods (bartering), money was used, and increasingly, people went into business for profit. Jewish traders, Knights Templars, and certain business families specialized in moneylending and the safekeeping of valuables. Italy was the richest part of Europe. Venice and Genoa were large independent seaports and banking centers, buying spices, silks, and other luxuries from the East. Goods from Asia came through Byzantium, Egypt, and Syria, and from Africa through Tunisia and Morocco. They were traded for cloth, furs, hides, iron, linen, timber, silver, and slaves.

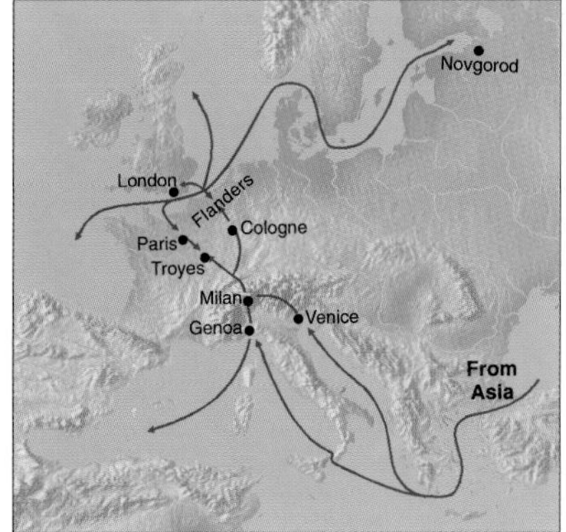

In the 1100s, cities and ports grew along trade routes in Europe. Italian merchants attended fairs such as that at Troyes to buy Flemish cloth and sell Asian goods.

Most of Europe's money was silver, but the Asian countries traded in gold. This caused problems, so the Templars, Jewish traders, and Italian merchants invented banking, with bills of exchange and "promissory notes" that could be used instead of cash. Industries grew in the Rhineland (Germany), northern France, Flanders, and England, importing materials like copper, alum, wool, and charcoal, and exporting goods and clothes.

In a medieval town, markets were usually held once a week. Livestock, food, metals, cloth, leather, and woodwork were all sold there, and people met to discuss local affairs.

THE GROWTH OF COMMERCE

A new class of merchants and skilled craftworkers appeared. Merchants grew rich through buying and selling, but they also risked loss because of highway robbery or piracy on the high seas where cargoes and fortunes could be lost. Trading companies, cities, and organizations like the Hanseatic League in the Baltic Sea worked together to protect trade, and opened offices in ports and marketplaces. To protect their trade, the Venetians and Genoese became Mediterranean naval powers. Around 1350, in Genoa, insurance services were offered, to protect traders against loss and bankruptcy. Banking families such as the Fuggers in Augsburg, Germany, and the Medicis in Florence, Italy, grew in wealth and influence. A new commercial order was developing, and kings, nobles, and clerics slowly lost power as they grew dependent on merchants and indebted to bankers. Soon, this new class began to influence the decisions of kings.

In Europe, posthouses and taverns were built along main roads. They provided refreshments, a place to stay, and a change of horse for merchants, pilgrims, and other travelers.

THE HANSEATIC LEAGUE

In 1241, two German towns, Hamburg and Lübeck, set up a *Hansa* or trading association, which developed into the Hanseatic League in 1260, and involved many former Viking towns. They carried food and raw materials from eastern Europe in exchange for manufactured goods from the west. The Hanseatic League dominated trade between England, Scandinavia, Germany, and Russia during the 1300s.

The seal of Danzig, one of the leading Hansa towns.

Hanseatic merchants used these sturdy ships to carry goods between Baltic and Atlantic ports. They established warehouses, customs, banking systems, and defensive structures.

CHARTER AND PARLIAMENT 1215–1485

In England, in the 1200s, there was a growing struggle between the kings and the lords. The absolute power of kings was being questioned by those they ruled.

King John (1199–1216), quarrelled with his nobles, who turned against him, and forced him to sign the Magna Carta.

King John of England, the youngest son of Henry II, was given to violent outbursts of temper. Not surprisingly, he soon angered his barons in English-ruled Anjou and Poitiers, and he lost those lands to France. In England, he taxed his barons heavily and ruled so harshly that they rebelled. The barons threatened John, and demanded that he recognize their traditional rights and obey the law.

This is the great seal of King John, affixed to the bottom of the Magna Carta. John's seal showed his consent, and so turned the charter into the law of the land.

In 1215, John was forced to put his seal on the Magna Carta at Runnymede. John did not actually sign the charter, and possibly could not even write.

THE MAGNA CARTA

In 1215, the barons met King John in a meadow called Runnymede, beside the Thames River. There, they forced him to put his seal on the Magna Carta, or "great charter." This document covered many important areas, including weights and measures, the powers of sheriffs, and the legal rights of freemen and boroughs (towns). The king agreed to obey the law himself, and he was not allowed to raise taxes without the agreement of his Great Council of nobles. No sooner had John agreed to the charter than he went back on his word. A civil war broke out, but John soon died, leaving the throne to his young son who became Henry III. The charter was reissued, and in 1225, it became the law of England. Henry III was incompetent and he spent large sums of money, so the barons banded together again, this time led by Simon de Montfort. They forced Henry to agree to consult the Great Council in all major matters. Like his father, Henry III went back on the deal, but de Montfort defeated him in battle at Lewes in 1264. Simon de Montfort and the Council then ruled England in Henry's name.

THE POWER OF PARLIAMENT

In 1265, Simon de Montfort called a new Parliament of two chambers, the House of Lords (previously the Great Council of nobles and bishops,) and the House of Commons. The House of Commons was made up of two knights from every shire and two people (burgesses) who represented each borough. Later, Edward I (1272–1307), a successful ruler, reformed England's law and administration; he created a Model Parliament which included even more representatives from the country. However, the king still held power. In 1388, there was a major clash and the "Merciless" Parliament removed some of King Richard II's rights.

As time went on, Parliament's powers gradually grew. The House of Commons slowly gained greater power, although it was mostly the richer classes that were represented in Parliament. Full-scale democracy only arrived in the 1900s.

KEY DATES	
1215	King John reluctantly affixes his seal to the Magna Carta
1216	King John dies. His nine-year-old son, Henry III, becomes king
1225	The Magna Carta becomes the law of England
1227	Henry III, now aged 20, begins to rule
1258	Council of nobles set up
1265	Simon de Montfort's Parliament is called
1272	Edward I becomes king of England
1295	Edward I's Model Parliament
1307	Edward II becomes king of England
1388	The "Merciless" Parliament (against Richard II)

▶ Simon de Montfort (c.1208–1265) was a Norman baron who became Earl of Leicester. In 1264–65 he virtually ruled the country on behalf of the king.

▲ Henry III, is pictured here at his coronation in 1216. He ruled for 55 years. He lost much of his power as king because he was not a good ruler. He was more interested in the arts and in building churches.

These were the different social classes of the time, in order of power from the king downward. The largest number of people were peasants, who had no power at all. Some lords and priests treated them fairly, allowing them to voice their concerns, but this was rare.

BENIN AND ZIMBABWE 1100–1480

Benin was an advanced kingdom in the tropical forests of West Africa. Zimbabwe was a gold-mining centre in the high grasslands of southeast Africa.

Benin was situated in what is now southeastern Nigeria. It was the longest lasting of the forest kingdoms of rain-forested West Africa. Its capital, Benin City, was founded in about A.D. 900 and was at its most prosperous during the 1400s. The city had wide streets lined with large wooden houses and was enclosed by walls 25 mi. (40km) long. The palace of the *oba* (king) was richly decorated with bronze plaques and carvings. The city's busy traders dealt in cloth, ivory, metals (especially bronze), palm oil, and pepper. Benin was famous for its art, especially sculptures using pottery, ivory, or brass.

During medieval times, there were four main kingdoms that flourished in Africa: Mali (later overwhelmed by Songhay), Ethiopia, Benin, and Zimbabwe.

This lifelike ivory mask shows an *oba* or king of Benin. The oba would have hung it around his waist on ceremonial occasions.

Benin flourished under the leadership of Oba Eware the Great, who ruled from 1440 to 1473. He modernized and expanded Benin. Usually, warring African states made slaves of their prisoners, but Benin avoided this—so when the Portuguese began buying slaves from West Africa in the 1500s, Benin did not join in the slave trade. This protected it from European colonialization until 1897.

This Benin bronze shows an oba seated on his throne, with two subjects. kneeling before him. The Benin cast bronzes by the "lost wax" process. A wax model was carved, then covered with clay to make a mold. The wax would be melted away, and molten bronze would be poured into the mold. Many copies could then be made using this process.

Many of the peoples of West Africa lived in tribal villages, herding animals and growing crops. The grasslands of central Africa (shown here) were very different environments from the tropical forests of the west.

ZIMBABWE

Zimbabwe grew prosperous from its large reserves of copper and gold. Dug from over one thousand mines, much of it was bought by Arab traders on the east coast from the 900s onward. They built the only towns in southern Africa, and Zimbabwe is best known for its walled palace city, Great Zimbabwe, built between 1100 and 1400. However, little is known of the Zimbabweans. They were not great warriors, so Zimbabwe did not expand its borders by military means.

Around 1450, Zimbabwe was absorbed into the Shona kingdom of Rozvi (Mwenemutapa), named after a line of strong kings. This warrior kingdom took control of most of what is now Zimbabwe and Mozambique. It continued to trade gold and copper with the Arabs and grew rich from this. This changed when the Portuguese settlers tried to gain control of the mines. Rozvi fought against this for some time, but by 1629, the mines had fallen under Portuguese control. Nevertheless, Rozvi survived until the 1830s.

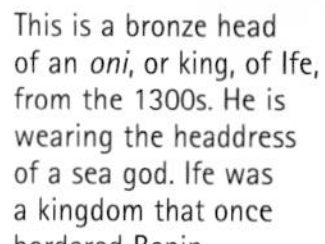

This is a bronze head of an *oni*, or king, of Ife, from the 1300s. He is wearing the headdress of a sea god. Ife was a kingdom that once bordered Benin.

GREAT ZIMBABWE

One intriguing African mystery is the walled city of Great Zimbabwe, after which modern Zimbabwe is named. The massive stone structures were built with granite blocks between 1000 and 1400, but nobody knows why or by whom. A *zimbabwe* is a stone-built enclosure, of which there were many in southeast Africa, but this was the largest and grandest.

The ruins of the Great Enclosure can be seen today on the 60-acre (24ha) site of Great Zimbabwe.

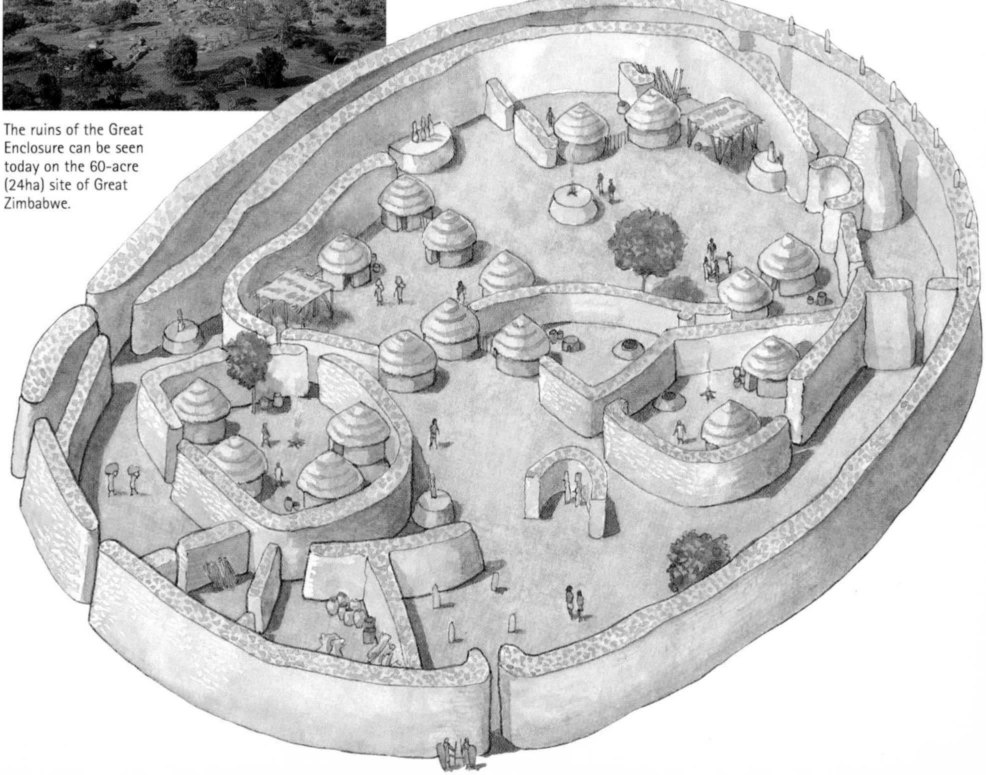

THE MONGOL EMPIRE 1206–1405

The Mongols created the largest empire in history. Their presence was felt strongly in China, Russia, and Islam, though their empire was not very long lasting.

Genghis Khan (c.1162–1227) was a great leader, general, and organizer. During one campaign, his army traveled at breakneck speed—275 mi. (440km) in just three days. He died after falling from a horse.

In 1180, a 13-year-old boy was made leader of his tribe when his father was poisoned. The boy was named Temujin, and his tribe, the Yakka Mongols, were a warlike nomadic people in Mongolia. Two thirds of the tribe promptly deserted him, but Temujin soon reunited them and went on to take over other Mongol tribes. In 1206, at a meeting of the *khans* (chiefs), Temujin was hailed as Genghis Khan, "Emperor of All Men." He promised that future generations of Mongols would lead lives of luxury. Genghis Khan began a career of conquest, by training a ruthless, fast-moving, and well disciplined army. His hordes terrified their opponents, killing anyone who did not surrender or change sides. In a series of outstanding campaigns, Genghis Khan conquered Turkestan, northern China, and Korea, then swung westward to overrun Afghanistan, Persia, and parts of Russia. Part of his success came from the fact that his opponents were not united.

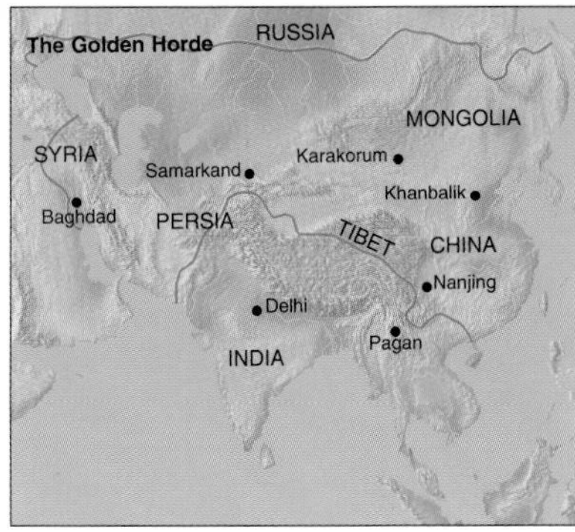

At its greatest extent, in the 1200s, during the reign of Kublai Khan, the Mongol Empire extended from the Pacific Ocean to the Black Sea.

MONGOL EXPANSION

After Genghis died, Ogodai and Monke Khan conquered Armenia, Tibet, more of China, and then ravaged eastern Europe. Ghengis's grandson, Kublai Khan, completed the conquest of China. He made himself first emperor of the Yuan dynasty (1271–1368). Some aspects of Mongol rule were good—they gave women status, encouraged scholars, respected different religions, and helped trade. They opened the Asian Silk Roads to East-West travelers. Other aspects were not so good—their ruthless armies destroyed cities and massacred many. However, the Song in southern China were able to resist them for 20 years before they fell, and the Delhi Sultanate stopped them from invading India. By 1260, Mongol expansion had ended.

In battle, the Mongols were unstoppable. Their bows fired farther than any had before, their horses were fast, and their tactics tricked many of their opponents.

The Mongols were a nomadic people from the plains of Mongolia who lived in portable *yurts*—large, round tents made of hides or cloth. They herded cattle, sheep, goats, and horses. Even when they invaded cities, their army stayed outside in yurt encampments.

In battle, the Mongols wore light armor made of leather and iron. They were so fast and ruthless that most of their opponents gave up in fear. Large silk flags streamed behind them. Anyone who opposed them was destined to die.

THE BARBAROUS TAMERLANE

From 1275, a Venetian merchant named Marco Polo spent 17 years at the court of Kublai Khan. His stories gave Europeans their first picture of China and its wealth. After Kublai Khan's death in 1294, the mighty Mongol Empire began to break up. Some khans, such as the Chagatais in Turkestan, the Ilkhans in Persia, and the Golden Horde in southern Russia, kept smaller empires for themselves. Cruel though the Mongols were, none was as barbarous as the great Mongol-Turkish ruler of Samarkand, Tamerlane, or Timur (1336–1405). His army went on the rampage between 1361 and 1405, and brutally overran Persia, Armenia, Georgia, Mesopotamia, Azerbaijan, and the Golden Horde.

Despite his cruel reputation, Tamerlane was a great patron of the arts, astronomy, and architecture in Samarkand. Generally, however, the Mongols left no lasting mark on the world, except for the destruction they brought. China and Russia became poor, the Muslim world was in turmoil, and even European countries like Poland and Serbia suffered greatly. After Tamerlane's death in 1405, the great, bloodstained Mongol adventure was over, except in Russia and Turkestan.

MONGOL SPORTS

The Mongols loved horseriding, wrestling, and archery. The great khans encouraged sport as a way of developing battle skills and discovering talented soldiers. There were many sports contests, and military promotion could be gained from success in these. Participating in sports also fostered teamwork, which was one of the Mongols' greatest strengths.

From an early age, Mongol boys practiced archery and wrestling.

The Mongols adopted the ancient Persian game of polo.

MEDIEVAL EXPLORERS 1270–1490

In the Middle Ages, many bold men made long, and often dangerous, journeys to distant lands. These new contacts improved trade and spread political influence.

Prince Henry the Navigator (1394–1460) was responsible for the port city of Ceuta in Morocco. This led to his fascination with ships. He sponsored expeditions and the work that led to a new ship, the caravel. He encouraged more precise mapmaking and seafaring instruments. The sailors he trained were the first Europeans to undertake long sea voyages. Soon the Portuguese opened up new routes around Africa to India and the Far East.

The first medieval explorers were the Vikings, who went as far as America, Morocco, and Baghdad. The first account of central Asia was written by a Franciscan friar, John of Pian del Carpine, who visited the Mongol khan on behalf of Pope Innocent IV in 1245. The best known European traveler was Marco Polo, a young Venetian who journeyed to meet Kublai Khan in China and remained there for many years. Returning in 1295, he composed a vivid account of his travels.

Between 1325 and 1350, Ibn Battuta, a Moroccan lawyer, traveled to Russia, central Asia, India, southern China, and Africa, writing detailed descriptions of his travels. Admiral Zheng He was sent by the Chinese Ming emperor Yongle on seven naval expeditions between 1405 and 1433. His fleet sailed to Indonesia, India, Persia, Mecca, and East Africa, establishing diplomatic relations and extending China's political influence over maritime Asia. Zheng He took back gifts to the emperor, including spices and exotic animals.

Camel caravans took Muslim travelers and traders across the deserts of Africa and Asia, making them some of the most traveled people of the medieval period.

PRINCE HENRY THE NAVIGATOR

Henry was a son of the king of Portugal. At the age of 21, he discovered treasures in Morocco that had been carried overland from Songhai and Senegal in West Africa. He was curious to know if these places could be reached by sea. So, after about 1420, Henry paid Portuguese sailors to explore the coast of Africa. Encouraged by their discoveries, he built a school of navigation at Sagres in Portugal, to train sailors for further voyages of discovery.

Kublai Khan sent Marco Polo on various journeys, including to the Chinese borders of Tibet. Polo told of how they burned bamboo on their campfire, which caused loud crackling noises that terrified the horses. However, the noise also scared off wild animals.

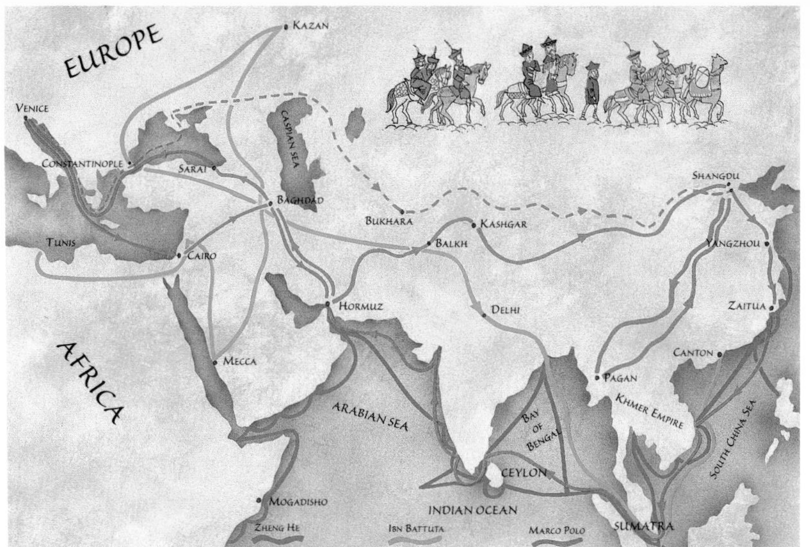

The incredible journeys of medieval travelers covered thousands of miles. The greatest of these travelers were Marco Polo, Ibn Battuta, and Zheng He.

Marco Polo first visited China with his father, a Venetian trader. He stayed there longer, playing an active role in the court of Kublai Khan. He was even sent on missions for the khan around China and to Pagan in Burma.

Marco Polo was away from Venice for 25 years. His overland journey to China took four years, and the return journey by sea from China to Persia, then overland, took three. He acted as a regional governor and ambassador for the khan while in China. The khan welcomed many foreigners, and he found Europeans to be very unusual, exotic visitors.

By the time Prince Henry died in 1460, Portuguese explorers had reached what is now Sierra Leone. Henry's work inspired later Portuguese explorers to sail farther down the coast of West Africa, seeking a sea route to India and the Far East. The world was now on the verge of a great expansion of international contact. The Chinese could have been the first international travelers, but its emperors preferred isolation, and traders were discouraged from travel. Muslims had also traveled far and wide, though by 1500 they had lost their urge to expand further. Meanwhile, the Europeans were about to change their inward-looking policies and seek new horizons.

Ibn Battuta (1304–68) was a lifelong traveler from North Africa who wrote lengthy accounts of his journeys. He traveled to Africa and Russia, to Morocco and India, and by sea to southern China. His stories were the most accurate and useful of all the accounts written by medieval travelers.

Admiral Zheng He's fleet of huge oceangoing junks were specially built for his expeditions. On his first voyage, his fleet consisted of 62 of these ships.

THE HUNDRED YEARS' WAR 1337–1453

The Hundred Years' War was a series of short, costly wars in which the English kings tried to dominate France, but met great resistance.

John of Gaunt (1340–1399) was one of the sons of Edward III. As regent (1377–1386) for his nephew Richard II, he was the most powerful man in England.

In 1328, Charles IV of France died. The French barons gave the throne to his cousin, Philip VI, but Charles's nephew, Edward III of England, challenged him. Philip confiscated Edward's French lands, and in 1337 war broke out. At the start of the conflict, which actually lasted 116 years, the English defeated a French fleet in the English Channel at Sluys, then invaded France, winning a major battle at Crécy, and capturing Calais. Both sides ran out of money and had to agree to a truce, which lasted from 1347 until 1355. In 1355, a fresh English invasion took place, led by Edward's heir, Edward, whose nickname was the Black Prince. He won a resounding victory at Poitiers. The Treaty of Brétigny in 1360 gave England large parts of France. But a new campaign followed, and England lost most of her French possessions.

The English longbow (left) shot farther and faster than ever before. The French crossbow (right) was easier to load and fire than a longbow, but much slower.

In the late 1360s, both thrones were inherited by children—Charles VI of France and Richard II of England. Richard's uncle, John of Gaunt (for Ghent in Belgium, his birthplace), ruled for him. In 1396, Richard II married Charles VI's daughter, Isabelle, and a 20-year truce was agreed.

▲ Edward, (1330–1376), father of Richard II, wore black armor and so was called "the Black Prince."

► Edward III, (1312–1377) invaded France in 1346. His army of 10,000 defeated a French army twice its size at Crécy. The English easily outshot the French crossbows.

BATTLE OF AGINCOURT

The Battle of Agincourt in 1415 was a notable English victory. Henry V commanded about 900 men-at-arms and 3,000 archers. The French had at least three times as many heavily armed troops, but they were badly led and organized.

THE END OF A COSTLY WAR

After a long truce the war began again in 1415. Henry V (1387–1422), England's adventurous king, revived his country's claim to the French throne. England still held Calais and parts of Bordeaux. Henry captured Harfleur in Normandy and heavily defeated the French at Agincourt. Henry then occupied much of northern France. Charles VI made him heir to the French throne in 1420. He also married Charles's daughter, Catherine of Valois. Henry died just 15 months later, leaving the throne to his infant son, Henry VI. Charles VI died soon after.

In support of the claim, Henry's uncle, John, Duke of Bedford, besieged Orléans. The French forces, led by a 17-year-old peasant girl, Joan of Arc, successfully defended the town. Joan claimed she saw visions and heard voices telling her to free France. She escorted the new but uncrowned king, Charles VII, to Reims to be crowned. However, Joan was soon defeated at Paris and captured by the Burgundians. They sold her to the English, who burned her as a witch. Sporadic fighting went on for some years afterward. The French recaptured their lands by 1453, ending the war. Only Calais remained English. This had been a kings' war—but it was the people who had paid the price.

KEY DATES

E = English victory, F = French victory

1340	Battle of Sluys (E), at sea
1346	Battle of Crécy (E)
1347	Battle of Calais (E)
1356	Battle of Poitiers (E)
1372	Battle of La Rochelle (F), at sea
1415	Battle of Agincourt (E)
1428	Battle of Orléans (F)
1450	Battle of Formigny (F)
1451	Battle of Bordeaux (F)

At the age of 17, Joan of Arc (1412–1431) led the French against the English, during France's darkest hour. The English accused her of being a witch, because she claimed she had visions and heard voices telling her to drive the English out of France.

Joan of Arc was burned at the stake in 1431. Six hundred years later, in 1920, she was made a saint.

THE BLACK DEATH 1347–1351

The Black Death was one of the worst disasters in history. It resulted in the death of around a third of the population of the Middle East and Europe.

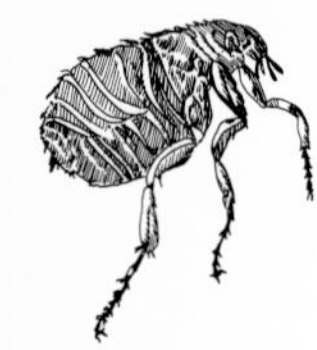
The Black Death was carried by fleas on rats. It may have spread from an area in southern China or Southeast Asia.

Rats were common in houses, ships, and food storerooms, so the disease spread rapidly through the population.

In the art of the time, the Black Death was depicted as a skeleton riding furiously on horseback.

The Black Death killed about 25 million people in Europe alone, and probably millions more in Asia. It began as bubonic plague. Its name comes from spots of blood under the skin that turned black and from swellings (buboes) in the groin and armpits. Most victims died horribly, shortly after symptoms appeared. Bubonic plague was transmitted to humans by fleas on rats—it could not be passed from person to person. But if pneumonia developed in a plague victim, the infection became pneumonic plague, which could be passed on to another person. It was highly contagious, spread rapidly, and most victims died.

The disease was carried from southern China or Burma, through central Asia, along the Silk Road to Baghdad and the Crimea. In 1347, it arrived by ship at Genoa, in Italy, and spread to Paris and London in 1348, and Scandinavia and Russia in 1349. No one was safe from it.

European towns were filthy, with rubbish, rats, and human excrement in the streets. Human waste was thrown out of windows and trodden underfoot. The lack of basic hygiene was the reason that the plague spread so fast.

THE IMMEDIATE EFFECTS

The Black Death devastated whole regions: houses stood empty, villages and towns were abandoned, and people in some trades and even some entire areas were completely wiped out. Baghdad and Mecca were emptied. Doctors, priests, and the people who buried the plague victims also died. In the end, fields were littered with unburied corpses. Society and the economy in Europe began to disintegrate.

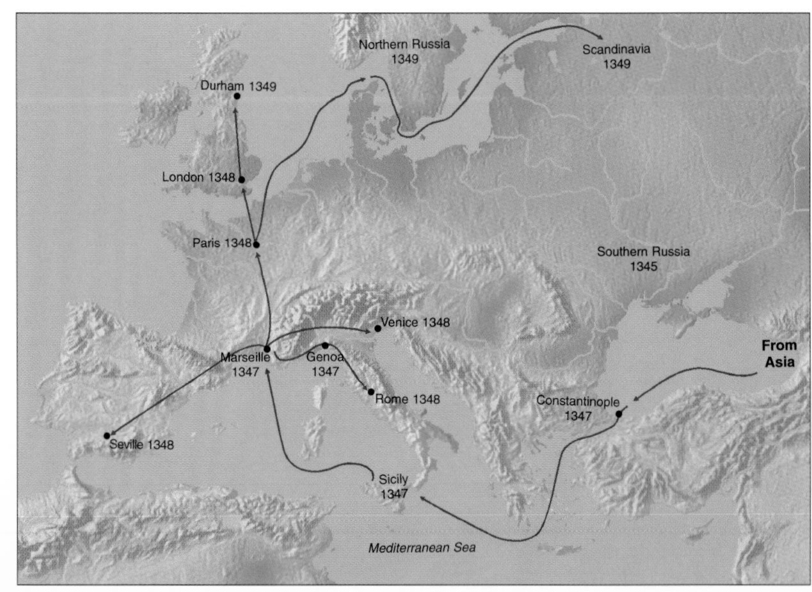

▶ The Black Death spread through Europe from Genoa. Some areas, including Ireland and parts of France lost 10 percent of their population. Other areas, including northern Italy, eastern England, and Norway, lost as much as 50 percent.

THE LONG-TERM EFFECTS

The Black Death destroyed many people's faith in God. To them it appeared to have no logic, killing good as well as bad people. Farms were abandoned and churches were empty. Until the onset of the Black Death, Europe usually had a surplus of labor and low wages, but the shortage of workers now made wages soar. Many country people began moving into the empty towns, working for actual money for the first time. The already weak feudal system collapsed. There were revolts. Europe and the Muslim world were in shock. Over the next 100 years, many things changed. The medieval period was making way for a new, more questioning, world.

People burned the clothes of the dead to try to stop the plague from spreading. This didn't work because the disease was caused by fleas living on rats that were found everywhere at the time.

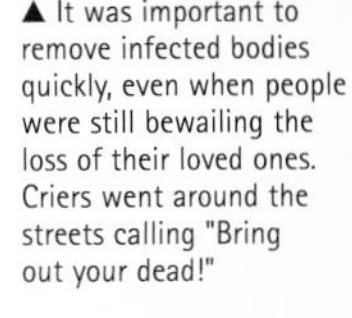

▲ It was important to remove infected bodies quickly, even when people were still bewailing the loss of their loved ones. Criers went around the streets calling "Bring out your dead!"

◀ At night, plague carts were loaded with corpses to be taken away and buried. The Black Death spread quickly in towns because of the crowded housing conditions and lack of hygiene. Even isolated monasteries did not escape since the disease was carried there by infected people pleading for help.

CHINA: THE MING DYNASTY 1368–1644

After a long campaign, the Mongols were driven out of China. There then followed 150 years of peace and prosperity under the Ming dynasty.

Emperor Hong Wu (1328–1398) reorganized the administration of China and set up colleges for training mandarins (civil servants). Candidates for these posts had to pass examinations in literature and philosophy.

Kublai Khan was a great Chinese emperor, but he was a foreigner. When he died in 1294, he was followed by a series of feeble Yuan emperors, famines, and much hardship. The last Yuan emperor, Sun Ti, was a bad ruler. The Chinese people were tired of being ruled harshly by foreigners. They found a Chinese ruler in Zhu Yuan Zhang, who had been a monk and, during bad times, a beggar. As a rebel bandit chief, he had a ready-made army. He also proved to be an excellent general.

After a 13-year campaign, he captured Beijing, drove the Mongols back to Mongolia, and became emperor in 1368. He founded the Ming ("bright") dynasty, and took the name Hong Wu ("very warlike"). He moved the capital south to the fortified city of Nanjing. Hong Wu ruled China for 30 years as a dictator, guarding against Mongol incursions and restoring order and prosperity to his country.

Art, literature, and ceramics had developed during the Song and the Yuan dynasties. This vase demonstrates another period of excellence in the arts under the Ming.

Hong Wu left his throne to a grandson, Jianwen (born Zhu Yunwen), but he was overthrown four years later by his uncle Zhu Di, who became Emperor Yongle (pronounced *Yong-lay)* in 1403.

▼ In Beijing, the Ming emperor Yongle built the Forbidden City, which only the emperor and his household were allowed to use. This is a typical building inside the imperial complex.

PEACE UNDER THE MING

China grew great again under Yongle, who was emperor from 1403 to 1424. Roads, towns, and canals were rebuilt, and when he moved to Beijing, he built the great halls, palaces, and temples of the Forbidden City. Learning and the arts flourished. Trade and industry were encouraged, and, unusually, China looked outward, exporting goods and spreading Chinese influence abroad. The Muslim admiral Zheng He was sent on long voyages to India, the Middle East, and Africa. After Yongle's reign, however, China lost interest in other countries. Many Chinese settled in Southeast Asia, and became involved with the growing "China trade." Government administration was improved and, apart from problems with piracy and Mongol attacks, flourished for a century.

From 1517 onward, the Portuguese and other Europeans arrived on the coast, trading mainly in Guangzhou (Canton). In the late 1500s, there was a series of emperors who were disliked and wasteful, and there were attacks on the borders. Trade declined, corruption and banditry grew, and there was famine and rebellion. In 1592, the Japanese invaded neighboring Korea, thereby threatening the security of China. Rebels eventually took over much of China, and in 1644, the Ming dynasty finally fell.

Gardening and landscaping developed into a very special art form in China and Japan. Water was an important ingredient in this exquisite Chinese ornamental garden.

KEY DATES

1353–54	The Black Death breaks out across China
1368	The Ming dynasty is founded by Zhu Yuanzhang
1403–24	The reign of Ming Emperor Yongle
1517	Arrival of the first European traders in southern China
1552–55	Major attacks on shipping by pirates off the coast of China
1582	Growing corruption and decline
1592	The Japanese invade Korea, threatening China's security
1644	Fall of the Ming dynasty

This brush holder, from the Ming period, is made of carved lacquer. Lacquer is a thick varnish painted in many layers onto wood. It sets hard, making a very strong material that is often used by the Chinese.

Landscape painting also became a highly developed art form under the Ming. This classic Ming landscape painting by Tang Yin is entitled "Dreaming of Immortality in a Thatched Cottage."

THE KHMER EMPIRE 802–1440

The Khmer Empire was created in 802, when the Khmer people were united by Jayavarman II. It reached its peak under Suryavarman I and Suryavarman II.

Around 400, the Khmer had created a state called Chen-la which was at its strongest around 700 under Jayavarman I. Previously Hindu, the Khmer adopted Buddhism during this time. Chen-la declined, and, after a brief occupation by the Javanese, a new Khmer state was created in 802 by Rajah Jayavarman II. He was a "god-king" or *devarajah* (like the Tibetan Dalai Lama today). He ruled from a city called Angkor Thom, near a lake called Tonle Sap. The Khmers wrote books on paper, palm leaves, and vellum. Fire, rot, and termites have long since destroyed them, but it is possible to learn about the Khmers from Chinese histories, and from the many carvings in the ruins of Angkor Thom ("great city") and Angkor Wat ("great temple") nearby.

The temple complex of Angkor Wat was richly decorated with many carved sandstone figures. After the temple was abandoned in the 1400s, they were swallowed up by the jungle and not rediscovered until the 1800s.

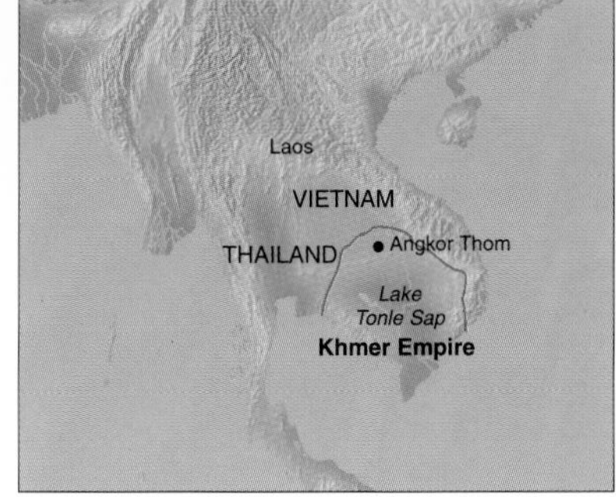

The Khmer lived in what is now Cambodia. Their armies conquered many of the surrounding lands, dominating mainland Southeast Asia during the 1100s.

The building of Angkor Thom, originally called Yasodharapura, was started just before 900. The richly decorated temple complex of Angkor Wat was built between 1113 and 1150.

▼ Angkor Wat, a huge temple complex built of red sandstone, was surrounded by walls and a moat 590 ft. (180m) wide and 2.5 mi. (4km) long. The temple had three main enclosures (representing the outer world) surrounding an inner holy shrine.

▲ Many of the temple carvings at Angkor Wat show the daily lives of the Khmer people as well as telling the stories of their sacred myths and battles.

The Khmer armies, which may have included hundreds of war elephants, fought many battles and conquered most of the surrounding lands, including Thailand and Champa (southern Vietnam). The empire reached its peak between 1010 and 1150, under Suryavarman I and Suryavarman II. During the 1200s, the people grew tired of serving the devarajahs through forced labor, and Khmer life began to break down. In 1444, invading Thai armies forced the Khmer to abandon Angkor. From then on, Cambodia was dominated by the Thai kingdom of Siam.

KHMER DAILY LIFE

The Khmer were builders, craftworkers, fishermen, farmers, and warriors. Many lived in houses perched on stilts around Tonle Sap. Their main food was rice, and their special irrigation systems produced three crops a year. The kings were still Hindus, but most of the population was Buddhist. They held elaborate religious ceremonies in connection with the seasons of the year. They traded with India and Java, and also with China, bartering spices and rhinoceros horn for porcelain and lacquerware. The royal women of the court wore skirts, leaving the upper part of the body bare. They were encouraged to study law, astrology, and languages. Men wore only a loose loin covering.

This masterpiece of carved architecture is one tower of the Bavon temple, built in the 1100s in the capital city Angkor Thom.

KEY DATES

c.400	Founding of Chen-la, after the fall of Funan
c.700	Chen-la reaches its peak of development
802	Jayavarman II founds the Khmer nation by uniting the people
880s	The Khmer conquer the Mon and Thai peoples
900	Angkor Thom founded
1050–1150	The Khmer Empire at its high point under Suryavarman I and Suryavarman II
1113–50	Angkor Wat is built
c.1215	Death of last Angkor king, Jayavarman VII; empire starts to fall into decline
1444	Angkor abandoned after Thai invasions led by Ayutthaya

These heavenly dancers were carved on one of the walls at Angkor Wat in about 1200.

THE RENAISSANCE

1461–1600

This period marks the start of modern history. Muslims still dominated much of Europe and Asia. The Ottomans in the Middle East and the Moguls in India took Islamic culture to new heights. The Aztecs and Incas dominated the Americas. In Europe, a new world was coming into being. Europeans questioned their traditions and beliefs. They sailed the oceans, explored new ideas, and European society changed greatly—becoming more complex, freethinking, and materialistic.

▲ The Inca celebrated two festivals of the sun. One was in June, the other in December. The emperor led the ceremonies, attended by officials from all over the empire, in the great square at Cuzco.

◀ This is a detail from "Madonna of the Magnificat," painted by Italian Renaissance artist Sandro Botticelli in 1465.

The world at a glance 1461–1600

Europeans started to emerge from the narrow confines of the Middle Ages to travel beyond their continent. In 1461, European seafarers, traders, and colonists were on the brink of setting out to find new routes to the Far East, and to explore and exploit the rest of the world. For the first time, continents were brought into direct contact with each other.

In Mexico and South America, the Aztec and Inca empires were at their height, but with the arrival of the Spanish, the Aztec capital of Tenochtitlan was destroyed and the Incas were forced to retreat to the mountains of Peru. By 1533, the Spanish had turned the native population into slaves and the original inhabitants were nearly wiped out by disease and mistreatment. The invaders turned their attention north, but it was some years before North America would feel the real effects of their arrival.

African civilizations also came under European influence, but it was confined to the coast. The heart of Africa remained undisturbed. China was still ruled by the Ming dynasty. Although the arts flourished, society had begun to stagnate under its rule.

In Europe, the movement now called the Renaissance was fueled by Greek scholars fleeing from the fall of Constantinople, who brought with them the knowledge of ancient Greece and Rome.

NORTH AMERICA

Europeans first arrived here about 1500, though colonies were not really started until the 1600s. The Mississippian culture was in decline from the 1450s, and the Pueblo peoples of the Southwest were now past their peak. Other native peoples were having their own political and religious problems, as well as matters of trade with other tribes—all the time unaware of the white man's impending threat to their way of life.

MESOAMERICA AND SOUTH AMERICA

Disaster struck the whole region. The richly advanced civilizations of Mexico and the Andean regions were generally on an upswing when the Spanish arrived. But both the Aztecs, in the 1520s, and the Incas in the 1530s, were quickly subjugated by these strange foreigners, whom they had welcomed at first. Trickery, followed by European diseases, killed millions. The Spanish and Portuguese quickly took over, establishing plantations, mines, and cities in the search for gold, wealth, and glory. The majority of early immigrants were actually Africans, brought over as slaves to work the plantations. But it was the European bosses and priests who, by 1600, ran what was to be become Latin America. Those indigenous Americans who survived were suddenly the subjects of new masters.

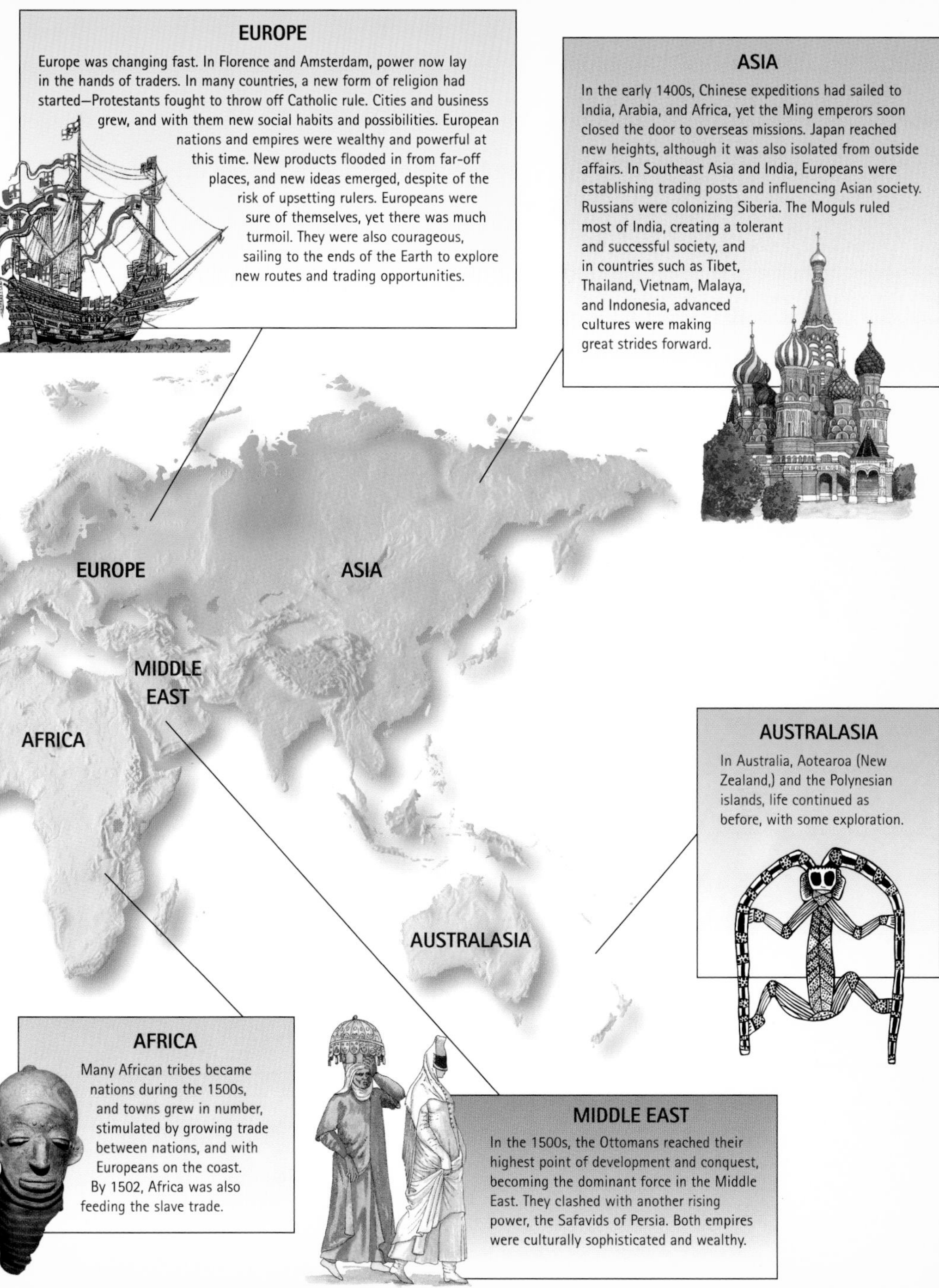

EUROPE

Europe was changing fast. In Florence and Amsterdam, power now lay in the hands of traders. In many countries, a new form of religion had started—Protestants fought to throw off Catholic rule. Cities and business grew, and with them new social habits and possibilities. European nations and empires were wealthy and powerful at this time. New products flooded in from far-off places, and new ideas emerged, despite of the risk of upsetting rulers. Europeans were sure of themselves, yet there was much turmoil. They were also courageous, sailing to the ends of the Earth to explore new routes and trading opportunities.

ASIA

In the early 1400s, Chinese expeditions had sailed to India, Arabia, and Africa, yet the Ming emperors soon closed the door to overseas missions. Japan reached new heights, although it was also isolated from outside affairs. In Southeast Asia and India, Europeans were establishing trading posts and influencing Asian society. Russians were colonizing Siberia. The Moguls ruled most of India, creating a tolerant and successful society, and in countries such as Tibet, Thailand, Vietnam, Malaya, and Indonesia, advanced cultures were making great strides forward.

AUSTRALASIA

In Australia, Aotearoa (New Zealand,) and the Polynesian islands, life continued as before, with some exploration.

AFRICA

Many African tribes became nations during the 1500s, and towns grew in number, stimulated by growing trade between nations, and with Europeans on the coast. By 1502, Africa was also feeding the slave trade.

MIDDLE EAST

In the 1500s, the Ottomans reached their highest point of development and conquest, becoming the dominant force in the Middle East. They clashed with another rising power, the Safavids of Persia. Both empires were culturally sophisticated and wealthy.

THE AZTECS 1430–1520

During the 1400s, the Aztecs dominated Mexico from the wondrous city of Tenochtitlan, dominated by pyramids, on an island in the middle of a lake.

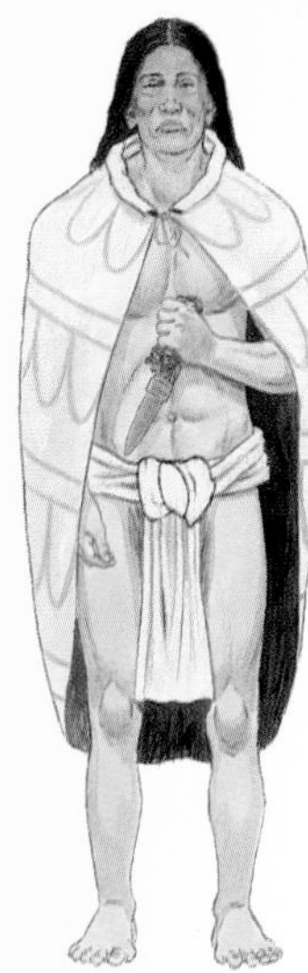

▲ Priests were powerful in Aztec society. They did not marry, and they were responsible for conducting all of the many ceremonies in the Aztec 260-day calendar. They also carried out human sacrifices, using knives with blades made from very sharp stone, such as chalcedony, flint, or obsidian.

The Aztecs had started to expand in 1430, under the emperor Itzcóatl, and by 1500, they controlled a large empire in Mexico. Tenochtitlan had a population of about 300,000, and was at its most powerful, under Montezuma II (also known as Moctezuma II). In order to feed everyone, food was grown on artificial islands, or *chinampas*, built up in Lake Texcoco, in the middle of which the city stood. Conquered lands provided corn, beans, and cocoa, cotton cloth, and gold, silver, and jade for Aztec craftworkers. Traders bought turquoise from the Pueblo Indians in the north, and from the south came brightly colored feathers, which were used to make elaborately decorated capes, fans, headdresses, and shields. Aztec society was organized along military lines. All young men served in the army from the age of 17 to 22. Some stayed longer than this, because even a peasant could rise to be an army commander if he was good enough.

The Aztecs dominated the center of Mexico from coast to coast, including several cities. They also influenced much wider areas to the north and south.

HUMAN SACRIFICES

One of the main tasks of the army was to take many prisoners of war. The prisoners were sacrificed in Tenochtitlan, at the huge pyramid-temples in the middle of the city. Religious blood sacrifice was important to the Aztecs who sacrificed to many different gods. All of these gods were believed to need a great deal of human blood—especially the god of war, Huitzilopochtli. This armed aggression and human sacrifice gradually turned the Aztecs' neighbors against them.

▶ Ordinary Aztecs lived in huts with thatched roofs. They ate pancakes made from cornmeal, with spicy bean and vegetable fillings, very like Mexican tortillas today.

This ceremonial headdress from the 1500s is made mainly of quetzal feathers. Parrot feathers in brown, crimson, white, and blue were also used.

The emperor was treated like a god, and he could be spoken to only by priests and nobles. Ordinary people had to keep their eyes down when the ruler traveled through the capital.

◀ This terracotta statue bears the hideously grinning skull face of the Aztec god of death. The Aztecs used human skulls to make masks. They encrusted them with turquoise and seashells and lined them inside with red leather.

RISE AND FALL OF THE AZTECS

The Aztecs traded far and wide around Mexico, into what is now the United States, and south to Colombia. They sold high-value items made by craftworkers—clothing, jewelry, and household and ceremonial items. They also exacted tribute—payments made by cities to keep the Aztecs from invading them. The capital, Tenochtitlan, was one of the world's best-planned cities. The streets and canals were laid out in a grid pattern on its lake island, and arranged around a huge ceremonial area of pyramids, temples, palaces, and gardens. Three wide causeways linked the city to the mainland. But the Aztecs' greed for sacrificial victims meant that, when the Spanish arrived in 1519, their neighboring societies helped them conquer the Aztecs by the following year.

▼ Three long causeways linked Tenochtitlan to the mainland. Traders traveled far and wide from the city, and some of them acted as spies for the emperor. The causeways were also a good defense for the city. When the Spanish arrived, it was trickery and disease, not direct attack, that helped them overcome the Aztecs.

THE INCA EMPIRE 1438–1533

For a century, the Incas ruled a vast, well-organized, mountaintop empire, high in the Andes in South America. Their empire was obliterated by the Spanish.

This golden pendant made by the Incas has markings showing mathematical patterns. These had a religious and calendrical significance for the Incas.

The Inca ruler was known as the *Sapa Inca*. He was believed to be descended from Inti, the sun god, who gave him the right to rule. He was also worshiped as a god himself. The Sapa Inca ran the country from Cuzco, thought to be Inti's home. Royal officials oversaw and directed everything in all parts of the empire. They looked after the affairs of the cities, and made sure the factories and workshops that produced pottery, textiles, and decorative metal objects, as well as the farms, were all working efficiently. Writing was unknown to the Incas, so they kept all their records on *quipus*. These were cords with knots tied in them to convey information, such as records of population and taxes. At its greatest period in 1525, the empire stretched for 2,200 mi. (3,500km). The cities, towns, and villages were all linked by a network of roads. Communication was provided by relay runners.

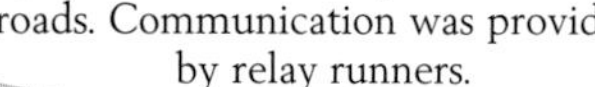

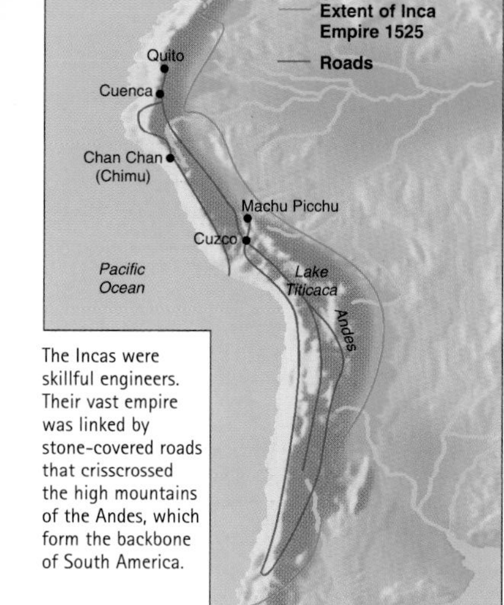

The Incas were skillful engineers. Their vast empire was linked by stone-covered roads that crisscrossed the high mountains of the Andes, which form the backbone of South America.

INCA EXPANSION

When Pachacuti became the Sapa Inca in 1438, he began to expand his lands around Cuzco. In 1450, he conquered the Titicaca basin; and in 1463, he went to war against the Lupaca and Colla tribes. Under his son Topa's command, the Inca army defeated the neighboring Chimu Empire in 1466, and Topa continued to expand the empire after he became the tenth Sapa Inca in 1471. During the next 15 years, he conquered lands far to the south, and later took control of lands to the north and west.

▲ A *quipu* was a length of string, or cord, from which several strings hung. These were in different colors, and each had knots in it. "Quipu" comes from the word for knot. By its style, color, and position, each knot was a valuable piece of information, usually a number. The Incas would hold up the long cord at the top and "read" the information in the downward rows.

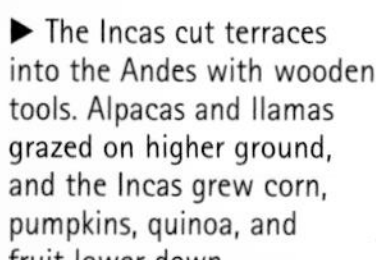

▶ The Incas cut terraces into the Andes with wooden tools. Alpacas and llamas grazed on higher ground, and the Incas grew corn, pumpkins, quinoa, and fruit lower down.

RISE AND FALL OF THE INCAS

The Incas reached a very high level of technology and organization, and came up with ingenious ways of farming on steep slopes, and building bridges, roads, and towns high in the mountains.

Topa built many of these roads and towns. Topa's son, Huayna Capac, the Sapa Inca from 1493, further expanded the empire, building a second capital at Quito. When he died in 1525, the empire was divided between his sons: Huascar ruled the south, and Atahualpa the north. This division led to civil war just before the Spanish landed in 1532. The invaders took advantage of the road system while the Incas argued among themselves, and the Spanish were able to destroy the empire by 1533.

▲ Two main roads ran the length of the empire. They were connected with every town and village by smaller roads. Goods were carried by trains of llamas. Quipus were delivered by relay runners.

KEY DATES	
1200	Manco Capac establishes the Inca dynasty and capital of Cuzco
1350	Local expansion of the Incas under Mayta Capa
1438	Pachacuti becomes the Sapa Inca
1450	Pachacuti greatly enlarges the Inca Empire
1466	Topa Inca overruns the Chimu Empire
1485	Topa Inca conquers Chile and Peru
1493	Quito becomes the second capital
1525	Huayna Capa dies, and civil war breaks out between Cuzco and Quito
1532	The Spanish invade the Inca Empire
1533	The Spanish destroy the Inca Empire

▲ Relay runners carried official messages and packages throughout the empire. Each runner ran about 1 mi. (1.5km) before the next one took over. To make sure of a quick changeover, a runner announced his approach by blowing on a conch shell.

◀ Each year, the Incas would celebrate the Great Festival of the sun, to give thanks for the growth of crops and the continuation of life, and to pray for blessings in the future—not unlike the Christian festival of Easter.

THE RECONQUEST OF SPAIN 1469–1516

The reconquest of Muslim-ruled Spain by the Spanish began during the 1100s. The country was fully reunited 300 years later, under Ferdinand and Isabella.

Ferdinand (1452–1516) succeeded to the throne of Aragon. He was a tough politician and ruled Spain together with his wife, Isabella.

Isabella (1451–1504) inherited the kingdom of Castile. She and her husband, Ferdinand, eventually became rulers of all Spain.

After the fall of the Roman Empire, Spain had been ruled by the Visigoths for 300 years. Then came the invading Berbers (Moors) from northern Africa in 711, establishing a Muslim caliphate which lasted from 756 until 1031. At this time, Christians in the north of Spain started pushing southward. They started a *reconquista* (reconquest) which, by 1235, had limited the Muslims to Granada in the south of the country.

However, Catholic Spain was divided into several countries—León, Castile, Navarre, and Aragon. In the 1400s, León had joined with Castile, making Castile and Aragon the two largest. The first step toward finally uniting Spain was made in 1469 when Ferdinand, heir to Aragon, married Isabella of Castile. When the king of Castile died in 1474, Isabella and Ferdinand succeeded him as joint rulers of his kingdom. Five years later, Ferdinand inherited Aragon and made Isabella joint ruler of Aragon as well.

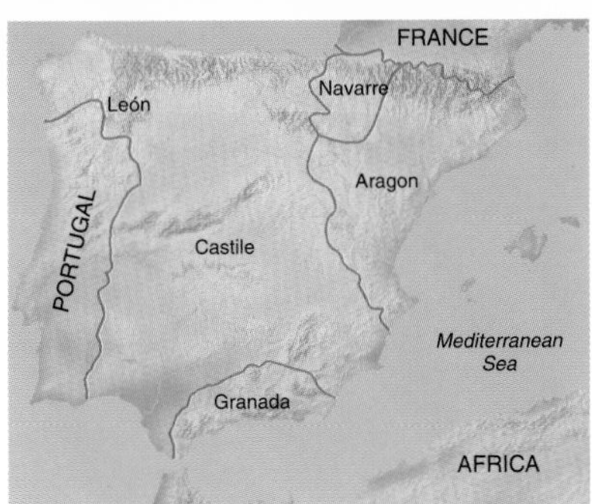

Spain was divided for much of the 1400s, though the uniting of Aragon and Castile in 1479 made the eventual union of Spain almost inevitable.

THE SPANISH INQUISITION

Many Muslims and Jews had converted to Christianity and stayed in Spain, making a great contribution to its culture. But their success was resented. The king and queen decided that all non-Christians should leave Spain. They wanted to find those who had "converted" but still followed the old religion secretly. Spain used religion as a political weapon. The pope gave permission for an Inquisition, a court that investigated heresy, but the Spanish misused the power and imprisoned, tortured, and killed thousands of people.

▼ The Christian armies of Aragon and Castile defeated the Moors in 1492, and the Moors were driven back to North Africa where they were shown no mercy.

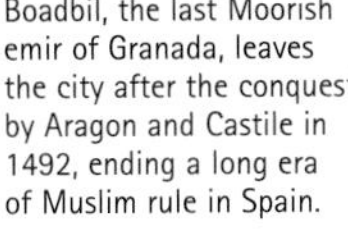

Boadbil, the last Moorish emir of Granada, leaves the city after the conquest by Aragon and Castile in 1492, ending a long era of Muslim rule in Spain.

During the Spanish Inquisition, books that were written by people suspected of heresy were burned. This painting by Pedro Berruguete not only celebrates the Catholic victory in Spain, but also vividly illustrates the power of the Inquisition.

THE REUNIFICATION OF SPAIN

In 1492, fourteen years after the Spanish Inquisition began, Moorish Granada was recaptured by Aragon and Castile. Many Muslims and Jews were expelled or forcibly converted—as many as 200,000 Jews left the country. This persecution resulted in many skilled and able people moving away to France, Germany, and the Ottoman Empire.

In the same year, Ferdinand and Isabella sponsored the voyage of Christopher Columbus—they were seeking a sea route to India and China, but instead found the Americas. This began a period of Spanish conquest that brought about the downfall of the Aztecs, Maya, and Incas.

Ferdinand and Isabella had five daughters, one of whom, Catherine of Aragon, married Henry VIII of England. But Ferdinand and Isabella had no son, and descent passed through their daughter Joanna the Mad. When Isabella died in 1504, Ferdinand acted as regent for the young Joanna. In 1515, Navarre joined Castile, and Ferdinand finally became king of a united Spain. Joanna's son, Charles V, eventually became the Hapsburg emperor, the most powerful ruler in Europe. Under his rule, Spain experienced its golden age.

KEY DATES

1248	The Christians reconquer most of Spain
1469	The marriage of Ferdinand and Isabella
1474	Isabella inherits Castile
1478	The Spanish Inquisition is established
1479	Aragon and Castile are united
1492	The conquest of Granada—end of Muslim rule in southern Spain. Christopher Columbus' expedition to India is financed by Isabella
1504	Isabella dies
1515	Navarre joins Castile—Spain is finally united
1516	Ferdinand dies

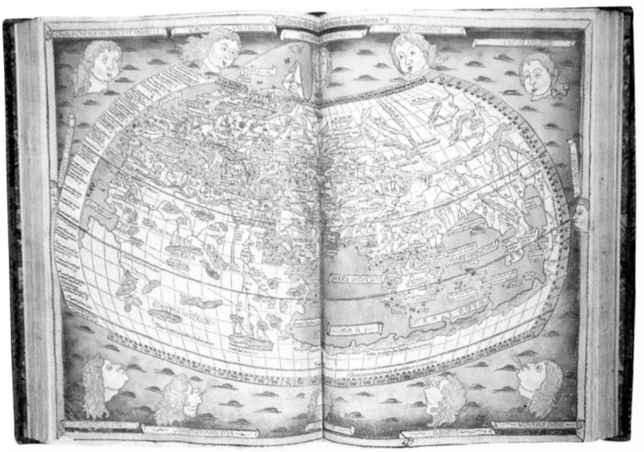

A map of the world taken from Ptolemy's *Geographia*, shows how the world was thought to look in 1486, before world exploration by Europeans really began.

ITALY 1460–1530

During this period, Italy was divided into small states. This made for great variation—some states were progressive while others were more conservative.

To further the ambitions of her father, Rodrigo, (Pope Alexander VI), Lucrezia Borgia (1480–1519) was married three times. With her third husband, the Duke of Ferrara, she became a great patron of the arts. Their court became a magnet for artists and writers. She is also known for her devotion to causes involving children and education.

Many Italian states, such as Florence, Venice, and Rome, were really large cities. Others were ruled by dukes, as in Mantua, Milan, Urbino, and Ferrara. Most of these states were ruled by families who had grown rich from trade and commerce in the late Middle Ages.

The most powerful family of the time was the Medici family of Florence. They had made a great fortune during the 1300s through banking and moneylending. The best known of the Medicis is Lorenzo, who became joint ruler of Florence with his brother in 1469. He was a cunning statesman and banker as well as a patron of writers, artists, philosophers, and scientists. He was eager to promote his family and saw his second son become pope. Under Lorenzo's influence, Florence became one of the most beautiful and prosperous cities in Italy, and a center of the Renaissance. Lorenzo helped make the form of Italian spoken in Florence into the language of the whole country.

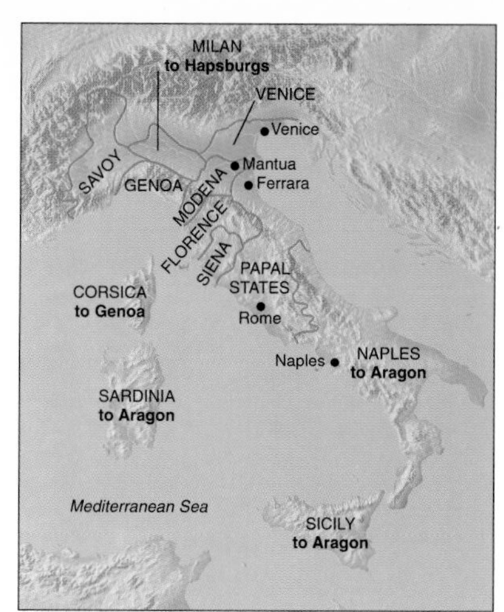

During the Middle Ages, much of Italy was controlled by the Holy Roman Empire. Following a power struggle between emperors and popes, many cities formed their own independent states.

Another family, the Borgias, sought power through the Church and the military. Two Borgias became pope. One of them, Rodrigo, schemed to help his children. When he died, the family's power collapsed.

The Medici villa at Florence was built in 1480 for Lorenzo the Magnificent by Renaissance architect Giuliano da Sangallo.

LORENZO DE' MEDICI

In 1469, when he was 20 years old, Lorenzo became joint ruler of Florence with his brother Giuliano. He was the grandson of Cosimo de' Medici, who was the second Medici to hold power in Florence. Lorenzo's brother was killed in a plot by a rival family in 1478. Lorenzo did everything he could to further his family's interests—his second son Giovanni became Pope Leo X—and to build a large gathering of scholars and creative people. He was the first patron of the artist Michelangelo. He maintained and expanded the family traditions of banking and government.

Lorenzo de' Medici (1449–1492)—"The Magnificent"—ruled Florence from 1478 to 1492.

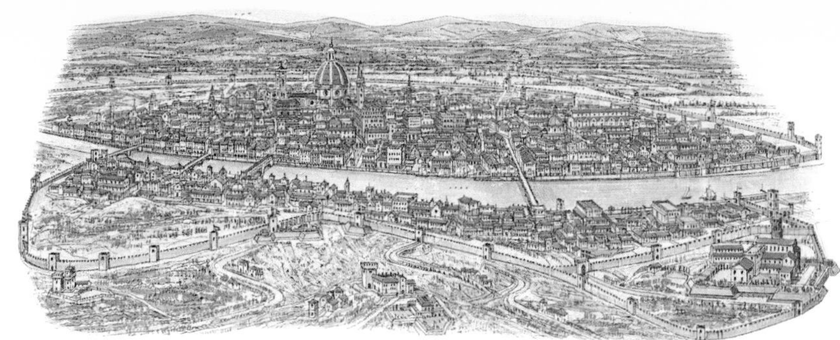

The magnificent city of Florence was at the height of its powers during the late 1400s. Ruled by the Medicis, it became home to many great artists, architects, writers, and scientists of the Renaissance. Florence also became one of Europe's main business and banking centers.

The Sforzas were a great family of Milan. Ludovico Sforza (1452–1508), was a man of taste, but also one with ruthless ambition. He ruled as regent for his nephew, the duke of Milan, but made himself the real center of power. He made alliances with Rodrigo Borgia and married a daughter of the powerful d'Este family, from Ferrara. Ludovico's court attracted great artists from all fields, among them Leonardo da Vinci.

Families like the Medicis represented "new money," with new values and ideas. They paid for exploration, centers of learning, public works, and new, imported products. People traveled to Italy to learn new ideas, which were taken back to other parts of Europe, and Europeans flocked to Florence, Venice, and Milan to gain support for their own ideas. Although future centers of modern development were to be in northwestern Europe, much of the energy of the early Renaissance came from the city-states of Italy.

Raphael was influenced by the work of Da Vinci and Michelangelo in Florence. This is his "Deposition of Christ," which he painted in 1507 at the age of 24. The following year Pope Julius II asked him to do a major work in the Vatican in Rome.

Wealthy Renaissance people enjoyed a very comfortable life. In addition to palaces or large city residences, many had country villas where they welcomed groups of visitors. They would spend time hunting, holding parties, discussing literature, and writing poetry.

EUROPEAN EXPLORERS 1460–1600

During the second half of the 1400s, European sailors and navigators planned voyages which would take them far beyond the limits of the world they knew.

In 1488, Bartholomeu Dias (1450–1500) sailed around Africa's Cape of Good Hope in a terrible storm—thereafter it was feared as the "Cape of Storms."

Vasco da Gama (1469–1525) rounded the Cape of Good Hope in 1497, and sailed up the east coast of Africa. With the help of an Indian sailor, he then crossed the Indian Ocean to Calicut in India, returning home with a cargo of spices. He went back to India to defend Portuguese interests and was made viceroy of India in 1524.

The urge to explore was partly a result of a new interest in the world, encouraged by the Renaissance; but the main intention was to bypass the Islamic world in order to set up new trading links with India and the Far East, the source of spices and other luxuries. Until the fall of the Byzantine Empire in 1453, spices were brought overland to Constantinople and then carried across the Mediterranean to Europe. In spite of their expense, spices were essential. The only way to preserve meat was by salting it. Adding spices helped hide the salty taste, and they also concealed the taste of meat which had spoiled despite being salted.

The Portuguese had set up harbors and forts along the west coast of Africa, trading with the Africans in gold, ivory, and silver. Gradually, they sailed farther south, and in 1488, Bartholomeu Dias sailed around the tip of southern Africa—pushed by a fierce gale. His frightened, exhausted crew refused to go any farther. Nine years later, Dias helped Vasco da Gama plan a voyage around the Cape of Good Hope to Calicut in India.

A sailor's personal property from the year 1536, salvaged from the wreck of Henry VIII's flagship, the *Mary Rose*. It includes a pouch, a whistle, a rosary, and a comb.

Vasco da Gama was followed by Pedro Cabral who returned from India with a cargo of pepper. This encouraged other navigators to try to sail farther east. In 1517, the Portuguese had reached China, and nearly 30 years later they had arrived in Japan. The Portuguese were driven not only by trading possibilities, but also by a determination to spread Christianity to the peoples of the East.

▶ Vasco da Gama's small ships were a development of the traditional caravel, with its triangular lateen sail. His ships had both square and lateen sails, making them more maneuverable and adaptable on the seas.

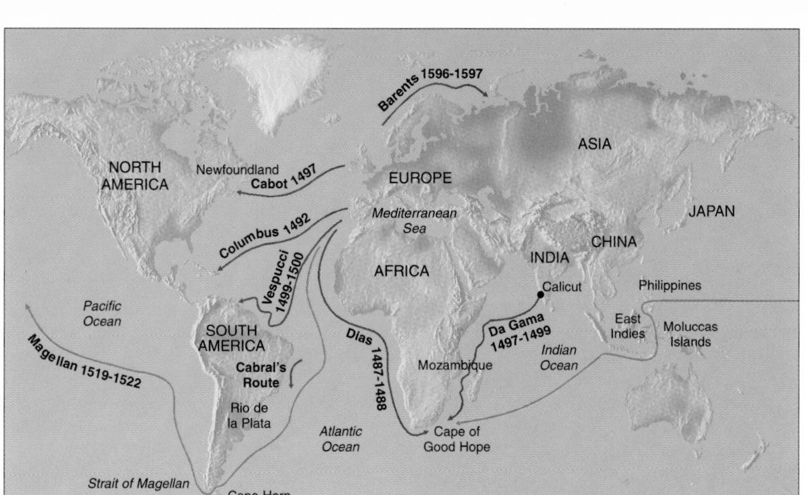

◀ Navigators from Europe tried many routes to reach the Spice Islands, the Moluccas. They discovered more than they expected, opening up new routes and laying the foundations of future empires.

▲ Although Portuguese by birth, Ferdinand Magellan (1480–1521) sailed for Spain. He led the first expedition to sail around the world, and gave the Pacific Ocean its name.

WESTWARD EXPLORATION

While the Portuguese sailed east, the Spanish sailed west. In 1492, Columbus found the West Indies. Amerigo Vespucci reached South America in 1499, but didn't realize until his voyage of 1501 that he had found a new continent. In 1497, John Cabot, a Venetian sponsored by England's Henry VII, discovered Newfoundland. In 1535, Jacques Cartier sailed up the St. Lawrence River, claiming the area for France. Ferdinand Magellan rounded South America in 1519. He died in the Philippines, but part of his crew returned to Spain in 1522—the first explorers to sail around the world.

CHRISTOPHER COLUMBUS

In 1492, Queen Isabella sponsored Christopher Columbus, a navigator from Genoa in Italy, to find a western route to India. It is possible that he knew of America from Viking tales he had heard in Iceland. Most people believed the world was much smaller than it really was. When Columbus reached a group of islands across the Atlantic, he called them the West Indies. They were in fact the islands of the Caribbean. Columbus made three more voyages there, but it is not known whether he really knew if they were America or Asia.

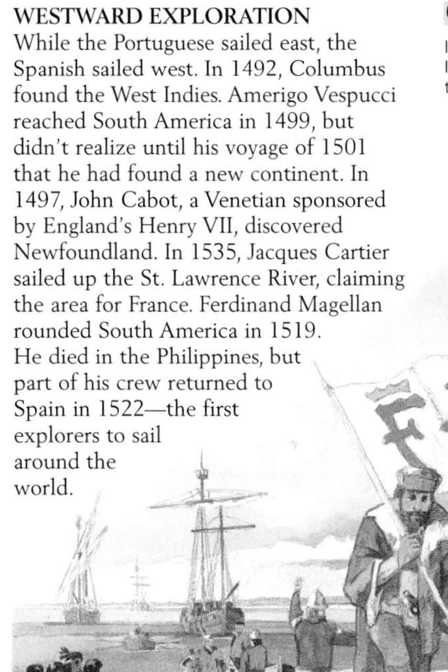

Christopher Columbus (1451–1506) first went to sea at the age of fourteen. He was shipwrecked and washed up on the coast of Portugal.

◀ When Christopher Columbus and his crew landed on Guanahani in the Bahamas, he claimed it for Spain.

TUDOR ENGLAND 1485–1603

During the Tudor period, England grew great and powerful. It forged a strong new identity, broke its ties with Rome, and sowed the seeds of an imperial future.

Henry Tudor (1457–1509) came to power in 1485.

Henry VIII (1491–1547) brought about great changes in England.

The Tudors, a Welsh family, rose to power after the confusion of a long civil war, the Wars of the Roses (1455–1485). The first Tudor king, Henry VII, banned private armies and put down any nobles who opposed him. He enriched his own finances and those of the nation. In 1509, when the young Henry VIII became king, England was an important power in Europe. Henry married Catherine of Aragon, daughter of Spain's Ferdinand and Isabella, and spent 15 years as a pleasure-seeking Renaissance-style ruler, while Thomas Wolsey ran the government. After wars against France and Scotland Henry became more politically aware. In 1521, he wrote a treatise attacking Luther, and the pope gave him the title Defender of the Faith. He had only one living child, Mary, and Henry wanted a male heir, so he asked the pope's permission to divorce Catherine. He was refused. At this time, new religious ideas and demands for Church reform were common, so Henry broke with Rome and made himself head of the Church in England.

Henry VIII loved banquets. He was well-educated, played several musical instruments, and wrote songs. He also enjoyed lively discussions on religion, art, and politics.

DISSOLUTION OF THE MONASTERIES

Between 1536 and 1540, Henry closed 800 monasteries. He turned 10,000 monks and nuns out and sold or gave away their lands. He did this to break the power of Rome in England, and to raise money. He founded the Protestant Church of England, though he was not enthusiastically Protestant—Protestantism really developed under Elizabeth I.

Henry VIII rebuilt the English navy, and his pride and joy was the *Mary Rose*. In 1536, he went to Portsmouth to watch it sail. However, the ship's balance was affected by the 700 sailors on deck, and it capsized and sank.

Henry married six times, and during his reign, strengthened English control of Wales and Ireland, established a large navy, and planned various colonial and commercial ventures. He was succeeded in 1547 by his only son, Edward VI (1537–1553) who died at the age of sixteen. During his reign, the Church of England grew stronger. Edward was followed by his half-sister, Mary I (1516–1558). Devoutly religious, she tried to restore England to Catholicism.

THE FIRST ELIZABETHANS

When Mary died, her sister Elizabeth I came to the throne. Elizabeth was hard-working, popular, and intelligent. She refused to marry, and she made her own decisions. The Catholic Mary, Queen of Scots, Elizabeth's cousin, was found guilty of plotting against her, but Elizabeth resisted pressure to have her executed for many years. Elizabeth aided European Protestants and sent out English pirates against Spanish ships. She made a settlement between English Catholics and Protestants, and fought a war with Spain, defeating the Spanish Armada. England began to develop overseas ventures, and at home its industries and economy grew. This was Shakespeare's time, when English culture and society flowered, laying the foundations for a period of imperial English greatness.

Elizabeth I (1533–1603) became queen of England and Ireland in 1558. She ruled for 45 years and, due to her active involvement in government, England went through a period of stability, as well as cultural and economic expansion.

MARY, QUEEN OF SCOTS 1542–1587

Mary Stuart became queen of Scotland in 1542 when she was only a week old. Her father, James V, was the nephew of Henry VIII, and this encouraged the Catholic Mary to claim the English throne. She was educated in France and married the heir to the French throne in 1558. After his death in 1560, Mary returned to Scotland where she proved unpopular. She abdicated and fled to England in 1568. As a focus for Catholic dissent against Elizabeth, Mary became involved in plots and was imprisoned in Fotheringay Castle, where she was executed in 1587 on a charge of treason.

THE PORTUGUESE EMPIRE 1520–1600

Portuguese seafarers and traders paved the way for European colonialism around the world. At its height, their trading empire spanned the whole globe.

This ornamental African mask from Benin shows the oba (king) wearing a headdress carved with representations of Portuguese merchants.

The Portuguese were the leading seafaring explorers of Europe. They had long been fishermen, accustomed to the high seas. Henry the Navigator began the training of sailors in the mid-1400s, and sent ships down the west coast of Africa. There were large profits at stake in the trade of exotic goods. Portuguese explorers reached the East Indies (Indonesia) in the early 1500s, following the Muslim trade routes to the Moluccas (Spice Islands), which were rich in the spices such as cinnamon, cloves, and nutmeg, that Europe wanted. To control this valuable trade, the Portuguese conquered the Moluccas and seized many of the best-placed ports on the Indian Ocean. They also visited China. Because Portuguese traders needed to sail around Africa in order to return to Lisbon, forts were set up at various places along the African coast to supply and protect the ships.

▲ The Portuguese were the first Europeans to trade with West African countries. This brass plaque from Benin shows Portuguese men symbolically holding up the pillars supporting the palace of the oba of Benin.

▼ The Portuguese Empire at its greatest extent in about 1600 was far-flung, but very profitable. Trading posts and ports to service ships were positioned in strategic locations along the major trade routes.

▲ In the 1500s, Benin craftspeople carved items such as this ivory saltcellar, for export to Europe. Around the base are figures of Portuguese noblemen.

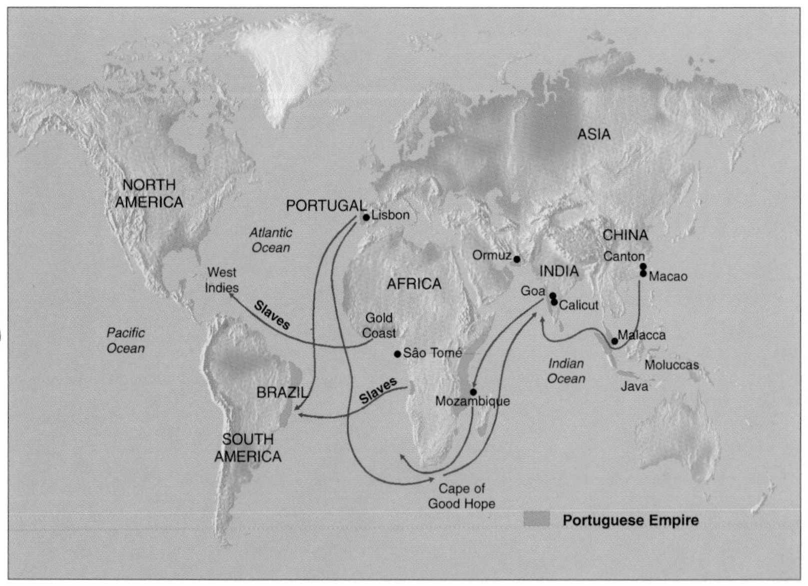

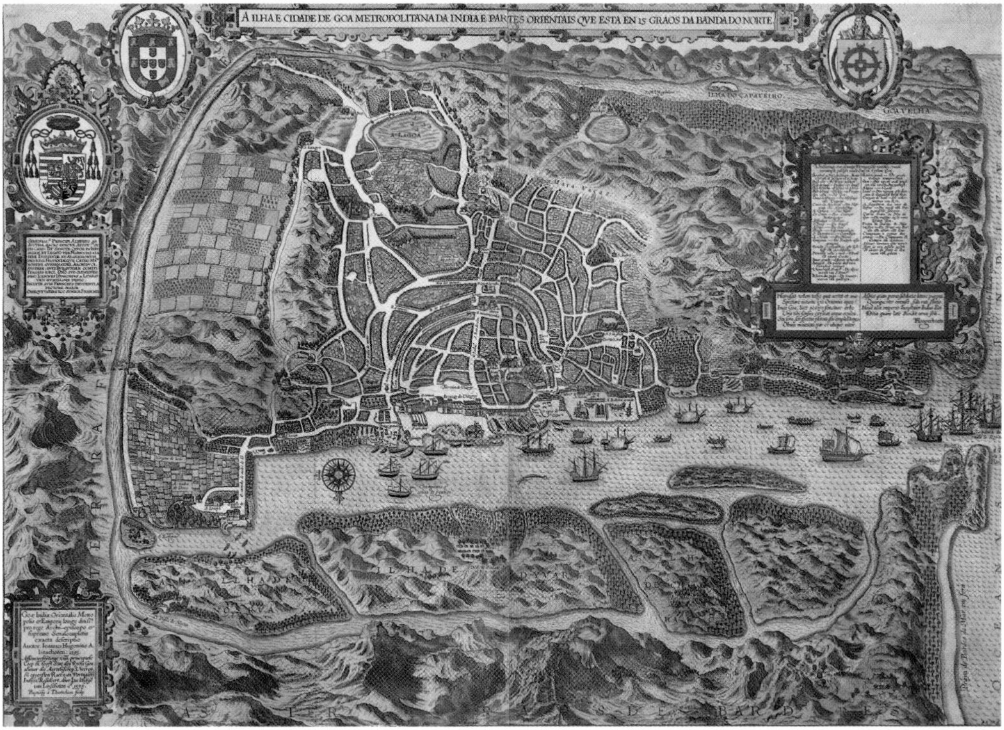

The port of Goa in India was an important trading link in the Portuguese Empire. It is shown here in a map made in 1595 by a Portuguese-Dutch engraver, Johannes Baptista van Doetechum the Younger.

THE START OF THE SLAVE TRADE

From Africa, the Portuguese bought gold and slaves to work on their sugar plantations. The first ones were on the African island of Sâo Tomé, but the sugar was inferior and the market collapsed. Problems grew. In the 1570s, a slave named Amador led a major revolt. Raids by pirates were a continuing threat. Sâo Tomé became only a place where slaves were loaded onto ships bound for Brazil—and so the transatlantic slave trade began.

At its height in the 1500s, the Portuguese Empire did not possess large areas of colonial land like the Spanish, but they did hold well-placed, valuable trading posts and plantations. These included Angola and Mozambique, the islands of Cape Verde, Madeira, and the Azores; the bases of Ormuz (Persia), Goa and Calicut (India), and Colombo (Sri Lanka); and trading posts in the Far East, such as Macao (China), the Celebes, Java, and Malacca.

KEY DATES

1419	The Portuguese reach Madeira
1471	The Portuguese reach Asante and Benin
1488	Dias rounds the Cape of Good Hope
1498	Vasco da Gama reaches India
1500	Cabral explores the coast of Brazil
1505–20	Asian trading posts founded in Goa and Malacca
1520	Magellan discovers the Moluccas (Spice Islands)
1530	First Portuguese colony established in Brazil
1534	First African slaves are brought to Brazil

Before the Portuguese arrived in the Moluccas, its rulers enjoyed high profits from the lucrative spice trade. Under Portuguese rule the local rulers were bypassed. Spices from the Moluccas included cloves, nutmeg, pepper, cinnamon, and ginger.

THE REFORMATION 1520–1618

During the Reformation, a new kind of Christianity, with many new groups and sects, developed. This led to social divisions and eventually war across Europe.

John Calvin (1509–1564) was born in France and was originally named Jean Chauvin. He was a strict Protestant and believed that God had already ordained the future and that only those chosen by God (the Elect) would be saved.

Europe suffered a series of violent religious civil wars. There were many massacres, and people accused of being heretics were burned at the stake.

By the early 1500s, the new ideas of the Renaissance led some people to challenge the teachings of the Roman Catholic Church. The way its leaders ran the Church was strongly criticized. Priests, monks, and nuns no longer led lives of poverty, celibacy, and simplicity, and popes and bishops were too interested in money and power. People sought Church reform. This became known as "the Reformation." It had started quietly over 100 years before, but gained momentum in 1517 when Martin Luther, a German priest, nailed a list of 95 statements (theses) to the church door at Wittenberg, criticizing the role of the Church. Luther hated the sale of "indulgences"—the forgiveness of sins in exchange for money. He hoped that his list would lead to healthy debate, but he was accused of heresy (going against Church beliefs), and excommunicated from the Catholic Church in 1521.

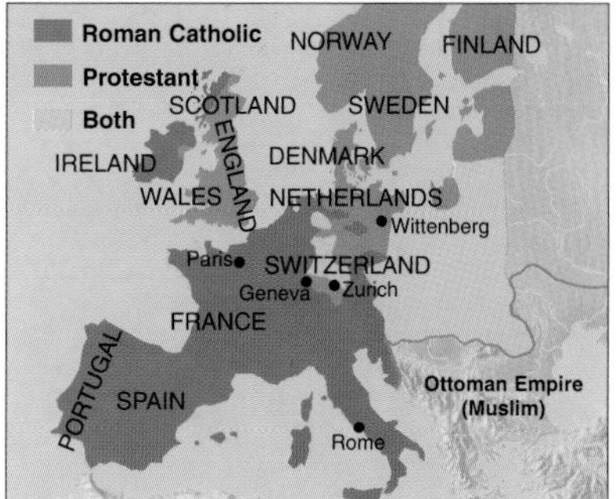

The Reformation in the 1500s meant that Europe was divided roughly north–south over religious beliefs—Protestant to the north and Roman Catholic to the south. This division also happened within individual countries such as France, and later led to civil war.

THE EARLY PROTESTANTS

Luther had gained support in Germany and Switzerland, setting up his own Lutheran church. Other groups, such as Quakers, Anabaptists, Mennonites, and Moravian Hussites did the same. After a conference in 1529, they were all called Protestants. Ulrich Zwingli led the Reformation in Switzerland. His views were more extreme, and this led to a civil war in which Zwingli was killed. He was followed by John Calvin, who gained followers in France, Germany, and Holland. He established the Reformation in Switzerland and influenced John Knox, who took the Reformation to Scotland. Some groups pooled all their property to form communities, taking over whole towns.

▲ Martin Luther (1483–1546) believed that people are saved by faith alone, not by buying indulgences. He wanted faith to be based on the Bible, not on corrupt religious traditions. He believed that church services should be in the local language, not Latin. The cartoon on the right shows the devil dictating Luther's sermons to him.

The Council of Trent met three times between 1545 and 1563. It began a major reform within the the Catholic Church and sought to stop the spread of Protestantism.

▲ The Catholic Church used pictures for teaching, and this 1470 woodcut from Germany shows a good Catholic on his deathbed, being given the last rites.

THE COUNTER-REFORMATION

In 1522, Pope Adrian VI admitted there were many problems in the Roman Catholic Church, but following his death, nothing more was done until 1534, when Paul III became pope. This was the year Henry VIII of England broke away from Rome. Paul began to reform the Church in a movement known as the Counter-Reformation. He began by encouraging the preaching and missionary work of an Italian order of friars called the Capuchins. Six years later, he approved the founding of the Society of Jesus, or Jesuits, which had been started by Ignatius Loyola, to spread Catholicism. He also called together a group known as the Council of Trent, in 1545, to decide on further Church reforms. The council enforced vows of poverty and set up Church colleges (seminaries) to educate monks, nuns, and priests. All this led to a revival of Catholic faith and active opposition to the Protestants.

However, the religious dispute in Europe grew into a political one when Philip II of Spain tried to restore Catholicism in England, France, and Holland by force. Other rulers took sides. Civil war erupted in France, and Protestant Holland revolted against Spanish domination. Eventually, the Thirty Years' War broke out in 1618.

▼ Julius II, pope from 1503 to 1513, was concerned with politics, and was a great patron of the arts. Popes after him were forced to reform the Church from within.

KEY DATES

1517	Luther's 95 Theses, announced at Wittenberg, Germany
1522	Luther's Bible is published in German
1523	Zwingli's Program of Reform established in Switzerland
1530s	Protestant social movements and revolts in Germany
1534	England separates from the Roman Church
1540s	Calvin establishes Protestant church in Geneva
1545	The first Council of Trent—the Counter-Reformation begins
1562–98	The Huguenot Wars in France
1566	Calvinist church founded in the Netherlands
1580s	Increase of tension between European rulers
1618	Outbreak of the Thirty Years' War (until 1648)

THE OTTOMAN EMPIRE 1453–1600

Following the taking of Constantinople in 1453, the Ottoman Empire soon became a force to be reckoned with in the Middle East and around the Mediterranean.

▲ The Ottoman *spahi*, or cavalry knights were given land in return for military service, and became a local ruling class across the empire.

When Constantinople fell to Mehmet II in 1453, the Ottoman Empire began its golden age. The former Byzantine capital was renamed Istanbul, and became the center of an enormous empire. which at its peak, stretched from Algeria to Persia and Hungary to Arabia. The empire was founded by Osman I in 1301, and by 1389, it had extended into Europe. The Mongols halted its expansion for a while, but, after taking Constantinople, Mehmet II quickly conquered 12 kingdoms and 200 cities in Anatolia and the Balkans. Then Selim I gained Syria, Arabia, and Egypt between 1512 and 1520.

SÜLEYMAN THE MAGNIFICENT

Süleyman the Magnificent ruled for 46 years from 1520. He conquered Belgrade and Hungary, but failed in his siege of Vienna, the capital of the Holy Roman Empire. He later took Mesopotamia, Armenia, and the Caucasus region. The Ottomans gained control of the eastern Mediterranean and Black Sea (thereby dominating Venetian and Genoan trade), and also North Africa and the Ukraine.

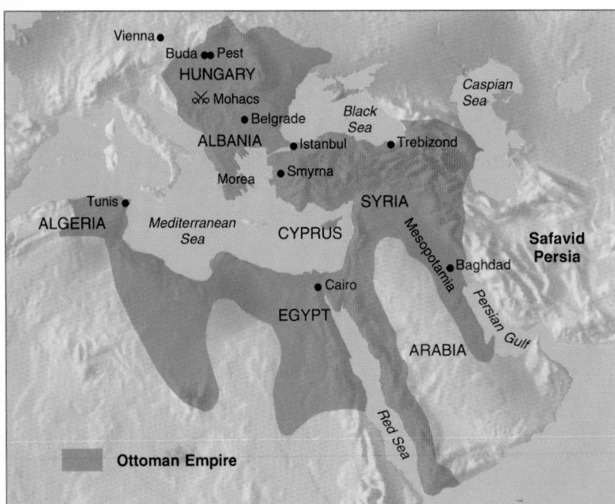

▼ By 1566, the Ottoman Empire stretched into three continents. Süleyman had built up a strong navy and won control of the Mediterranean. He also dominated the Red Sea and Persian Gulf.

Women in the Ottoman Empire led a secluded life. Outside their home they had to wear a veil and could only meet men from their own families.

To his own people, Süleyman was known as *Qanuni*, the Lawgiver, because he reformed the Ottoman administration and the legal system. He gave shape to the Ottoman Empire, enriching everything from architecture to courtly life. He was a poet, scholar, and patron of the arts, and he rebuilt much of Istanbul.

Europeans called him Süleyman the Magnificent because of the splendor of his court and his military victories in Europe. These included a series of campaigns in which he captured Belgrade in Yugoslavia in 1521, and threw the Crusader Knights of St. John out of Rhodes in 1522. His greatest victory was at Mohacs in Hungary in 1526; his siege of Vienna in 1529 threatened the heart of Europe; and he took the Muslim holy city of Mecca in 1538. Meanwhile, the Turkish fleet, under the pirate Barbarossa (Khayr ad-Din Pasha), attacked and ravaged the coasts of Spain, Italy, and Greece.

Süleyman the Magnificent (1494–1566), became sultan in 1520 and turned the Ottoman Empire into a vast and rich Sunni Muslim empire straddling three continents.

MUSLIM WARS

Süleyman waged three campaigns in the east against the Safavid Empire of Persia. This was a war between Muslims—between the Sunni Ottomans and the Shiite Persians. Süleyman took Baghdad, but the eastern border of the empire was never secure. The wars between the two empires lasted throughout the 1500s and diverted Ottoman attention so that they did not advance further into Europe.

THE START OF A SLOW DECLINE

When Süleyman died, his son Selim II became sultan. Selim led a life of leisure, while his ministers and generals ran the empire. The Ottomans themselves were not many in number. They relied on taking Russian and North African slaves, and drafting one in five boys from their European territories, to train them as administrators and soldiers. Ordinary people were left alone as long as they were obedient and paid taxes, and no one was forcibly converted to Islam. The Ottomans relied on Greeks, Armenians, Venetians, and other foreigners as traders, making the Ottoman Empire international in character. However, by 1600, the empire had begun a long, slow decline.

KEY DATES

1453 The Ottomans take Constantinople
c.1460 Greece, Serbia, and Bosnia taken
1512–20 Selim I takes Syria, Arabia, and Egypt
1522 Süleyman takes Rhodes from the Knights of St. John
1526 Battle of Mohacs: Hungary taken
1529 Siege of Vienna (failed)
1534 Süleyman takes Baghdad and Armenia
1538 Süleyman takes the holy city of Mecca
1540s onward The flowering of Ottoman culture
1566 Death of Süleyman, the Ottoman Empire passes its peak

▲ Süleyman's greatest victory was at the battle of Mohacs in 1526 where he crushed the Hungarian army. His army overwhelmed an alliance of central European nations and killed the king of Bohemia.

▼ Süleyman's failure to capture Vienna, the capital of the Holy Roman Empire in 1529 prevented him from moving farther into Germany and central Europe. Ottoman advances halted there. The use of cannons was a fairly recent development in warfare.

INDIA: THE MOGULS 1504–1605

The Islamic world was changing. India, a divided subcontinent, was invaded by the Moguls. They established a strong Empire in the north of India.

Babur (1483–1530), born in Turkestan, was the first Mogul emperor in India. He died in Agra.

Babur, a descendant of Genghis Khan and Tamerlane, led a tribe in Turkestan called the Moguls—the name Mogul is a variation of the word "Mongol." Driven out by the Uzbeks, they invaded Kabul in Afghanistan in 1504. Then they set their sights on India, a patchwork of often-warring Hindu and Muslim states. After an experimental attack in 1519, 12,000 Moguls swept through the Khyber Pass into India in 1526, invading the Delhi sultanate, the greatest power in India.

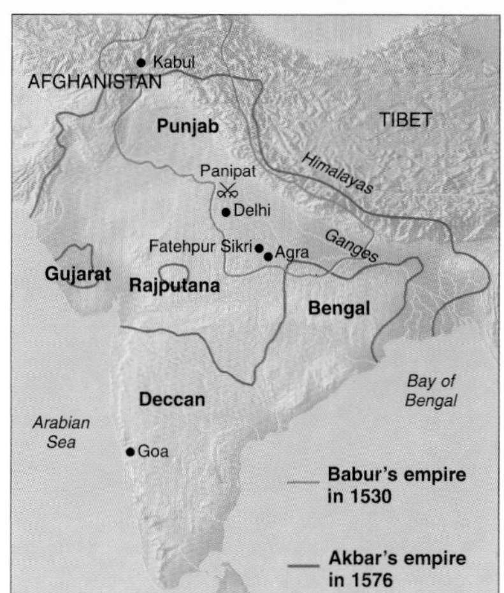

Expanding outward from Delhi, the Mogul Empire grew to cover all of northern India and much of central India. Although it was Muslim-ruled, it accommodated the many faiths and cultures of India.

Babur and his followers were Muslims. When they invaded India, the Ottoman Empire supplied them with guns and soldiers. Babur's troops also rode swift horses which easily outmaneuvered the Indians' slower elephants. This helped them defeat a much larger Indian army at a battle in which the sultan of Delhi was killed. After this victory, Babur made Delhi his capital. When Babur died in 1530, his son Humayun became ruler.

◀ Painted by a Persian, this picture shows Babur (left), his ancestor Tamerlane, and Babur's son Humayun (right).

▲ Babur had a full-scale account of India written. It details the nature, people, and customs of his empire.

Humayun invaded western India, but in 1540, the Surs chased out the Moguls, forcing them back into Persia. Humayun returned in 1555, overcame the Surs, and moved back to Delhi. A year later, before he was able to win back the whole empire, Humayun was killed in an accident.

AKBAR EXPANDS THE EMPIRE

Humayun's succesor was Babur's grandson, Akbar. He became emperor at the age of 13 and ruled until his death in 1605. Akbar was a great military leader and wise ruler. His army pushed west into Gujarat and east into Bengal—the richest province in northern India. It produced rice and silk, which provided Akbar with his main source of income. By 1576, Akbar controlled all of northern India.

Although Akbar was a Muslim, many of his subjects were Hindus, and to keep the peace, he married a Hindu princess. He believed in religious tolerance, bringing the Hindus into the government and encouraging their overseas trade. He set up a well-organized empire with professional administrators.

MOGUL GREATNESS

During this period, India traded profitably with Africa, the Ottomans, Europe, and the Far East. By this time, the Portuguese had trading posts and ports in India. The country also had the world's largest textile industry. Akbar welcomed Christian Jesuits and Persian artists to his court, and he tried unsuccessfully to create a new religion for India. He built schools for children as well as a new capital city at Fatehpur Sikri. The city combined Muslim and Hindu styles of architecture.

KEY DATES	
1504	The Moguls seize Kabul
1526	Delhi becomes the Mogul capital in India
1556	Akbar the Great, the greatest Mogul emperor, begins reign
1571	Fatehpur Sikri becomes the new capital
1605	Jahangir becomes Mogul emperor (Nur Jahan rules 1611–22)
1628	Shah Jahan, Mogul emperor
1658	Aurangzeb, the last great Mogul emperor
1707	Beginning of the decline of the Moguls
1803	The fall of the last Mogul stronghold to the English

AKBAR, THE THIRD MOGUL EMPEROR

Akbar inherited the Mogul Empire at the age of 13, and he ruled for nearly 50 years. He invaded Rajasthan, Gujarat, Bengal, Kashmir, and the Deccan to rule most of India. He taxed farming peasants less, encouraged traders, and introduced a very efficient government and military service. This served later Mogul emperors and their people well. Though Akbar could not read, he welcomed scholars of all religions, artists, and foreign travelers to his court. His greatest success was in making peace with the Hindu majority of the Indian population, ending many Hindu–Muslim conflicts.

Akbar (1542–1605) believed in religious toleration. His own beliefs included ideas from different religions. In 1575, he set up a center for the study of religion through the exchange of ideas. Akbar found, however, that the scholars were not as broad-minded as he had hoped—each one argued without really listening to anyone else's point of view.

◀ Although some local rulers rebelled against Akbar's rule, they were soon defeated. Here, the rebel Bahadur Khan is shown yielding to Akbar.

▼ At Fatehpur Sikri, Akbar built a capital city with a mixture of Muslim, Hindu, and other architectural styles as the center for his new religion. He was buried in this tomb.

THE CONQUISTADORES 1519–1550

The Spanish conquistadores were soldiers and adventurers who invaded the Americas. In doing so, they destroyed the great Aztec and Inca civilizations.

Hernán Cortés (1485–1547) returned to Spain where he died in poverty.

Francisco Pizarro (c.1475–1541) marched on the Incas in 1532. He was murdered in Lima.

Soon after the navigators had found the Americas, Spanish adventurers, known as *conquistadores* (conquerors), followed them. After conquering many Caribbean islands, they explored the American mainland, hoping to find treasure. In 1519, about 500 Spanish soldiers, led by Hernán Cortés, reached the Aztec city of Tenochtitlan, where, at first, they were welcomed. It is thought that the Aztec emperor, Montezuma II, believed that Cortés was the god Quetzalcóatl, whose return he had been awaiting. The Spanish tricked and captured Montezuma, and Cortés ruled in his place. When Cortés left, the Aztecs rebelled and defeated the remaining Spanish. With the help of an interpreter, Cortés then won the support of the neighboring tribes who had been conquered by the Aztecs. In 1521, he returned to Tenochtitlan with a native army and destroyed the city.

At first Montezuma welcomed Cortés to Tenochtitlan, showering him with gifts. This goodwill died when the Spanish seized power. Most of the Aztecs soon died of diseases brought by the foreigners.

THE END OF THE INCA EMPIRE

Another conquistador, Francisco Pizarro, landed in Peru in 1532, seeking to conquer the Incas. An Inca civil war was already in progress between Huascar and Atahualpa, the sons of Huayna Capac. Atahualpa killed Huascar with the help of the Spanish, but Pizarro then had Atahualpa executed. The Incas soon surrendered, and by 1533 their vast empire was in Spanish hands.

THE CAPTURE OF ATAHUALPA

In 1532, Pizarro, with only 159 men against a large Inca army, kidnapped the Inca leader, Atahualpa. He was a god to the Incas, which, to them, made Pizarro more powerful than the gods. The Incas soon yielded, and Atahualpa was executed. Like the Aztecs, the Incas were tricked into submission, and a whole civilization died.

THE SPANISH EMPIRE 1533–1600

Spain's occupation of large areas of the Americas brought harsh conditions and disease to the Native Americans. By 1600, Spain had the largest empire.

After the fall of the Aztecs and Incas, the king of Spain added their territories to his empire. The Aztec Empire became the Viceroyalty of New Spain in 1533. Later in the 1500s, it also included parts of California, Arizona, and New Mexico. The land of the Incas became the Viceroyalty of Peru. Many people from Spain emigrated to live in this new Spanish Empire. The colonies were ruled by the Council of the Indies, based in Spain. Many of the laws made for the colonies show that the Spanish government tried to make sure that the Native Americans were not badly treated. But it was impossible to prevent the colonial Spaniards from treating them cruelly. Native Americans were forced to mine silver and work as slaves. Millions died because they had no resistance to European diseases such as measles and smallpox. The colonists were followed by Spanish missionaries, who destroyed temples and idols and set up churches in their place, trying to convert the Native Americans.

The conquistadores were followed by missionaries, who tried to convert the Native Americans—by force, if necessary. They destroyed their temples and made the people build churches in their place.

The Spanish forced the Native Americans to mine gold and silver, which was then sent back to Spain. The harsh conditions and new diseases brought by the Spanish decimated the population of Mexico, which fell from 25 million in 1500 to just one million in 1600.

The Spanish Empire continued to expand under the reign of Philip II (1556–1598). Most of the Philippine Islands were conquered in 1571. Then, in 1578, King Sebastian of Portugal was killed in Morocco. Philip was his closest relative, so he inherited the Portuguese Empire. By 1600, the Spanish had the world's largest empire, but they were losing power. Philip's opposition to the Protestants in Europe led to expensive wars that used up the gold and silver from the Americas.

▲ The Spanish took new foods, such as pineapples, tomatoes, potatoes, cocoa, peppers, and sunflowers back to Europe.

▶ The Spanish Empire was large and yielded vast wealth, especially from gold and silver mined in Mexico and Peru.

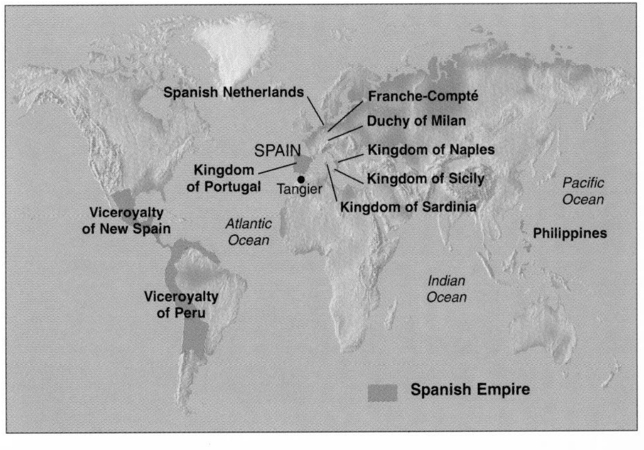

RUSSIA 1462–1613

During this period, Russia grew from a collection of small principalities into a great country. Its isolation ended, allowing it to play a major role in history.

Ivan III (1440-1505) was the first ruler of all Russia. He made Moscow his capital. By the time he died from alcoholism, he had set Russia on a new course.

▲ Ivan III adopted the Byzantine symbol of the double-headed eagle as his own emblem—both Byzantium and Russia looked east and west.

After the decline of Kiev around 1060, Russia survived as an assortment of separate small principalities such as Novgorod, Smolensk, Kiev, and Vladimir. This suddenly changed when the Mongols, under Batu Khan, invaded in 1238. They burned Moscow and damaged Kiev. The Khanate of the Golden Horde (or Tartars) dominated Russia by demanding tribute in money and soldiers, and the Russians cooperated to avoid trouble. (In the 1300s, Kiev was absorbed into Lithuania for a time.)

In 1263, Moscow had a new ruler, Prince Daniel, who gradually expanded its territories. Slowly, Moscow began to dominate the other Russian states. In 1380, the Muscovites defeated the Golden Horde, although the Tartars carried on raiding Moscow and demanding tribute until 1480, when Ivan III finally defeated them. Ivan III, or Ivan the Great, came to the throne of Moscow in 1462. He expanded Moscow and gave it a sense of pride, introduced a legal code, and declared himself "ruler of all Russia." In 1472, he married Sophia, the niece of the last Byzantine emperor, and appointed himself as the protector of the Eastern Orthodox Church, calling Moscow "the third Rome."

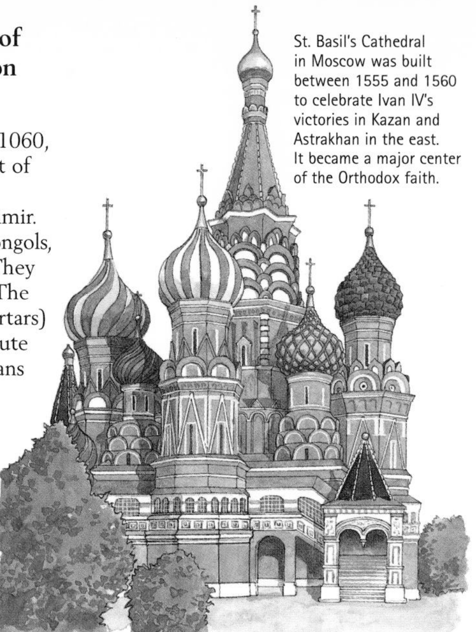

St. Basil's Cathedral in Moscow was built between 1555 and 1560 to celebrate Ivan IV's victories in Kazan and Astrakhan in the east. It became a major center of the Orthodox faith.

By 1480, Ivan III had brought Novgorod and other cities under his control. He rebuilt Moscow's famous *Kremlin* (citadel). When he died in 1505, he was succeeded by his son Vasili, who ruled until 1533. Vasili was succeeded in turn by Ivan IV, his three-year-old son.

▼ The boyars of Russia had been independent until Ivan the Terrible brought them under his control. They then joined the growing trade with the West in fur, timber, and other raw materials.

▲ The Kremlin was the center of Moscow. It was actually a fort and many palaces, churches, and cathedrals were rebuilt within the protection of its walls by Ivan III. It became the symbol of the centralized power of the czars.

IVAN THE TERRIBLE

Ivan IV, or "Ivan the Terrible," was the Grand Prince of Moscow from 1533 to 1584. He was crowned as the first *czar* (emperor) in 1547. His harsh upbringing left him with a violent and unpredictable character, but his nickname meant "awe-inspiring" rather than "terrible." He improved the legal system as well as reforming trading links with England and other European countries—Russia had until then been isolated. He captured Kazan and Astrakhan from the Tartars, pushing on toward Siberia. Ivan reduced the power of the boyars (the nobility) by instituting a kind of secret police, to bring the country under stronger control. He set many patterns for the future, and established strong central control by the czars. In 1581, in a fit of anger, he killed his son and heir Ivan, and so was succeeded by his second son, Fyodor, who was mentally unstable.

THE ROMANOV CZARS

After Ivan IV died in 1584, Boris Godunov ruled as regent until Fyodor died in 1598. Boris made himself czar, despite opposition from the boyars. He promoted foreign trade and defeated the Swedes, who sought to invade Russia. When he died in 1605, Russia entered eight years of civil war, as rival forces fought for the throne. Eventually, Ivan IV's great-nephew Mikhail Romanov (1596–1645) gained the throne in 1613. He was czar for thirty years, founding the Romanov dynasty, which ruled until 1917.

◀ Ivan the Terrible visited the seat of the patriarch of the Russian Orthodox Church at Zagorsk, in order to have himself anointed and confirmed as the head of the Orthodox Church.

KEY DATES

1238	Invasion of Russia by the Mongols
1263	Moscow begins to grow larger
1462–1505	Ivan III, the Great, strengthens Moscow
1472	Ivan III appoints himself protector of the Eastern Orthodox Church
1480	End of Tartar dominance of Russia
1505–33	Vasili is ruler
1533–84	Ivan IV, the Terrible, expands Russia
1584–98	Fyodor is czar and Boris Godunov regent
1598–1605	Boris Godunov rules as czar
1605–13	Civil war between rival boyars
1613	Mikhail Romanov, first of the Romanovs, becomes czar

Ivan IV (1530-1584) was a strong ruler who truly set the course of Russia's expansion. Known as the Ivan the Terrible, he had a formidable personality.

DUTCH INDEPENDENCE 1477–1648

The Netherlands was a fast-developing Protestant area with a promising future, but ruled by Catholic Spain. The Dutch wanted to control their own affairs.

William of Orange (1533–1584)—"the Silent"—became Spanish governor of part of the Netherlands in 1559. He disagreed with Philip II's treatment of the Protestants and turned against Spain. He led the Dutch Revolt from 1567 to 1572, and in 1573 became a Calvinist. Philip offered a reward for his death. In 1584, having escaped one assassination attempt, he was killed by a fanatical Catholic, Balthasar Gérards.

After the collapse of Charlemagne's empire in the 800s, the Netherlands, made up of 17 provinces in what is now Belgium, Luxembourg, and the Netherlands, were very fragmented since they belonged to various ruling families. In the 1300s and 1400s, the dukes of Burgundy, Philip the Bold and John the Fearless, acquired Flanders (Belgium) and the Netherlands. These lands stayed under Burgundy's control until Charles V, inheritor of Burgundian lands and a member of the Hapsburg dynasty, made them a Spanish possession in 1516. This did not suit the people of the Netherlands, since most of them were Protestant. The fight for independence started when Charles's son Philip II became king of Spain in 1556. He resisted the Protestant tide and tried to take complete control. He sent the Duke of Alba as governor to the Netherlands with orders to use terror, if necessary, to crush any opposition.

The Duke of Alba executed two leaders of the independence movement, and this resulted in the Dutch Revolts—led by William of Orange. The more ruthless the Duke of Alba became, the more the opposition grew. There were public executions, towns were pillaged, and whole populations were massacred. The Dutch used many guerrilla tactics, such as the flooding of the lowlands, to halt the Spanish advance. In 1576, Spanish troops sacked Antwerp, one of Europe's richest ports, and ended its prosperity.

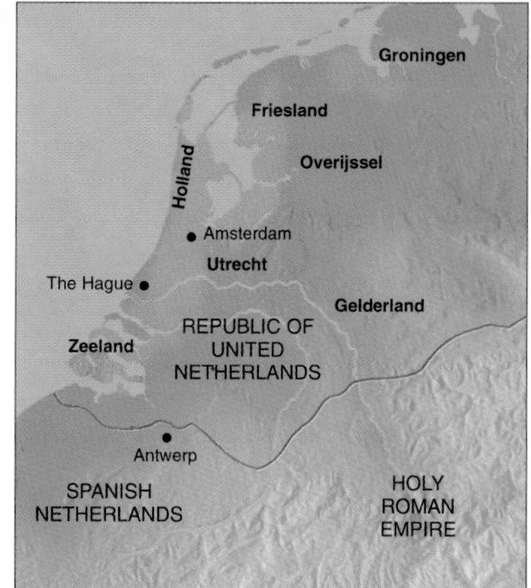

The United Provinces grew richer as the marshy land was drained and developed. As a Protestant country with growing trade and industry, independence from Spain, an old-fashioned imperial power, became necessary.

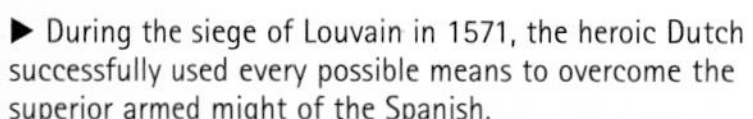

▲ A cartoon of the time shows the aristocratic Duke of Alba trying to stamp out heresy in the Netherlands by trampling on the bodies of executed Protestants.

► During the siege of Louvain in 1571, the heroic Dutch successfully used every possible means to overcome the superior armed might of the Spanish.

▲ Battle is joined on the Zuider Zee, east of Amsterdam, between the naval might of Spain and the small boats of the Dutch in 1573. As with the Armada, the smaller boats outmaneuvered the Spanish vessels and sank many of them.

STRUGGLE AND INDEPENDENCE

Many merchants and bankers moved to Amsterdam, rebuilding it into a fine city defended by canals and a growing navy. They developed modern trade, banking, and industry, becoming one of Europe's main Protestant centers. Spain brought the Catholic southern provinces (Belgium) back under its control, but in 1581, seven Protestant northern provinces declared themselves independent. Fortunately for them, Spain was busy fighting France, England, and the Ottomans, and so was unable to stop the Dutch.

This struggle for independence was a religious war and a fight between modern Dutch town-dwelling burghers and the traditional Spanish royal hierarchy. Led by William of Orange, the Dutch declared the Republic of the United Netherlands. A truce followed in 1609, but it was not until 1648 that Spain officially recognized Dutch independence.

KEY DATES

1477	The Netherlands become a Hapsburg possession
1516	The Spanish take control of the Netherlands
1568	The Dutch Revolt begins
1576	The sack of Antwerp—a turning point
1581	The Northern Provinces declare independence
1609	Truce—the Dutch effectively win the war
1648	Dutch independence fully recognized

▶ The plundering of the rich city of Antwerp by the Spanish in 1576 was the last straw for the Dutch. From then on, they were determined to get rid of the Spanish.

NORTH AMERICA 1460–1600

North America was a land of many different peoples, each with their own traditions, way of life, and culture. The arrival of the Europeans was disastrous for them.

The tribes of the Iroquois wore masks during important tribal ceremonies. The masks represented the spirits of mythological creatures.

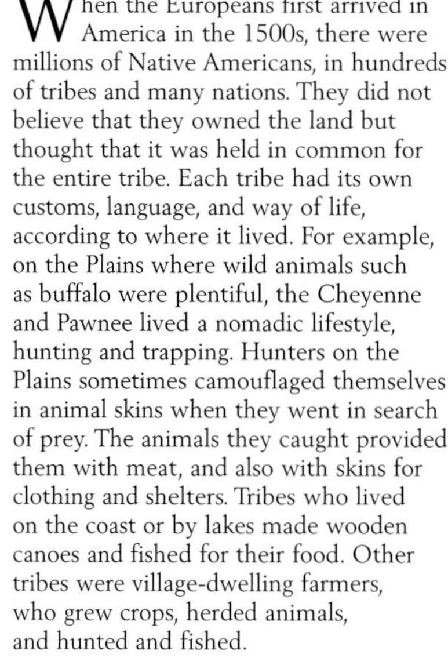

When the Europeans first arrived in America in the 1500s, there were millions of Native Americans, in hundreds of tribes and many nations. They did not believe that they owned the land but thought that it was held in common for the entire tribe. Each tribe had its own customs, language, and way of life, according to where it lived. For example, on the Plains where wild animals such as buffalo were plentiful, the Cheyenne and Pawnee lived a nomadic lifestyle, hunting and trapping. Hunters on the Plains sometimes camouflaged themselves in animal skins when they went in search of prey. The animals they caught provided them with meat, and also with skins for clothing and shelters. Tribes who lived on the coast or by lakes made wooden canoes and fished for their food. Other tribes were village-dwelling farmers, who grew crops, herded animals, and hunted and fished.

▲ The French explorer Jacques Cartier (1491–1557) sailed up the St. Lawrence River in what is now Canada, and claimed the area for France. One of his men drew this map of the Huron town of Hochelaga—now the city of Montreal.

Some Native Americans built totems to the spirits of nature, often with an eagle at the top to represent the farseeing powers of Great Spirit.

In the Southwest, people living in villages, called *pueblos*, grew crops of corn, squash, and beans by building dams to irrigate the dry land. They had roads, complex societies with strong religious traditions, and they traded with the Aztecs and other native peoples.

Along the Mississippi River, an advanced city civilization had thrived, although it was in decline from 1450 onward. The Mississippians supplied Native American tribes with tools, cloth, valuables, and goods brought from far away.

People on the east coast lived by farming corn, beans, and tobacco in plots around their villages, and they engaged in local trade and barter. In the Northeast, Native American fields and clearings reminded European settlers of home—with the result that the region gained the name "New England." Many tribes were part of confederations or nations related by blood, tradition, or political agreements. Sometimes disagreements between tribes led to war.

▶ The Miami tribe of Ohio made clothing from hides and furs. Skins were cleaned and stretched, then cut and sewn into garments and moccasins. Women did most of the domestic work and crop-growing, but they also held power in tribal decision-making.

The people of the northeastern woodlands made decorated moccasins and ceremonial pipes which were used to celebrate special occasions.

The American tribes were very diverse. The map shows where the main tribes of Native Americans lived in 1500, before Europeans arrived and started driving them off their lands. At this time there were about six million Native North Americans. These numbers fell drastically as the colonists spread west across the continent.

▼ The Chippewa lived in wigwams made of bent branches and covered with an outer layer of skins or birchbark to fend off the winter cold.

THE ARRIVAL OF THE EUROPEANS

Like the Aztecs and the Incas, none of the Native American tribes had horses or wheeled transportation before the Europeans arrived. Their knowledge of metal was limited, and most of their tools were made from wood or stone. Their weapons were bows and arrows, slingshots, and spears. At first, some tribes were friendly to the Europeans, and even helped them survive. But things changed disastrously for the native peoples when more aggressive European settlers arrived. Whole villages of Native Americans died from European diseases such as smallpox and the measles. Others were killed in disputes, and the rest were driven off their lands.

▶ The nomadic Plains Indians lived in *tepees*. In the evenings, stories were told, both to entertain and to pass on the history, customs, laws, and ways of the tribe. They also held tribal councils to settle disputes and decide the tribe's future.

TRADE AND EMPIRE

1601–1707

The Europeans were now beginning to take over the world. The biggest impact was in the Americas. British and French settlers occupied the east coast of North America, and Spanish *conquistadores* had already taken over Mexico and South America. European trading posts were now dotted around the world—only Japan kept them out. In Europe, this century brought a tragic mixture of wars, revolution, and devastation, as well as enormous growth and progress in the sciences and arts.

▲ In 1620, a ship called the *Mayflower* sailed from Plymouth in England, carrying pilgrims to a new life in North America.

◀ The Taj Mahal, near Agra in India, was built in the 1600s by Shah Jehan as a mausoleum for his wife, Mumtaz Mahal.

THE WORLD AT A GLANCE 1601–1707

The 1600s were the age of the absolute ruler. In Europe, India, China, and Japan, power was concentrated in the hands of the kings, emperors, and shoguns who ruled the land. The great exception was England where an elected, rebellious Parliament overthrew and executed the king, Charles I. Although his son, Charles II, was later invited to take the throne, he was only granted limited powers.

At this time, although embroiled in wars, Europe spread its influence worldwide, while countries such as India and China enriched Europe with their products, art, and ideas.

Many thousands of Europeans sailed across the ocean to North America to seek a better life, or to try to set up communities where they could worship as they wished, free from the interference of hostile governments.

The 1600s also saw another kind of movement of people. The terrible trade in slaves tore millions of Africans from their homes and transported them across the Atlantic to work on American plantations.

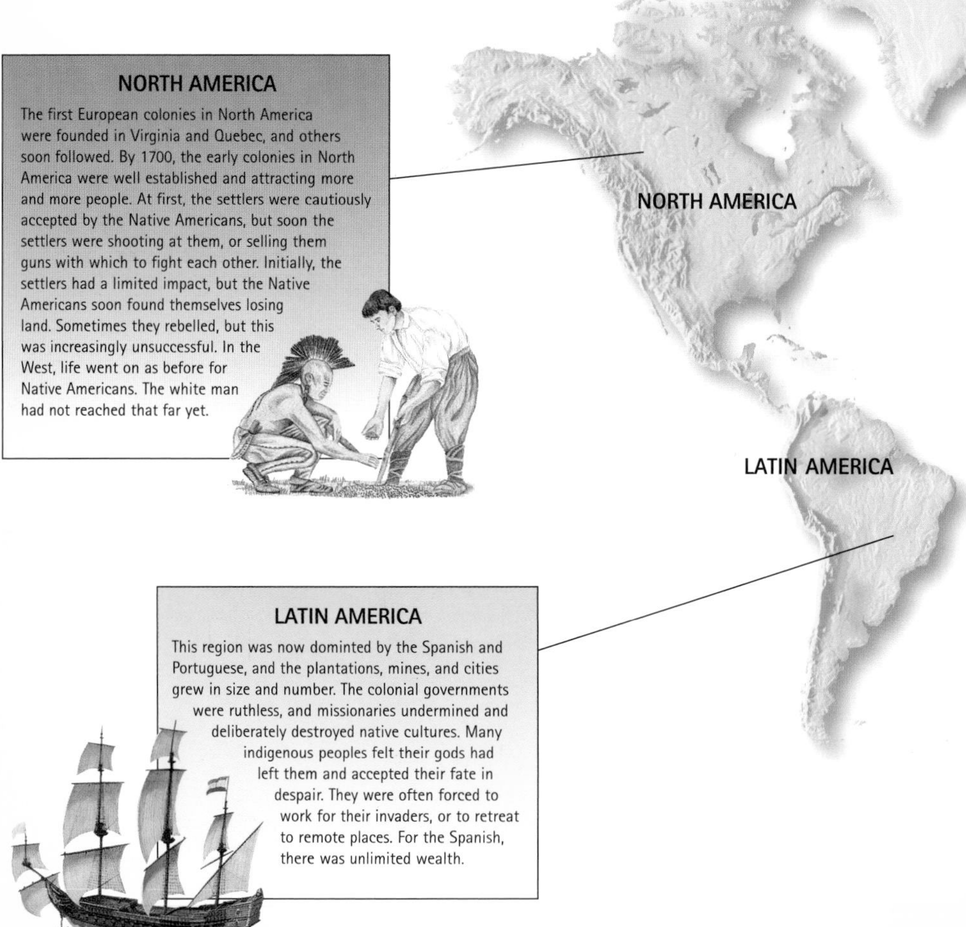

NORTH AMERICA

The first European colonies in North America were founded in Virginia and Quebec, and others soon followed. By 1700, the early colonies in North America were well established and attracting more and more people. At first, the settlers were cautiously accepted by the Native Americans, but soon the settlers were shooting at them, or selling them guns with which to fight each other. Initially, the settlers had a limited impact, but the Native Americans soon found themselves losing land. Sometimes they rebelled, but this was increasingly unsuccessful. In the West, life went on as before for Native Americans. The white man had not reached that far yet.

LATIN AMERICA

This region was now dominted by the Spanish and Portuguese, and the plantations, mines, and cities grew in size and number. The colonial governments were ruthless, and missionaries undermined and deliberately destroyed native cultures. Many indigenous peoples felt their gods had left them and accepted their fate in despair. They were often forced to work for their invaders, or to retreat to remote places. For the Spanish, there was unlimited wealth.

EUROPE

During the Thirty Years' War, many countries in Europe were devastated by troops and cannons, as rulers fought for power. Rivalry between Catholics and Protestants caused much bloodletting, and in England, a civil war. Yet rulers, while causing much of the turmoil of this century, also grew rich and powerful. They built great palaces and estates and became patrons of music, science, and the arts. Underneath, European society was transforming itself, with people moving into cities, reading more books, and exchanging new ideas in the streets and coffeehouses. Their attitudes were changing faster than those of their rulers, which would lead to trouble. The ports, banks, and warehouses became busy as Europe's trade with the world expanded.

ASIA

The Manchus invaded China and set up the Qing dynasty, which would last until 1911. But Europeans were knocking at their door, looking for trade. Japan kept them out, India and Southeast Asia let them in, and China allowed access only to Canton. A fight for control of India and the East Indies broke out between rival European trading companies. In India, friction between Hindus and Muslims grew stronger, and the Mogul Empire weakened. Asian products were sought by Europeans, bringing wealth and major changes to the affected countries. In the more isolated parts of Asia, though, people had not yet encountered Europeans.

EUROPE

ASIA

MIDDLE EAST

AFRICA

AUSTRALASIA

AUSTRALASIA

Australia, called *Terra Incognita* (meanding "unknown land"), and New Zealand were first visited by Dutch sailors in the 1600s. However, life for the Aborigines, Maoris, and Polynesians carried on undisturbed. This relatively isolated part of the world was still untouched by Europeans or Asians.

AFRICA

Africa lost much of its population through the slave trade, though its chiefs gained in wealth as a result, and new trading nations grew, such as Ashanti and Congo. European settlers moved into South Africa, and trade with Europe, particularly in West Africa, increased.

MIDDLE EAST

The Ottomans and the Safavids in Persia continued to dominate the Middle East, though both were now past their peak. The Ottoman Empire was beginning a very long, slow decline, which was to be gradually worn away from the inside as well as the outside. The Persians thrived on contact with India and Asia, but had little to do with Europeans.

JAPAN IN ISOLATION 1603–1716

The Tokugawa shoguns brought stability to Japan after years of chaos. Fearing disruptive influences from foreigners, they sealed Japan from the outside world.

Shinto religious traditions remained strong under the Tokugawas, but the role of the temples in politics and the economy was reduced.

In 1603, Tokugawa Ieyasu (1543–1616), head of a powerful family, became shogun—largely by political maneuvering and military force. Edo (later renamed Tokyo), the small fishing village that had been his headquarters, became his capital. Here, Ieyasu began to build what became the world's largest castle. He retired in 1605, and made his son Hidetada shogun. But Ieyasu continued to control the government until his death.

Ieyasu thought that there were two threats to Japan: the violent rivalry between *daimyos* (lords) that had caused great instability, and the growing foreign influence. He placed the daimyos under constant watch in Edo and kept them so busy organizing—and paying for—the building of the palace there, that they had no time to make trouble and no money for soldiers.

Japan is a fertile and well-populated country, with many valleys and plains separated by mountains. These geographical extremes made it difficult to unify during this period.

Hokkaido
JAPAN
Honshu
Edo
Kyoto
Nagasaki
Deshima

When the foreign missionaries and traders began to involve themselves in Japanese politics, Ieyasu realized that their ideas could lead to more violence. For the sake of harmony, the shogun placed restrictions on them. The strongest Christian influence was in Nagasaki. In 1638, after a revolt there, the shogun had 37,000 converts killed, and banned Christianity.

▲ There were important technical and cultural advances in Japan during this time. However, because of Japan's "closed door" policy to foreigners, these advances were not seen by the outside world. These exquisite Japanese porcelain figures date from this period.

▶ Nijo Castle in Kyoto was built in the 1600s for the Tokugawa Bakufu, the ambassador to the emperor. Even though the emperor was by now largely powerless, it was still important for the shogun to remain on friendly terms with him.

JAPAN BECOMES PROSPEROUS

Following the rebellion by Japanese Christians in Nagasaki, only a few Dutch and Chinese traders were allowed into Japan. Japanese people were not allowed to go abroad, and those who lived away from the country were not allowed to return. Christian priests were ordered to leave or be killed, and their churches were torn down. Japanese Christians were executed. Life became strictly regulated, and the country was sealed off from outside influences. Tokugawa rule gave Japan almost 250 years of peace.

Japan grew more prosperous because it now operated as one country. Merchants and farmers were encouraged to expand their businesses, and traditional *daimyos* and samurai warriors lost their positions and grew poor. Like Europe, Japan was changing from a feudal society into a trading economy. Cities and towns grew larger, and the population expanded greatly during the 1600s and 1700s. Though Japanese society still kept its strict rules of behavior, people were becoming better educated.

There were temporary setbacks to Japan's growth during this period. In 1684, the fifth Tokugawa shogun, Tsunayoshi, introduced some reforms inspired by Buddhist scholars of the 1100s. They were not popular. In 1703, the capital, Edo (Tokyo), was destroyed by an earthquake and fire. However, in 1716, a reforming shogun, Yoshimune, came to power and Japan's isolation from the rest of the world began to break down.

▲ The Tosho-gu Temple at Nikko, built during the 1600s, was dedicated to Ieyasu, who, after his death, was looked on as a saint.

◀ Sumo wrestling began in 1624. It was encouraged as an alternative to samurai warriors killing each other. Wrestlers were selected when young. They trained for many years.

◀ The Dutch were permitted to occupy the island of Deshima in Nagasaki Bay as a trading base. A few ships were allowed to visit each year, exchanging foreign goods for Japanese silks and other products. The Dutch were not allowed to cross onto the Japanese mainland.

KEY DATES

1603 Ieyasu founds the Tokugawa Shogunate
1609 Small Dutch trading base established on the island of Deshima in Nagasaki Bay
1612 Persecution of Nagasaki Christians begins
1637 Portuguese traders banned and expelled
1637–38 The Shimabara Rebellion in Nagasaki
1684 Hardship after Tokugawa Tsunayoshi's reforms
1703 Edo (Tokyo) destroyed by earthquake and fire
1716 Yoshimune, a reformer, comes to power

THE STUARTS 1603–1649

The Stuart dynasty came from Scotland. In England, they faced a complicated political situation that led to six years of civil war and the downfall of a king.

Apparently, James I (1566–1625) stammered and dribbled. But he was an intelligent king who did his best in a difficult situation, and during his time, England and Scotland moved closer to being united. He was not popular. He believed in divine right, which claimed that a ruler could do as he wished and was responsible only to God.

Queen Elizabeth I, the last Tudor monarch of England, died in 1603 without an heir. James VI of Scotland, son of Mary, Queen of Scots, succeeded her as James I of England. James was descended from Henry VIII's sister and Elizabeth's aunt, Margaret Tudor, who had married the Scottish king, James IV, in 1503. His family, the Stuarts, had ruled Scotland since 1371.

England and Scotland now had the same king, but they still remained separate countries. James dreamed of uniting them, but many English and Scottish people were opposed to this. He tried to make peace between Catholics, Anglicans, and Puritans. The Puritans were extreme Protestants who wished to abolish church ceremony and music, bishops, church hierarchies, and other "popish" traditions. James angered them by refusing to go as far as they wanted. But he ordered a new translation of the Bible, the King James Bible, to try to bring Christians together.

As England's prosperity grew under Tudor and Stuart rule, many towns were renewed. They were not planned, but rebuilt along existing winding streets.

JAMES THE SPENDER

James made peace with Catholic Spain to try and ease tensions between European Catholics and Protestants, and Britain was at peace for 20 years. But in 1624 James was drawn into the Thirty Years' War in Germany on the Protestant side, supporting his son-in-law, Frederick. James fell deeply into debt. The cost of running the country was growing and James himself was a lavish spender. He believed Parliament should obey him without question and grant whatever he asked for. But Parliament and the king's ministers had grown stronger in Tudor times, and he clashed with them when his demands for money were refused.

THE GUNPOWDER PLOT

Catholics in England were frustrated by Protestant intolerance toward them, and, although James I tried to please everyone, opinions pulled in conflicting directions. Some Catholics saw violence as the only way to gain toleration for Catholicism, though many disliked this idea. A small group plotted to kill both the king and parliamentarians by blowing up Parliament during its ceremonial opening on November 5, 1605. One of the conspirators was Guy Fawkes, who was discovered guarding barrels of gunpowder in the cellars of Parliament. He and the other plotters were arrested, tortured, and put to death. After this, attitudes toward Catholics hardened.

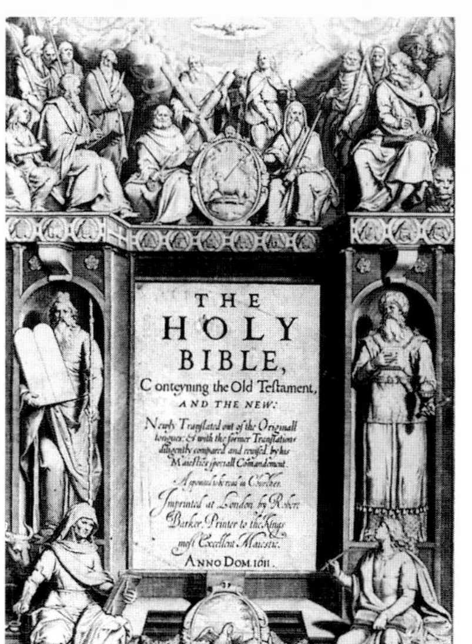
THE HOLY BIBLE, Conteyning the Old Testament, AND THE NEW: Newly Translated out of the Originall tongues: & with the former Translations diligently compared and revised, by his Maiesties speciall Comandement. Appointed to be read in Churches. Imprinted at London by Robert Barker, Printer to the Kings most Excellent Maiestie. ANNO DOM. 1611.

The King James Bible, or Authorized Version, published in 1611, was carefully translated under James I's guidance, in order to serve as the one Bible for Anglicans, Puritans, and Catholics. It was admired because of the beauty of its language, and has survived to this day. It is still used in some churches.

KEY DATES

1603	James I becomes king of England
1605	The Gunpowder Plot to blow up Parliament
1608	James disagrees with Parliament over money
1621	James again disagrees with Parliament
1625	Charles I becomes king
1629	Charles closes Parliament
1637	Charles's court splits after a crisis
1640	Charles recalls Parliament—clashes follow
1642	The English Civil War begins
1649	Charles I is executed by parliamentarians

CHARLES I

James I tried to please everyone. He was unpopular in England because he made mistakes, and because he was Scottish and his Danish wife, Anne, was Catholic. His belief in the rights of the king was also disliked. When he died in 1625, his son Charles became king and inherited his lack of popularity.

Charles I (1600–1649) also disliked parliamentary interference, and handled situations badly. People took sides and supported either the king or Parliament. This became a battle between traditional and modern ideas. When, in 1629, Parliament refused to give Charles more money and allow him to rule in his own way, he sent the parliamentarians home and tried to govern without them.

Charles ruled without Parliament for eleven years, but his court and ministers were divided over many important questions. Charles also angered the Scots, who thought he had become too English, and lost their support. Parliament, called back in 1640, united against him. It tried to limit his powers and suppress his supporters. In 1642, Charles tried to arrest five parliamentary leaders, but Parliament, including the nobility, opposed him fiercely.

Charles left London and raised an army. He was defeated in 1646, and handed power to Parliament, but he then escaped to continue the Civil War. Finally, Charles was recaptured, brought to trial, and executed in 1649. For 12 years following the English Civil War, England had no king.

▼ During Tudor and Stuart times, the wealthy gained more power and influence. However, disagreements increased between the different groups, especially over money, business, and religious matters.

THE THIRTY YEARS' WAR 1618–1648

The Thirty Years' War was the world's first modern war. Starting as a religious conflict between Catholics and Protestants, it ended as a fight for power in Europe.

Ferdinand II of Austria (1578–1637) was a Catholic. He tried to impose his religion on all his subjects.

Frederick (1596–1632), the "Winter King" of Bohemia, was the son-in-law of England's James I.

In 1618, tensions exploded in Bohemia between Catholics and Protestants, and between the Hapsburgs and other royal houses. Ferdinand II, the Holy Roman emperor, had inherited the Bohemian throne in 1617 and two years later, in 1619, the Austrian throne. Until that time, the Hapsburgs had been neutral in matters of religion. Bohemia had long been Protestant, but Ferdinand was Catholic, and he unwisely forced Bohemia to become Catholic. This resulted in the Bohemians revolting against him.

In 1619, the German rulers who elected the Holy Roman emperor met at Prague. They deposed Ferdinand II as king of Bohemia and made Frederick, a Protestant, king in his place. This resulted in a series of wars, fought mainly in Germany, which eventually involved most of Europe for the next thirty years.

At first, the Catholics won most of the battles, with Spanish Hapsburg help and money. In 1625, the Danes joined the Protestants, but to no avail. The Catholics had two outstanding generals, Count Wallenstein and Count Tilly, whose troops fought well, and by 1629, the Protestant allies were in trouble.

The use of guns and cannons increased the destruction and cost of the war. The matchlock musket was improved by the Swedes to make it lighter and faster to reload.

SWEDEN ENTERS THE WAR

Frederick fled and a Catholic prince, Maximilian of Bavaria, was appointed king of Bohemia. The struggle then moved northward. Led by Wallenstein, the emperor's army defeated the Danes and overran northern Germany. It seemed that nothing could stop Ferdinand from forcing Germany to become Catholic until, in 1630, Protestant Gustavus Adolphus of Sweden entered the war. He took back northern Germany, soundly defeating the Catholics in battles at Breitenfeld and Lützen. But the battles took their toll. Tilly was killed at Breitenfeld, and Gustavus Adolphus died at Lützen.

THE DEFENESTRATION OF PRAGUE

In Prague, in 1618, a group of Bohemian Protestant nobles met with representatives of the Catholic Hapsburg emperor. Their arguments became so heated that the Bohemians threw the emperor's men out of a window—in other words, defenestrated them—of Hradcany Castle, the Hapsburg stronghold. This violent action is known as the "Defenestration of Prague" and sparked the Thirty Years' War.

The French entered the war in 1635, a year after the Swedes were beaten at Nördlingen. The French minister Cardinal Richelieu already supported the Protestants because he opposed the ambitious Hapsburgs. The same year, the German Protestant princes withdrew from the war, bankrupt and defeated. Many alliances switched, and the conflict grew even more complicated. The French advanced into Catholic Bavaria to overcome the Spanish Hapsburgs and Sweden defeated the Austrian Hapsburgs. When the French and Swedes were poised to take over Bavaria and threaten Austria, the Hapsburg emperor asked for peace.

▲ One of the worst events of the Thirty Years' War was the destruction of the German city of Magdeburg by the Catholics under Count Tilly in 1631. Until then, Tilly had been highly respected across Europe.

THE RESULTS OF THE WAR

During this long war, large guns and mercenary troops had been used. This had been expensive and caused great devastation. Troops looted whole areas of Germany and at times even switched sides. Germany was ruined, and the Netherlands and Switzerland gained independence; however, France, Sweden, and Holland grew stronger. Some states gained land and others lost it. One German state, Brandenburg–Prussia, grew stronger and was to become even more important. The Hapsburgs lost their power, and the Holy Roman Empire grew weaker. Germany broke down into 300 small states. Many European governments became secular, which meant that they no longer forced religious beliefs on their subjects. The Peace of Westphalia, which ended the war, was the first major European treaty of modern times.

▶ The Catholic Count Albrecht Wallenstein (1583–1634) was an outstanding general. He became rich from the war, and tried to build his own empire in northern Germany. This made him very unpopular with the emperor, and eventually led to his downfall.

▼ Wallenstein and his men were murdered at Eger in Germany in 1634, when it was discovered that he was using the war as a way of creating power for himself.

KEY DATES

1618–20 Bohemian revolt against Austria
1625–27 Denmark joins the Protestants
1629 Protestant Germans losing the war
1630 Gustavus Adolphus of Sweden joins the war, overrunning northern Germany
1631 Tilly storms and destroys Magdeburg
1631–32 Protestant victories at Breitenfeld and Lützen
1634 Protestants are defeated at Nördlingen. Count Wallenstein is murdered
1635 Protestant Germans make peace—France joins the war
1645 French and Swedish victories in Germany
1648 The Peace of Westphalia treaty ends the war

FRANCE AND RICHELIEU 1624–1661

Louis XIII became king at the age of nine. He later appointed as his chief minister the man who was to make France the leading nation in Europe.

Marie de Médicis (1573–1642) was queen of France, then regent to her son Louis XIII. She clung to power, but was banished in 1617. Richelieu helped her make peace with her son in 1620. But when she tried to replace Louis in 1630, she was permanently exiled to Brussels.

In 1624, Louis XIII of France appointed Cardinal Richelieu as his chief minister. They worked together for eighteen years. Richelieu's ambition was to unify France into one centrally ruled country and make it great. Regional dukes held a lot of power, so he set out to reduce their influence. In 1628, he also dealt harshly with the troublesome French Protestant Huguenots. Richelieu was disliked by Catholic leaders, nobles, and judges because he stopped many of their privileges, and the high taxes he levied caused mass revolts. He believed in strong control, and used force to get his way.

The clothing of the French nobility was elaborate. Wigs, hats, and clothes were a sign of status. This was a French army officer's clothing when on campaign.

Abroad, Austria and Spain were the main threats to France. The Hapsburgs ruled both countries and, if they joined forces, France would be vulnerable. By 1631, during the Thirty Years' War, Hapsburg Austria controlled most of Germany and threatened to dominate Europe.

Louis XIII (1601-1643) was the son of Henry IV and the second king of the Bourbon line. He became king as a boy in 1610 and assumed power in 1617. He was very influenced by Cardinal Richelieu, but he outlasted Richelieu by one year, and left the throne to his young son, Louis XIV.

CARDINAL RICHELIEU

Armand du Plessis, the Duke of Richelieu (1585–1642), became a bishop in 1607 and a cardinal in 1622. He entered the council of the regent, Marie de Médicis, in 1616, and became chief minister in 1624. Richelieu believed in absolutism—the right of the king to do what he wanted. He believed the king was responsible to God, not to the Church, the nobility, or the people. Richelieu used spies effectively and suppressed all opposition. He trained his successor, Cardinal Mazarin, who continued Richelieu's policies and ruled as regent for the young Louis XIV until 1661. In many European countries, this was a time when chief ministers were very powerful.

La Rochelle was the stronghold of the Protestant Huguenots, who had developed their own army and navy. Richelieu besieged the port in 1628 and broke their power. In this painting, Louis XIII is depicted visiting the scene of the siege in October of that year.

FRANCE BECOMES STRONGER

To weaken Austria, Richelieu paid Sweden, the Netherlands, and Denmark to fight a common enemy, the Hapsburgs. In 1635, France declared war on Spain (which ruled Belgium and Burgundy). The fighting went on until 1648 and outlasted Richelieu, but his plans succeeded. He tried to extend France to what he thought were its natural frontiers—the Pyrenees in the southwest and the Rhine in the east.

When Richelieu died in 1642, his follower Cardinal Mazarin continued his policies. France replaced Spain as Europe's greatest power. A revolt by the French nobility, called the Fronde, was put down in 1653. When Louis XIV came to the throne he was only five, and Mazarin ruled as regent. By the end of Mazarin's life, in 1661, France had changed greatly. It had grown larger, stronger, and richer; its armies had become the finest in Europe, and Louis XIV was to be its greatest king.

▶ The royal flag of the ruling Bourbon kings of France acted as the French flag until 1790, the time of the French Revolution.

▼ Richelieu allowed the Protestant Huguenots religious freedom, but he fought to break their political and military power. This grisly massacre of Huguenots was initiated by Richelieu.

EAST INDIA COMPANIES 1600–1700

The East India Companies were powerful trading organizations set up by the English, Dutch, and French to protect their business interests in southeastern Asia.

The ships of the East India Companies, first used for trading, were also converted into warships for use against pirates, Asians, and ships from other companies.

In 1600, the English East India Company was formed in London. Its purpose was to unite the English traders doing business in southeastern Asia. There was cut-throat competition for trade in this area which had first been controlled by the Spaniards and the Portuguese. During the 1600s, the contest for this lucrative trade with the East was between the Dutch, English, and French.

The Netherlands followed England and set up a Dutch East India Company in 1602, with its headquarters in Amsterdam and also at Batavia (Jakarta) on the island of Java. The French formed their own East India company later, in 1664.

These organizations became immensely powerful. Trading was only one of their activities—they also had a political influence. They armed their ships to fight at sea and maintained private armies. The East India companies set up military as well as trading bases and made treaties with local rulers around them. They waged war on neighboring nations and on each other. In many ways they behaved like independent states.

In the 1600s, many European travelers visited India. Through them, knowledge of the impressive history and culture of India began to reach Europe.

The English lost the contest to control the spice trade in the East Indies to the Dutch. India then became the center of English activities, and by 1700, they had sole trading rights in India, with a number of key ports, notably Calcutta, Madras, and Bombay. The Dutch had ports on the Cape in South Africa, in Persia, Ceylon, Malaya, and Japan, and also dominated the Spice Islands (now Indonesia). The French were less successful in their attempt to dominate India. Many private fortunes were made. Sailors and traders often died of disease or fighting. Some made homes in Asia, founding European centers in India, Southeast Asia, and China.

▲ In 1652, the Dutch founded a base at the Cape of Good Hope (Cape Town) as a staging post for ships on the long voyage from Europe to the Far East. This later became a Dutch colony.

▶ The English colony of Madras was a major port for exporting cotton goods. It was also the center of a region noted for making cloth with brightly colored designs and scenes from Indian life.

THE DUTCH EMPIRE 1660–1664

The Dutch Empire was founded on worldwide trade. During the 1600s, their huge merchant fleet helped the Dutch to become a powerful trading nation.

▲ Peter Stuyvesant (c.1610–1672) was the harsh governor of the New Netherland colony in North America from 1647 to 1664. He was against religious freedom. He was hated both by the Native Americans and the colonists. In 1664, they surrendered without a fight to a small English fleet.

By 1600, Amsterdam was Europe's busiest port, with warehouses, banks, and trading houses, as well as a large fleet of ships. Frustrated by their exclusion from South America by the Spanish and Portuguese, the Dutch headed for the Far East. They founded an East India Company for their traders. They took control of trade from the Spice Islands or "East Indies," seizing Java and the Moluccas from the Portuguese.

The Dutch East India Company established its headquarters at Batavia (Jakarta) on the island of Java (now part of Indonesia) in 1619. The company maintained an army and a powerful fleet of ships that drove the English and the Portuguese out of the East Indies and seized Ceylon, the port of Malacca, and several ports in India. The company even set up a trading post in Japan—the only Europeans allowed to do so.

In 1652, the Dutch occupied the Cape of Good Hope on the southern tip of Africa, as a midway point on the long journey from the Far East to Europe. From there, Dutch ships were able to take the shortest route to the East Indies, straight across the Indian Ocean.

Amsterdam was the center of European banking in the 1600s. A bank was founded there in 1609 that deposited and loaned money to finance trade.

EXPANSION AND CONTRACTION

The huge merchant fleet of the Netherlands was also busy elsewhere. In 1621, the Dutch West India Company was founded across the Atlantic. By 1623, 800 Dutch ships were engaged in the Caribbean, trading in sugar, tobacco, animal hides, and slaves. The company established a colony in Guiana, and they captured Curaçao. For a while, they controlled northeastern Brazil.

In North America, the company founded the colony of New Netherland along the Hudson River in 1624. From there they exported furs, timber, and other goods bought from Native Americans.

Eventually, the Dutch lost their naval supremacy to the English and their empire suffered. They lost Ceylon, Malacca, and the Cape to the English, and were left with just their Southeast Asian empire.

▼ The Dutch Adrian Reland made this folding map of Java around 1715. Java had been ruled by many different local rulers until the Dutch East India Company took control in 1619. Java remained a Dutch colony until 1949.

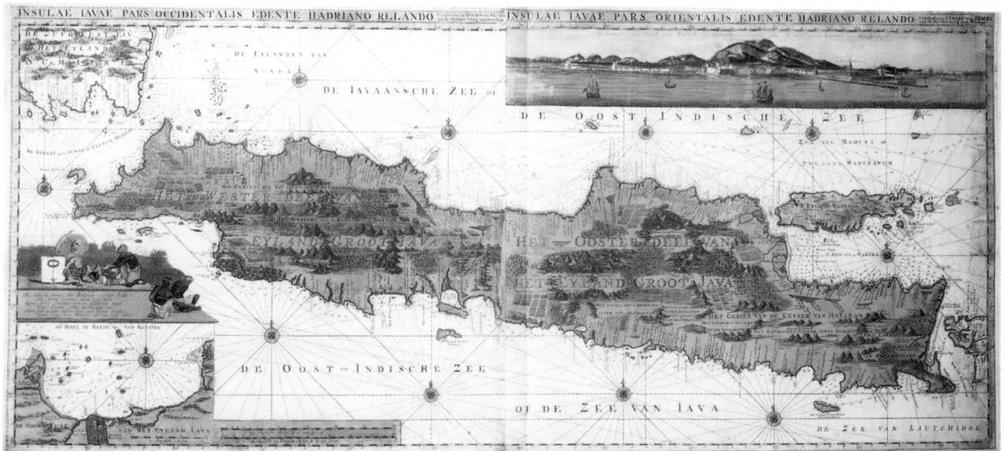

ENGLISH CIVIL WAR 1642–1660

The English Civil War was fought between supporters of the king and supporters of Parliament. For five years the country was run by a dictator, Oliver Cromwell.

Charles I (1600–1649) came to the throne of England in 1625, the same year that he married Henrietta Maria of France. His belief in the divine right of the king first led to clashes with Parliament and eventually to the English Civil War.

▲ Oliver Cromwell (1599–1658) went to college in Cambridge and studied law in London. He was first elected to Parliament in 1628, representing Cambridge. He recruited and trained Parliament's New Model Army. He was a strict Puritan and believed that God had chosen him to perform His will.

The English Civil War was fought between supporters of King Charles I and supporters of Parliament. Like his father, James I, Charles believed in divine right, claiming that his right to rule came directly from God. This belief put Charles at odds with Parliament.

Charles became king in 1625 and immediately began to quarrel with Parliament over his right to imprison people who opposed him over religion, and taxes. In 1629, he dissolved Parliament, and, for 11 years, tried to rule alone.

In 1637, Charles attempted to impose the Anglican form of public worship on the Scots. The Presbyterian Scots rebelled, raising an army that, in 1640, occupied part of northern England. Charles recalled Parliament to ask for money to put down the rebellion by the Scots, but Parliament demanded reforms. Civil war broke out after Charles tried to arrest his five leading parliamentary opponents. In 1642, fighting broke out all over the country between Royalists (supporters of the king), known as Cavaliers, and supporters of Parliament, known as Roundheads.

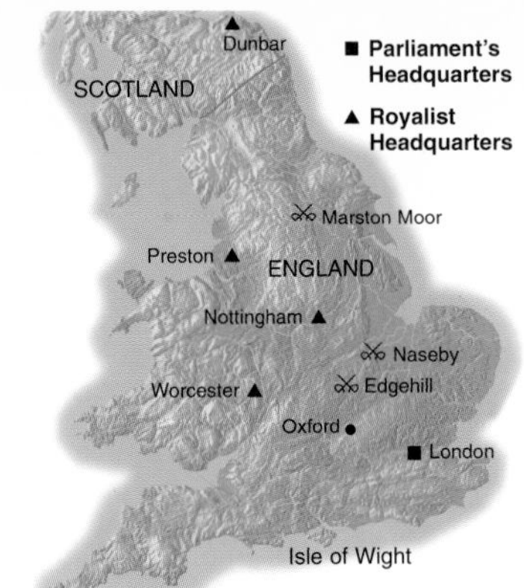

During the Civil War, the west and north generally supported the king, and the south and east supported Parliament, though there were local divisions across the country. The first major battle took place at Edgehill in 1642; the last at Worcester in 1651.

The king made Oxford his capital, and his forces at first held the advantage. However, Parliament secured the support of the Scottish army, and in the long run, proved superior, for it had the money to maintain a professional army. This New Model Army led by Sir Thomas Fairfax decisively defeated Charles's forces at Naseby in 1645. The king surrendered in 1646, after Oxford fell to the Roundheads.

▶ The king's Cavalier forces were crushingly defeated by the New Model Army of the Roundheads at the battle of Naseby in 1645. This was the decisive victory for Parliamentary forces during the English Civil War.

Charles was imprisoned on the Isle of Wight, where he plotted to start the war again with Scottish help. A second phase of fighting broke out, with Royalist risings and a failed invasion attempt by the Scots. In 1648, parliamentarians who still respected the king were removed from Parliament by Oliver Cromwell. The remaining Rump Parliament, as it was called, found Charles guilty of treason and executed him in 1649.

OLIVER CROMWELL

After Charles' execution, Parliament abolished the monarchy, and England became a Commonwealth. Parliament governed the country, but had an ongoing struggle with the army. In 1653, Oliver Cromwell emerged as a strong leader and ruled the country as Lord Protector. Cromwell clashed with some parliamentarians and was forced to govern with the help of army generals. He fought a war with the Dutch over trade and control of the seas, took control of Ireland, and planned colonial expansion.

His dictatorship was not universally popular because of his use of force and high taxes he imposed. But he introduced education reforms and gave more equality to the people. In 1658, Cromwell died and was succeeded by his son Richard. He was not an effective ruler and the army removed him. The English people wanted a king again, and in 1660, the son of Charles I took the throne as Charles II.

THE TRIAL OF CHARLES I

Charles was unpopular because he married a Catholic. He also imposed high taxes to pay for wars that people did not want, as well as trying to limit the powers of Parliament—he dissolved it for 11 years. At his trial and execution, he behaved with great dignity, and this won him some sympathy. At his execution, Charles put on an extra shirt so that people would not think that, when he shivered from the cold, he was shivering with fear. His body was secretly buried by his supporters at Windsor Castle.

◀ The seal of the House of Commons depicts the Commonwealth Parliament in session in 1651.

▼ Shortly after the end of the Civil War, there were two disasters in London. The first was the Great Plague, which arrived from Europe, and killed about 20 percent of London's population in 1665. Then, in 1666, the Great Fire destroyed most of the city.

CHINA: THE QING DYNASTY 1644–1770

The Qing dynasty was founded by the Manchus, a Siberian people who lived in Manchuria. The Qing dynasty would rule China from 1644 to 1911.

This intricate gold flower-shaped brooch was made during the Manchu period and was exported to Europe.

▼ The grand houses and ornamental gardens of the upper-class Qing Chinese are depicted on this ebony paneled Coromandel screen, made in 1672. Such screens could have up to 12 panels and were shipped to Europe from the Coromandel coast in India.

The Ming dynasty of emperors had ruled China since 1368. But heavy taxation had made their rule unpopular and rebellions broke out all over the country. The last Ming emperor, Chongzhen, hanged himself as peasant rebels overran his capital, Beijing. In the confusion that followed, the Manchu chieftain Dorgon led an army south from Manchuria. He occupied Beijing and set up the Qing ("pure") dynasty. His nephew Shunzhi was the first Qing emperor.

Resistance to the Manchus continued in China's southern provinces, and 40 years went by before all of China submitted to their rule. The Manchus lived separately from the Chinese in closed-off areas. Marriage between Chinese and Manchus was forbidden. Chinese men were even compelled to wear their long hair in *queues* (pigtails) to show that they were inferior to the Manchus.

The Manchus came to conquer China from lands lying north of the Great Wall. During the Manchu period, the size and population of China grew, and the troublesome Mongols were finally defeated.

However, both Chinese and Manchus were employed as civil servants to run the empire. As time passed, the Manchus adopted Chinese customs and were eventually accepted. They were few in number, so they had to be careful not to be too excessive in their treatment of the Chinese. They brought new life and efficiency to the country without disturbing the nation's customs.

A RICH AND POWERFUL EMPIRE

At first China prospered under Qing rule. The empire grew and trade increased, particularly with Europe. Chinese silk and porcelain were considered the finest in the world, and their cotton goods were inexpensive and of high quality. Huge quantities of Chinese tea were sold abroad when tea drinking became fashionable in Europe in the 1700s.

The empire became so rich and powerful that its rulers were able to treat the rest of the world with contempt. Under Emperor Kangxi's rule (1661–1722), foreign traders were forced to kneel whenever his commands were read out. The Manchus also forced several nations into vassal status, including Tibet, Annam (now Vietnam), Burma, Mongolia, and Turkestan, making the Chinese Empire the world's largest at the time. They made a deal with the Russians over land and trade.

Early on, there were some rebellions in southeast China and among ethnic minorities, who protested against Chinese people moving into their areas. But, on the whole, the Qing period brought peace, prosperity, and security to China. The population grew dramatically from 100 million in 1650 to 300 million in 1800, and Chinese (Han) people spread out to the west and southwest of China. In the late 1700s, however, corruption and decline began to set in.

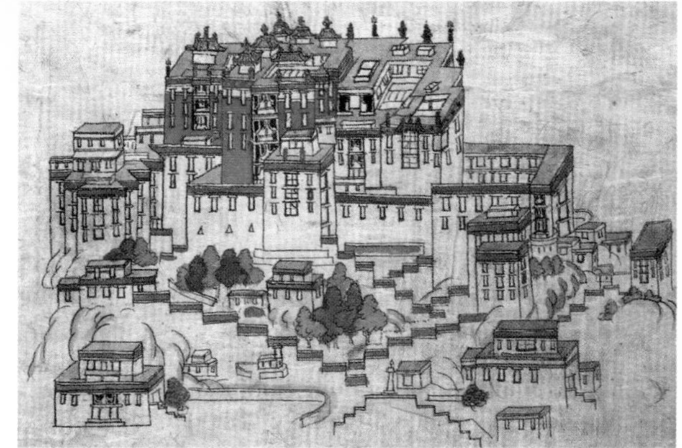

▲ Tibet (Xizang) was ruled by a Buddhist leader called the Dalai Lama. The third Dalai Lama rebuilt the Potala monastery in Lhasa, the capital, as his residence in 1645. The Dalai Lamas came under the influence of the Mongols, but the Qing army invaded and by the mid-1700s, Tibet was part of the Chinese Empire.

◀ This enameled porcelain vessel from the late 1600s imitated the shape and design of the bronze ritual vessels of ancient Shang China.

◀ The Chinese silk industry employed thousands of workers, especially women, to weave silk into cloth on looms. Silk cloth was made for use in China and for export to Europe. Cotton was also imported and then made into cloth for export. The weavers of the port of Su-Chou were particularly famous for their silks.

KEY DATES

1644 The Manchus found the Qing dynasty in Beijing
1644–60 Manchu forces conquer most of China
1661 The island of Formosa is captured from the Dutch by supporters of the defeated Ming; Kangxi becomes second Qing emperor
1674–81 Rebellions in the south, soon suppressed
1683 Manchu forces capture the island of Formosa from supporters of defeated Ming
1689 Russians swap Siberian land for trade in China
1696 The Manchus defeat the Mongols in Mongolia
1717–20 War against the Mongols for the control of Tibet
1750s Chinese invade Tibet and Turkestan
1760s Chinese invade Burma, making it a vassal state

THE OTTOMAN EMPIRE 1602–1783

After the reign of Süleyman the Magnificent, the Ottoman Empire entered a long and slow decline. Nevertheless, the empire survived until 1923.

In 1565, Süleyman the Magnificent decided to invade Malta, occupied at the time by the Crusader Knights of St. John. Although the Turks greatly outnumbered the Knights, their invasion was not successful, and they had to withdraw after several months. Süleyman died in 1566. In 1571, when the Ottomans tried to invade Venetian-ruled Cyprus, their invasion force was destroyed by a combined fleet from the navies of Venice, Spain, and the Papal States, at Lepanto off the coast of Greece. In 1602, a long and costly war broke out with Safavid Persia, with no gain. Plagues and economic crises also hit Istanbul. Once-profitable trade routes linking Asia, Africa, and Europe were bypassed as new sea routes around Africa and land routes through Siberia opened.

Sultan Osman II (1603–1622) ruled from 1618. He was young, strict, and fond of archery. He restricted the power of the Janissaries (senior army officers), but they took over, had him killed, and replaced him with Mustafa I.

THE EMPIRE FADES

The Thirty Years' War in Europe gave the Ottomans some peace. But when, in 1656, they tried to invade Crete, the Venetians blocked the Dardanelles (the narrow sea passage from the Mediterranean to the Black Sea), threatening Istanbul itself. This caused panic, and the sultan, Ibrahim, was deposed by army officers. A new grand vizier (chief minister), Mehmet Kuprili, took charge. He reformed the economy and army, and Ottoman fortunes revived.

The next vizier, Kara Mustafa, tried to invade Hapsburg Vienna for a second time in 1683. The defenders of Vienna held out for two months until an army of Germans and Poles arrived to defeat the Turks. The Austrians invaded Hungary, the Venetians took part of Greece, and the Russians threatened Azov in the Ukraine. Another vizier, Mustafa Kuprili, took office in 1690. He managed to drive back the Austrians, but he was killed in 1691. During the 1690s, the Ottomans finally lost Hungary and Azov. Their European empire was saved only because Austria went to war with France.

▲ Sultan Mustafa I (1591–1639) was mentally unstable. He ruled twice—between 1617–1618 and again between 1622–1623.

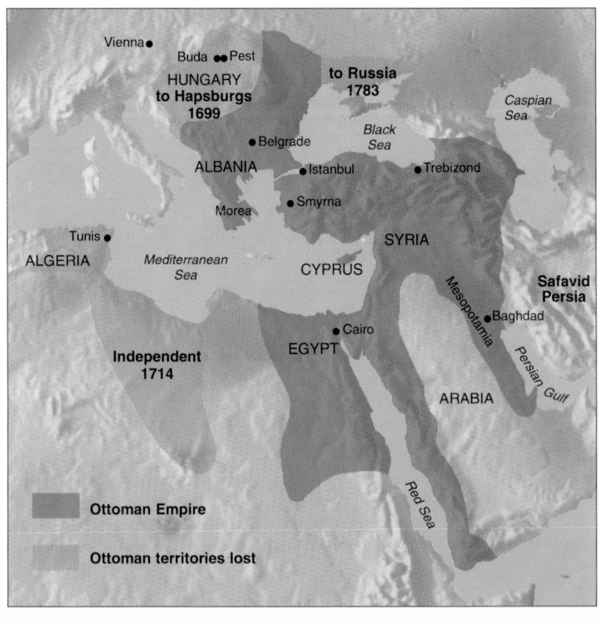

▶ The Ottoman Empire was still large, but it was slowly falling apart at the seams as its prosperity dwindled.

THE EMPIRE SHRINKS

Between 1710 and 1720, the Ottomans regained Azov and Greece, but they lost Serbia and parts of Armenia. They also lost control of most of northern Africa—Algeria, Tunisia, and Libya. Officially, these countries were still Ottoman, but were actually independent. In 1736, the Russians attacked again, and by 1783, they had taken the Crimea and most of the Ukraine—the Ottomans no longer controlled the Black Sea. In Anatolia, local chiefs were rebelling, and in Istanbul, people were worried about the future.

The Ottoman Empire was still strong, but it had lost much of its trade and wealth. The progress made in the early days of the Ottoman Empire in religion, the arts, and social advances, slowed. The Ottomans' only friends, the Moguls, were also in decline, while the Europeans were advancing rapidly. But the Ottoman Empire was not yet finished.

▶ A Turkish miniature, made in 1610, shows a festival of musicians called to entertain the sultan in Istanbul. To keep the sultans separate from politics and the people, they were looked after lavishly. The authority of the sultans was finally weakened by a series of bloody contests for power among the ruling families.

▼ The siege of Vienna in 1683 marked the farthest point of the Ottoman Turks' advance into Europe. The defenders of Vienna held out for two months, just long enough for a slow-moving army of Germans and Poles to arrive. The Turks were utterly defeated in a 15-hour battle on September 12, 1683.

SLAVERY AND PIRATES 1517–1810

The early development of many colonies in the Americas was carried out by pirates, the owners of sugar plantations, and millions of African slaves.

Within a hundred years of Columbus' landing in 1492, most of the native peoples of the Caribbean islands, the Arawaks and Caribs, were dead as a result of European mistreatment and diseases. By the early 1600s, the Caribbean was a battleground. The Spanish, French, English, and Dutch all fought for the islands they called the West Indies. Some islands changed hands several times in a fierce contest for trade and for land to establish European colonies.

West Africa was rich in gold. Arabs called the area "Guinea" and Europeans borrowed the word. In 1663, a guinea coin of Guinea gold was issued by order of Charles I.

English, French, and Dutch privateers became pirates to make their fortune. They were often sponsored by their governments, since they caused trouble for the Spanish, captured islands, established settlements, and made good profits. Some were later sent out as admirals or colonial governors. Francis Drake sailed around the world between 1577 and 1580, raided Spanish ships, and returned home rich. Captain Kidd was enlisted to help control pirates, but joined them instead. Edward Teach (Blackbeard) and Captain Morgan raided Spanish settlements and galleons in the Caribbean. They paved the way for the establishment of colonies. The Spanish lost gold to the pirates, but this did not stop them from colonizing the Americas.

Newly captured slaves were chained together by the neck or feet. Iron collars stopped the slaves from running away.

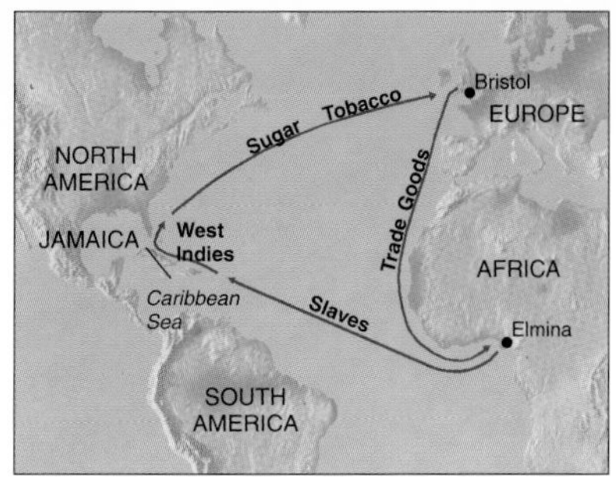

From ports such as Bristol, finished goods were shipped for sale in West Africa. Once the goods had been sold in Africa, the ship would be loaded with slaves to take to the West Indies. The final leg of the voyage would bringa cargo of sugar back to Europe.

THE SLAVE TRADE

In Europe, tea and coffee were becoming fashionable, and this led to a huge demand for sugar to sweeten them. Sugar grew well in the climate of the West Indies, but its cultivation needed many workers. Local labor could not be found, because many of the original islanders had died, and so the colonists imported slaves from West Africa.

Europeans saw nothing wrong with using Africans as slaves. They were bought cheaply, crammed into ships, and then sold to plantation owners. Two thirds of them died, either on the voyage or from disease, harsh treatment, and overwork. Even so, by 1800, there were nine million African slaves in the Americas.

▲ Iron manacles (handcuffs) that could not be opened without special tools were used to hold slaves' arms together.

▶ Whole families and villages of Africans were shipped to the Americas as slaves. Many did not survive the journey. West Africa, the Congo, and Angola lost much of their populations.

Slaves harvested the sugarcane on plantations in the Caribbean. Landowners grew wealthy. They often returned to Europe where they lived well, and left their plantations in the hands of managers.

▶ Long before Europeans arrived, the Arabs had traded slaves on the eastern African coast. When the Portuguese arrived they used the slaves in their colonial ventures.

THE TRIANGLE OF TRADE

The European-owned sugar plantations in the Caribbean were often very large. They had warehouses, boatyards, churches, slave quarters, and the landowner's grand house. A triangle of trade developed, taking finished goods from Europe to West Africa, slaves from West Africa to the Americas (the Middle Passage), and plantation products back to Europe. The profitable markets in Europe for sugar, tobacco, oils, and other products were exploited. Piracy, plantations, and slavery were driven by the urge for profit. Slavery continued into the 1800s. Most of today's African–Americans are the descendants of slave ancestors.

HENRY MORGAN

Welsh Captain Morgan (1635–1688), pirate, was the scourge of the Caribbean between the 1660s and 1680s. He organized fleets of buccaneers, attacked Spanish galleons in midocean, and seized their treasures. Much of the booty went to England, to reward investors who sponsored his voyages. He captured Porto Bello in 1668, sacked Maracaibo in 1669, and took Panama in 1671. Later, he was knighted for his services against the Spanish, and was made lieutenant governor of Jamaica in 1674. He died in 1688, aged 53. Buccaneers like Morgan helped England's economy to prosper.

AFRICAN STATES 1550–1700

In the 1600s, Africa was a patchwork of different peoples and kingdoms. Each had its own customs, form of government, language, and gods.

The West African kingdom of Benin is famous for its bronzes. This ram's head was made in the 1600s for a chief, who would have worn it on his belt.

During this period, the nations of Africa were developing rapidly. If the Europeans had not arrived, the African nations would probably have advanced their cultures much farther. Although Europeans did not have a great influence until the 1800s, they bought gold, exotic items, and slaves, and sold guns, cloth, tools, and finished goods. By doing so, traditional African trade and society were changed. Some areas, such as West Africa, lost many people to slavery. Social divisions increased as chieftains and traders made profitable deals with the Europeans. Some chiefs even sold their own people into slavery.

The largest African state was Songhay. European traders on the coast took the gold and slave trade away from Songhay, and its wealth collapsed. In 1591, a Moroccan army crossed the Sahara and invaded the country. South of the Sahara, new states had emerged, including Mossi, the city-states of Hausaland, and Kanem-Bornu, and Darfur. These Muslim states traded with the Ottomans and Arabs.

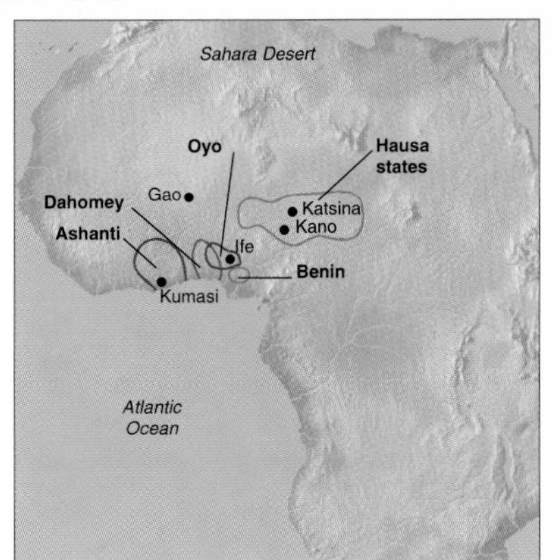

Gao, Katsina, and Kano adopted the Muslim faith, brought to West Africa across the Sahara by the Arabs. The coastal kingdoms kept their own religions. Much of northeast Africa was under Ottoman control.

In the east, Christian Ethiopia was surrounded by Muslim countries. Muslims in some parts of the country rebelled, ravaging Ethiopia. The Portuguese arrived and drove out the Muslims in 1543, and Ethiopia was left in peace. Along the east and west coasts, the Portuguese built forts and slave depots. These attracted Africans to the coasts and encouraged chiefs to grow rich by joining in the slave trade.

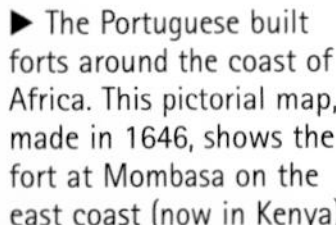

▲ This Ashanti helmet was decorated with gold animal horns and charms. Europeans were unable to buy slaves with gold from the Ashanti because they had all they needed. Instead they paid for them with guns that increased Ashanti military power.

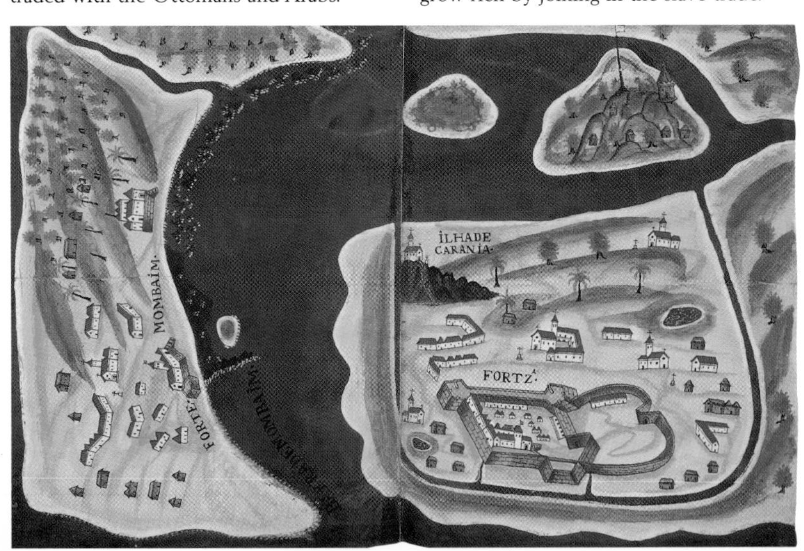

▶ The Portuguese built forts around the coast of Africa. This pictorial map, made in 1646, shows the fort at Mombasa on the east coast (now in Kenya).

DAHOMEY AND ASHANTI

A number of states occupied the forest zone along the west African coast. In 1625, a new kingdom called Allada was founded by King Akaba. Between 1645 and 1685, it merged with two other kingdoms to become Dahomey. This new state grew wealthy from the gold and slave trades. Dahomey was overrun in 1747 by Yorubas from Oyo (now in Nigeria). Dahomey became notorious to Europeans because, when its chief died, thousands of slaves were sacrificed so they could accompany him to the afterlife.

West of Dahomey lay Ashanti. In 1689, Osei Tutu founded the powerful Ashanti confederacy and built its capital at Kumasi. It grew wealthy from trade in cola nuts, gold, and slaves. The important Portuguese-controlled fort and trading post at Elmira in Ashanti was taken over by the Dutch in 1637.

Africa provided the slaves needed to work the rapidly growing plantations in the Americas. Millions were shipped across the Atlantic. Many died either during slave wars between African states to capture slaves or on the terrible voyage across the Atlantic ocean—the Middle Passage. To lose such an enormous number of its people was a catastrophe for Africa.

▲ A tribal celebration in the kingdom of Lovango in the Congo region in 1686. After the arrival of the Europeans, tribal security and unity gradually gave way to increased social distrust and control by greedy chiefs.

▶ A European trader offers brandy to the chief of the Alcaty tribe, in Senegal, West Africa, in exchange for water, around 1690.

KEY DATES

1570	Rise of Kanem-Bornu as a major nation
1575	Portuguese first settle in Angola
1588	The English Guinea Company is founded
1600	Mwenemutapa at its zenith
1625	New kingdom of Allada set up by King Akaba
1637	Dutch drive Portuguese from the Gold Coast
1652	Dutch East India Company founds Cape Town
1660s	Rise of Bambara kingdoms in West Africa
1685	Founding of Dahomey from three kingdoms
1689	Osei Tutu founds the Ashanti Empire
1701	Military expansion of Ashanti by Osei Tutu

◀ Here an *oba* (ruler) of Benin rides in a procession of his people. Once the richest state in West Africa, by 1700, the kingdom of Benin was on the wane. It was overwhelmed by the growing strength of the Yoruba people and the kingdom of Oyo.

IRELAND 1540–1800

English Protestant rule in Ireland was finally and forcibly imposed during the 1600s. There was resistance, but this was brutally crushed by the English.

The Irish never liked English rule. Henry II of England had conquered most of Ireland in 1171, and for the next 400 years English monarchs had struggled to maintain their authority there. Relations became more strained as time passed. The problem was mainly religious. The Irish were Catholic and the English had become Protestant. Irish priests encouraged rebellion by teaching that the English were heretics with no rightful authority over Ireland. But the English took strong measures to keep the Irish under their control. They dissolved many old monasteries and sold the land to families who supported their rule. The Irish reacted with frequent revolts. In 1556, Mary I sent troops into central Ireland to forcibly remove some of the native Irish and give their land to English settlers.

▲ James Butler, the Duke of Ormonde (1610–1688), governed Ireland for Charles I of England.

PLANTATIONS AND REVOLT

The established hold of the English was further extended in 1580. English colonists were promised wealth and opportunity, and they quickly developed the land and new towns. But their colony was destroyed in 1598 by an Irish attack. A revolt broke out in Ulster, a purely Irish area, but was suppressed by 1603. The English started a plantation there, mostly with Puritan Scots settlers, strengthened by fortified towns such as Londonderry. Some Irish fought back, but many left. By the mid-1600s, the Catholics of Ulster were outnumbered by Protestants.

In 1642, an Irish uprising began, and thousands of Protestant settlers were killed. Engaged in the English Civil War, Cromwell did not tackle the uprising until 1649. He arrived with a large army and crushed the Irish with a brutality that has never been forgiven. Local people were moved to poor land in the west of the country, and English soldiers were given the land to settle. Catholics now owned less than half the land in Ireland.

▼ The town of Drogheda was beseiged in 1641 by Catholic Irish forces led by Sir Phelim O'Neill.

HARSH PROTESTANT RULE

Irish hopes were briefly raised when Catholic James II became king of England. His daughter married William of Orange from Holland, commander of a grand alliance of countries fighting France. William became king of England in 1688. James, the "Old Pretender" escaped to Ireland. Eventually James's army (the Jacobites) met William's at the battle of the Boyne in 1690, and William triumphed.

This series of events marked a turning point in Irish history. Harsh laws were introduced that banned Catholics from owning guns. They were also forbidden to be involved in politics, to hold land, to receive education, and even to own large horses. Catholics converting to the Protestant faith were given land taken from those that remained Catholic. Communities broke apart, with some Irish accepting their lot, others resisting, and yet more leaving the country. But, while the 1700s were relatively peaceful, new trouble was brewing. When Wolfe Tone led a rebellion in the 1790s, many Irish people were killed, a French invasion was fought off, and the rebellion cruelly crushed. However, the English were forced to realize that the Irish Catholics were there to stay.

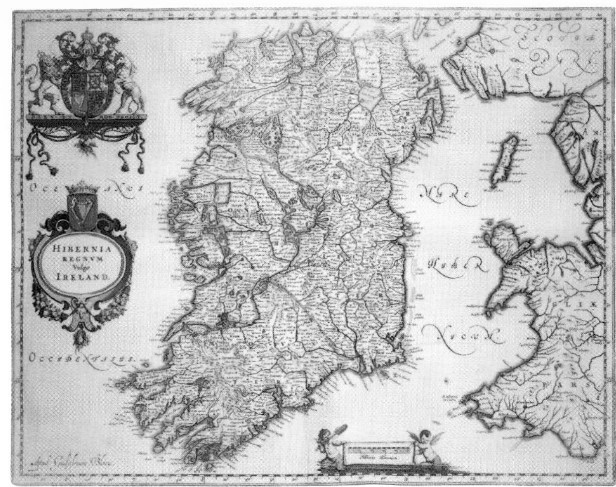

This map of Ireland was made by a Frenchman in 1635. Fourteen years later, Cromwell arrived with a large army and brutally suppressed an uprising against English rule. Many Irish people were moved to poor land in the west.

KEY DATES	
1556	Mary I starts Protestant plantations in Ireland
1580	Further plantation settlements established
1598	Revolts across Ireland, especially in Ulster
1642	Irish uprising against English control
1649	Cromwell's suppression of the Irish revolt
1690	Battle of the Boyne—a Protestant victory
1798	Wolfe Tone's nationalist rebellion

Being Catholic, James II was the great hope of the Irish Catholics. However, European power politics became caught up in the Irish question, and the English, under William III, had to defeat James.

THE BATTLE OF THE BOYNE

This decisive battle took place near Drogheda in 1690. The army of the recently deposed James II, last of the Stuart kings, was outnumbered by the Protestant army of William III. When William's troops crossed the Boyne River, James's troops fled. James went into exile in France, and William's rule in England was strengthened by the victory.

THE GREAT NORTHERN WAR 1700–1721

Following a war between Sweden and other northern European countries, Sweden lost most of its empire, and Russia became the leading power in the Baltic.

This painting shows King Charles XI of Sweden (1655–1697) and his family. The future Charles XII (1682-1718) is held by his mother, Queen Eleonora.

The Great Northern War was fought between Sweden and other northern European powers, led by Peter the Great of Russia. At stake was control of the Baltic Sea and the lands around it. In 1700, Sweden was attacked by Denmark, Saxony, Poland, and Russia. Sweden's Charles XII was only 18, and his enemies hoped to take advantage of his inexperience. But Charles proved to be a born leader. He defeated the Russians at Narva in Estonia, forcing Saxony, Poland, and Denmark out of the war and putting a new king on the Polish throne. Eight years later, Charles invaded Russia. But the bitter winter of 1708–1709 set in, and the Russians retreated, destroying everything as they went. The Swedes ran short of food, and struggled against repeated Russian attacks. By the spring, Charles's army was just half its original size.

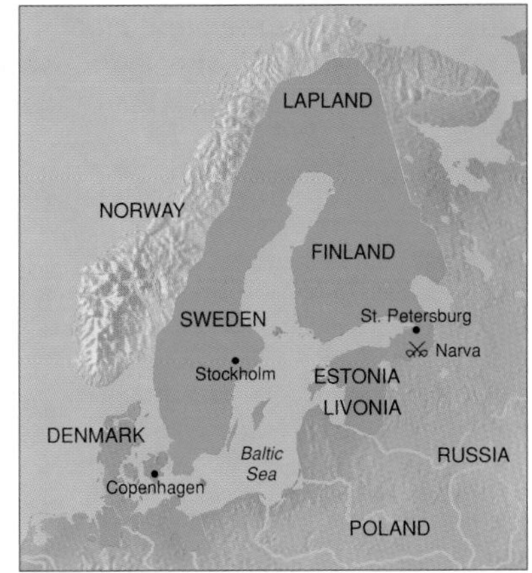

This map shows the Swedish Empire at its greatest extent in 1660. Sweden was the largest military power in northern Europe and was in an ideal position to invade Russia in 1708.

At the battle of Poltava in June 1709, the Russians beat the Swedes, and Charles fled to Turkey. He returned to Sweden in 1714, and beat off a Danish invasion in 1716. He invaded Norway and was killed there in 1718. Without Charles, and exhausted by 20 years of fighting, the Swedes agreed peace terms in 1721.

▲ This bronze plaque shows the taking of Narva in Estonia by the Swedes. During the battle, 40,000 Russian soldiers were crushingly defeated by an army of 8,000 Swedes. This was a tremendous victory for the young Charles XII of Sweden.

▶ The Battle of Poltava, near Kiev, in the Ukraine, in 1709, brought Sweden's power and dominance in the region to an end. Peter the Great's army was larger and better equipped, and the Swedes were tired, hungry, and far from home.

THE SPANISH SUCCESSION 1701–1713

When Charles II of Spain died in 1700 he left no heir. The question of who should succeed him led to the War of the Spanish Succession.

John Churchill, Duke of Marlborough (1650–1722), commander of the allied forces, won great battles at Blenheim, Ramillies, Oudenarde, and Malplaquet.

Prince Eugene of Savoy (1663–1736) fought the Turks at the siege of Vienna in 1683. By 1701, he had become commander-in-chief of the Austrian forces and fought at the battles of Blenheim and Oudenarde.

The French Bourbons and the Austrian Hapsburgs both claimed the Spanish throne. Before Charles II died in 1700, they had signed an agreement dividing his empire. But Charles's will left his lands to Philip of Anjou, the grandson of Louis XIV of France. Louis ignored his earlier agreement with the Hapsburgs, and chose to back Philip instead. But an alliance between France and Spain was not acceptable to every country in Europe.

By 1701, western Europe was at war. Organized by William III of England, England, the Netherlands, most German states, and Austria formed a grand alliance against France. In 1704, a French army was overwhelmed at Blenheim by a combined force under the Duke of Marlborough. He won three more victories over the French in the Spanish Netherlands. In 1706, an Austrian army under Prince Eugene of Savoy drove the French from Italy.

At the Treaty of Utrecht in 1713, France retained her frontiers. Austria took the Spanish Netherlands and Naples, England gained Gibraltar and Newfoundland. Philip V remained king of Spain.

The allies then invaded Spain, but the French forces pushed them out again, leaving Louis' grandson Philip V on the Spanish throne. The long war had exhausted both sides and, in 1713, a peace treaty was signed at Utrecht.

THE BATTLE OF BLENHEIM

In 1704, the Battle of Blenheim was fought in Bavaria among four armies and several nations. The French and Bavarians were marching on Vienna. The armies of Marlborough and Eugene intercepted them at Blenheim, and in the ensuing battle, 12,000 allies and 30,000 French and Bavarians were killed. However, it was a victory for Marlborough and Eugene, and Vienna was saved.

COLONIAL AMERICA 1600–1700

Settlers were arriving on the North American continent in large numbers. These European peoples shaped the character of future life in the "New World."

▲ William Penn (1644–1718) was a wealthy Quaker who founded Pennsylvania in 1681. He set out to welcome people who had suffered religious persecution and hardship.

The French and Spanish made up the majority of the early European settlers, but they were later overtaken by the English and Germans. The majority were Protestants who had suffered persecution. Within 20 years of the first Puritans arriving, there were 20,000 English people living in Massachusetts. The colony developed rapidly, with Boston as its capital. Some of these colonists preferred the land in Connecticut. Others founded Rhode Island because they disliked Puritan religious restrictions.

In 1625, at the mouth of the Hudson River, New York had started out as a Dutch colony. When the English took over in 1664, English, German, and a variety of other nationalities settled there. It soon grew into a large cosmopolitan city of traders and craftspeople. Farther down the coast in 1681, in repayment of a debt, the English king gave Pennsylvania to a group of Quakers led by William Penn. Penn was a religious idealist and dreamed of a "holy experiment"—a new society. He helped poor people from Europe settle in the colony. Many English, Scottish, Irish, and German settlers moved there to start a new life.

▼ The Quaker Society of Friends was founded in England in the mid-1600s. They were Puritans and disliked priestly control of the Church. Quakers, including women, were encouraged to preach and speak out.

Settlers worked hard to build a new life. This is a small family farm in Maryland (previously New Sweden). The family kept cattle, pigs, and chickens and grew wheat, vegetables, tobacco, and cotton.

Farther south, the Carolinas and Virginia grew in size after the English Civil War, when King Charles II granted land there to his royalist supporters. They established profitable plantations growing tobacco, cotton, rice, and indigo. The settlers imported slaves from Africa to work the land from 1619 onward. Soon the majority of the people were slaves.

The Puritans of New England had a high regard for education. In 1636, the Massachusetts government founded Harvard College in Cambridge.

PIONEERING SETTLERS

In the southwest, Spanish–Mexican pioneers pushed up into New Mexico, and built a capital at Santa Fe in 1609. This was a colony of forts, mines, and trading posts. With Florida also in their hands, the Spanish might have taken all of North America, but Spain lost its control over the seas and they missed their chance. The French had settled around the St. Lawrence, the Great Lakes, and the Mississippi. As colonists, traders, fur-trappers, and pioneers, they were few in number. By 1700, there were 12 English colonies along the Atlantic coast, with some 250,000 English compared to only 20,000 French. Germans, Dutch, Swedes, Lithuanians, Bohemians, and other nationalities all found homes in different areas. The new America was being built by hardworking, ordinary people rather than distant European governments.

NATIVE PEOPLES

At first, the Native Americans and European settlers both gained from mixing together and in some cases, coexisting peacefully. But as more settlers arrived, native lands were seized. There were several atrocities, and native distrust of and resistance to the settlers grew. Local conflicts arose, leading to war in the 1670s. The settlers won, and native resistance declined. Some native peoples were actively driven from their homelands. As European takeover became certain, a gradual tide of Indian migrations began.

▼ The first elected representatives of the colony of Virginia, together with its governor and council, met in 1619 at Jamestown to make the laws.

▼ Fur was an important commodity that the settlers exported to Europe. Here, two French fur traders meet Native Americans near Lake Superior.

SALEM WITCH TRIAL

In 1692, several young girls in the town of Salem, Massachusetts, claimed that they had been bewitched by a West Indian slave, named Tituba. Most people of the time believed in witchcraft and the Puritans of Salem took fright. This led to the trial and execution of 14 women and 6 men accused of witchcraft. Several people died in prison, and 150 more awaited trial. Eventually, the madness was stopped by the governor, William Phips, and by a respected Congregational preacher, Increase Mather.

REVOLUTION AND INDEPENDENCE

1708–1835

The 1700s are often called "the century of revolutions." Between 1708 and 1835, there were revolutions against governments and growing colonial power in many parts of the world—some were successful, some were not. Political revolutions happened because people were dissatisfied with the way their countries were run. There were also revolutions in farming techniques, and industry, in science, technology, and medicine, in transportation, and in the arts—especially literature.

▲ The Jacobite Rebellion against Hanoverian rule in England ended at the Battle of Culloden in 1746, when the Jacobites were defeated by English troops led by the king's son, the Duke of Cumberland.

◀ Generals Rochambeau and Washington give orders for the attack at the siege of Yorktown during the American Revolution in 1781.

The world at a glance 1708–1835

In North America, the United States won its independence from British rule, but this brought problems for the Native Americans. Many people emigrated from Europe and took up more and more land. In Mexico and South America, the colonies fought for freedom from Spain and Portugal and won.

In Europe, Prussia and Russia rose to become major European powers, while the French Revolution of 1789 marked the end of the monarchy in France.

In Africa, the Fulani, Zulu, and Buganda peoples established new kingdoms. African states in the north threw off Ottoman control. The Mogul Empire in India collapsed and Britain and France fought for control of its land. China conquered Tibet, but faced problems at home. Japan banned contact with the West. In the Pacific, the arrival of Europeans threatened the traditional way of life.

NORTH AMERICA

The 1700s saw the birth of the United States of America and of Canada. The American Revolution had been caused by bad British colonial government. The United States became the world's first democratic, constitutionally ruled country, with a declaration of rights embracing everyone (except Native Americans and slaves). A declaration of independence was made, and after a while, the new republic began to spread its wings westward, reaching toward the Pacific Ocean. Migrants from war-torn Europe, seeking a new future, swelled the population. American towns, trade, and culture took shape and grew larger and richer. The British held on to Canada, which eventually gained greater control of its own affairs. Meanwhile, many Native Americans in the East were thrown off their lands, and made to migrate westward. In the South, slaves worked the cotton and tobacco plantations, catering for the appetites of Europe and fueling the wealth of their landowning masters.

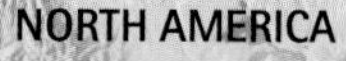

LATIN AMERICA

LATIN AMERICA

The Napoleonic Wars in Europe forced Latin Americans to think for themselves, and in the early 1800s, new independence movements fought against the Spanish and Portuguese for control of their colonies. The riches of the mines and slave-run plantations had declined in importance, and Latin Americans now had to fight for a place in a fast-changing world. But the independence movements were run by the landowners, so there was little gain for ordinary people. Native peoples suffered greatly under the rule of Europeans.

EUROPE

For much of the 1700s, a gap was developing in European society. Wealthy, autocratic rulers lived in great palaces, while the growing middle classes with "new money" developed a different, forward-thinking outlook. Society changed greatly. Cities grew, bankers and inventors were busy, foreign goods and ideas arrived. New inventions enabled factories to start making manufactured goods in large quantities. During the Napoleonic Wars, the old order was swept away across much of Europe, and the rule of law and business grew stronger. Russia expanded into the Far East, knocking on China's door. Europe now dominated the world, mainly as a result of trade, industry, bravado, and cannons, and its influence was still growing.

ASIA

During this time, India was slowly taken over by the British. China resisted such changes, growing conservative and refusing to entertain new ideas and foreign contact. Japan was still isolated, yet modernizing faster than China. Other Asian countries found themselves with both new friends and new enemies in the Europeans, who meddled in their affairs—always to their own advantage. Rivalry between Russia, China, and Britain for control of central Asia grew stronger. Asian traditions and stability were being undermined, and if Asian rulers resisted, the Europeans came in the back door.

EUROPE

ASIA

MIDDLE EAST

AFRICA

AUSTRALASIA

Following the explorations of Captain Cook, Australia and New Zealand became targets for British colonization. Settlers started arriving in the early 1800. The Maoris, who were warriors, fought back, but the Aborigines of Australia, who lived simpler lives, were easily controlled

AFRICA

Though Europeans and Arabs controlled a few coastal colonies, many African nations were now strong. However, their power came from trade with Europeans. Some tribes dominated others, and some, such as the Zulus and Ashanti, were aggressive toward their neighbors. African disunity made it easier for Europeans to turn one nation against another.

MIDDLE EAST

The Middle East was weak at this time because of the decline of the Ottomans. In North Africa and Egypt, Ottoman control was lost. Persia remained stable, largely unaffected by outside influences.

AUSTRIA AND PRUSSIA 1711–1786

The Austrian Empire was by now passing its peak, and Brandenburg–Prussia was growing stronger. They both sought to dominate the other states of Germany.

Maria Theresa (1717–1780) was Hapsburg empress from 1740. She slowly improved conditions in the Austrian Empire with the help of well-chosen ministers, and reformed local government, education, and the army.

Frederick the Great (1712-1786) became King of Prussia in 1740. He was stern, brave, and ambitious. Under his leadership, Prussia became a strong nation. He established religious tolerance in Prussia and freed his serfs. But many men died as a result of the wars he entered.

Charles VI, Archduke of Austria, became Holy Roman Emperor in 1711. This made him the most powerful man in Europe, and added the lands of the Holy Roman Empire to Austrian territory. After he died in 1740, three men claimed that they, not Charles's daughter Maria Theresa, should be crowned. The rivals were Charles of Bavaria, Philip V of Spain, and Augustus of Saxony.

The situation became more complicated as other European states got involved. The War of the Austrian Succession (1740–1748) began when the Prussians invaded the Austrian province of Silesia. Prussia was supported by France, Bavaria, Saxony, Sardinia, and Spain. But Britain, Hungary, and the Netherlands backed Maria Theresa. In the end, Maria Theresa kept her throne, but Austria was weakened, and Prussia kept Silesia. The balance of power in Germany shifted to Prussia, and the Holy Roman Empire declined. Over a century later, in 1870, it was Prussia which united Germany, and Austria was left out.

The enormous Schönbrunn Palace in Vienna, built between 1696 and 1730, is a grand example of decorative Rococo architecture.

BRANDENBURG–PRUSSIA

The Hohenzollern dynasty of Brandenburg inherited Prussia in 1618. By 1700, Brandenburg–Prussia had become a leading Protestant power, with Berlin as its capital. Its electors (kings) built an efficient government and helped its industries thrive. Prussia's rise to power began under Frederick William I. He reigned from 1713 to 1740 and built up the army. His successor, Frederick the Great, used the army to challenge Austria, France, and Russia. During his reign, he doubled the size of Prussia, improved its business and industry, and made it a cultural center of the Enlightenment. Over the next 100 years, Prussia gained more lands, and increasingly dominated Poland and northern Germany.

In the Battle of Fontenoy in Belgium, in 1745, France had a major victory over Austria and its allies. In this painting, the French king Louis XV, points to the victor of the battle, Marshal de Saxe.

SCOTLAND: THE JACOBITES 1701–1746

During the early 1700s, the grievances of the Scottish people and Stuart claims to the English throne led to two fateful and bloody Scottish rebellions.

Charles Edward Stuart (1720–1788), or "Bonnie Prince Charlie" was half-Scottish, half-Polish, and raised in Rome. He led a rebellion in Scotland and was beaten at the Battle of Culloden in 1746.

Flora Macdonald (1722–1790) was the daughter of a laird who worked with the English, but she supported Bonnie Prince Charlie and helped him escape, disguised as her maid.

▲ The Jacobites were beaten at Culloden by English troops led by the Duke of Cumberland. He had all the wounded killed, and the others were chased and punished.

Scottish Highlanders, many of whom were Catholic, felt threatened by Mary, daughter of James II, and the Dutch and Protestant William III on the throne. They actively supported the return of a Scottish Stuart. To control such sentiment, the English tried to break down the Highland clan system. The lairds (clan chiefs) were forced to live in Edinburgh or London. As a result, they needed more money. They raised rents and cleared people from the highlands so that they could create large areas of farmland to increase production. Family feeling in the clans broke down, and relatives just became tenants, without any clan rights.

When Mary's sister Queen Anne died in 1714, her German cousin, George of Hanover, became king. He was the great-grandson of James I and a Protestant, but a foreigner. Some people felt that the Scottish James Stuart (1688–1766), son of James II, had a better claim. Many Scottish people were also unhappy about being joined with England in the "United Kingdom" in 1707.

The Jacobites supported James Stuart. They planned rebellions both in England and Scotland, but these failed. James returned from France in 1715, but it was too late; 26 soldiers were executed and 700 sent to the West Indies as punishment. In 1745, there was another uprising. James's son, popularly known as "Bonnie Prince Charlie," or the Young Pretender, landed secretly in Scotland. He overran Scotland, then invaded England. They got only as far south as Derby. In 1746, the Jacobites were cruelly defeated at the Battle of Culloden.

Bonnie Prince Charlie fled, and returned to France in disguise. The English gained control of the Highlands, and their revenge was severe. Highland lairds were executed and clansfolk disarmed. Until 1782, they were forbidden to wear kilts or play bagpipes. Over the years, clan lands were forcibly cleared of people to make way for grazing sheep, in order to earn money by supplying wool to the woolen mills of England. Clansfolk were sent to live in the cities, Northern Ireland, and the colonies.

▼ Bonnie Prince Charlie traveled from France and landed secretly in the Hebridean Islands off northwest Scotland on his way to lead the rebellion of 1745.

AGRICULTURAL REVOLUTION 1650–1800

During the 1700s, the landscape changed dramatically in parts of Europe as profitable new farming methods were introduced.

This cartoon shows a farm worker carrying all the tools he needed to use on the new farms of the 1700s.

European farming methods had not changed for centuries. But by 1700, landowners, botanists, and breeders, particularly in England, were discussing better ways of running farms and growing crops. Scientists did research into animal breeding, land management, and raising crops. Cities and industries were rapidly growing larger, and there was more money to be made in farming. As profits rose, landowners studied and experimented even more. All this led to an agricultural revolution.

New plows were designed, and in 1701, the English farmer Jethro Tull (1674–1741) invented the horse-drawn seed drill, which allowed the mechanized planting of seeds in rows for ease of weeding. By rotating crops, soil fertility was increased, and by careful breeding, animals were improved. These methods all required financial investment and larger farms.

In many villages, the poor were forced to leave their homes to clear space for the new enclosed fields and modern farming methods.

The rural landscape changed greatly during the 1700s. In many parts of England, land had been farmed in large, open medieval fields. Villagers rented strips of these fields, where they worked alongside their neighbors. This system provided enough food to keep people alive, but it did not produce a surplus to sell to town dwellers for profit.

▲ Thomas William Coke (1752–1842), Earl of Leicester, was a wealthy landowner and a member of Parliament. He was famous as a leader in the Agricultural Revolution. He changed the way soil was treated and the kinds of crops that were grown.

▶ Each year, Thomas Coke held a conference at his country house, Holkham Hall. Landowners and breeders from all over Europe met to discuss new farming and breeding methods. Here, he inspects some of his sheep with a visiting sheep breeder.

The British Royal Agricultural Society held outdoor meetings each year, to show pedigree animals and discuss farming. This meeting, near Bristol in southern England, took place in the early 1800s.

THE ACTS OF ENCLOSURE

Landlords decided that their fields could be farmed more efficiently if they were enclosed. Hedges and walls were built across fields, to create smaller units that were easier to work. The Acts of Enclosure, passed by Parliament between 1759 and 1801, also meant that common grazing land was enclosed. In total, 7,400,000 acres (3 million ha) of English land were enclosed during the Agricultural Revolution.

Many tenants lost their livelihoods, and had to move to towns. Rich landlords established enormous estates with grand houses. Their farms grew large, and some estates were redesigned as beautiful parkland by landscape gardeners like Lancelot ("Capability") Brown. This was all supported by the government, which itself was made up of landowners. But it brought hardship to ordinary farmers.

Experimental breeding of farm animals produced new, improved strains, such as this Old English breed of pig.

KEY DATES

1701	Jethro Tull invents seed drill for faster planting
1730	Lord Townshend introduces the system of four-crop rotation
1737	Linnaeus develops a system of plant classification
1754	Charles Bonnet publishes a study of the food value of various crops
1804	French scientist Sussure explains how plants grow

Growing the same crop every year eventually weakens the soil. Using crop rotation increases soil fertility, especially if clover is sown every fourth year. This enriches the soil and lets it rest. Crops planted in the next three years grow better.

THE SEVEN YEARS' WAR 1756–1763

The Seven Years' War was a battle between the European powers for continental dominance, and for control at sea and of overseas colonies.

William Pitt, the 1st Earl of Chatham (1708–1778) was British secretary of state from 1756 to 1761. He directed the British involvement in the Seven Years' War with a sharp sense of strategy.

▼ The Seven Years' War was costly in lives and money for all the participants and fought on a large scale, as this skirmish involving Prussian and British soldiers demonstrates.

During much of the 1700s, Austria, Prussia, Russia, and France each wanted to take control of Europe. This was unfinished business left over from the War of the Austrian Succession, which ended in 1748. But none of the European powers was strong enough to win on its own, so they made alliances. As a result, there was an uneasy balance of power.

Austria, France, Sweden, Russia, and Spain were opposed to Prussia, Britain, and Hanover. Austria wanted to recapture Silesia from Prussia, and England and France were already fighting over their Indian and Canadian colonies. But wars were expensive in time, money, weapons, and lives, and they drained the warring states' resources. Fighting started in 1756 and lasted for seven years. At first, it seemed as if the Austrians and French would win.

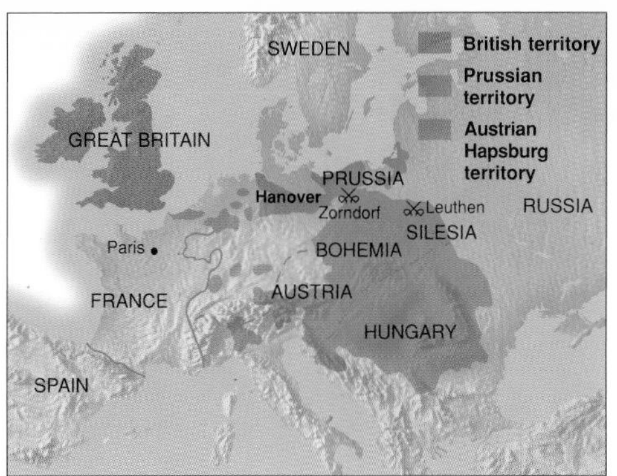

The Seven Years' War involved many nations, each with its own aims. Prussia and Britain gained the most. Prussia kept Silesia, and Britain gained greater control of Canada, India, and the seas.

Then the British, under secretary of state William Pitt ("Pitt the Elder"), joined the Prussians. Prussian victories in 1757 at the battles of Rossbach (against France), Leuthen (against Austria), and Zorndorf (against Russia), along with British success against the French at Plassey in India and in Quebec, restored the balance of power.

HOW THE WAR ENDED

In 1759, a British–Prussian army defeated the French at Minden in Germany, and the British navy defeated the French fleet at Quiberon Bay, northwest France. In 1760, the British took Montreal in Canada. Then, in 1761, William Pitt was forced to resign because his policies were unpopular with other politicians. Elizabeth, the czarina of Russia died in 1762, and the new czar, Peter III, withdrew Russia from the war. However, this did not bring an end to the hostilities. What actually ended it was the expense and destruction it brought to all sides as they ran out of money and military materials.

Ministers and diplomats now controlled governments and, after prolonged deprivation, many countries preferred to talk rather than make war. In the Treaty of Paris in 1763, it was agreed that Britain would get French lands in Canada and India, and the Prussians would keep the rich province of Silesia.

In the Battle of Quiberon Bay, off Brittany in November 1759, the British navy defeated the French and, from then on, dominated the high seas.

This medal was made in honor of the alliance forged at Versailles in 1756 between Austria and France.

KEY DATES

1740–48 War of the Austrian Succession
1756 The Seven Years' War breaks out
1757 Battle of Plassey—British control of India grows
1757–58 Prussia battles for survival—victories at battles of Rossbach and Leuthen
1759 British gains in Canada and at sea; Battle of Minden—British-Prussian victory
1760 British take Montreal, Canada
1762 Russia withdraws from the war
1763 Treaty of Paris ends the war

▼ The Battle of Zorndorf was fought between the Russians and the Prussians in 1758. The battle was fierce, and neither side really won, but Prussia benefited most, since it fended off a Russian invasion.

NORTH AMERICA 1675–1791

The mid-1700s saw a conflict for control of North America between settlers and the Native Americans, and between the English and the French.

Joseph Brant, also known as Thayendanegea, (1742–1807), was a Mohawk. He was befriended by an English official, who gave him an English name and education. Brant fought with the British when he was just 13, and became a captain in 1775. He later visited London and was received at the British court.

French and British colonists had been fighting for many years. First came King Philip's War (1675–1676), in which the New England Wampanoag tribes rose up against the settlers. The Wampanoag lost, but not before killing 10 percent of the adult males in Massachusetts. King William's War (1689–1697), between English and French settlers, did not achieve much. In Queen Anne's War (1702–1713), the English took Acadia (Nova Scotia) and destroyed Spanish St. Augustine in Florida. Finally, in King George's War (1744–1748), the British captured Louisbourg, a French fort, but it was returned in 1748 in exchange for Madras in India.

These wars were all related to European conflicts. Each side had one long-term aim: they wanted to control North America. Each side was helped by Native Americans, who fought in all the wars, hoping to receive support in their own disputes with colonists in return. But the Native Americans generally lost out to the settlers, who did not respect them. For example, between 1730 and 1755, the Shawnee and Delaware peoples were forced from their lands.

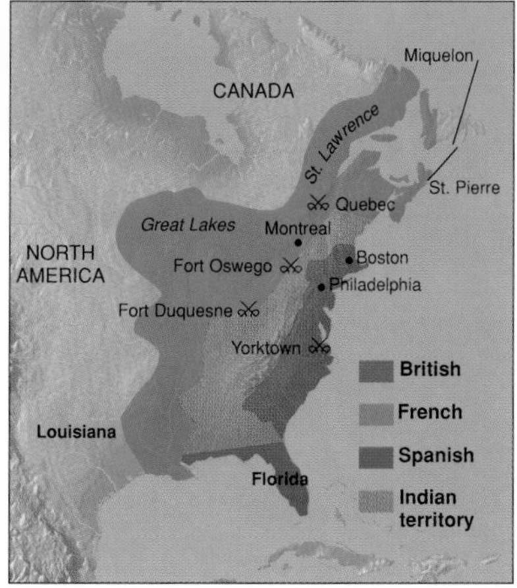

European possessions in North America at the beginning of the Seven Years' War in 1756. By the end of the war in 1763, Britain controlled most of France's lands.

PONTIAC'S REBELLION

In 1763, there was a Native American uprising. Pontiac (1720–1769) was chief of the Ottawa and of a confederacy of Algonquin tribes. To drive the British out, the tribes attacked places from the Great Lakes to Virginia. Some 200 settlers were killed. The British retaliated, and in 1766, Pontiac made peace. He was assassinated in Illinois in 1769 by a British-paid Native American.

CAPTURE OF ACADIA

Acadia, or Nova Scotia, was claimed by the French in 1603 and settled by them. Britain also claimed it, and attacked it several times during the 1600s. Finally, they captured it in 1710, though the French held on to nearby Cape Breton Island. In the late 1750s, the British threw out 10,000 of the Acadians. Many went to Louisiana, settling around the mouth of the Mississippi, where they became known as Cajuns. Nova Scotia was then populated by Scottish people, many of whom had lost their lands in the Highland Clearances.

The British taking of Quebec in 1759 meant the beginning of the end of New France. The battle took place in the fields outside the city. The British and French generals, James Wolfe (1727–1759) and the Marquis de Montcalm (1712–1759), both died during the fighting.

CANADA

The French and Indian War (part of the Seven Years' War) was fought from 1754. French colonists had settled in the Ohio Valley, and the British claimed it for themselves, so the French built a chain of forts and refused to leave. The French won some important battles in 1755 (Fort Duquesne) and 1756 (Fort Oswego). But the British captured Acadia in 1755, Quebec in 1759, and Montreal in 1760. The Treaty of Paris in 1763 gave Britain many former French colonies, and New France became British. Britain now controlled all of the lands east of the Mississippi River, and some French lands were given to Spain in exchange for Florida, which became British.

After the American Revolution, many colonists loyal to the crown, but with strong feelings about freedom, moved north to Canada. So, in 1791, the British Constitutional Act split Quebec into English-speaking Upper Canada (Ontario) and French-speaking Lower Canada (Quebec). The Act set up a government with an elected body in each of the two provinces. The British hoped that this would satisfy the growing demand for a government in which people felt they had a say. The French were also guaranteed continuing freedom of religion.

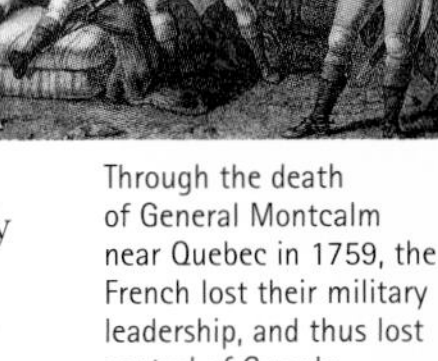
Through the death of General Montcalm near Quebec in 1759, the French lost their military leadership, and thus lost control of Canada.

KEY DATES

1675–76 King Philip's War
1686–97 King William's War
1710 Acadia taken by the English
1739–41 The British fight Spanish Florida
1744–48 King George's War
1754–63 French and Indian War
1760 British gain control of Canada
1763–66 Pontiac's Rebellion
1775 American Revolution begins

In 1775, Ethan Allen (1738–1789) and the Green Mountain Boys attacked the British garrison at Fort Ticonderoga. This was the first colonial victory in the American Revolution.

TRADE WITH CHINA 1700–1830

Trade with China was profitable, but the government there did not want "barbarian" influences introduced. European merchants looked for other ways to trade.

Throughout the 1700s, Chinese silk, cotton, tea, lacquerware, and porcelain were highly prized in Europe. They were expensive and in short supply. Merchants from Portugal, Britain, Italy, and the Netherlands tried to expand trade with China. But the powerful Chinese emperors, who controlled all contact between their people and foreigners, were simply not interested. Qianlong (Ch'ien-lung), emperor for 60 years, was a scholar and traditionalist who had no time for "barbarians." The Europeans' problem was that they had to pay for everything in silver, because Chinese traders were not allowed to exchange foreign for Chinese goods. Also, Europeans were permitted to trade only in Guangzhou (Canton), where they were penned up in "factories" (fortified warehouses), and forced to trade through Chinese intermediaries. European traders were competitive, and fought to get the best Chinese goods and to ship them to Europe quickly to fetch the highest prices.

Qianlong (1711–1795) ruled China for 60 years from 1735. He was a philosopher-emperor who supported the arts, wrote poetry, and created libraries.

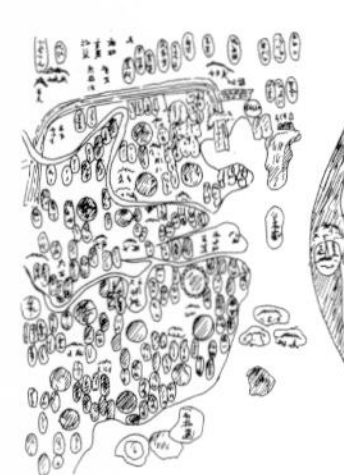

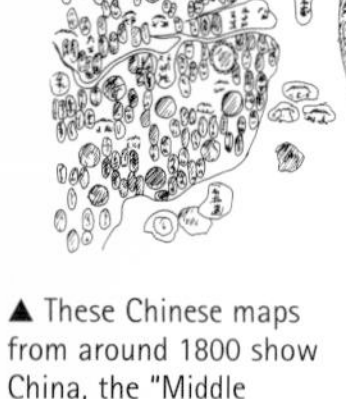

▲ These Chinese maps from around 1800 show China, the "Middle Kingdom," sitting at the center of the world. At the time, China was isolated—but the world was knocking at its door.

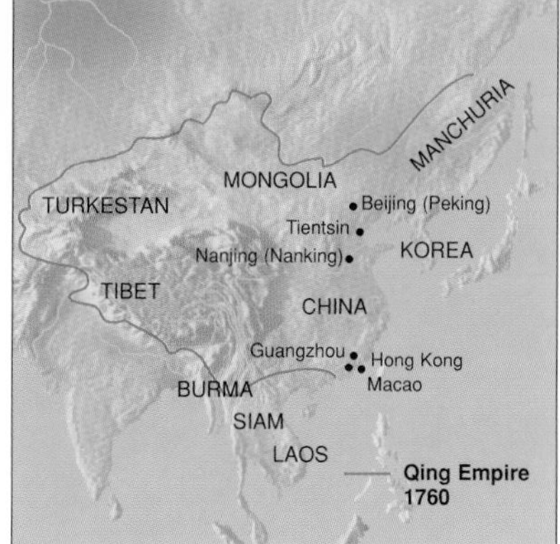

China reached its largest size during the reign of Qianlong, spreading its tentacles into central Asia and Tibet—but this expansion was expensive and brought few benefits except keeping out the British and the Russians.

THE OPIUM TRADE

Opium had long been used in China for medicinal purposes. Since European merchants were looking for other ways to trade, they established links with Chinese drug dealers, and sold them vast quantities of opium (5,000 barrels every year by the 1820s), from countries such as Burma. In return, they received precious Chinese goods for Europe. The trade grew steadily in the late 1700s, and the Qing government tried to stop it. By the 1830s, opium use was spreading through China, making people lazy, harming society and the economy, and costing China dearly.

▶ In 1793, the British diplomat Lord Macartney visited the Chinese emperor to encourage trade relations. Such relations were rejected, so people resorted to illegal deals. China and Britain had little respect for each other.

The foreign trading stations or "factories" at Guangzhou were the only places where trading with China was permitted. Europeans could not travel outside their compound, and they could trade only during certain months.

THE QING DYNASTY

The Qing emperors were not keen to develop trade because they had urgent problems at home. Years of peace and prosperity had led to huge growth in the population (400 million by 1800), and there were now food shortages. Taxes were high, corruption was growing, and the population was moving from place to place.

The Qing were very conservative, remote, and stubborn. As as result, there were protests and uprisings, often organized by secret societies with political ambitions. The White Lotus sect caused a peasant rebellion which lasted from 1795 to 1804. The effect of this was to weaken people's respect for the Qing dynasty.

Foreigners—Russians, Japanese, Tibetans, and other ethnic minorities, as well as the Europeans—were also nibbling at China's edges.

EUROPEAN INTERVENTION

The Qing emperors believed that China was the center of the world—"the Middle Kingdom, surrounded by barbarians." When a British ambassador traveled to Beijing in 1793, Qianlong refused to discuss trade. From then on, foreigners decided to get their way by other means, and the opium trade increased. By 1800, life was oppressive for many Chinese. They were heavily taxed, and He Shen, a corrupt official, had gained power. Smoking opium provided an escape. In 1839, when the Chinese tried to stop the trade, the British went to war. Even control of the world tea supply was almost at an end. During the 1840s, Robert Fortune stole several tea plants in China, took them to India, and set up rival plantations.

▲ The Temple of Heaven was rebuilt in 1751 during Qianlong's reign. The wooden prayer hall was enormous and highly decorated, and the roof was covered with blue ceramic tiles.

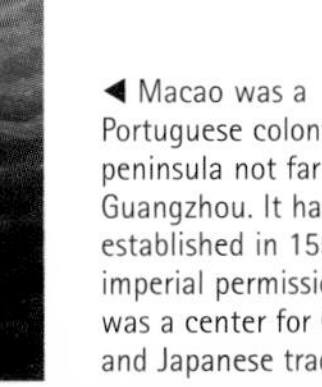

◀ Macao was a Portuguese colony on a peninsula not far from Guangzhou. It had been established in 1557, with imperial permission, and it was a center for Chinese and Japanese trade.

AFRICA 1700–1830

Africa was now strongly affected by its increasing trade with Europeans and Arabs. Many African kingdoms grew strong and rich as a result.

Shaka Zulu (1787–1828) became Zulu leader in 1816. He taught them battle skills and expanded their lands in southeastern Africa.

During the 1700s, the continent of Africa was relatively peaceful. In the north, the Ottoman Empire, which controlled Egypt, continued to decline. The Ashanti people on the west coast grew increasingly rich by selling slaves. In the southeast, the Portuguese were slowly building up a colony in Mozambique. The lands of the east coast (now Kenya) were ruled from Oman, a kingdom to the north, on the Arabian Sea. At the southern tip, the Cape of Good Hope, Dutch settlers began to explore the inland territory.

Zulu warriors were armed with stabbing spears known as *assegai*. They wore battle headdresses and ornamental shields to frighten their enemies and also to recognize each other in battle.

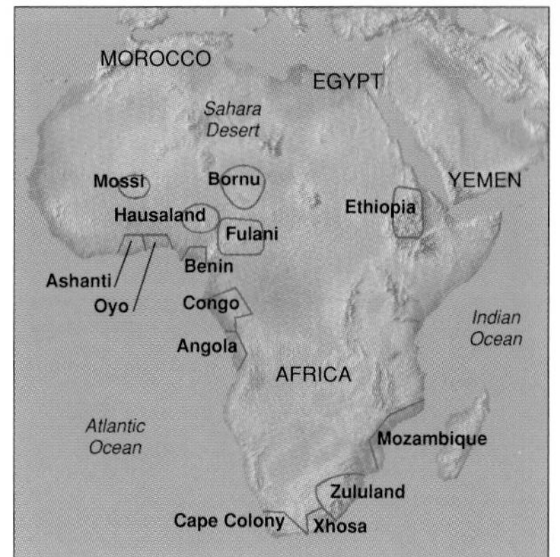

Many new states were growing in Africa, and there was much movement of peoples. Europeans and Arabs had small coastal colonies, but their influence inland was mainly felt through trade, rather than invasion.

NEW AFRICAN STATES

During the 1700s, an average of 35,000 slaves each year were being sent from western Africa to the Americas. But, by the end of the century, the British were having second thoughts, and in 1787, they established Sierra Leone as a refuge for freed slaves. In 1822, Liberia was founded for freed slaves from the United States. Most European countries stopped trading in slaves in the early 1800s, but Portugal continued until 1882.

The Yao and Nyamwezi empires in eastern Africa virtually emptied that area to provide slaves. Ashanti and Oyo dominated the West African slave trade into the 1800s, then they started selling timber, ivory, hides, gold, and beeswax to the Europeans instead. This changed the West African farming practice of growing cash crops for export. Meanwhile, in eastern Africa, slaves continued to be sent by the Omani Arabs to Arabia and India.

The Zulu nation in southern Africa, led by King Shaka, fought constantly with its neighbors. The bloodshed was so great that the years from 1818 to 1828 became known as *mfecane*, or the time of troubles. There were migrations from the Sudan, the Tutsi moved into Rwanda, and the Masai into Kenya from farther north.

AFRICAN MUSLIM STATES

On the southern edge of the Sahara, there was an Islamic revival. Many Muslims expected a *mahdi*, or savior, to appear, and various African caliphs, moved by this possibility, founded new, well-organized states such as Sokoto, Mossi, Tukulor, and Samori in inland West Africa. In Egypt, Mehmet Ali Pasha took control from the Mamluks in 1811, modernized the country, and invaded Sudan in the 1820s.

Africa was changing rapidly. Most of it still belonged to Africans, but they were not united against their common threat, the Arabs and Europeans. As a result, Africa was vulnerable.

▲ In 1809, the Hausa city of Kano in northern Nigeria was captured by the Muslim leader Usman dan Fodio, of the Hausa kingdom of Gobir. The Hausa cities converted to Islam, and became part of an Afro-Islamic state called the Sokoto Caliphate.

Mehmet Ali Pasha (1769–1849) was the Ottoman governor of Egypt, but he made Egypt virtually independent of the Ottomans and invaded the lands up the Nile River in Sudan, making Egypt the leading power in the eastern Mediterranean. He ruled Egypt from 1805 to 1848.

MASSACRE OF THE MAMLUKS

The Mamluks were originally slaves, captured in the 800s by Muslim armies in the Caucasus and Russia. They were mostly Cossacks and Chechens by origin, trained to serve as soldiers and administrators in Egypt. By 1200, they had become palace guards and ministers. They then overthrew the sultan and ruled Egypt from 1249 to 1517. When the Ottomans took Egypt, the Mamluks became the ruling class under the Ottomans. As Ottoman power declined in the 1700s, they regained power in Egypt. After Mehmet Ali Pasha conquered the Mamluks in 1811 and took control of Egypt, he invited all the surviving Mamluk commanders to a banquet in Cairo where he had them massacred.

MODERNIZING RUSSIA 1730–1796

The rulers who followed Peter the Great continued his strategy of westernization and expansion, making Russia into a great European power.

Peter III (1728–1762) was czar for half a year. A grandson of Peter the Great, he did not have the character to be czar, and he was not liked. Czarina Elizabeth forced him to marry Catherine.

When Peter the Great died in 1725, his wife became Czarina Catherine I. However, she died after only a few years. Anna Ivanovna ruled for ten years from 1730, continuing Peter's pro-Western policies, and welcoming many foreigners at court. The Russian people themselves suffered. The czarina's court in St. Petersburg cared more about music, poetry, and wars against the Ottomans or the Europeans, than about the welfare of the peasants.

From 1741, Peter's daughter, Elizabeth (1709–1762), made Russia even more westward-looking and industrial, and she declared war on Prussia in the Seven Years' War. In 1745, she forced her son Peter, the heir to the Russian throne, to marry Catherine, who was from a poor but noble Prussian family. The marriage was not a happy one. When Elizabeth died in 1762, Peter III ruled briefly.

▼ Winter was often a good time to travel in Russia, because the snow made progress faster. Catherine the Great traveled in an enclosed sled drawn by horses.

Catherine the Great (1729–1796) ruled Russia for 34 years. Other European leaders respected Catherine for her achievements in foreign policy, but feared her power.

CATHERINE THE GREAT

Peter III was a weak man, and Catherine despised him. Six months after his coronation, he was deposed and murdered. Catherine declared herself empress and ruled in his place. Although she was intelligent and cultured, she carried her private ruthlessness into public life.

To support Catherine's wars and her lavish court, Russia was drained of wealth in tax and young men. She planned to improve education and social conditions, but there were few educated officials to carry out these plans. So she asked the nobility for help, and gave them extra powers. This made the peasants' situation even worse, and led to Pugachev's Rebellion in 1773–1774. Rebels took the city of Kazan, and promised to abolish tax, serfdom, landlords, and military service. But Pugachev was brutally crushed.

◀ From the 1500s to the 1700s, the Russian Empire had more than doubled in size. During Catherine's reign, it gained ports on the coasts of the Baltic and Black seas.

FOREIGN POLICY

Catherine's appointment of a reform commission in the 1760s failed, so she chose autocratic rule, and divided the country into regions, each ruled by nobles. Then she left the nobles to take care of Russia's internal affairs.

Her claim to greatness comes from the way she expanded Russia's lands. This strategy of expansion was masterminded by two ministers, Count Alexander Suvarov and Grigori Potemkin. In the north and west, new lands were won from Sweden in 1790. Most of Poland was seized when it was partitioned (divided). These gains gave Russia important seaports on the Baltic coast.

In the south, Russia took Azov from the Ottomans, then the Crimea, and, by 1792, the whole northern shore of the Black Sea. The Ottomans no longer controlled the Black Sea and Russia built up a powerful navy. To the east, Russia's gradual development of Siberia was also stepped up.

But Catherine was very cruel. Courtiers were flogged, and peasants who dared to complain about their situation were punished. Many poor people faced starvation, yet Catherine continued to collect heavy taxes to pay for her wars and extravagant lifestyle.

Life at the Russian court was rich and elegant, sheltered from reality, and out of touch. In contrast, the peasants lived in poverty. When Catherine the Great traveled through Russia in 1787 to see how her subjects lived, the streets of the towns were lined with healthy, well-dressed actors. The real peasants were kept hidden from view.

KEY DATES

1741 Elizabeth becomes czarina
1756–63 Russia joins the Seven Years' War
1762 Catherine the Great becomes czarina
1772 First partition of Poland
1783 Russia annexes the Crimea
1792 Russia gains Black Sea coast
1793–95 Second and Third partitions of Poland
1796 Death of Catherine the Great

This painting of the inside of the Winter Palace in St. Petersburg shows how impressive life in St. Petersburg was. Tropical plants thrived indoors, while people sometimes froze to death just outside the palace.

EXPLORATION IN OCEANIA 1642–1820

The exploration of Oceania came about quite late compared with other parts of the world. It was pioneered by Tasman, Cook, and other explorers.

Between 1768 and 1779, the navigator Captain James Cook (1728–1779) made three voyages of discovery to the Pacific. In 1770, he landed at Botany Bay and claimed Australia for Britain.

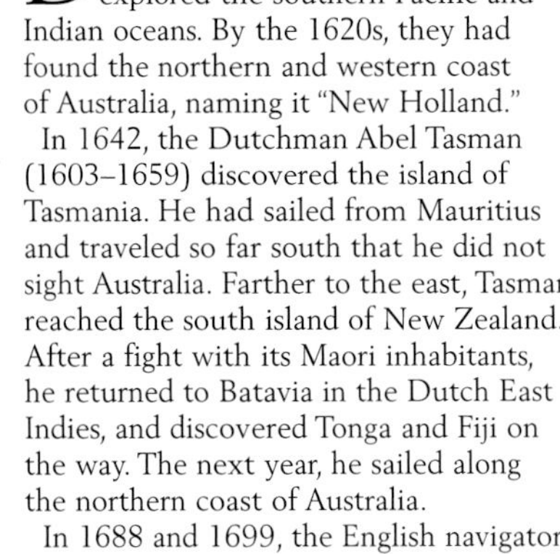

During the 1600s, Dutch seamen explored the southern Pacific and Indian oceans. By the 1620s, they had found the northern and western coast of Australia, naming it "New Holland."

In 1642, the Dutchman Abel Tasman (1603–1659) discovered the island of Tasmania. He had sailed from Mauritius and traveled so far south that he did not sight Australia. Farther to the east, Tasman reached the south island of New Zealand. After a fight with its Maori inhabitants, he returned to Batavia in the Dutch East Indies, and discovered Tonga and Fiji on the way. The next year, he sailed along the northern coast of Australia.

In 1688 and 1699, the English navigator William Dampier (1652–1715) explored the western and northwestern coastline of Australia. These explorers proved that Australia was an island, but they did not settle there. The Pacific remained largely unknown since it was too distant and too poor to attract European trading interest.

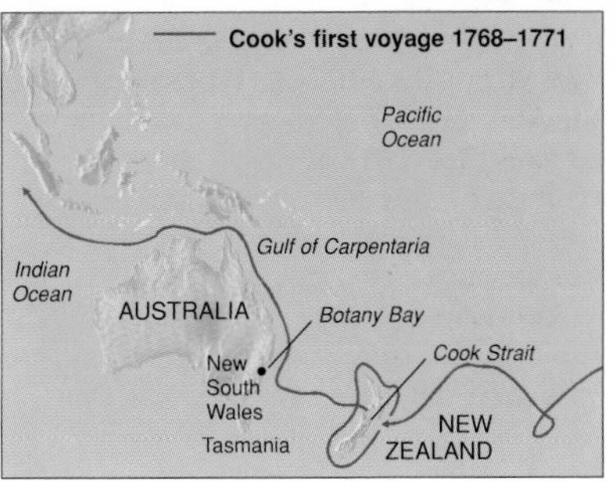

On Cook's first voyage, he sailed from the tip of South America to New Zealand and proved that there was no large continent in between as many people thought.

The first scientific exploration of these southern lands was undertaken by Captain James Cook, who made three voyages. The first voyage (1768–1771) took him around New Zealand. Then he landed at Botany Bay in Australia, claiming it for Britain. On his second voyage (1772–1775), he explored many Pacific islands and Antarctica. On his last voyage, started in 1776, he visited New Zealand, Tonga, Tahiti, and finally Hawaii, where he was killed in a quarrel with the islanders.

Jean-François La Pérouse (1741–1788) was sent by Louis XVI to sail around the world on a scientific expedition. He traveled the oceans with a crew of scientists, charting, observing, and collecting samples while visiting Canada, Siberia, and Australia. His ships disappeared in 1788.

THE VOYAGES OF CAPTAIN COOK

Captain Cook was commissioned to sail to Tahiti to observe the passage of Venus in front of the sun. After this, he was secretly sent south to chart New Zealand and Australia for the British government. On his second voyage, he was the first explorer to visit the Antarctic, but he was driven back by pack ice. Cook discovered the value of carrying vegetables and fruit for his sailors, so preventing scurvy (caused by lack of Vitamin C). He also took well-trained artists with him because he was determined that the findings should be scientifically recorded. He died in Hawaii, in 1779, while on his third voyage.

NATIVE PEOPLES

The "new" lands explored by Cook had been inhabited for hundreds of years. The Maoris lived in New Zealand, and the Aborigines lived in Australia. Both peoples lived according to ancient traditions. Understandably, they were wary of Cook and his men—the first Europeans that they had ever seen.

Aborigines had lived in Australia for thousands of years, spread out over a vast continent. They lived by foraging and hunting, and using their advanced knowledge of nature. They were so different from Europeans, and there was such a culture clash, that Aboriginal culture was almost entirely destroyed.

The Maoris, it is thought, had sailed to Aotearoa (New Zealand) from Polynesia around A.D. 750, and were farmers, warriors, and village dwellers. They resisted the efforts of the Europeans to move into their land.

The first settlers in Australia arrived in 1788. They were convicts who had been transported there from Britain as punishment. Free settlers started to arrive in 1793. In New Zealand, whalers, hunters, and traders were soon followed by missionaries. Many of the early settlers came from Scotland, Ireland, and Wales. The settlers introduced diseases that often killed the local peoples.

▲ The Maoris were skilled sailors and craftworkers who decorated their canoes with elaborate religious carvings. When Cook arrived, there were about 100,000 Maoris in New Zealand. Many were killed in later wars against British settlers and troops.

KEY DATES

1642–44 Tasman's voyages to Tasmania and New Zealand
1688/1699 Dampier explores western and northwestern coastline of Australia
1766–68 Bougainville discovers Polynesia and Melanesia
1768–71 Cook's first voyage
1772–75 Cook's second voyage
1776–79 Cook's third voyage
1829 Britain annexes all of Australia
1840 Britain claims New Zealand

In 1779, while on his third voyage to the Pacific, Captain Cook was killed in a skirmish with Hawaiians over the theft of a boat. Initially, the British had been welcome, but after this event, his crews had to sail home without their captain.

THE BIRTH OF THE U.S.A. 1763–1789

People in the Thirteen Colonies in America were dissatisfied with British rule. They fought for their independence, and a new nation was born.

George Washington (1732–1799) was an officer in the British army and a wealthy landowner. He was made commander in chief of the new American army, fighting the British. In 1789, he became the first president of the United States.

At the end of the Seven Years' War in 1763, both the British government in London and the English colonists in America felt satisfied. They had defeated France and gained territory from them in Canada, as well as land as far west as the Mississippi River. With the French threat gone, the colonists no longer needed the British to defend them.

But the British wanted to govern the old French territories and collect higher taxes to pay for soldiers to defend these newly won lands, so they raised taxes in the 13 colonies. Local colonial assemblies argued that it was unfair for Britain to tax the American colonies, since they had no say in running the British government. They said "taxation without representation is tyranny." The colonies decided to ban all British imports. On July 4, 1776, representatives from all 13 colonies adopted the Declaration of Independence, claiming the right to rule themselves.

The Boston Tea Party, in 1773, was a protest against British taxation. A band known as the Sons of Liberty, led by Samuel Adams (1722–1803), dressed up as Mohawks, boarded two ships in Boston Harbor, and threw tea chests into the sea. The British closed Boston Harbor until the lost tea was paid for.

▲ The British soldiers were well-drilled professionals, while the Americans were mostly volunteers. But the Americans were highly motivated because they felt strongly about their cause. On the left is a uniformed British grenadier, and on the right is an American revolutionary soldier.

At the Battle of Bunker Hill, near Boston, in 1775, the British lost twice as many men as the Americans. It took three uphill assaults for the British to win.

INDEPENDENCE

Guided by the ideas of Thomas Jefferson, and influenced by the Enlightenment, the American Declaration of Independence stated: "We hold these truths to be self-evident, that all men are created equal, that they are endowed by their Creator with certain inalienable Rights, that among these are Life, Liberty, and the Pursuit of Happiness."

The American Revolution had begun in 1775. At first the British were successful, despite the problems of fighting nearly 3,000 mi. (5,000km) from home. But the Americans had an advantage because they were fighting on home territory, and they believed in their cause. Six years after the conflict began, the British army surrendered at Yorktown, Virginia, having been defeated by Washington's troops. Britain eventually recognized American independence in the Treaty of Paris in 1783.

KEY DATES

1763	End of the Seven Years' War; British troops sent to North America
1764	Sugar Act taxes imported molasses
1765	Stamp Act adds tax on documents
1775	American Revolution begins; Battle of Bunker Hill takes place
1776	Declaration of Independence
1781	British army surrenders at Yorktown
1783	Britain recognizes American independence
1787	Draft American Constitution drawn up
1789	American Constitution becomes law; George Washington becomes first president
1791	Bill of Rights is adopted

THE U.S. CONSTITUTION

At first, the United States of America was run by the governing body that was set up during the Revolution, the Continental Congress, under the laws called the Articles of Confederation. But the Congress was weak. It was little more than an assembly of representatives from the states and could only make decisions that affected all of the states. It could borrow money, for example, but could not collect taxes from the states to raise money to repay the loan.

Some thought a whole new system of government that would unite the states into a nation was needed. In May 1787, at the Constitutional Convention in Philadelphia, they designed this system. They decided to have a president, elected every four years. He would rule with the help of a Congress (consisting of a House of Representatives and a Senate, made up of representatives from every state), and a Supreme Court.

In addition, each of the states would have an elected assembly, and run their state government as they liked. A system of checks and balances would make sure that neither the president, the Congress, nor the Supreme Court would be allowed to control the federal government.

Finally, many people worried that the Constitution did not protect all the rights they had fought so hard for. So, in 1791, ten amendments were added to the Constitution. They are the Bill of Rights.

A Liberty Medal was made to mark the victory of the Americans over the British in 1781.

The Liberty Bell in Philadelphia symbolizes American independence.

Thomas Jefferson (1743–1826) became the third president in 1801. He was a political leader whose ideas greatly affected American politics.

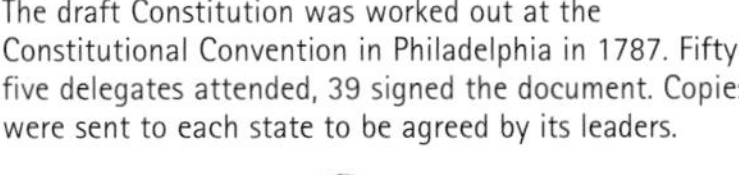

The draft Constitution was worked out at the Constitutional Convention in Philadelphia in 1787. Fifty-five delegates attended, 39 signed the document. Copies were sent to each state to be agreed by its leaders.

THE FRENCH REVOLUTION 1789–1799

In 1789, the discontented people of France overthrew their king, demanding freedom and equality. The revolution that followed changed France forever.

Marie Antoinette (1755–1793) was Louis XVI's Austrian wife. The people thought she was arrogant and extravagant.

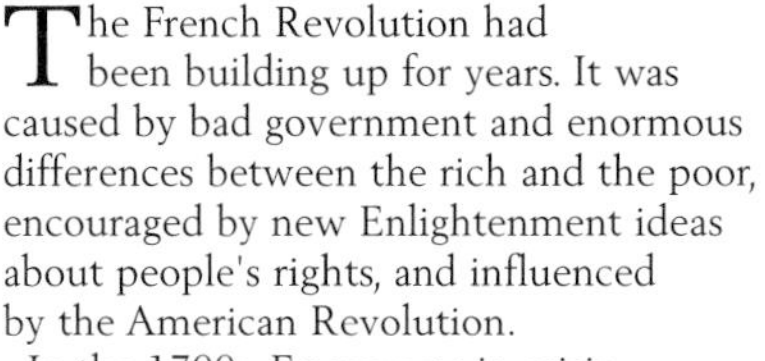

The French Revolution had been building up for years. It was caused by bad government and enormous differences between the rich and the poor, encouraged by new Enlightenment ideas about people's rights, and influenced by the American Revolution.

In the 1700s, France was in crisis. Food was scarce, prices were high, and the government was facing bankruptcy. To get more money, Louis XVI could either borrow it or raise state taxes. But first he needed approval and support from a traditional assembly, the Estates-General, which had not met for 175 years.

At the assembly, the representatives of the professional classes rebelled against the nobles and clergy. They took an oath to start a new National Assembly and demand reform. They wrote a new constitution that abolished the old order, nationalized Church lands, and reorganized local government. Louis sent troops to try and dismiss the Assembly.

Louis XVI (1754–1793) became king in 1774. He was shy and not a strong ruler. His wrong decisions led to the Revolution.

When the citizens of Paris heard this, they rebelled. On July 14, 1789, a mob stormed the Bastille, the king's prison in Paris. The riot marked the beginning of a bloody revolution in which the rebels demanded "Liberty, Equality, Fraternity."

▲ Maximilien Robespierre (1758–1794) became the leader of a revolutionary group called the Jacobins in 1793. He was the head of the Committee of Public Safety and backed the execution of the king and queen. Executions grew so frequent that this time was known as the Reigin of Terror. Robespierre may not have been responsible for this, but he did make enemies. In 1794, he was accused of treason and executed.

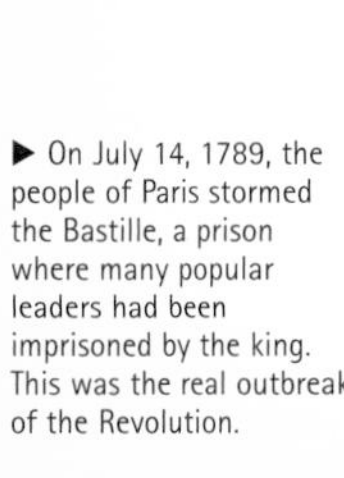

► On July 14, 1789, the people of Paris stormed the Bastille, a prison where many popular leaders had been imprisoned by the king. This was the real outbreak of the Revolution.

THE STRUGGLE FOR POWER

In 1791, Louis XVI fled, but was captured and imprisoned. In 1792, the monarchy was abolished, and the following year, Louis and his wife were tried and executed. By this time, the revolutionary government was at war with most other European states, who were afraid that revolution might spread to their countries.

Predictably, chaos broke out, and there was a struggle for power. The new revolutionary government began rounding up its rivals, royalist or popular, calling them "enemies of the revolution." There was a political battle between two groups, the Jacobins and Girondins, which the Jacobins won. They then dominated a new ruling body, called the Committee of Public Safety. The committee mobilized French armies against foreign invasion, and from September 1793 to July 1794, they executed all who opposed them in what is known as the Reign of Terror.

During the Terror, around 18,000 people were guillotined. Soon, one man, Robespierre, wielded dictatorial power. Even he was not safe, and in 1794, he was accused of treason and executed.

THE DIRECTORY

A new constitution was written in 1795 and a weak government, called The Directory, was formed. War had already broken out, and French revolutionary armies had conquered the Netherlands and south Germany. A young general, Napoleon Bonaparte, took over the army, and invaded Italy, Switzerland, and Egypt. The Directory came to rely on him. He grew popular and powerful. In 1799, he removed the Directory and took control.

The so-called *sans culottes* (named because they did not wear knee-length pants, like the middle class and aristocracy), preserved public order in the streets during the Reign of Terror. Many people lost their lives as a result of the hatred of the *sans culottes*.

KEY DATES

1788	Estates-General called to a meeting
1789	National Assembly and storming of the Bastille; Declaration of the Rights of Man
1791	The New Constitution and Legislative Assembly
1792	The Revolutionary Wars and French Republic
1793–94	The Reign of Terror
1794	Robespierre's dictatorship; Holland invaded
1795–99	The Directory rules France
1796	Napoleon becomes chief army commander
1799	Napoleon takes power

THE REIGN OF TERROR

After Louis XVI had been executed in 1793, the Committee started to attack and execute anyone suspected of opposing the revolution. A Tribunal was set up to bring "enemies of the revolution" to trial, but these trials were often hurried and unfair. Aristocrats, royalists, priests, and any suspected people went to the guillotine. Once Robespierre had rid himself of rivals in the Committee of Public Safety, he ruled alone for a short time, until he too was sent to the guillotine in July 1794. The Reign of Terror then ended.

Here, people celebrate the end of the Reign of Terror by dancing around a tree decorated with rosettes in red, white, and blue, the national colors.

THE NAPOLEONIC WARS 1797–1815

Restoring order after the French Revolution, Napoleon attempted to change the whole of Europe. But Britain stood against him and Napoleon was finally exiled.

Napoleon was born in Corsica, the second son of an Italian lawyer. As a young man, he had joined the French army, and his courage and quick thinking led to rapid promotion. At the age of 24, he became a general. He led a number of successful campaigns, capturing northern Italy in 1797. The new government, the Directory, feared his popularity and power. They offered Napoleon the job of invading Britain, but he suggested invading Egypt to disrupt Britain's trade route to India. In 1789, he did invade Egypt, but his plan failed after the British, led by Lord Nelson, destroyed his fleet.

In this 1803 cartoon, Napoleon is shown straddling the world while the comparatively tiny John Bull (representing Britain) tries to fight him off alone.

In 1799, Napoleon returned to France and seized control. He dismissed the government, and appointed three consuls (officials), to run the country. He made himself first consul, and ruled for 15 years. In 1804, he crowned himself emperor.

Napoleon introduced many lasting reforms that brought new laws, a better educational system, a reorganized government, and a new national bank.

In 1799, Napoleon (1769–1821), already a war hero, took over the government by force. Many disagreed, but France was in disorder and Napoleon became first consul.

He was a brilliant general, who moved his troops quickly and used new battle tactics. He also had a very large army, because Robespierre had introduced a draft system in which all adult men were forced to serve. The army numbered 750,000 soldiers in 1799, and another two million men joined up between 1803 and 1815. Napoleon used this massive force to try to conquer Europe.

Napoleon wanted to create a society based on skill rather than on noble birth. To encourage achievement he founded the Legion of Honor in 1802 "for outstanding service to the state." Members of the Legion received a medal and a pension for the remainder of their lives.

THE BATTLE OF MARENGO

One of Napoleon's many military successes, the Battle of Marengo was fought against the Austrians in Italy in 1800. Napoleon was a brilliant leader, inspiring his troops with speeches, "leading from the front," and using very innovative tactics. He modernized warfare, used cannons and large armies, and outwitted his opponents. His control of Europe pushed many countries into the modern world.

THE NAPOLEONIC WARS

Napoleon defeated Austria and Russia at Austerlitz in 1805, Prussia at Jena in 1806, and Russia faced a second defeat at Friedland in 1807. Napoleon created new republics allied to France and ruled by placing his relatives in positions of power. He also created Europe-wide laws and governments—known as the Continental System.

In 1805, Britain won a major sea battle against France at Trafalgar in Spain. The British admiral, Horatio Nelson (1758–1805) died, but his victory saved Britain from invasion. In 1808, Napoleon invaded Spain. This began the Peninsular Wars in which Britain supported Spain and Portugal.

The British sent troops led by the Duke of Wellington to Spain. There, he won battles at Salamanca (1812) and Vittoria (1813), pushing the French out of Spain.

Napoleon's disastrous invasion of Russia in 1812 left over 500,000 French dead of cold or hunger, or killed. In 1813, he was also crushed at Leipzig by a combined European force, led by the Prussian general, von Blücher. Finally, in 1814, France was invaded, and Napoleon was exiled. He escaped and was defeated by Wellington and von Blücher at Waterloo in Belgium. He died in exile on the remote South Atlantic island of St. Helena in 1821.

Napoleon believed Russia had allied with Britain, so he invaded. When his army reached Moscow, the Russians had already burned it down. Eventually, the winter took its toll. Napoleon entered Russia with 510,000 men—but left with only 10,000.

KEY DATES

1796–97	Napoleon invades Italy
1798	Campaign in Egypt
1799	Napoleon takes over French government
1804	Napoleon crowns himself emperor
1805	Battle of Austerlitz against Austria and Russia; Battle of Trafalgar—British sea victory
1807	Peace of Tilsit with Russia and Prussia
1812	Russian campaign
1813	Napoleon loses Battle of Leipzig; Spain freed at Battle of Vittoria
1814	France invaded; Napoleon exiled to Elba
1815	Napoleon's last battle, at Waterloo

Irish-born Arthur Wellesley, Duke of Wellington (1769–1852), fought Napoleon's armies in Spain where it took four years to push out the French. Wellington was involved in the Congress of Vienna after the Napoleonic Wars. A national hero, he became prime minister of Britain in 1828.

The Battle of Waterloo in Belgium, in 1815, was closely fought. It was Napoleon's last battle, fought against Wellington of Britain and von Blücher of Prussia.

THE END OF SLAVERY 1792–1888

The European colonies in the Americas depended heavily on slave labor. But by the mid-1700s, many people were questioning the morality of this.

William Wilberforce (1759–1833) was the member of Parliament for Hull, a busy slave trading port. The trade horrified him. He and other humanitarian Christians campaigned against the slave trade from 1788 onward.

Throughout the 1700s, Britain, France, and Spain grew rich on taxes and profits from their colonies. Much of this wealth was created by slave labor. Denmark, Sweden, Prussia, Holland, and Genoa (Piedmont) also traded in slaves. Africans were sold to Europeans by slave dealers and local rulers, who saw slave trading as a means of punishing criminals, getting rid of enemies, disposing of captives, and getting rich. Nobody knows how many slaves were sold in all, but historians have estimated that 45 million slaves were shipped between 1450 and 1870, although only 15 million survived—many died on the voyage across the Atlantic. Many Europeans disapproved of the slave trade, but they believed it was the only way to supply labor to colonial plantations.

However, some protested, saying it was against God's law and human decency. Rousseau, a French philosopher, wrote in *The Social Contract*, in 1762, "Man is born free, but everywhere he is in chains." His writings inspired the revolutions in America and France, and individual freedom became regarded as a social right, not a gift from a king. Rousseau's ideas also inspired people to fight on behalf of others who were unable to help themselves. Politicians, clergy, and ordinary people began to think how they might help the slaves. But moral arguments did not have as much force as the profits that slavery generated.

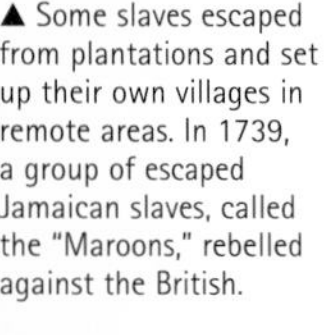

▲ Some slaves escaped from plantations and set up their own villages in remote areas. In 1739, a group of escaped Jamaican slaves, called the "Maroons," rebelled against the British.

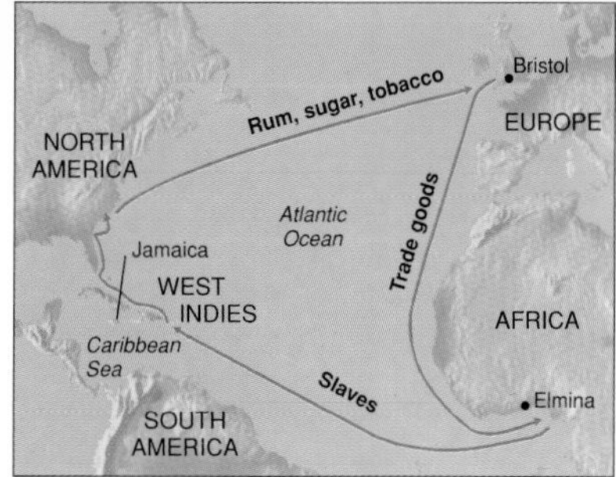

Before abolition, slave ships followed a triangular Atlantic sailing route, taking goods to Africa, slaves to the Americas, and products such as sugar back to Europe.

ENDING THE SLAVE TRADE

Between 1777 and 1804, slavery was made illegal in the northern United States. Denmark withdrew from the slave trade in 1792, and Britain in 1807. But slave smuggling continued. The British navy clamped down on slave trading from 1815, but slavery was still legal elsewhere. A slave revolt in the French colony of Santo Domingo in 1791–1793 led to abolition by France but, in 1803, they made slavery legal again. In 1831, a slave uprising in Virginia led by Nat Turner led to harsh laws and increased support for slavery among white southerners.

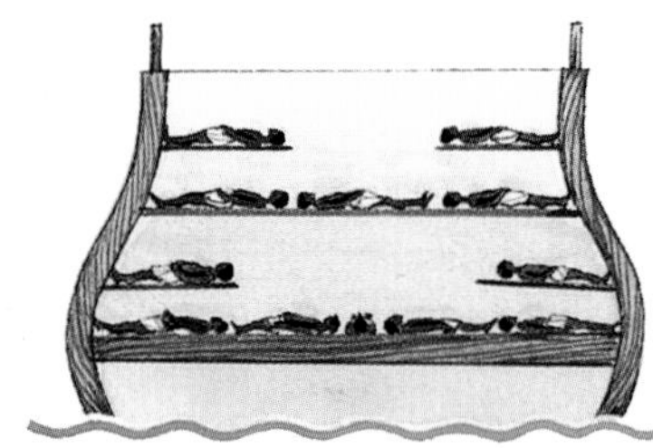

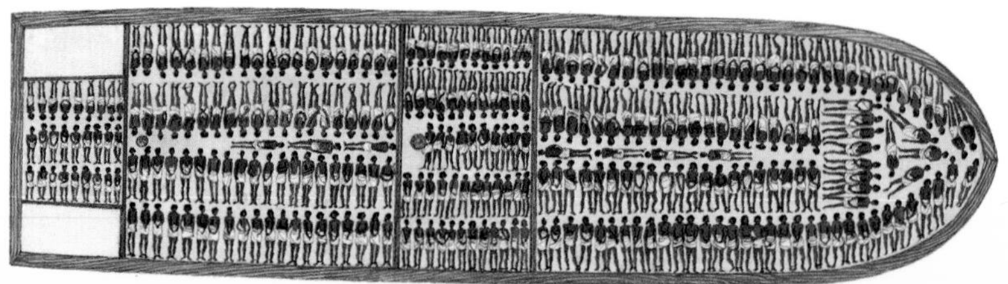

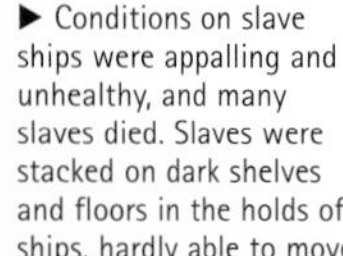

▶ Conditions on slave ships were appalling and unhealthy, and many slaves died. Slaves were stacked on dark shelves and floors in the holds of ships, hardly able to move.

PHILANTHROPY

In Britain, Thomas Clarkson (1760–1846) and William Wilberforce had led an antislavery campaign, which resulted in the abolition of slave trading in 1807. However, slaves were not actually freed for some time. Wilberforce died just before all of the slaves in British hands were freed. Europeans had by now grown disgusted with slavery, and the British navy blocked slave-trading ships.

Slavery continued in Cuba, Costa Rica, Brazil, and the southern United States. The plantations had been built on slave labor. There was a thriving market in Europe for cheap, slave-grown cotton and tobacco, and plantation owners were reluctant to change.

In the U.S., the northern states supported freeing the slaves, but the situation in the South grew worse. Nat Turner's 1831 revolt in Virginia led to new laws designed to control the slaves. Slavery finally ended in the United States in 1863, in Cuba in 1886, and in Brazil in 1888. The Arabic slave trade in Africa ended in 1873.

◀ The leader of the Virginia slave revolt of 1831, Nat Turner (1800–1831), killed his master and 60 whites, and encouraged 75 slaves to revolt. Their revolt lasted for some weeks. He and his followers were eventually captured, tried and hanged.

KEY DATES	
1517	Regular slave trading started by Spain
1592	British slave trading begins
1739	Jamaican "Maroon" slave revolt
1760s	Slave trading at its peak
1791–1804	Santo Domingo slave revolt
1792	Danish slave trade abolished
1807	British slave trade abolished
1834	Slavery abolished in British colonies
1865	13th Amendment abolishes slavery in U.S.
1888	Slavery abolished in Brazil

The economy of the southern states relied on black slave labor. Cotton picking was one of the slaves' main jobs. The cotton was profitably exported to supply the cotton mills of industrial Europe.

THE SLAVES' REVOLT IN SANTO DOMINGO

The French Revolution spread to French colonies overseas. In 1791, the National Assembly in Paris decided to give the vote to slaves in Santo Domingo (now Haiti) in the Caribbean. Plantation owners refused to obey. When they heard this, about 100,000 slaves rebelled. Many slave owners were killed, houses destroyed, and sugar and coffee plantations set on fire. Napoleon sent troops to the island and there was a long civil war led by Toussaint l'Ouverture (1746–1803), an ex-slave who declared himself ruler of the island in 1801.

THE BRITISH IN INDIA 1774–1858

The hold on India by the British East India Company gradually grew stronger. The British came to dominate Indian society, becoming its ruling caste.

By 1750, the British East India Company controlled the very profitable trade between Britain, India, and the Far East. Its officials were skillful businessmen who had built up a knowledge of Indian affairs, especially through the Indians they employed. They made friends with Indian princes, and struck bargains with both the friends and the enemies of the declining Mogul rulers. Many British people in India lived like princes themselves. By working for the East India Company many became very rich. Some of these "nabobs" (from the word *nawab*, for local ruler or rich man) built fine houses; they were designed by British architects, and furnished with luxuries from England, India, and the colonies. In Calcutta, they held horse races, tea parties, and dances. Gradually, wives and families arrived to share this way of life and a community developed.

This mechanical toy, called "Tipu's Tiger," shows a tiger devouring a European. It was made for Tipu Sahib of Mysore. Between 1767 and 1799, with French support, Mysore tried to resist British control of its lands.

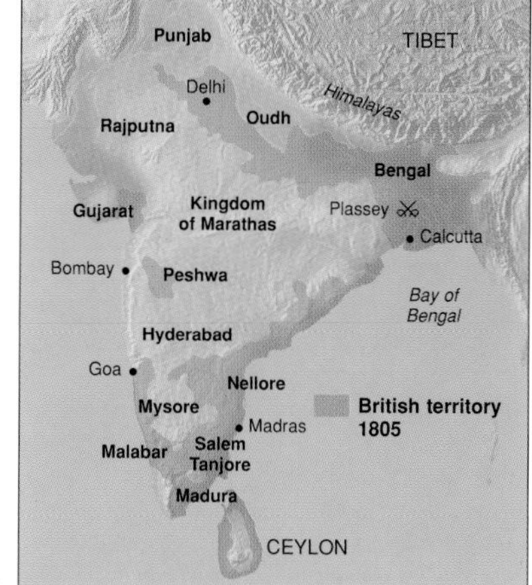

By 1805, the British controlled the rich clothmaking districts of Bengal in northeastern India, as well as the prosperous coastal lands in the south.

However, some British people were attracted to Indian art, culture, and architecture, even wearing Indian clothes, at least at home. They learned Indian languages and studied Indian religions and writings. They took Indian ideas back to Britain when they went home.

▲ Tipu Sahib (1749–1799) of Mysore owned an ivory chess set which was made up of pieces with Indian princes and men on one side, and East India Company administrators and soldiers on the other.

► At first, the British mixed easily with Indians. Here, the Scottish governor Sir David Ochterlony smokes a water pipe at an Indian musical performance.

BRITISH EXPANSION

By 1780, the East India Company controlled many of the more prosperous parts of India, but in 1784, the British government decided to stop it from expanding any further—a policy the company's managers were not happy about. Around 1800, the British were frightened by Napoleon's ambition to build an empire in India, and the government changed its policy. From 1803 to 1818, the company fought the Marathas, who ruled central India, and broke their power. In many cases, they took a soft approach, and used trade to favor certain Indian states, stationing troops there "for their protection."

The company fought in Burma, where the local rulers threatened Bengal, as well as on the Northwest Frontier and in Afghanistan, where they feared Russian influence. Between 1843 and 1849, they annexed Sind and the Punjab. Whenever a dynasty failed, or if a state was weakly governed, the company moved in. During the 1830s, the company's governor had arrogantly overruled local traditions, and brought in missionaries to convert Indians to Christianity. The company built roads, railroads, and buildings, and expanded British businesses. They insisted on using English as the language of education and business. As a result, Indian opposition gradually grew stronger.

Some Indian rajahs and princes made friends with the British and gained many advantages as a result. To be protected by British soldiers guaranteed a prince's power, and the British gained from the deal by having easy influence and trade in a prince's state, without having to govern it.

THE INDIAN MUTINY

Trouble broke out among the *sepoys*, the Indian soldiers in the company's army. Sparked by a terrible famine, a mutiny started in 1857. Several towns, including the capital, Delhi, were captured by the sepoys, and British men, women, and children were massacred. The mutiny was suppressed violently by British troops. Each side now became suspicious of the other side. The British started to live a more separate life, and Indians were "kept in their place." The British government took control of the East India Company in 1858, and closed it down. While India was perhaps the richest and most developed European colony of all, the British had to work very hard to control it.

HOMES FOR NABOBS

Nabobs were officers of the East India Company who had made fortunes in India. Many nabobs had themselves grown up in tough conditions, and had gone to India to escape hard times, seek a fortune, or build a new life. They worked hard, risking their lives through war or disease. They lived in conditions that reflected the opulence of Indian rulers and combined them with the trappings of the British aristocracy. They built great mansions in cities like Calcutta and Delhi, and often had many servants.

Unification and Colonization

1836–1913

The world map changed dramatically during this period—new nations were formed and some were unified. Africa was carved up by nations seeking new colonies, and China's power was fractured. There were more revolutions in Europe. The United States, Canada, and Russia expanded to the farthest frontiers of their countries. Railroads, telegraph wires, and steamships suddenly made the world seem smaller. New cities such as New York, Buenos Aires, Johannesburg, Bombay, and Shanghai became centers in a new global order.

▲ The coming of the railroad opened up North America, but also led to the first national strike. The strike spread along the railroad, from coast to coast, uniting the workers in their fight for decent wages.

◀ During the Second Boer War in South Africa, the Boers (Dutch settlers) were finally defeated by the British in 1902.

THE WORLD AT A GLANCE 1836–1913

In North America, settlers moved west to colonize the vast lands taken over by the United States and Canada. However, the opening up of these new territories caused much hardship for the native peoples, whose way of life was being threatened.

In Africa, religious wars strengthened the influence of Islam in the kingdoms of the north. European explorers and missionaries began to visit lands in the interior. Led by a desire to exploit the resources of Africa, European powers quickly established colonies throughout the continent. The power of the great trading nations of Europe grew.

In Asia, Europeans also took control of India, Burma, and Southeast Asia, and began to trade with China and Japan. Europe's expansion into other continents did not stop internal conflicts, and many wars were fought between countries or empires that wanted more power and territory.

NORTH AMERICA

The United States grew strong during this period. Its territories now extended west to Texas and California, and the Wild West was being opened up by railroads, settlers, and soldiers. This took place at great cost to the Native Americans, who were killed or squeezed into small, isolated reservations. Despite attempts to revive their fortunes, their culture was dying, and it gained little respect from the new Americans. In the 1860s, the Civil War broke out, a destructive, modern-style war over political principles. One result of it was the abolition of slavery. The cities of the East and the Midwest then grew larger and more industrial, and more settlers arrived from Europe. Canada was united, and it pushed west, too, becoming a prosperous independent dominion within the British Empire. By 1900, North America had become wealthy and strong. The United States became an imperial power itself. Its financiers, corporations, and armies were to help it dominate the world from the 1900s onward.

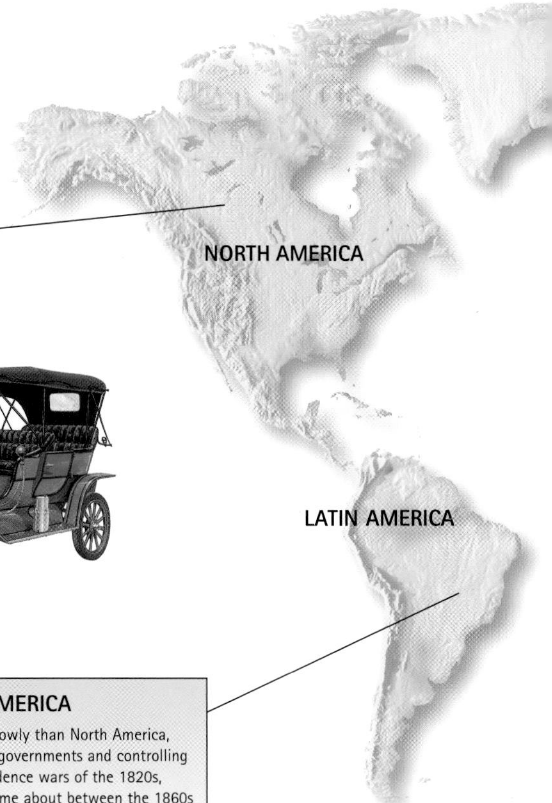

NORTH AMERICA

LATIN AMERICA

LATIN AMERICA

Latin America developed more slowly than North America, partly because of its dictatorial governments and controlling landowners. After the independence wars of the 1820s, a second wave of changes came about between the 1860s and 1880s, when South American countries fought each other. There followed a spate of development brought by railroads, population growth, and increasing wealth earned from exports. But the old Spanish ways lived on, in the form of tough governments, rich landowners in their *haciendas* (ranches), and a large mass of poor people.

EUROPE

This was Europe's century. Europe's incessant wars almost stopped, and its armies went overseas, staking out claims to empires elsewhere. Industrial cities grew large, linked by railroads and telegraph wires. Politicians, industrialists, and the middle classes gained increasing power. The new working classes formed workers' movements, leading, by 1905, to the first—unsuccessful—workers' revolution, in Russia. Immense achievements were made in engineering, science, ideas, the arts, and in exploring the world. Europe now governed and financed the world, and grew rich as a result. Yet times were hard for some—there were famines, strikes, economic downturns, and mass emigrations. These hardships eventually led to another new invention—social welfare systems for the poor.

ASIA

Trouble hit China and Japan in the mid-1800s. Foreign traders forced their way in, and in China, major rebellions broke out. China's, isolationist Qing dynasty eventually fell in 1911. Japan, inspired by the West, began modernizing. In India, British rule became total—though not without being challenged by an Indian mutiny first. The West now dominated the East. For some Asians, employed by Westerners, this was advantageous. But many Asians simply became cheap labor on plantations and in Asian colonial cities. Railroads, missionaries, soldiers, and traders opened up the interior of Asian countries. But Asian traditions survived better than those of other cultures elsewhere.

EUROPE

ASIA

MIDDLE EAST

AFRICA

AUSTRALASIA

AUSTRALASIA

British settlers took over most of Australasia, and, in growing numbers, overwhelmed the indigenous peoples. Australia and New Zealand made a name for themselves as exporters of food, wool, and gold.

AFRICA

First came explorers, then traders, missionaries, governors, and administrators. In the 1880s, Europe carved up Africa and took over. Gold rushes made South Africa rich, though ruled by whites. The slave trade had now ended, but all of Africa fell to European exploitation and government instead,dominated by the British and the French.

MIDDLE EAST

The long, slow decline of the Ottomans continued, and the Persians had to fight the British to fend them off. The Middle East became something of a backwater, held in check by traditional rule, and untouched by change. By the same token though, it also avoided colonialization.

INDUSTRIAL REVOLUTION 1836–1913

The continuing revolution in industry was shaping a new world. The rapid growth of opportunities for employers and workers also brought exploitation and injustice.

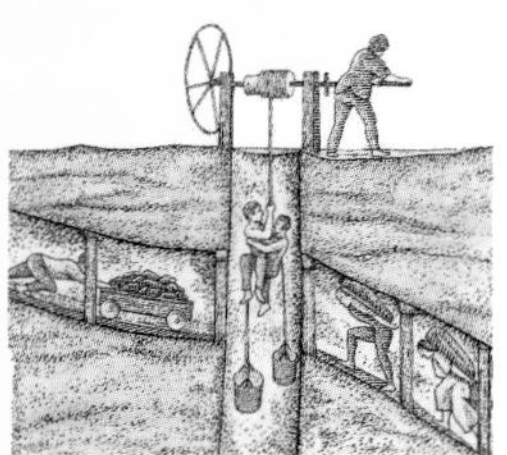

Many children worked in mines and factories, but this was banned in most countries by 1900.

The British inventor Isambard Kingdom Brunel (1806–1859) built railroads, bridges, tunnels, train stations, ports, and the world's largest ship.

During the 1700s, many people in Britain worked at home, usually producing goods by hand. There were also many farmers and farm laborers who worked on the land to grow crops to feed their families. By the middle of the 1800s, all this had changed. Many British people now lived in towns and worked in enormous factories, or in stores, offices, railroads, and other businesses designed to serve the inhabitants of these industrial centers. Leading the world, British inventors continued to develop revolutionary new machines that performed traditional tasks such as spinning and weaving much faster than they could be done by hand. Machines were also used to make iron and steel. These metals were, in turn, used to make more machines, weapons, and tools.

Jobs in factories, such as textile mills, often required skill rather than strength. This gave women a chance to earn a living wage, both in the towns of the New England states and in the north of Britain.

Four factors brought about the change: coal mining, a canal system, capital (money), and cheap labor. Coal was used to smelt iron and steel and to make steam to power the new machines. Barges carried raw materials and finished goods along the canals. The profits from Britain's colonies gave businessmen the money to invest. And badly paid farmworkers flocked to the towns for better paid work.

▼ New factories were built near rivers or canals and railroads This meant that raw materials could be delivered, and finished goods taken away. Houses for workers were often built close to the factory.

BUSINESS BOOM

New coal mines were dug to supply coal for steam engines and coke for ironworks. By the mid-1800s, Britain's canal and rail systems linked all the major industrial cities. The new machines made goods faster and more cheaply. Factory and mine owners made huge profits, some of which they spent on more machines, so creating new jobs. Investors saved small amounts of money in banks. The banks then lent large amounts to industrialists. This developing capitalist system raised money to build factories, offices, and houses.

For many workers, life in the factories and mines was hard and dangerous. Men, women, and children worked 12 or more hours a day, often for low wages. Many workers were killed or injured by unsafe machinery before new safety laws were enforced. Towns grew rapidly and without any real planning, leaving some areas without drains or clean water. Diseases such as cholera (from dirty water) became common and killed thousands of people.

The arrival of the railroad opened up North America but also led to the first national strike—the Great Strike of 1877. When railroad workers had their wages cut, their protests stopped the trains.

In time, laws to shorten working hours and prohibit child labor were introduced. Trade unions, at first banned, campaigned for better pay and conditions for workers. Reformers won better working conditions, and schooling for all children. Slums were cleared and new laws were brought in to control factories and houses.

In 1842, James Nasmyth (1808–1890) invented the steam hammer, used to make parts for the new steamships.

▶ A big step forward in steelmaking was made by Henry Bessemer (1813–1898). In a Bessemer Converter, hot air was blasted through melted iron to convert it into steel. Steel was stronger and more useful than iron, but before Bessemer's invention in 1856, it was very expensive to make.

KEY DATES

1838	Brunel builds the steamship *Great Western*
1842	James Nasmyth invents first steam hammer
1865	George Pullman invents railroad sleeping car
1869	George Westinghouse invents air brake; Suez Canal completed, easing travel to India
1886	Samuel Gompers sets up American Federation of Labor
1893	Frank Sprague invents electric trolley
1900	United States and Germany both overtake Britain's steel production

THE OPIUM WARS 1830–1864

European merchants used the addictive power of opium to gain important trading links with China—a country that wished to remain closed to foreigners.

The wife of an opium smoker publicly destroys her husband's pipe. The sale and smoking of opium had been banned in China from the early 1700s, by order of the emperor.

Ships, like this British merchant ship in Lintin Harbor, in 1834, would have carried quantities of opium. Foreign merchants traded the drug for the precious goods that were so greatly desired by customers in Europe.

The Chinese had almost no contact with the rest of the world for centuries. Many European merchants were eager to trade, especially in the rare Chinese silks and porcelain that were so popular in Europe. However, the Chinese government allowed trading to take place at only one port, Guangzhou (Canton). To get around this problem, foreign traders began to smuggle the drug opium into the country, so that the Chinese would trade their precious goods in exchange for the drug. The Chinese government tried to stop this. In 1839, Chinese officials, under the orders of Lim Tse-hsu, the Chinese high commissioner of Guangzhou, visited British warehouses where they seized and burned up to 20,000 chests of opium.

The British would not tolerate what they saw as the confiscation of private property. In response, they sent warships that threatened the Chinese and besieged the port. The Chinese refused to pay compensation, banned trade with Britain, and fired on the British forces. Thus started the First Opium War (1839–1842) fought by the Chinese and the British.

TREATY OF NANJING

The war was one-sided. The British had superior forces, and they bombarded Guangzhou and captured Hong Kong from the Chinese. When this first war was over, the British forced the Chinese to sign the Treaty of Nanjing (Nanking), which opened up Chinese ports to Britain. China also had to pay compensation and give the island of Hong Kong to the British.

Britain's aggressive approach to the Chinese owed a great deal to the British foreign secretary Henry Temple, 3rd Viscount Palmerston. He was always ready to use force in what he saw as the defense of British interests overseas. In this, and later treaties, the Chinese were forced to give in to European demands. The Chinese, however, continued to fear that foreign trade meant that the country would come under foreign influence.

Hong Kong Island became a British colony in 1842. It soon grew into a center of trade. In 1860, the Kowloon Peninsula was added, and in 1898, the British gained the New Territories on a 99-year lease.

SOCIAL UNREST

Trouble, largely promoted by the British, erupted again in the mid-1850s and resulted in the Second Opium War (1856–1860). This war was also eventually won by the British and it ended with another treaty. The Treaty of Tianjin (Tientsin) was signed in 1858, and it forced the Chinese to open even more ports to trade with European merchants. Other countries, including France and the United States, also signed treaties, which gained their citizens special rights and increased Western influence in China. Eager traders and missionaries rushed in.

At the same time, the huge Chinese Empire was gradually breaking down. The ruling Qing dynasty was faced with rebellions started by starving peasants. The Taiping Rebellion (1851–1864) was begun by people who wanted the land to be divided equally among ordinary people. The foreign powers helped to crush the rebellion because they wanted the Qing dynasty to continue so that the treaties would be honored.

KEY DATES	
1839	Chinese officials destroy British opium stocks; Outbreak of First Opium War
1842	Chinese sign the Treaty of Nanjing
1844	Treaty of Wanghia with the United States; Treaty of Whampoa with France
1851	The Taiping Rebellion breaks out
1856	Outbreak of Second Opium War
1858	Chinese sign the Treaty of Tianjin
1898	Britain obtains 99-year lease on New Territories

Britain's vastly superior navy could easily destroy Chinese junks during the opium wars.

The Taiping Rebellion (1851–1864) was crushed by the Chinese with help from foreign powers who wanted Qing rule to continue.

EUROPE: YEAR OF REVOLUTION 1848

In 1848, protests broke out all over Europe. They demonstrated how unhappy people were with how they were governed.

Giuseppe Mazzini (1805–1872), seen here in prison, was a tireless campaigner for democracy and the unification of Italy.

The reasons for many of these rebellions were similar to those that sparked the French Revolution. One of the main factors was that people in many countries in Europe began to feel that they should have a say in their own government. In response to the rebellions and violent protests, many rulers just ignored the pleas of their people and tried to restore older systems of government, but the events of 1848 showed that change was inevitable.

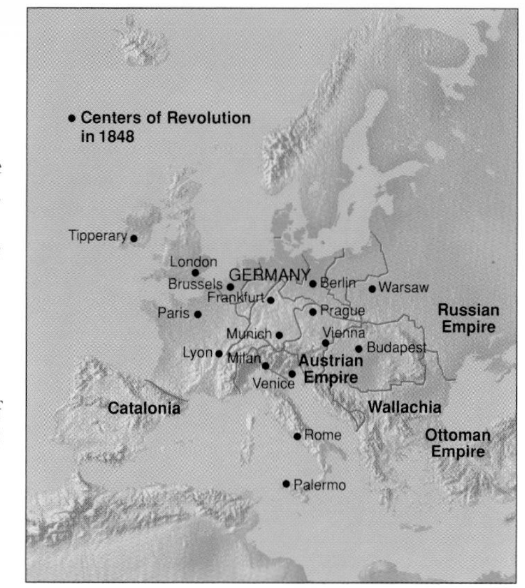

Revolution in Europe had been simmering since 1815, and in 1848, most European countries experienced rebellions. The map above shows where the most serious outbreaks were.

One powerful reason for the revolutions of 1848 was nationalism—the desire of people who spoke the same language to form their own independent nations. Nationalism was especially strong in Italy and Germany, which were divided into many small states, and in parts of the Austrian Empire. Other rebellions were led by people who wanted cheaper food, or changes in laws that would give land to working people.

▲ Paris revolutionaries demanding "Bread or Death" stormed government buildings in Paris. They overthrew the king, Louis-Philippe, and declared a republic with Louis Napoleon, nephew of Napoleon Bonaparte, as "prince president."

▶ The People's Charter, drafted by William Lovett (1800–1877) in 1838, demanded political reforms, including votes for all men. It gave its name to the Chartist movement. The last and biggest Chartist demonstration took place in London, in 1848.

CHARTISM

In some countries, people were demanding the right to vote. This was one of the reforms that the Chartist movement in Britain wanted. The People's Charter was first published there in May 1838. A petition said to have 1,200,000 signatures on it was handed in to Parliament in June 1839, but was rejected a month later. By February 1848, and following the revolution in France, a final petition was formed. When it was complete it was said to have over 3,000,000 names on it. On April 10, 1848 a mass march traveled across London to the Houses of Parliament to present the petition. Again, it was rejected, and Chartism lost its momentum.

Recent changes had made rebellion easier. More people were now able to read and newspapers told them what was happening in other countries. Few police forces existed, so troops had to be used against rioters. Most of the revolts of 1848 failed in their immediate demands, but over the next few years, nationalist feeling grew stronger, and many governments began to see that democratic reforms would soon be necessary.

The rebellions in Vienna and other cities resulted in the resignation of the Austrian chancellor, Prince Metternich, in March 1848. Emperor Ferdinand abdicated in favor of Franz Josef in December 1848.

Frankfurt, in Germany, also witnessed street fighting and rebellion. The people did succeed in forcing a change in their country's leadership. Peasants were given rights and protection.

REVOLUTION IN EUROPE

In France, the Second Republic was founded with Louis Napoleon, nephew of Napoleon Bonaparte, as "prince president." In the Italian states, revolts were widespread, but were crushed by the end of the year. The Austrian chancellor, Prince Metternich,was forced to flee, and the emperor abdicated in favor of Franz Josef.

There were uprisings in Berlin, Vienna, Prague, Budapest, Catalonia, Wallachia, Poland, and Britain. In Germany, the National Assembly met in Frankfurt, and in the Netherlands, a new constitution was introduced.

In Belgium, the *Communist Manifesto*, written by Karl Marx and Friedrich Engels, was published. Elsewhere, the armies and peasants remained loyal to their monarchs. Revolts were crushed in Prussia and Italy, but there were some reforms.

JAPAN 1853–1913

Under the Tokugawas, Japan had been closed to foreigners for more than 200 years. In the early 1800s, it began to experience Western influence.

After 1868, the Meiji government improved educational standards. By 1914, the Japanese were among the best-educated people in the world.

During the first half of the 1600s, Japan's rulers decided that contact with the West must end. In particular, they feared that Christian missionaries might bring European armies to invade Japan. They therefore banned almost all foreigners from entering Japan and the Japanese from leaving their own country. As a result, people in the West were unable to appreciate the great beauty of the Japanese art of this period until the mid-to-late 1800s. In 1853, Millard Fillmore (1800–1874), the 13th President of the United States, sent four warships, under the command of Commodore Matthew Perry, on an important journey to Japan designed to bring about the opening of trade there.

The warships anchored in Tokyo Bay. The threat of American naval power helped Commodore Perry persuade the Japanese to resume trading with the West. The Japanese were impressed by Perry's steamships and by the other machinery he showed them. The two countries went on to sign the Treaty of Kanagawa a year later, in 1854, in which they agreed to open two ports to American trade.

▲ U.S. Commodore Matthew Perry (1794–1858) is known as the man who opened up Japan to trade with the rest of the world. In 1853, he sailed to Japan, and in 1854, signed the Treaty of Kanagawa with the Japanese.

The ships of Commodore Perry's fleet were the first steamships that the Japanese had ever seen. They realized that they would be unable to beat them.

Soon, similar treaties had been signed with Britain, the Netherlands, and Russia. The Tokugawa were criticized by their opponents for allowing these treaties to be signed, and for many other problems they could not solve.

▶ This Japanese woodblock print shows Yokohama Harbor in the late 1800s. Following the Treaty of Kanagawa, the Japanese agreed to open ports to trade with the United States and several European countries.

RESTORATION OF THE EMPEROR

People were tired of the near total isolation that the Tokugawa family had imposed for so long. In 1868, the Tokugawa were finally overthrown and the emperor, Mutsuhito, was restored as ruler (the Meiji Restoration). Now that their country had opened up to the West, the Japanese began to modernize.

Although the Japanese wanted to keep some of their own traditions, they were also eager to learn from the industrial nations of the West. They changed and adapted both their government and their schools. Improved education meant that by 1914 the Japanese were among the best-educated people in the world. They began to import machines and introduced new industries such as cotton manufacture. Many Japanese people adopted European fashions in music and clothes. At the same time, foreigners gradually learned to respect Japanese success and culture.

With industrialization, the Japanese soon began to expand their country. They tried to take over Korea, which led to a war with China in 1894. Japan also fought Russia over this issue in 1904–1905 and finally annexed Korea in 1910. This helped make Japan the most powerful nation in its region. By 1913, Japan had become an industrial power of great importance—the first country in Asia to make such advances.

▲ Russian soldiers flee after the Battle of Mukden, in northeast China, in which the Japanese won a decisive victory in March 1905.

▼ In May 1905, Japan's fleet, led by Admiral Togo, annihilated the Russian fleet. This led to the Treaty of Portsmouth and gave the Japanese control over Korea.

AMERICAN CIVIL WAR 1861–1865

By the mid-1800s, the United States was badly divided. The North and South strongly disagreed about questions of states' rights and ownership of slaves.

Ulysses S. Grant (1822–1885) was appointed commander of the Union forces in 1863. He was a tough and determined general.

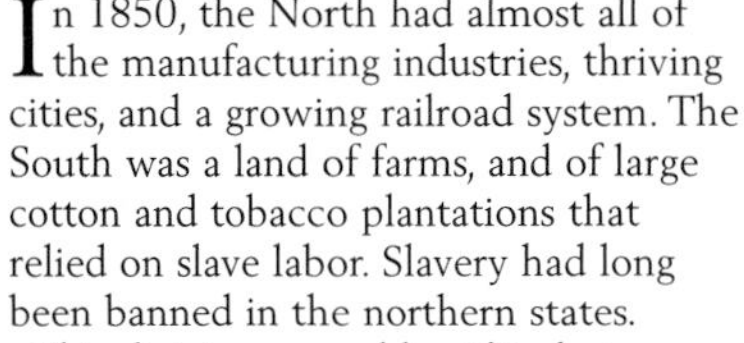

In 1850, the North had almost all of the manufacturing industries, thriving cities, and a growing railroad system. The South was a land of farms, and of large cotton and tobacco plantations that relied on slave labor. Slavery had long been banned in the northern states.

This division caused hostility between North and South. The Kansas–Nebraska Act (1854) gave new states the right to choose whether or not they allowed slavery. The Compromise of 1850 helped northern states protect the rights of runaway slaves—the South felt threatened.

The southern states were sure that the economy of the South would be ruined if the slaves were freed. Furthermore, the southern states believed that they had the right to make their own laws without interference from the federal government.

In 1860, Abraham Lincoln (1809–1865) was elected president. He belonged to the Republican Party, which opposed slavery, although he himself was not an abolitionist. Many southern states refused to live under such a government, and led by Jefferson Davis (1808–1889), they announced in December 1860 that they were seceding from (leaving) the Union and forming the Confederate States of America. The United States government declared they had no right to do this.

Union soldiers wore the blue uniform of the U.S. army. The Confederates usually wore gray.

Robert E. Lee (1807–1870) was in the U.S. army when civil war broke out. He resigned, and first advised, then took command of, the Confederate troops.

BATTLE OF GETTYSBURG

The Battle of Gettysburg (July 1–3, 1863) was a turning point in the Civil War. The battle was the bloodiest ever fought on American soil, but was an important Union victory by General George Meade. He stopped an invasion of the North by General Robert E. Lee's Confederate army. From this point onward, the South's chances of winning the war declined.

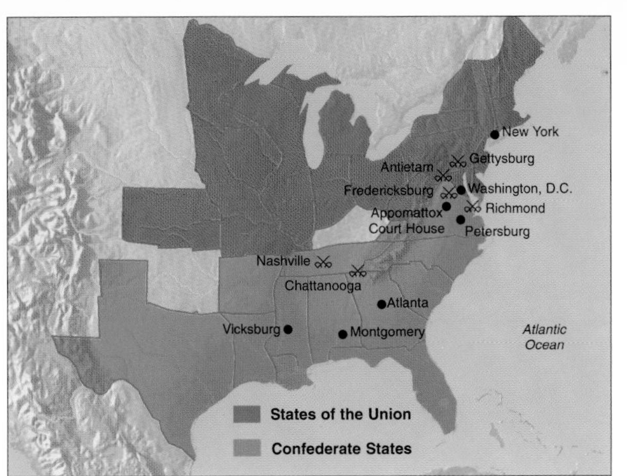

◀ This shows the division of the United States at the beginning of the Civil War. Eleven of the 34 states made up the Confederacy. Most of the battles were fought in the east and southeast.

▲ The Battle of Spotsylvania, Virginia, in May 1864, was one of the many Union victories of the Civil War. In all, more than 600,000 soldiers died on both sides in the conflict.

THE TWO SIDES

The North (Union), made up of 23 states, had more men, more money, and more industry than the South. The North also controlled the navy and started a naval blockade that prevented the South from receiving help or supplies from abroad. The 11 states of the South (the Confederacy) were much weaker, but they had the benefit of good generals and a great fighting spirit. Civil war broke out on April 12, 1861 when the forces of the South opened fire on Fort Sumter in South Carolina. The Confederates won a number of victories early in the war.

The South won the first battles in 1861, including Fredericksburg and Chancellorsville, but the turning point in the struggle came in July 1863, when the North won the biggest battle of the war, at Gettysburg. The Union forces, under the command of General George Meade, stopped an invasion of the North by General Robert E. Lee's Confederate army. Each side had over 20,000 soldiers killed or wounded.

Union flag

Confederate flag

During the Civil War, the Confederates rejected the Stars and Stripes and adopted their own flag.

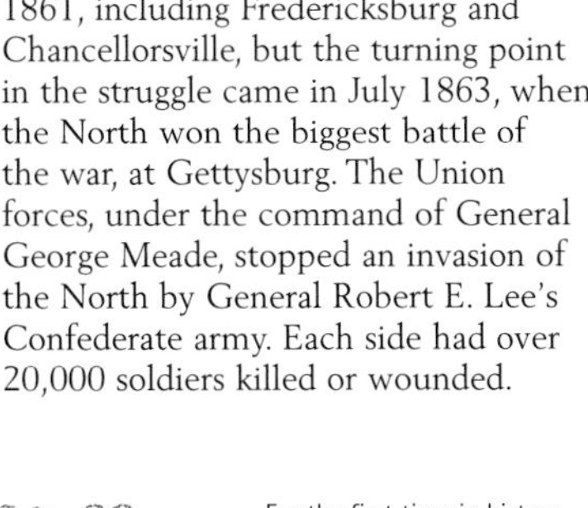

For the first time in history, railroads played a vital part in warfare by moving troops, ammunition, and supplies swiftly over great distances.

Harriet Tubman (1820–1913) was an escaped slave who made trips through southern territory, helping slaves escape.

THE END OF THE CIVIL WAR 1865

Slavery was completely abolished in 1865, with the 13th Amendment to the Constitution. The country was reunited, but new problems emerged.

General Lee's presentation sword was not handed over during the surrender ceremony, as was customary. Instead, it remained by his side.

In 1864, despite Lee's skillful tactics, General Grant captured Richmond, the capital of the South. General Sherman marched through Georgia and the other southern states, capturing Atlanta. He followed this victory with a "march to the sea," during which he destroyed towns and farms. Short of men, money, weapons, and food, Lee surrendered on April 9, 1865, ending the Civil War. More than 600,000 soldiers had died, many from diseases such as typhoid and dysentery. Five days later, Abraham Lincoln was assassinated.

The Civil War settled two important questions. First, it confirmed that the United States of America was a single nation and that no state had the right to break away. Second, it brought slavery in the southern states to an end. After the Civil War, arguments raged over how the South should be "reconstructed." Ideas included the opening of schools and the building of railroads. Abraham Lincoln's successor, Andrew Johnson (1808–1875), a Democrat, wanted better conditions for black Americans. The Republicans wanted a harsher policy, and it was they who won the argument in the end.

General Lee surrendered to General Grant at Appomattox Court House, Virginia, on April 9, 1865. His men were outnumbered, exhausted, and starving.

The people of the South resisted most aspects of Reconstruction. Many former slaves who had fought on the Union side returned home expecting more freedom in the South. However, the Ku Klux Klan and other racist organizations began a campaign of murder and terrorism in 1866 that tried to stop black Americans from enjoying civil rights. Northern troops withdrew, Reconstruction ended, and the Democrats took over the South.

Abraham Lincoln (1809–1865) was the 16th President of the United States. Many people believe he was the greatest of all of the presidents. "Honest Abe" was known for his integrity and the force of his arguments.

THE GETTYSBURG ADDRESS

In November 1863, President Lincoln was invited to make a "few appropriate remarks" at the dedication of a national cemetery at Gettysburg. His speech lasted about two minutes and is today regarded as a masterpiece. Abraham Lincoln summed up the central issue of the war—the survival of a nation dedicated to freedom.

CANADA 1763–1913

The peace terms of 1763 effectively gave Canada over to British rule. In 1791, the British Constitutional Act split Canada into British- and French-speaking territories.

Louis Joseph Papineau (1786–1871) was a French-Canadian politician. He led the French-speaking Canadians' demand for reform and equality.

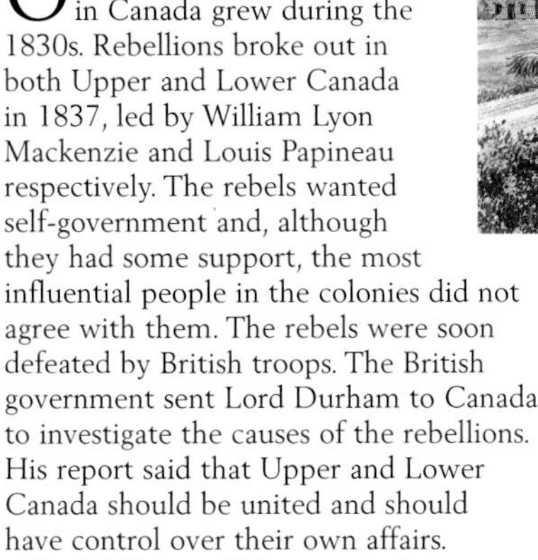

William Lyon Mackenzie (1795–1861) was a member of Canada's Reform Party. He wanted Canada to have more freedom from British rule. He led the 1837 rebellion in Upper Canada.

Opposition to British rule in Canada grew during the 1830s. Rebellions broke out in both Upper and Lower Canada in 1837, led by William Lyon Mackenzie and Louis Papineau respectively. The rebels wanted self-government and, although they had some support, the most influential people in the colonies did not agree with them. The rebels were soon defeated by British troops. The British government sent Lord Durham to Canada to investigate the causes of the rebellions. His report said that Upper and Lower Canada should be united and should have control over their own affairs.

The 1840 Act of Union united the two colonies, which became known as the Province of Canada. However, many Canadians still felt that these reforms did not go far enough. This was partly because the Canadians were concerned that the United States might invade if Canada looked weak. In 1867, the British North America Act was passed, and Canada became self-governing. The act united four Canadian provinces in a dominion. The French Canadians of Quebec were promised equality, and French and English became the official languages.

Winnipeg, a center of the fur trade, was still a small town in 1870. In that year, the settlement became the capital of the province of Manitoba.

WESTERN TERRITORIES

The vast lands to the west, which belonged to the Hudson's Bay Company, later also became part of Canada. The Northwest Territories joined the dominion in 1870, and the Yukon Territory in 1898. The Yukon had been the location of a gold rush in 1896, which led to tens of thousands of hopeful prospectors making their way over the Rocky Mountains to the goldfields and, they hoped, great wealth. Completion of the Canadian Pacific Railway in 1885 united the country. Unlike the American railroads, it formed one continuous system from the St. Lawrence River to the Pacific Ocean.

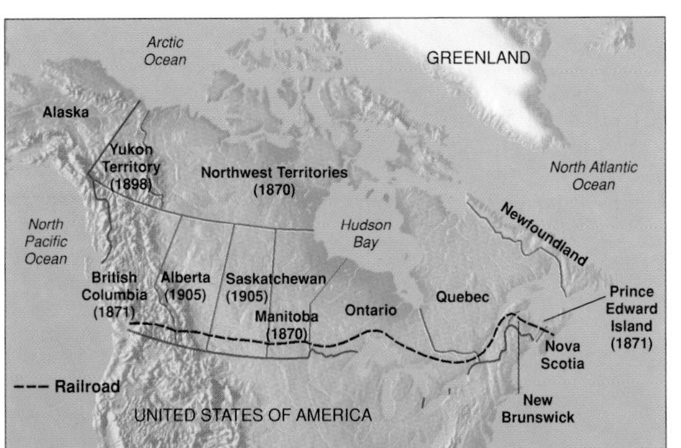

◀ The British North America Act of 1867 united the provinces of Nova Scotia, New Brunswick, Ontario (formerly Upper Canada), and Quebec (Lower Canada) in the Dominion of Canada.

▲ The Canadian Pacific Railway was completed in 1885. It linked the east and west coasts, reducing the journey time from five months to five days.

ITALY 1833–1878

The birth of the Italian nation was brought about with the help of an aristocrat, Count Camillo Cavour, and a man of the people, Giuseppe Garibaldi.

Victor Emmanuel II (1820–1878) was the popular king of Piedmont–Sardinia. He eventually became king of all Italy.

▼ Piedmont–Sardinia took the lead in uniting Italy in 1859–1860. Nice and Savoy were given to France in 1860.

In the early 1800s, Italy was made up of a number of small states. Apart from the Kingdom of Piedmont–Sardinia and Rome, which was ruled by the pope, these states were governed by foreign countries. In the 1830s, an independence movement known as the *Risorgimento* ("resurrection") began to grow. In 1848, many revolutions against foreign rule broke out, but they were quickly suppressed. In 1849, Victor Emmanuel II became king of Piedmont–Sardinia (a northern state in the Piedmont region, which also ruled the island of Sardinia), and made Turin his capital. He was a very popular man, at least in part because he restricted the powers of the clergy, who were less well-regarded in the north than in the south. He was known as "the cavalier king."

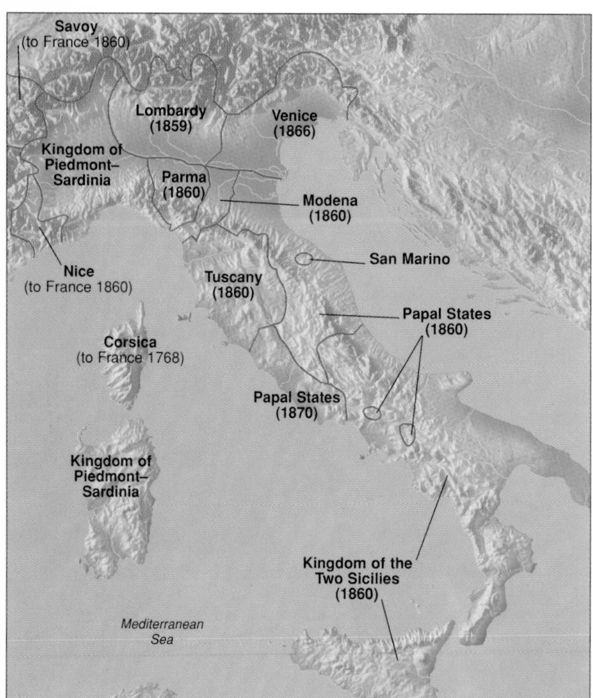

The rebellion in Venice in 1848 was one of the last in Italy to hold out. Severely weakened by hunger and disease, the people of Venice gave up in August 1849.

SKILLFUL POLITICIAN

Count Camillo Cavour, an Italian aristocrat with very liberal views, became the chief minister of the Kingdom of Piedmont–Sardinia in 1852. He made an alliance with France in 1858. Together, they defeated the Austrians in 1859. Austria ceded Lombardy to France who then handed it to Piedmont in exchange for Savoy and Nice. Most of northern Italy then joined with Piedmont–Sardinia.

In 1860, rebellion broke out in southern Italy, which was part of the Kingdom of the Two Sicilies. Giuseppe Garibaldi led a revolt and conquered the kingdom. His men were known as "red shirts" because of their dress, and faithfully followed their romantic and patriotic leader. It took them a mere three months to conquer all of Sicily.

Cavour was now very concerned that Garibaldi, and his seemingly unstoppable men, would attack Rome, which might in turn lead Austria or France to come to the aid of the pope. Cavour invaded the Papal States (but not Rome) and then marched his army south. Garibaldi's forces had taken Naples, and Cavour, being careful to go around Rome itself, finally met up with him.

Giuseppe Garibaldi (1807–1882) was a patriot who fought against foreign rule in Italy. With his "red shirts," he conquered the kingdom of the Two Sicilies in 1860, and it became part of the Kingdom of Italy.

Count Camillo Cavour (1810–1861) was the politician who made most of the plans for a unified Italy. He was also able to harness the talents of Giuseppe Garibaldi to help his own plans.

AGREEMENT AND UNITY

Count Cavour reached a detailed agreement with Garibaldi and his red-shirt soldiers that allowed the Kingdom of Piedmont–Sardinia to take over Sicily, Naples, and the Papal States. In February 1861, the first national parliament was held in Turin and, one month later, Victor Emmanuel II was proclaimed king of all Italy.

Two small areas were not included. Venice was still part of the Austrian Empire and Rome was ruled by the pope but occupied by France. Venice was given to Italy after Austria was defeated in the Austro–Prussian War (1866). In Rome, Pope Pius IX was totally unwilling to bend to what he still saw as a northern king. The Franco–Prussian War of 1870 forced the French to withdraw their garrison in Rome for other duties, and the Italian army immediately took over Rome. The city then became the capital of Italy. Pope Pius would not negotiate and thought of himself as a prisoner in the Vatican until he died in 1878. The people of Rome wanted unity and so it was that the ruling house of Piedmont–Sardinia reigned over a totally united country.

KEY DATES

1830s	Mazzini founds the "Young Italy" movement
1848	Revolutions break out in Europe
1849	Victor Emmanuel II—King of Piedmont–Sardinia
1852	Cavour—chief minister of Piedmont–Sardinia
1859	Piedmont–Sardinia and France defeat Austrians
1860	Garibaldi and his army conquer Sicily
1861	First national Italian parliament held
1870	Rome joins greater Italy

▼ A meeting between Victor Emmanuel II and Garibaldi at Teano, northeast of Naples, in 1860 eventually led to the unification of Italy.

GERMANY 1848–1871

In the second half of the 1800s, the military might of France was overtaken by a German state, Prussia. A new and powerful Germany emerged.

The diplomatic skills of Otto von Bismarck (1815–1898), prime minister of Prussia, kept his enemies isolated.

▲ Napoleon III (1808–1873) became emperor of France in 1852. He was captured at the Battle of Sedan during the Franco-Prussian War and sent into exile in 1871.

After the failure of the revolutions of 1848, the German Confederation, made up of over 40 states, stayed as disunited as it had been for centuries. The two strongest states, Austria and Prussia, jostled for power over all of Germany. Although weaker at first, Prussia's trade and industry grew in the 1850s. Its increasing strength was supported by the Prussian kaiser and his new prime minister, Otto von Bismarck.

Austria and Prussia went to war against Denmark over control of the duchies of Schleswig and Holstein. Although both duchies belonged to the royal family of Denmark, many Germans lived there. Denmark was defeated, and both duchies now came under German control. But Austria and Prussia soon clashed over how they should be administered.

WHO WOULD LEAD GERMANY?

In 1866, Bismarck dissolved the German Confederation, and Austria declared war on Prussia, confident of victory. They had, however, not taken sufficient account of the skill and strength of the Prussian army. The Prussian forces swept through the Austrian territory at an alarming speed. The power of the Austrian Hapsburg Empire was forever weakened when they were defeated on July 3, 1866 at the Battle of Sadowa. Bismarck then set up the North German Confederation, with Prussia as the most powerful member.

The Peace of Prague was an excellent example of the skillful diplomacy and statesmanship of Bismarck. He knew that it would be dangerous to humble Austria, and he wanted to make an ally and not an enemy. Accordingly, the Hapsburgs only lost the two duchies, which they did not really want anyway, and Venice. Prussia did, however, make huge gains within the rest of Germany.

► In September 1870, during the Franco-Prussian War, the Prussian army laid siege to Paris. Rather than make a full assault on the city, the Prussians simply surrounded it and waited. The poor were soon facing starvation, and the wealthy were reduced to eating the animals from the Tuileries Zoo. Peace came in May 1871.

THE BATTLE OF SEDAN

The Battle of Sedan, in northern France, on September 1–2, 1870, was the scene of an unequal conflict between Prussian forces and the French. The French forces were outnumbered two to one. Although Leboeuf, the French war minister, had claimed that the French preparation was total, once the battle began, it was found that not all of the French riflemen even had a rifle. Surrounded and unable to break out, Napoleon III, along with 85,000 French troops, was forced to surrender.

THE FRANCO–PRUSSIAN WAR

The French emperor, Napoleon III, a poorly supported, ill-advised leader, felt threatened by Prussia's increasing power. He demanded Germany hand over some of its territory to balance out the Prussian gains. Bismarck ignored this demand, and Napoleon's threats only served to bring the previously reluctant southern German states behind Prussia.

Bismarck provoked the French when he altered the report of a conversation between the Prussian king and the French ambassador so that it looked like an insult to France. When the document, the "Ems Telegram," was published in 1870, Napoleon III was furious and declared war. In the Franco–Prussian War, Prussia defeated France in 1871 and took over Alsace and Lorraine. The remaining German states also joined in 1871. Bismarck then formed the German Second Reich, with the king of Prussia (William I) as emperor.

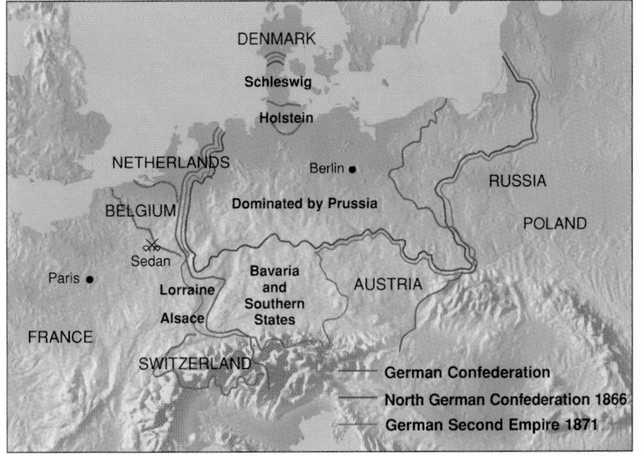

▲ The North German Confederation, dominated by Prussia, was formed in 1867. It was a union of states in which the members kept their own governments, but military and foreign policy was decided by a federal government.

KEY DATES	
1852	Napoleon III becomes emperor of France
1862	Bismarck becomes Prussian prime minister
1864	Danish plans to take over Schleswig-Holstein
1866	Schleswig-Holstein taken over by Prussia
1867	North German Confederation formed
1870	Outbreak of the Franco–Prussian War
1870	French defeat at the Battle of Sedan, Napoleon III captured
1870	Prussian siege of Paris begins
1871	Franco-Prussian War ends at Peace of Frankfurt
1871	Second German Reich proclaimed at Versailles
1873	Napoleon III dies in exile

◀ This cartoon shows Bismarck and Kaiser Wilhelm riding on Napoleon III as a pig as they make their triumphal entry into Paris in 1871.

SCRAMBLE FOR AFRICA 1880–1912

With their greater wealth and technology, the major European powers were able to conquer large parts of the world. They claimed the territory as their own.

Toward the end of the 1800s, the European powers ceased to squabble among themselves for territories and trade within Europe itself. With the sudden emergence of the new force of Germany under the political control of Otto von Bismarck, all European nations looked farther afield for economic gain. Rival European nations now rushed to carve out their respective colonies in Africa. This process became known as the "scramble for Africa."

Britain and France undoubtedly led the scramble, but Germany, Belgium, and Italy were very close behind. Numerous conflicts flared up between Britain and France over colonies in West Africa. Where Britain had been happy to control a relatively small number of coastal towns and ports, by the end of the century they had taken over all of what is now Ghana and Nigeria, and effectively controlled Sierra Leone and The Gambia.

This cartoon shows the German eagle, poised to take as much of Africa as it can. Germany was just one of many European powers seeking new lands.

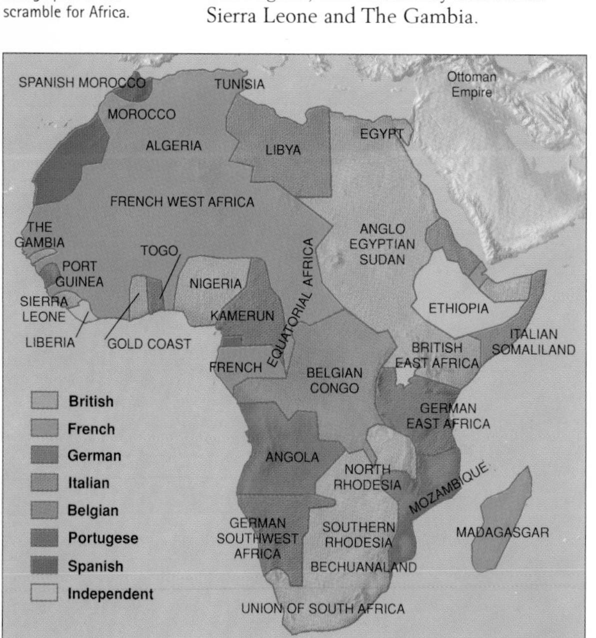

▼ During the latter part of the 1800s, rivalry between the different European powers played a large part in the scramble for Africa.

Dr. David Livingstone, lost while seeking the source of the Nile, had a historic meeting with Welsh-born American journalist H. M. Stanley by Lake Tanganyika in 1871.

THE SUEZ CANAL

Opened in 1869, the Suez Canal cut the sea journey between Britain and India from three months to three weeks. The Khedive of Egypt was in financial difficulties, and the British bought his half of the shares in the Suez Canal in 1875.

Relations between Britain and France worsened when the British occupied Egypt in 1882 to protect their interests during a local uprising against the Europeans. In 1885, General Gordon and many British soldiers were killed when the Mahdi, the leader in Sudan, took Khartoum on the White Nile. The Italians invaded Eritrea (now part of Ethiopia), and King Leopold of the Belgians took over the Congo.

Europeans traded guns in exchange for gold and ivory. The guns had a devastating effect in Africa.

CONSTANT EXPANSION

The scramble for Africa became a formal process at a conference in Berlin in 1884. The rival European countries cut up Africa like a cake. Only Liberia and Ethiopia, which held off an Italian invasion, remained independent. The colonization of Africa had a number of effects on Africans. The Europeans took no notice of the different African nations and tribal boundaries when the new borders were drawn. They brought new forms of government to Africa, but few Africans could vote. Profits from the colonies went back to Europe, and European colonists often took the best farmland.

KEY DATES	
1869	Suez Canal opens to shipping
1871	Stanley meets Livingstone at Lake Tanganyika
1876	Leopold II of Belgium takes over the Congo
1882	British occupy Egypt to protect the Suez Canal
1884	European nations meet in Berlin to divide Africa among themselves
1885	The Mahdi besieges Khartoum
1898	British defeat the Mahdi's troops at Omdurman
1893	The French take Timbuktu, Mali, West Africa
1899	British-Egyptian rule of Sudan
1912	The African National Congress (ANC) forms in South Africa

▲ The French conquest of Mali in West Africa was symbolized by the raising of the French flag in Timbuktu in 1893. Their advance along the Niger River was held up by the resistance of the local people, the Mande.

◀ Designed by French engineer Ferdinand de Lesseps (1805–1894), the Suez Canal considerably reduced the journey from Britain to India, and helped trade goods reach England more quickly. In 1875, the British, under the leadership of Disraeli, heard that the Khedive (viceroy) of Egypt faced bankruptcy, and they bought his share of the canal for £4 million.

IRELAND 1800–1913

Ireland went through a period of great suffering when disease struck the potato, the staple food of the poor. At least a million people died, and a million emigrated.

Daniel O'Connell (1775–1847) was a fighter for the rights of Catholic people in Britain. He was the first Irish Catholic to be elected to the British Parliament. He served from 1829 to 1847.

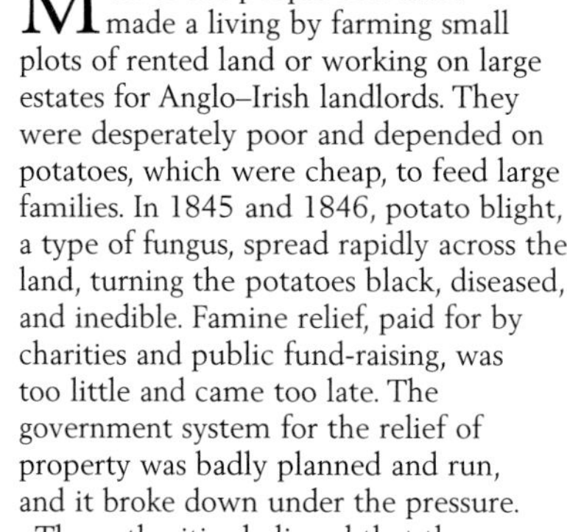

Most of the people of Ireland made a living by farming small plots of rented land or working on large estates for Anglo–Irish landlords. They were desperately poor and depended on potatoes, which were cheap, to feed large families. In 1845 and 1846, potato blight, a type of fungus, spread rapidly across the land, turning the potatoes black, diseased, and inedible. Famine relief, paid for by charities and public fund-raising, was too little and came too late. The government system for the relief of property was badly planned and run, and it broke down under the pressure.

The authorities believed that the food supply would adjust itself to meet the demand, and they opposed the distribution of free food until it was too late. Efforts to bring down the price of wheat by repealing the Corn Laws also came too late. Because landlords evicted tenants who could not pay their rent, entire families were left to starve to death by the side of the road.

On May 6, 1882, in Phoenix Park in Dublin, Lord Frederick Cavendish, the Irish chief secretary, and T.H. Burke, his undersecretary, were stabbed to death by Irish Nationalists. Five were later hanged for this offense.

IRISH EMIGRATION

To escape the famine, hundreds of thousands of Irish people emigrated, mostly to the British mainland, but great numbers also went to the United States and Canada. Blight also hit potato crops in Britain and other countries. But only in Ireland did it have such disastrous consequences, including the shadow it was to cast over Irish–British relations in future generations.

▲ Irish tenant farmers were ruined when the potato blight struck in 1845. The harvest was poor and they could not pay their rent. Many of the farmers and their families starved to death.

▶ Most Irish people lived a hard life with little food and comfort. Their homes were usually not very different from the barns in which their Anglo-Irish landlords kept their cattle.

During the potato famine, many Irish people had to choose between possible starvation or leaving their country. About one million people starved to death and another million emigrated over the next five years, mostly to England, Scotland, and Wales, as well as the United States. A typhoid epidemic in 1846–1847 is thought to have killed another 350,000 Irish people.

Charles Stewart Parnell was the leader of the Irish Nationalists in the British Parliament. He led the struggle for Irish home rule and supported the Land League, which wanted land to be given to Irish farmers.

The Irish Republican Brotherhood, or Fenians, was founded in 1858 by James Stephens (1825–1901). It was an organization that wanted to set up an Irish republic.

IRISH LEADERS

The demands of Irish politicians, particularly Charles Parnell (1846–1891), became increasing vocal in the British Parliament. Parnell had entered Parliament in 1875, and became president of the Irish Land League in 1879. His party demanded rent reductions and resisted the evictions of tenant farmers. The Irish politicians, and the strength of public feeling among the Irish, led to some law reforms, especially relating to land ownership rights.

However, these reforms were not enough to keep the Irish happy with British rule. Almost all of the Irish wanted home rule, or self-government. After the failure of both the 1886 and 1893 Home Rule Bills, the British Parliament finally passed the third Home Rule Bill in 1912—but it was not put into operation because of the outbreak of World War I, in 1914.

KEY DATES	
1801	Irish Parliament abolished by the British
1829	Daniel O'Connell enters the British Parliament
1845	First potato blight leads to widespread famine
1846	Second potato blight causes worse famine
1846	Typhoid epidemic kills 350,000 Irish people
1875	Charles Parnell enters the British Parliament
1879	Parnell becomes president of the Land League
1912	Third Home Rule Bill passed, but not enacted

▼ The Fenians sometimes resorted to acts of violence in Britain. In 1867, they attacked a police van in Manchester to rescue some of their members.

SOUTHEAST ASIA 1800–1913

Southeast Asia was dominated by the Dutch, French, and British in the late 1800s. They grew rich on the profits from crops grown by local people.

In Malaya, the British ruled through the local sultans. This beautiful mural of the tree of life comes from a family home in Sarawak, now part of Malaysia.

Southeast Asia was colonized by Europeans who set up plantations that were worked by the native population. The French colony of Indochina included Cambodia, Laos, and Vietnam. The French gradually conquered the area during the 1800s, despite local resistance. In Annam, the emperor, Ham Nghi, waged a guerrilla war until 1888.

The Dutch had been established in Indonesia since the 1620s. They had already taken over Indonesian trade, and from 1830, they also took over agriculture. The peasant farmers were forced to grow the crops the Dutch wanted, especially coffee and indigo (a plant from which a blue dye was made). By 1900, a nationalist movement was growing in Indonesia itself. The Indonesians made efforts to improve education and to regain some control over their business and trade.

The merchant ships of the British East India Company were known as East Indiamen.

Faced with Burmese expansion at the end of the 1700s, the British colonized Burma and the Malay Peninsula during the 1800s because they wanted to protect India, which they regarded as the most valuable part of their empire.

Rubber packing in Ceylon (now Sri Lanka) in the late 1800s. Rubber plants were introduced to Southeast Asia by the British from seeds collected in Brazil.

The Burmese resisted British rule in a series of bloody wars between 1824 and 1885, but by 1886, Britain controlled the whole country and made it into a province of India. It was not until 1937 that Burma was separated from India and regained some independence.

In Malaya, the situation was calmer because of British rule through the local sultans. During the early part of the 1800s, the British East India Company had set up trading posts; in 1826, Singapore, Malacca, and Penang were united to form the Straits Settlements.

▲ Indonesian princes and Dutch colonists benefited from the profits made by growing cash crops on the islands. For ordinary Indonesians, this way of life meant great hardship.

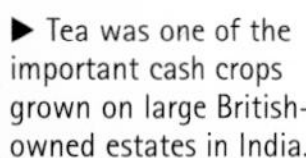

▶ Tea was one of the important cash crops grown on large British-owned estates in India.

BRITISH INFLUENCE

In later years, the British went on to become responsible for other states in the Malay Peninsula and formed the Federated Malay States in 1896, with the capital at Kuala Lumpur. Demand for rubber grew rapidly in the 1800s, but the only source of supply was South America. Rubber seeds were collected in Brazil and shipped to Kew Gardens, in London, where they were raised. In 1877, 2,000 young plants were shipped and distributed to countries such as Ceylon, Malaysia, and Indonesia, where the plants flourished.

By the 1880s, British engineers, surveyors, and architects were helping to build railroads, roads, bridges, factories, and government buildings in Southeast Asia. They drew on the experience gained from the Industrial Revolution in Britain. Banking and investment were geared toward financing the empire by trading raw materials from the colonies for homemade manufactured goods.

The British also figured out how to improve the techniques used for mining the large deposits of tin and other precious metals that had been discovered in Malaya and other countries. Toward the end of the 1800s, many people went to live and work in Southeast Asia as traders, soldiers, engineers, diplomats, and government administrators.

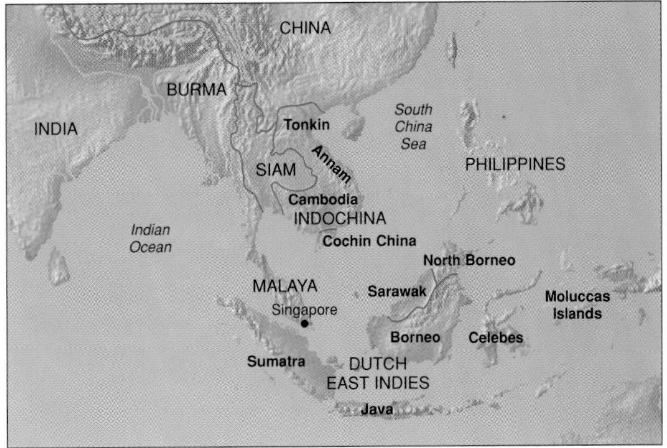

Southeast Asia was dominated by three European powers in the late 1800s—the French, British, and Dutch controlled every country except Siam.

KEY DATES

1813	East India Company's trade monopoly ends
1819	Thomas Raffles of the East India Company founds Singapore as a free port
1824	British and Dutch interests settled by treaty
1859	French naval forces capture the citadel in Saigon
1867	Singapore and the Straits Settlements apply to be a Crown colony
1877	Brazilian rubber plants, grown in Kew Gardens, in London, exported to Southeast Asia
1884–1885	Chinese-French War
1885	At the Treaty of Tientsin China recognizes French rule over Annam and Tonkin
1886	British annexe Upper Burma
1887	Union of Indochina formed from Vietnam, Cambodia, and Laos
1898	U.S.A. takes Philippines from the Spanish

▼ The French gradually conquered Indochina during the 1800s. Their forces captured the citadel in Saigon, Annam, on February 17, 1859. In 1862, the French signed a treaty with the local leader, Tu Doc.

THE BRITISH EMPIRE 1815–1913

During the 1800s, the British extended and consolidated their empire. Britain took over more land than any other nation in history.

When William IV died in 1837, the English crown passed to his niece, Victoria (1819–1901), who was just 18 years old. When Victoria died, her reign had lasted 63 years, the longest in British history.

▼ Between 1870 and 1913, the British Empire expanded further to take in land in Africa and Southeast Asia. This provided jobs for many British people. At its height, it included a quarter of the world's land and people.

At its height, during the reign of Queen Victoria, the British Empire included a quarter of the world's land and people. From the end of the Napoleonic Wars in 1815 to the start of World War I in 1914, Britain acquired so many new colonies that the empire stretched around the world. Britain was able to control this vast empire by its domination of the seas and world trade routes. Throughout the 1800s, British naval strength was unbeatable, and its boats constantly patrolled countries that belonged to the empire.

Because the empire covered both hemispheres it was known as "the empire on which the sun never sets." Colonies in the Caribbean, Africa, Asia, Australasia, and the Pacific were ruled from London, and were all united under the British monarch. Strategic harbors such as Gibraltar, Hong Kong, Singapore, and Aden came into British hands. Vital trade routes such as the Cape route to India, or the Suez Canal (via Egypt) to the spice and rubber plantations of Southeast Asia were also controlled by Britain.

Soldiers from the countries that were part of the British Empire were frequently used to make sure that British power and influence continued and expanded.

RAW MATERIALS

The empire provided the British with raw materials for manufacturing, and British demand for colonial products such as silk, spices, rubber, cotton, tea, coffee, and sugar led to the gradual takeover of many countries. Several countries became colonies when the British government acquired a bankrupt trading company. India was an example of a country where the British had come to trade and stayed to rule. It was the most prized colony in the empire. In 1850, India was still under the rule of the British East India Company. After the rebellion, of 1857, India was placed under the rule of the British government, and its policies were more cautious. British officials left control of local affairs to the Indian princes.

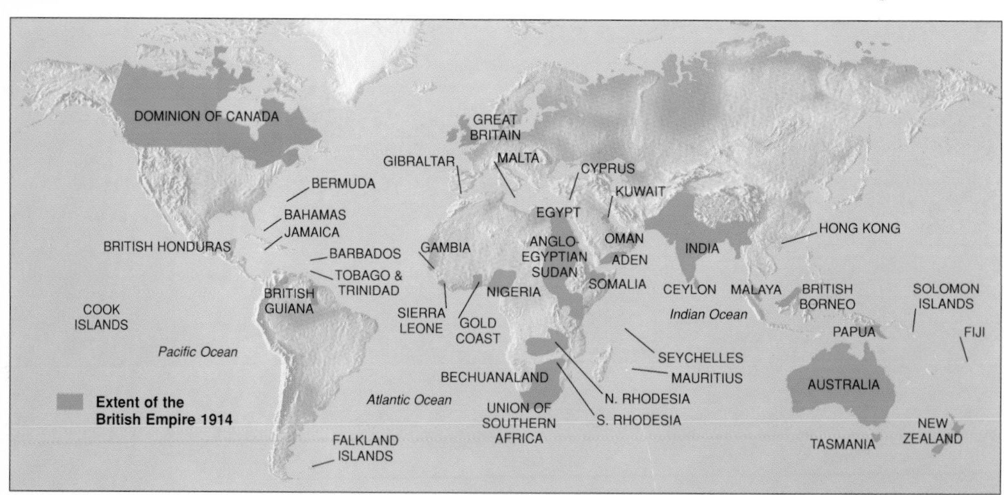

CONSOLIDATION

The British took over Egypt in 1883 to guard the Suez Canal and the route to India. After a rebellion in the south of Egypt led by a religious leader, the Mahdi, Britain entered Sudan in 1898. The British set up trade links throughout the empire by appointing an agent in every port. They organized local produce for export and markets for British imports. The British navy protected their interests and kept the sea routes safe for shipping.

British influence extended into mainland settlements in Central and South America, and into China where it had trading outposts. Queen Victoria, herself empress of India since 1876, was a keen supporter of a foreign policy that pursued colonial expansion and upheld the empire.
As more British people emigrated to countries within the empire, these lands were given more freedom to govern themselves. Many colonies, notably Canada, Australia, and South Africa, became dominions rather than colonies and were allowed self-government.

KEY DATES	
1824	Penal colony established in Brisbane, Australia
1829	Britain claims West Australia
1837	Victoria becomes queen of England
1850	Australian Colonies Government Act gives limited independence to Australia
1852	New Zealand is granted a constitution
1857	Indian mutiny against British rule begins
1867	British North American Act grants home rule to Canada
1875	Britain buys controlling interest in Suez Canal
1876	Queen Victoria becomes empress of India
1884	Britain annexes southeastern New Guinea
1890	Zanzibar becomes a British protectorate
1901	New South Wales, Queensland, Victoria, South Australia, Western Australia, and Tasmania become the Commonwealth of Australia; Queen Victoria dies
1907	Dominion of New Zealand is founded

The British government passed the Australian Colonies Government Act in 1850. This gave limited independence to the country. In 1901, the colonies of New South Wales, Queensland, Victoria, South Australia, Western Australia, and Tasmania became the Commonwealth of Australia.

END OF EMPIRE

Toward the end of the 1800s, some colonies began to break away from British rule. Home rule was granted to Canada in 1867, and independence to Australia in 1901. Both countries became dominions although they remained part of the British Empire. The gradual loosening of ties with the British Empire reflected the fact that Britain had ceased to be the leading industrial nation in the world. Germany and the United States had overtaken it, with France and Russia close behind.

◀ This cartoon from the 1800s shows the colonies of the British Empire constantly worrying the imperial lion.

▼ In 1897, Victoria celebrated her Diamond Jubilee. The guests of honor included Indian princes, African chiefs, Pacific Islanders, and Chinese from Hong Kong.

THE PLAINS WARS 1849–1913

The plains of the American Midwest had once seemed vast and endless. In the 1800s, they became the scene of a struggle for land ownership.

The Pawnee were one of the Plains tribes. They lived by hunting buffalo.

General George Custer (1839–1876) died in the Battle of the Little Bighorn.

Sitting Bull (1831–1890) was a Dakota (Sioux) medicine man and war chief.

Many groups of Native Americans lived on the Great Plains of the American West and had done so for thousands of years. This vast area stretched from the Mississippi River in the east to the Rocky Mountains in the west, and from Canada in the north to Texas in the south. Until the 1600s, many Plains tribes were farmers. They grew corn, beans, and other food, but they also hunted buffalo, on foot, using bows and arrows. Their way of life on the plains began to change during the 1600s when the Spanish introduced the horse.

With horses, the Native Americans could easily follow the buffalo. The buffalo not only provided them with meat, but also with tools and weapons fashioned from the animals' bones, and tepees and clothing made with the skins. Some of the larger tribes of Native Americans became known as the Plains tribes. Early white settlers forced some tribes to move west from their original homelands east of the Mississippi River.

WESTWARD HO!

After the Civil War, the land between the Mississippi River and the Rocky Mountains was thought of as a wilderness of plains and mountains. The government encouraged pioneers to migrate westward. Settlers traveled west together in wagon trains for protection on the long journey across plains, rivers, and mountains, which could take up to eight months.

Native Americans depended on buffalo for their food, clothing, and shelter. Many buffalo were also killed to supply meat to workers laying track for the railroads.

SETTLERS MOVE WEST

The government encouraged people to migrate westward. Under the Homestead Act of 1862, a family could have 160 acres (65ha) for a small fee, as long as they did not sell the land for five years. More land was given to those who made improvements by drilling wells or planting trees. The Act encouraged farmers to move into and settle on the Great Plains.

The government also encouraged the building of railroads, which carried people into unsettled regions. It gave land to the railroads so generously that many lines were built simply to obtain land. By 1869, the Union Pacific Railroad was finished—connecting America from coast to coast.

STRUGGLE FOR SURVIVAL

The expansion of the railroads soon changed the face of the United States. They brought even more settlers to the Native American homelands. The two cultures came into conflict. Local Native American chiefs made land agreements with the settlers, without realizing that they were signing away their rights. The settlers' idea of private property meant nothing to the Native Americans. They thought they could continue to hunt on the land. Many bought guns and attacked the settlers' homesteads, their wagon trains, and the railroads.

Between 1860 and 1885, the number of buffalo was reduced—largely by white hunters—from 15 million to only 2,000. Starting in 1866, a series of wars took place. The goal was to claim land for white settlers. To do this, the Native Americans were driven onto reservations, or destroyed if they resisted. President Rutherford B. Hayes (1822–1893) said, in 1893, "Many, if not most, of our Indian wars had their origin in broken promises and acts of injustice." By then, it was too late—the few survivors of the Plains tribes had been forced onto the poor quality land of the reservations.

Virginia City in Nevada began in 1859 when gold and silver were found. By 1876, it was a large town, but when the gold and silver ran out, it became a ghost town.

In 1848, gold was discovered at Sutter's Mill, in California, and the gold rush started. By 1855, San Francisco's population had grown from 800 to 50,000.

The Native Americans were used to hunting and did not want to be farmers. They were not allowed to become American citizens and had few civil rights. Fierce battles with soldiers resulted in the deaths of thousands of Native Americans. The last battle was at Wounded Knee in South Dakota, in 1890, when soldiers slaughtered 200 Sioux. Soon, all the tribes were moved onto reservations, and the Native American way of life was changed forever.

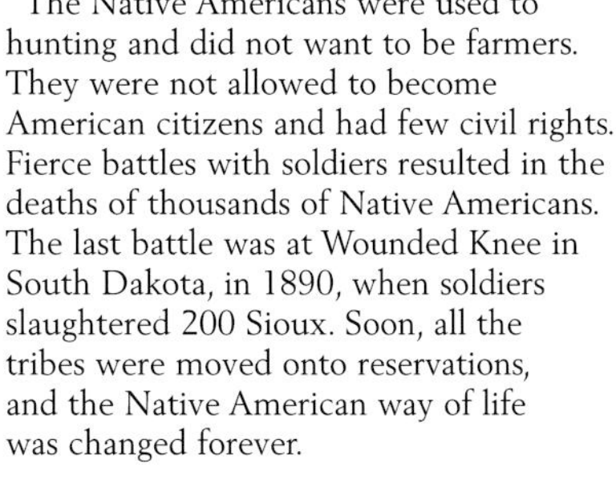

▲ The possibility of making their fortune attracted people of many nationalities to the American goldfields. Thousands of Chinese people traveled to California in the 1850s and the 1870s to work as laborers.

◀ In the 1830s, the Chickasaw tribe was forced to move to a reservation in Oklahoma where they were told that the land was theirs "as long as the grass grows and the waters run." But the central and western parts were thinly populated, and very sought after by white settlers. In 1906, the Chickasaw rose up to stop their land from being taken, but were suppressed by the United States Cavalry.

AUSTRALIA 1788–1913

The original inhabitants of Australia, the Aborigines, faced a growing threat to their way of life, as white settlers encroached ever farther into their territories.

Aborigines led a way of life based around tribal territories and customs. Although the spread of white settlements destroyed much of this, they still kept a strong cultural identity.

During the 1800s, the new nation of Australia was created. More than 174,000 convicts had been shipped from Britain to Australia, mainly to Sydney, to serve their sentence in work gangs, for periods varying from a few years to life. Transportation to the colonies, which had begun in the reign of Elizabeth I, was an extension of the older punishment of banishment, and it did not end until 1868.

For many convicts, Britain held only bitter memories, so many of them chose to settle in Australia after their release. Early settlements were founded along the coast, but explorers gradually opened up the interior. They were followed by pioneers looking for grazing land for the ever-growing flocks of sheep.

▲ Robert O'Hara Burke (1820–1861) and William Wills (1834–1861) were the first white men to cross Australia. Their expedition contained 18 men and set out in 1860 to travel north from Melbourne to the Gulf of Carpentaria. They suffered terribly from starvation and exhaustion on the way back and only one man survived.

As the wool industry grew, so did the demand for land. Many drove their sheep beyond the official settlement limits, earning themselves the name "squatters." Though they were later granted grazing rights, the name stuck. These early farmers gradually spread into the interior, acquiring land as they went. But eventually they came into conflict with the native Australians, the Aborigines.

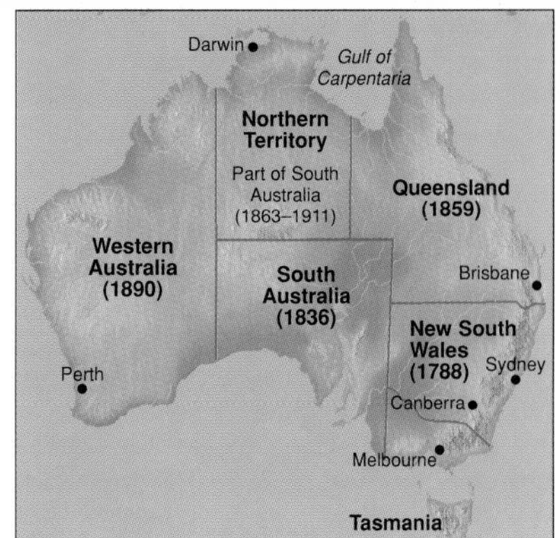

The colonies were granted self-government by 1890. New South Wales originally occupied all of eastern Australia, but was eventually divided.

ABORIGINAL PEOPLE

Australia's first inhabitants, the Aborigines, arrived from Southeast Asia 50,000 years earlier. They lived in nomadic groups, traveling around their territories, hunting with spears and boomerangs, fishing from canoes, and gathering fruit and vegetables. They had no written language, but passed on valuable knowledge by word of mouth and in song.

When the British settled in Australia, Aboriginal culture was threatened and their land was taken over by squatters. In the late 1700s, there were more than 300,000 Aborigines. Many were killed or driven off their land by settlers, and the population fell to under 45,000.

▶ On arrival in Australia, immigrants were housed at first in large wooden buildings. This one was designed to accommodate more than 70 people.

In Van Diemen's Land, later renamed Tasmania, the Aboriginal population was completely wiped out by the 1870s. Some had perished from European diseases, and white settlers had murdered the rest.

THE GOLD RUSH

In 1851, many people rushed to Australia at the news that gold had been found in New South Wales and Victoria. This event became known as the Gold Rush. Melbourne, the capital of Victoria, became a wealthy city, and Australia's population more than doubled. In 1854, gold miners at the Eureka Stockade rebelled against their colonial rulers, and put on pressure for reform and self-government.

GROWING UNREST

Squatter settlement also created problems when the immigrants and ex-convicts demanded that land be made available for farms. Many failed to gain land because of opposition from existing squatters. At the same time, a sense of nationalism was growing. Britain had granted self-government to all her colonies by the 1890s, and the leaders of the colonies had come to realize that some form of union was needed.

None of the Australian colonies were willing to give up their individual independence, so in 1890, after fierce arguments, the colonies agreed to unite in a federation. The Commonwealth of Australia was proclaimed on the first day of 1901, and the city of Canberra was chosen as the federal capital.

▲ In 1851, thousands of people from many countries moved to Australia after they heard that gold had been found in New South Wales and Victoria.

▶ Ned Kelly (1855–1880) and his gang of bushrangers roamed the country staging holdups and bank raids. Kelly, who often wore homemade armor, was hanged in 1880.

KEY DATES	
1797	Sheep ranching introduced to Australia
1836	City of Adelaide founded
1851	Gold Rush starts in New South Wales
1854	Rebellion of gold miners at Eureka stockade
1855	Van Diemen's Land renamed Tasmania
1860	Burke and Wills set out to cross Australia
1868	Britain stops sending convicts to Australia
1880	The outlaw Ned Kelly is captured and hanged
1901	Commonwealth of Australia declared

SHEEP RANCHES

Introduced to Australia in 1797, sheep ranching became the major agricultural activity in the country. Because the land was often far from fertile, enormous areas of pasture were needed to keep the sheep healthy and well fed. This meant that more and more land was taken from the Aborigines.

The World at War

1914–1949

In the years from 1914 to 1949, the world went through a period of rapid, intense, and painful change. The Great War, the "war to end all wars," was followed by a massive worldwide influenza epidemic. The 1917 Bolshevik Revolution made Russia the world's first socialist state. Then came the Great Depression, a collapse of capitalism that led to mass unemployment worldwide. This, followed by World War II, meant that European world dominance was replaced by that of the United States and the Soviet Union.

▲ World War I saw the first widespread use of aerial warfare. These early airplanes were used to spy on enemy positions and drop bombs.

◀ After the defeat of Nazi Germany in 1945, the victors, Marshal Zhukov (U.S.S.R.), General Eisenhower (U.S.A.), and Field Marshall Montgomery (Britain) meet in the ruins of Berlin.

THE WORLD AT A GLANCE 1914–1949

Almost the whole world was affected by World War I, the Great Depression, and World War II. In North America, the United States adopted a policy of isolation between the wars, but joined the Allies in World War II. In South America, right wing governments came to power in Argentina and Brazil.

In Europe, civil wars broke out in Ireland, Spain, and Greece, and revolution in Russia led to civil war there, too. In the Middle East, the Ottoman Empire collapsed after World War I, and Israel was founded in 1948 as a homeland for the Jewish people.

Italy's attempts to build an empire in Africa failed. Many countries began clamoring for independence. India gained independence from Britain, but it was partitioned to form Pakistan. Civil war divided China, while Japanese expansion was one of the causes of World War II, with the Pacific becoming a battle zone. Science, in the form of the atom bomb, ended the war.

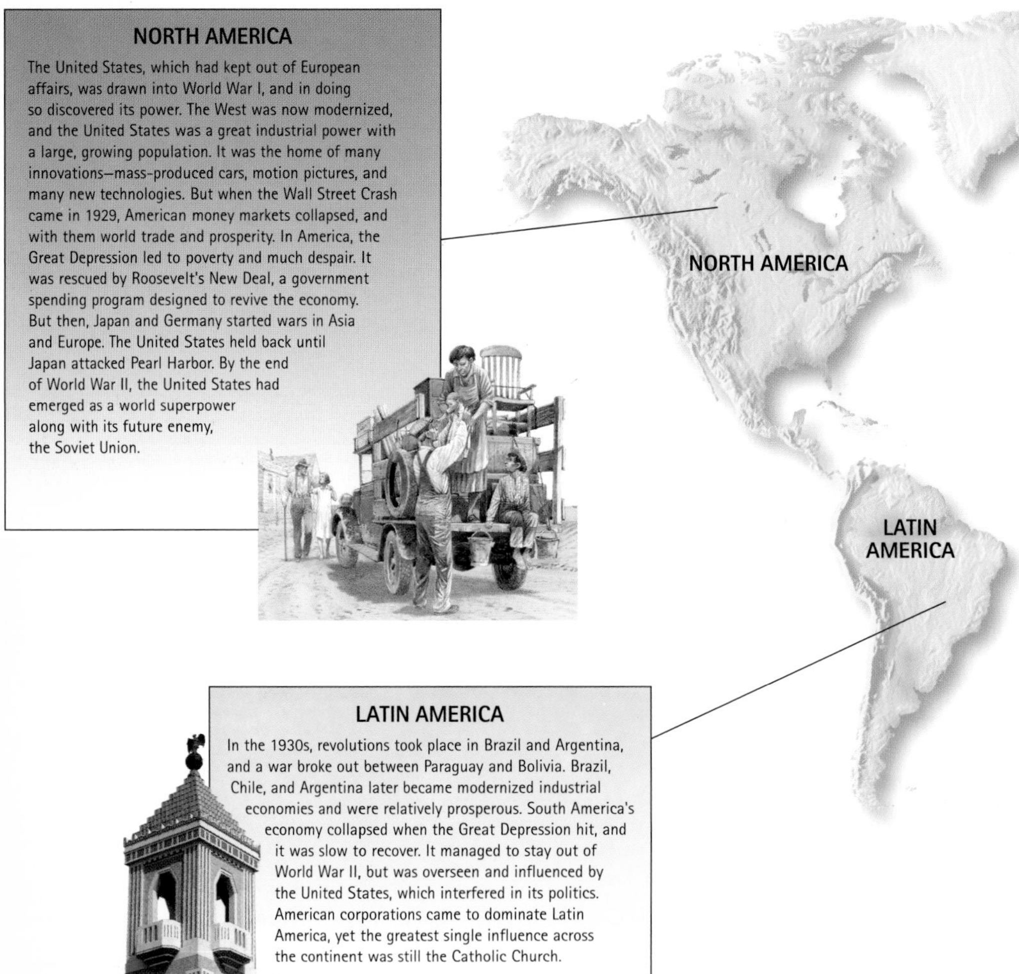

NORTH AMERICA

The United States, which had kept out of European affairs, was drawn into World War I, and in doing so discovered its power. The West was now modernized, and the United States was a great industrial power with a large, growing population. It was the home of many innovations—mass-produced cars, motion pictures, and many new technologies. But when the Wall Street Crash came in 1929, American money markets collapsed, and with them world trade and prosperity. In America, the Great Depression led to poverty and much despair. It was rescued by Roosevelt's New Deal, a government spending program designed to revive the economy. But then, Japan and Germany started wars in Asia and Europe. The United States held back until Japan attacked Pearl Harbor. By the end of World War II, the United States had emerged as a world superpower along with its future enemy, the Soviet Union.

LATIN AMERICA

In the 1930s, revolutions took place in Brazil and Argentina, and a war broke out between Paraguay and Bolivia. Brazil, Chile, and Argentina later became modernized industrial economies and were relatively prosperous. South America's economy collapsed when the Great Depression hit, and it was slow to recover. It managed to stay out of World War II, but was overseen and influenced by the United States, which interfered in its politics. American corporations came to dominate Latin America, yet the greatest single influence across the continent was still the Catholic Church.

EUROPE

The fall of the Hapsburgs and the Ottomans put many new countries on the map. Ireland gained independence and Poland reappeared as an independent country. The Bolshevik Revolution turned the Soviet Union into a massive power, with large-scale industrialization and collectivization of farms under the dictatorship of Stalin. Germany, though it lost World War I, grew strong again under Hitler, taking over much of Europe in World War II. Europe was vulnerable as a result of the Depression, and there was a desire to keep peace and to appease the Nazis. Despite these difficulties, Europe came to lead the way in the creation of social welfare, social insurance, and education systems. After World War II, much of Europe was devastated, and American aid was necessary for its recovery. Overseas colonies were made independent, public opinion held sway, and Europe approached 1950 shell-shocked by the violence of the previous decades.

ASIA

After the Chinese Revolution of 1911, life for the people did not improve. In the 1930s, China became a dictatorship, opposed by Mao Zedong's communists. The Japanese invaded in 1937, and China was devastated. Mao's communists fought back and took power in 1948. Before World War II, Japan had risen to military and industrial greatness. Its aggressive expansion during the war was finally halted by two atom bombs and occupation by the United States. India avoided the war, but Indians could no longer tolerate British rule, and in 1947, India and Pakistan separated and gained independence. Indonesia and the Philippines also gained independence.

EUROPE

ASIA

MIDDLE EAST

AFRICA

AUSTRALASIA

AUSTRALASIA

As more settlers arrived, Australia and New Zealand became richer, exporting agricultural products and metals. Auckland, Sydney, and Melbourne joined the list of world cities. After World War II, many European immigrants moved there. Polynesia suffered because of the war—the islands were dragged into the modern world.

AFRICA

Under colonial administration, African states were rapidly modernized. South Africa became a strong white-ruled nation. Except in North Africa, World War II did not greatly affect the continent.

MIDDLE EAST

After the fall of the Ottoman Empire, the Middle East was split up into separate countries, governed by the British and French. The discovery of oil made Iraq, Iran, Kuwait, and Saudi Arabia economically important. British and French rule ended after World War II, and the Arab states became independent. Controversially, the Jewish State of Israel was formed in their midst.

THE START OF WORLD WAR I 1914

The assassination of Archduke Franz Ferdinand, heir to the Austro–Hungarian Empire, in Sarajevo in June 1914, triggered the bloodiest conflict in human history.

A British recruiting poster at the start of World War I featured the War Minister, Lord Kitchener.

Jealous of Britain's trade and colonies, Germany—which already had the world's largest army—had begun to build up its navy. Kaiser Wilhelm II's ambition to acquire more colonies overseas, along with his aggressive foreign policy, worried other European countries. In the years leading up to 1914, Britain and Germany competed to build bigger and better ships for their navies. The rivalry of other European countries over trade, colonies, and military power had also been growing, and the European powers had grouped together in defensive alliances.

Under Kaiser Wilhelm II (1859–1941), Germany built a battle fleet to rival Britain's navy.

DEFENSIVE ALLIANCES

The main alliance was the Triple Alliance: Germany, Italy, and Austria–Hungary. An attack on any one country would bring its allies to its defense. The purpose of the alliance was to block Russian aggression in the Balkans (mainly the European areas of the old Ottoman Empire).

The Triple Entente, between Britain, France, and Russia, was not a military alliance, but its members had agreed to cooperate against German aggression.

World War I began after Serbian terrorist Gavrilo Princip killed the heir to the Austro–Hungarian throne, Archduke Franz Ferdinand, in Sarajevo on June 28, 1914.

HOW THE WAR BEGAN

The war began when a Serbian terrorist, Gavrilo Princip, assassinated the heir to the Austro–Hungarian Empire, Archduke Franz Ferdinand, and his wife in Sarajevo on June 28, 1914. This led Austria to declare war on Serbia on July 28. Russia's Czar Nicholas II mobilized his country's troops to defend Serbia from Austria. In return, Germany declared war on Russia on August 1. Russian armies were defeated by the Germans at Tannenberg and in the Battle of the Masurian Lakes. To the south, the Austro–Hungarian armies were defeated by the Russians in September.

A WAR ON TWO FRONTS

Germany had always dreaded a war on two fronts, so it put the Schlieffen Plan into operation. Drawn up by General von Schlieffen, the plan aimed to defeat France in six weeks, so that Germany could concentrate its forces against Russia.

On August 3, Germany declared war on Russia's ally, France. When the German army marched into neutral Belgium to attack the French from the north, they were faced with determined Belgian resistance. This slowed down their advance and allowed the French, under General Joffré, time to reorganize their forces.

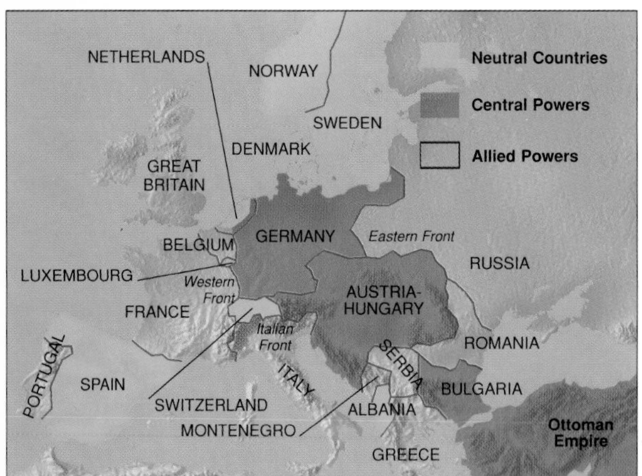

◀ In 1914, Europe was divided in two. Britain, France, and Russia, known as the Allies, combined to fight the Central Powers, comprising Germany, Austria–Hungary, and its allies. Fighting took place simultaneously on an eastern front and a western front.

GERMANY INVADES FRANCE

The British then acted on the Treaty of London (1839), in which they had agreed to protect Belgian neutrality. It was on these grounds that Britain declared war on Germany on August 4. Britain went to Belgium's defense and sent the 100,000-strong British Expeditionary Force to France to help slow the German advance at Mons and Charleroi.

However, in the face of a determined German advance, Joffré retreated until he was behind the Marne River. Here, the French forces halted the Germans on September 8. Both sides then took up defensive positions and within three months, a line of trenches was dug from the English Channel to the Swiss frontier.

During the war, Britain, France, and Russia were known as the Allies, or Allied Powers. Germany, Italy, Austria–Hungary, and their allies were known as the Central Powers. Both sides raced to produce more and more deadly weapons, such as poison gas. They thought that by using these weapons they would shorten the war, but it lasted for four years and was the bloodiest conflict in human history. It has been estimated that the war cost the United States alone over $20 billion. The total number of men killed or wounded amounted to about 30 million.

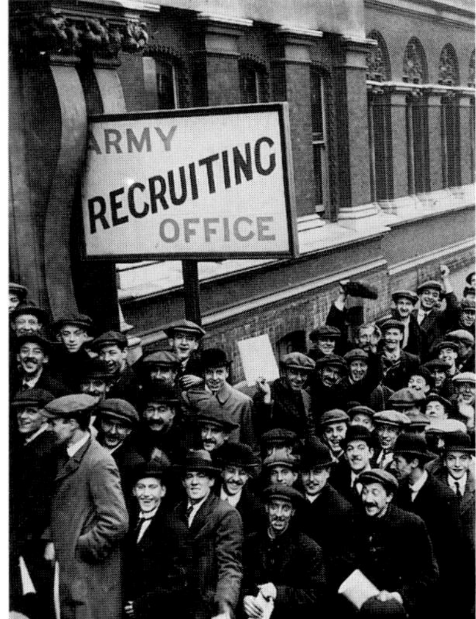

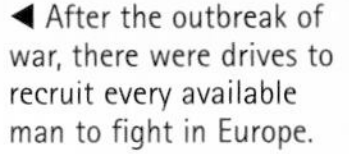
◀ After the outbreak of war, there were drives to recruit every available man to fight in Europe.

The French army had the difficult task of defending hundreds of miles of frontier against the enemy.

KEY DATES	
June 28	Archduke Franz Ferdinand assassinated in Sarajevo by a Serbian terrorist
July 28	Austria declares war on Serbia; Russia mobilizes its troops to defend Serbia
Aug. 1	Germany declares war on Russia
Aug. 3	Germany declares war on France
Aug. 4	Germany invades Belgium; Britain declares war on Germany
Sept. 8	German advance on Paris stopped at the Marne River

The German army was the largest and best trained in the world.

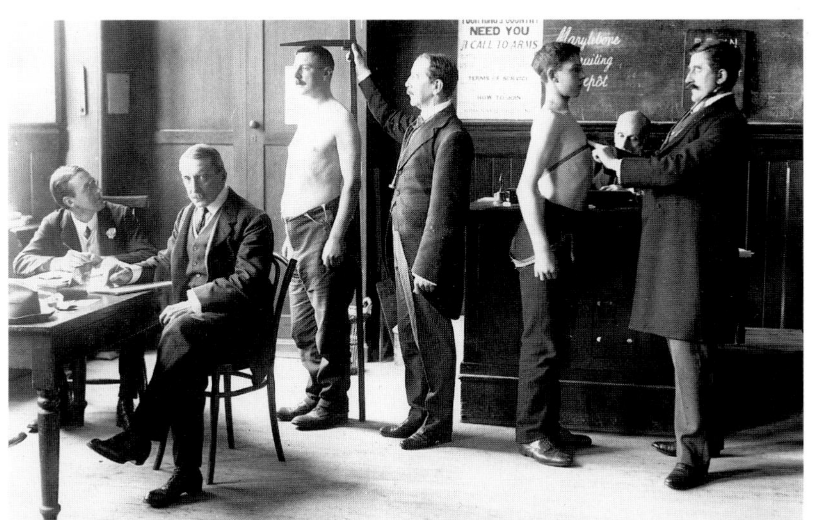

Britain had the smallest army, but it consisted of professional career soldiers.

◀ Motivated by patriotism and inspired by the call for volunteers to defend their countries in August 1914, millions of men of all ages across Europe joined up to fight the enemy.

BATTLES OF WORLD WAR I 1914–1917

In a series of horrific battles along the Western Front, millions of lives were lost to gain only a few miles. The land war soon reached a stalemate.

Gas masks were introduced in World War I to protect the troops against poison gas attacks by the enemy.

During World War I, fighting took place in several areas. The Western Front was between Germany and northern France, and the Eastern Front between Germany and the Russian forces. There was also fighting at sea and in the Middle East, where the Allied Powers attacked the Ottoman Empire. In Africa, British and French troops attacked German colonies.

On the Western Front, French and British troops, together with thousands of men from the British Empire, occupied a network of deep trenches from September 1914. Facing them, across a few hundred yards of ground known as "no man's land," were trenches occupied by the Germans. Millions of men were killed on the Western Front in battles including Ypres, Verdun, and the Somme. One of the worst was the Third Battle of Ypres, or Passchendaele, in 1917. The troops had to wade through mud up to waist level. In 102 days, the Allies advanced just five miles at a cost of 400,000 lives.

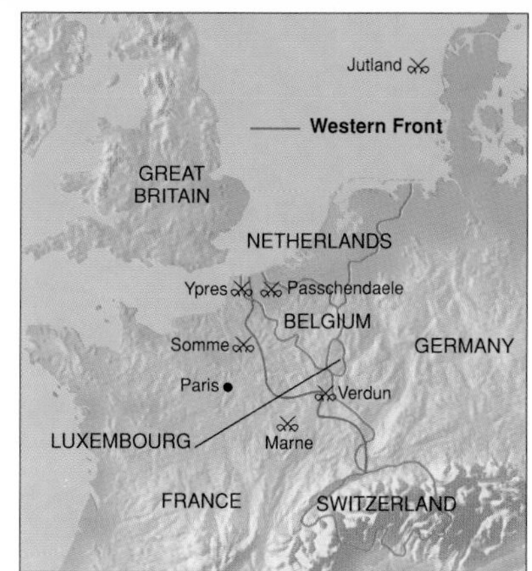

The Western Front stretched across Belgium and northeastern France. Millions of soldiers were killed in battles along it between 1914 and 1918.

For four years, the Western Front did not move more than 20 mi. (32km) in any direction. Barbed wire and machine-gun and artillery defenses made attack futile. Tanks, first used in 1916, could crush barbed wire or machine guns, but were unreliable. Aircraft were more successful, and were used to spot enemy troops, target shells, and drop bombs. The Eastern Front ran from the Baltic to the Black Sea and also had lines of trenches, to which the Russians retreated in September 1914.

▲ Only 12 years after the Wright brothers made their pioneering flight in North Carolina, aircraft were being used in warfare. Although control of the air was not a deciding factor in World War I, the war led to many advances in flight technology.

▶ In September 1914, the German advance toward Paris was stopped short of the capital when the Allies precariously held the line of the Marne River. The French government fled to Bordeaux. The Allied line held, and in their great counterattack, known as the First Battle of the Marne—regarded as one of the decisive battles of the war—the Allies drove the Germans back to the line of the Aisne River.

The war along the Western Front was fought from trenches guarded by barbed wire and machine guns. The conditions were appalling, with knee-deep mud, constant shelling, sniping, and raids. The battles of the Somme and Verdun in France in 1916 cost over two million casualties, but neither side was able to advance more than a few hundred yards.

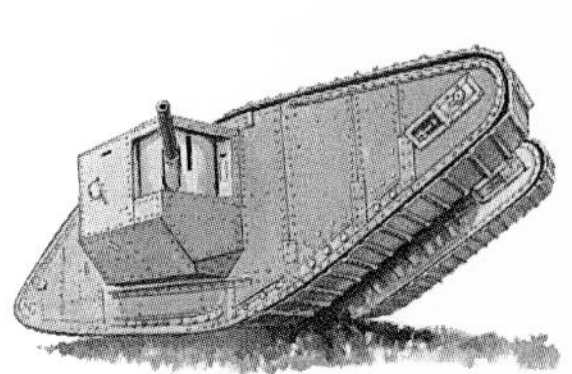

Invented by two British scientists, Tritton and Wilson, the first tanks were used in the Battle of the Somme in 1916. These vehicles, fitted with machine guns, terrified the German soldiers, but suffered from too many mechanical failures to be fully effective.

THE WAR AT SEA

There were only two significant sea battles in World War I. The first, in 1914, was when a German fleet was destroyed by the Royal Navy off the Falkland Islands. In 1916, the Battle of Jutland took place and both Germany and Britain claimed victory. However, the German fleet did not leave the port of Kiel again until the end of the war, when it surrendered to the Allies.

German submarines, called U-boats, attacked ships bound for Britain and France. U-boats sank hundreds of Allied ships, nearly crippling Britain. When the U.S.S. *Housatonic* was sunk in 1917, the United States declared war on Germany.

Jutland was the major sea battle of World War I. Although the German fleet inflicted far more serious losses than they sustained, Britain and Germany both claimed victory. After the battle, on May 31, 1916, the German fleet escaped in darkness and returned to port, where they remained for the rest of the war.

DISASTER AT GALLIPOLI

During 1915, in an attempt to assist the Russians on the Eastern Front, Allied forces bombarded Turkish forts guarding the Dardanelles. Allied troops, including ANZAC forces from Australia and New Zealand, then landed at Gallipoli to try to capture the strategic positions overlooking the narrow straits. But the Allied powers grossly underestimated the strength of the Turkish forces. Almost 15 percent of Australian deaths in the war came from this battle.

Turkish officer

Australian private

IRELAND: CIVIL UNREST 1916–1923

Irish frustration at home rule being first granted, and then delayed by World War I, led to rebellion and civil war. Southern Ireland became self-governing in 1921.

James Connolly (1868–1916) led the Irish Citizen Army. After the Easter Rising, he was shot in jail, even though he was already mortally wounded.

▲ On Easter Monday, April 24, 1916, the Republicans made their headquarters inside Dublin General Post Office. Fighting went on for a week. The Republicans surrendered on April 29. The British army fired heavy guns at the building, and it caught fire.

Many Irish people wanted home rule, and a Home Rule Bill was approved by the British Parliament in 1912. This would have become law, and given Ireland its own parliament to deal with domestic affairs, but it was suspended when war broke out in 1914.

In the north, Protestants opposed home rule because they would be a minority in a Catholic country. Some people (Republicans) wanted Ireland to be an independent republic. Many supported a political party called Sinn Féin ("We alone"). Some belonged to the Irish Volunteers, the Irish Republican Brotherhood, or the Irish Citizen Army.

On Easter Monday 1916, members of the Irish Volunteers and the Irish Citizen Army, led by Patrick Pearse and James Connolly, took control of public buildings in Dublin. This event became known as the Easter Rising. From their headquarters in the General Post Office, Pearse and Connolly declared a republic, but were soon defeated by the British army. In the 1918 election, Sinn Féin won 73 of the 105 Irish seats in the British Parliament.

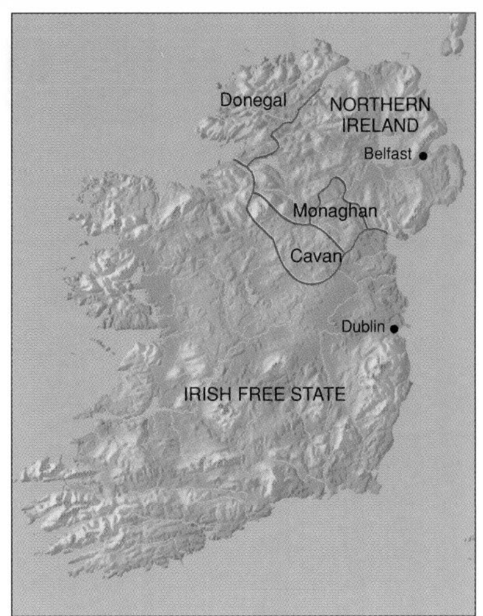

The Anglo-Irish Treaty of 1921 made southern Ireland into a self-governing country. In 1949, it became a republic, completely independent of Britain.

Sinn Féin set up their own parliament, the Dáil Eireann, and declared Ireland to be an independent republic in 1919. This led to war between the Irish Republican Army (IRA) and the Royal Irish Constabulary (RIC). Armed police, the Black-and-Tans, were sent to support the RIC. The fighting continued until 1921.

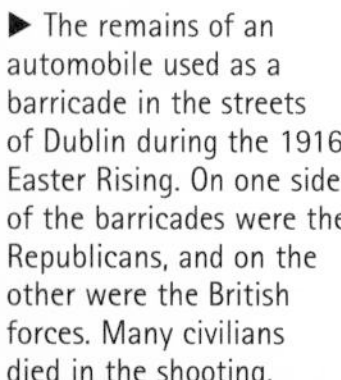

▶ The remains of an automobile used as a barricade in the streets of Dublin during the 1916 Easter Rising. On one side of the barricades were the Republicans, and on the other were the British forces. Many civilians died in the shooting.

◀ Michael Collins (1890–1922), center, took part in the 1916 Easter Rising, and was arrested and imprisoned by the British. He became leader of Sinn Féin and head of intelligence in the Irish Volunteers. He was elected to the Irish parliament in 1918 and negotiated the peace treaty with Britain in 1921. He became head of the provisional government in 1922, but was killed in an ambush that same year.

▲ Éamon de Valera (1882–1975) was born in the United States. He was arrested and imprisoned by the British for his part in the 1916 Easter Rising. In 1926, he founded the Fianna Fáil ("Soldiers of Destiny") Party. Between 1937 and 1959, he served as prime minister of Ireland three times. He then became president until 1973.

THE ANGLO–IRISH TREATY

The British government wanted to divide Ireland into two countries, with six of the counties of Ulster, in the north, separate from the rest. Under the 1920 Government of Ireland Act, both countries would have some self-government. The six Ulster counties had a Protestant majority, who did not want to be ruled from Dublin. They agreed to the act and formed the new state of Northern Ireland. The Dáil Eireann, led by Éamon de Valera, opposed the act because they wanted complete independence for all Ireland.

In an attempt to bring peace to the country, the Anglo–Irish Treaty of 1921 made southern Ireland into a dominion of Great Britain. Called the Irish Free State, it was established in 1922. But this action led to civil war. On one side were the Free Staters who agreed to the treaty's terms. On the other side were the Republicans.

The civil war lasted until 1923, when de Valera ordered the Republicans to stop fighting. In 1926, he founded a new political party, called Fianna Fáil. In the general election of 1932, he defeated the Free Staters. The new constitution of 1937 changed southern Ireland's name to Eire, but it stayed within the British Commonwealth. It became independent and left the Commonwealth in 1949.

KEY DATES	
1916	Easter Rising in Dublin is crushed by the British after a week
1918	In elections, Sinn Féin wins 73 of the 105 Irish seats in the British Parliament
1919	Sinn Féin declares Ireland independent—this leads to civil war
1922	Southern Ireland, known as the Irish Free State, becomes a self-governing dominion of Britain
1923	Civil war ends
1926	Fianna Fáil Party founded
1937	New constitution renames southern Ireland Eire

▼ Both the Free Staters and the Republicans were well supplied with weapons during the civil war. This gun belonged to the Free Staters and was used in County Limerick.

RUSSIA 1917–1924

After years of rule by a corrupt and inept government, the people of Russia rose against the czar and his advisers and seized power in November 1917.

Czar Nicholas II (1868–1918) was forced to abdicate in 1917. He and his family were then imprisoned and killed by the Bolsheviks in 1918.

Following the defeat of Russia by Japan in 1904, there were workers' strikes and revolts throughout Russia. The new czar, Nicholas II, issued a declaration promising civil rights and a national government, called the Duma. The Duma did not keep its promises. Elections were rigged so that reformers were kept out of government. Opponents of the government were arrested, and the leaders fled. But the Russian people thought that the czar was out of touch with the population and that his advisers were corrupt. The government, which had not been very efficient in peacetime, was even less effective during World War I. Soldiers who thought that they would be sent to fight in the war began to question their loyalty to their country.

Grigori Rasputin (1871–1916) was adviser to Czar Nicholas II and his wife Alexandra. They thought he was a holy man who could make their sick son better. But he was hated by the people of Russia.

During the March 1917 riots in Petrograd, many soldiers refused to obey orders and attached the Red Flag to their bayonets as a sign of support for the rioters.

Food and fuel were in short supply, and many people in the cities began to starve. The economy was on the way to collapse. In March 1917, riots broke out in the capital, St. Petersburg, which had been renamed Petrograd at the start of World War I. Rioting crowds were usually broken up by troops, but this time they refused to obey their orders. When the troops joined the rioters, the czar abdicated, and his advisers resigned. A temporary government was set up, led by Prince George Lvov.

Armed workers and Bolshevik-led soldiers and sailors attacked the Winter Palace in Petrograd on November 7, 1917. Although it was the headquarters of the czar's government, it was not well defended and was soon in Bolshevik hands.

◀ Vladimir Lenin (1870–1924) became a Marxist in 1887 after his brother was executed for trying to assassinate the czar.

Leon Trotsky (1879–1940) was the most influential person after Lenin in the revolution. During the Russian Civil War, he led the Red Army to victory. He hoped to become president after Lenin's death, but lost to Stalin.

THE BOLSHEVIKS SEIZE POWER

The government found it difficult to carry on with the war. Alexander Kerensky succeeded Prince Lvov as chief minister. After the March revolution, the Bolshevik Party was still determined to seize power. In April, their leader, Vladimir Lenin, returned from exile.

The Bolsheviks in Petrograd wanted Russia to become a communist state. After struggling with the government, the Bolsheviks, led by Lenin, seized power in November 1917. In March 1918, the new government signed the Treaty of Brest-Litovsk which made peace with Germany. It moved the capital from Petrograd to Moscow, broke up the large estates, and gave the farmland to the peasants. Control of factories was given to workers. Banks were taken into state control, and Church property was seized.

The White Russians (anticommunists) opposed these moves and, in 1918, the Russian Civil War broke out. The White Russians were finally defeated by the Bolshevik Red Army in 1922. By this time, around 100,000 people had been killed and two million had emigrated. That year, the country's name was changed to the Union of Soviet Socialist Republics (U.S.S.R.), or Soviet Union. Lenin led the U.S.S.R. until his death in 1924, when a new power struggle began between Leon Trotsky and Josef Stalin. Stalin won and dominated Soviet politics until 1953.

Josef Stalin (1879–1953) joined the Bolshevik Party in 1903. In 1922, Stalin became general secretary of the Communist Party and in 1924, leader of the U.S.S.R.

▶ When Josef Stalin became leader of the U.S.S.R. in 1924 he carried out the Great Purge—millions of people were arrested and murdered. He decided to strip farmers of their land in order to reorganize farming into larger state-owned units called collectives. His orders were brutally carried out by the army and secret police. Villages were burned and the villagers killed or evicted.

WORLD WAR I: THE AFTERMATH 1918–1923

Germany, freed from Russia, launched an assault on the Western Front in 1918. Newly arrived U.S. troops helped stop the attack and Germany asked for peace.

World War I involved whole populations. Women went to work to produce armaments and keep industries going while the men were at war.

The arrival of American troops in Europe in 1917 meant that the Allies could launch fresh attacks on the Western Front. In 1918, Russia withdrew from the war, so German soldiers were no longer needed on the Eastern Front. By 1918, more than 3.5 million German soldiers were fighting on the Western Front. In March, they broke through the trenches and advanced toward Paris. The French counterattacked in July, and in August, British tanks broke the German line at Amiens. As the United States poured troops into France, the Germans retreated.

The fighting in World War I left many areas of Belgium and northeastern France devastated. Cities such as Ypres, in northwestern Belgium, were left in ruins.

By October, the fighting was nearing the German border and a naval blockade was causing starvation in Germany. Early on the morning of November 11, Germany signed an armistice. Kaiser Wilhelm II abdicated, and at 11 o'clock, fighting in World War I ended. Almost 10 million people had been killed and over 20 million wounded. Most were young men, and their loss changed the social structure of several countries. As a result, many women gained more equality and freedom than they had had before the war. In many places, they also gained the right to vote.

▶ German submarines, or U-boats, attacked ships on the surface by firing torpedoes at them from under the water. They were so successful in attacking Allied ships that Britain came close to defeat in 1917.

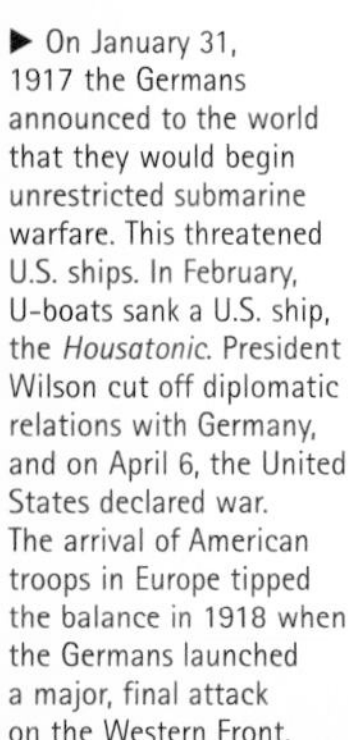

▶ On January 31, 1917 the Germans announced to the world that they would begin unrestricted submarine warfare. This threatened U.S. ships. In February, U-boats sank a U.S. ship, the *Housatonic*. President Wilson cut off diplomatic relations with Germany, and on April 6, the United States declared war. The arrival of American troops in Europe tipped the balance in 1918 when the Germans launched a major, final attack on the Western Front.

THE TREATY OF VERSAILLES

World War I was formally ended by the Paris Peace Conference, which was held between 1919 and 1920. All the nations that had been involved in the war (except Germany) met to draw up a peace agreement, but the United States, Britain, France, and Italy led the process. Five separate treaties were proposed.

The most important was the Treaty of Versailles, which punished Germany for its part in World War I. Vast amounts of reparations (compensation) were to be given to the Allies. The size of Germany was reduced and seven million people were removed from German rule. Germany had to surrender all its overseas colonies and reduce its army to 100,000 men. The German economy collapsed and this led to hyperinflation. Other nations also suffered as they tried to pay back money they had borrowed during the war. This led to political and economic upheaval.

Further strife was caused by the redrawing of international boundaries in Europe following the collapse of the German, Austro–Hungarian, Russian, and Ottoman (Turkish) empires.

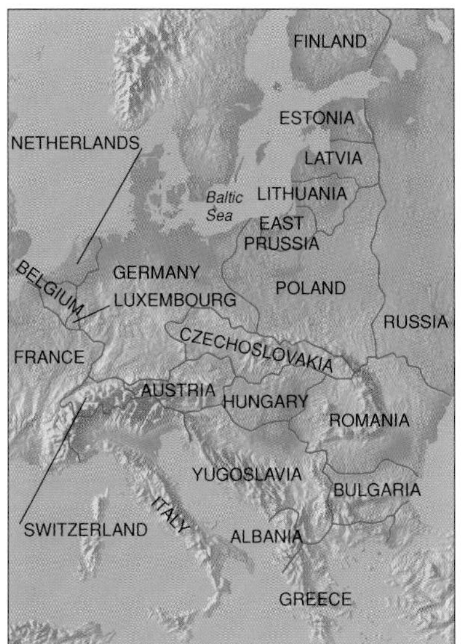

After the Paris Peace Conference (1919–1920), Germany gave back lands to France and Belgium. The Hapsburg monarchy was ended, and Poland, Czechoslovakia, Hungary, and Yugoslavia all became new states.

The Treaty of Versailles was signed on June 28, 1919. It declared that Germany's rulers were solely responsible for the outbreak of war, and so Germany had to make reparations (pay money) to the Allies.

THE LEAGUE OF NATIONS

The League of Nations was also set up at the Paris Peace Conference. Its aim was to help keep world peace, settling disputes by discussion and agreement, but it failed. The reasons for this were that it had little power because the United States refused to join, and there were still rivalries among the 53 members. These weakened the League and reduced its power, so by the late 1930s, few countries took any notice of it.

HYPERINFLATION

German industry was totally destroyed in the war and the country was unable to repay the reparations demanded by the Allies in the Treaty of Versailles. The Germans regarded the Treaty as unjust and indefensible. One of the outcomes was that the German economy was hit by hyperinflation in the 1920s. Hyperinflation is fast inflation that causes the value of money to drop very quickly. People needed enormous amounts of money to buy just a loaf of bread.

Because of hyperinflation, this million mark note issued in Germany during the 1920s was worth virtually nothing.

THE RISE OF FASCISM 1922–1939

The political philosophy known as fascism became popular in many European countries during the 1930s. To many, it offered a way out of economic decline.

Fascist ideas gained support after World War I. The first fascist government appeared in Italy in the 1920s. The term "fascism" comes from the Latin *fasces*—a bundle of rods with an ax that was a symbol of power in ancient Rome. Fascism was based on the idea that a nation would only succeed through disciplined, ruthless action and a determined will. To many people, it offered a way out of economic decline.

Fascists believed that achieving a worthwhile aim made any action they took acceptable. Schools, religion, newspapers, and the arts and sciences were expected to serve the nation. Military power and a secret police organization supported the fascist governments. Fascists believed that their race was superior to others. They opposed communism and encouraged national pride and racism (prejudice against other races). In Germany, this hatred was directed especially at Jews and gypsies.

Benito Mussolini (1883–1945) became the fascist dictator of Italy in 1922.

ITALY AND BENITO MUSSOLINI

In Italy, the Fascist Party was founded by Benito Mussolini in 1919, when economic depression and the threat posed by the communists helped its rise to power. In 1928–1929 he imposed one-party government.

To avenge a humiliating defeat in 1896, Mussolini's army invaded Abyssinia (Ethiopia) in 1935–1936. Britain, France, and other countries condemned the invasion. So, Italy, keen to become a major power, then formed an alliance with Germany. They became known as the Axis Powers. In May 1939, Mussolini and the German fascist dictator, Adolf Hitler, agreed a military treaty—the Pact of Steel. Mussolini's leadership led Italy to defeat in World War II, and he was dismissed and imprisoned by King Victor Emmanuel in 1943. He was later released by German soldiers and set up fascist rule in the north of the country. In April 1945, he was captured and executed by Italian partisans.

Young Italian fascists march past Mussolini during a March of Triumph in Rome in October 1935.

GERMANY AND ADOLF HITLER

The terms of the Versailles Treaty were harsh on Germany, and the economic recession of the early 1930s saw large-scale unemployment in the country. The fragile Weimar Republic was under threat from the communists and Adolf Hitler's National Socialist German Workers' Party (known as Nazis). Hitler promised to end unemployment and poverty, and to build the country into a great state after its humiliation in World War I. Amid political turmoil and violence, President Hindenburg appointed Hitler as chancellor in January 1933. As *Führer* (leader), Hitler crushed all opposition, and ordered the murder of millions of Jews, gypsies, and others. In 1939, he led Germany into World War II, but killed himself when faced with defeat.

THE SPREAD OF FASCISM

In other countries, economic difficulties and the threat of communism in the postwar period led to the establishment of many fascist governments. In Spain, the army leader, General Miguel Primo de Rivera, took power in 1923, and ruled until 1930. In 1933, his son José Antonio formed the fascist Falange Party.

To avenge Italy's humiliating defeat in 1896, Mussolini sent his army to invade Abyssinia. In 1936, Italian troops under General Badoglio victoriously entered the capital, Addis Ababa. The invasion led to a worldwide outcry and Italy's withdrawal from the League of Nations.

◀ Sir Oswald Mosley (1896–1980) resigned from Ramsay MacDonald's Labour government in 1931 to form the British Union of Fascists. The party stirred up anti-Semitism, especially in the East End of London, where many Jewish people lived.

The Falangists supported General Francisco Franco's nationalist forces during the Spanish Civil War (1936–1939). With the support of Germany and Italy, they took power in 1939. Franco ruled as dictator until his death in 1975.

Fascism also won support in Portugal, Austria, the Balkan states, and South America in the years before World War II. Juan Perón ruled Argentina with his wife Eva in the 1940s and 1950s. Antonio Salazar was dictator of Portugal from 1932 to 1968. In England, former Cabinet minister Sir Oswald Mosley founded the Britsh Union of Fascists in 1931, during a period of economic depression and mass unemployment. His public meetings were known for the violence between his supporters and his opponents.

KEY DATES

1919	Italian Fascist Party founded by Mussolini
1922	Mussolini becomes prime minister of Italy
1923	Primo de Rivera takes power in Spain
1928	Mussolini becomes dictator of Italy
1933	José Antonio Primo de Rivera forms Spanish Falange Party; Hitler appointed chancellor of Germany
1936	Italian troops invade Abyssinia
1939	General Franco becomes dictator of Spain; World War II begins

This antifascist poster was issued by the Socialist Party of Catalonia in Spain.

José Antonio Primo de Rivera (1903–1936) founded the Spanish Falange nationalist movement in 1933.

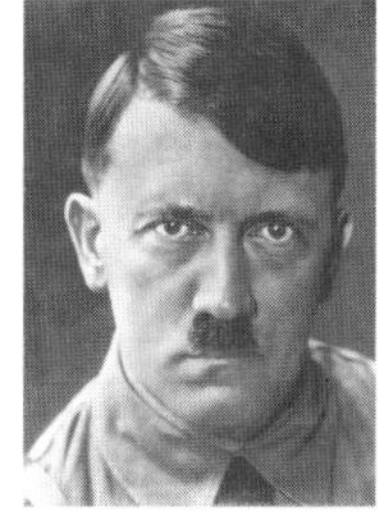

Adolf Hitler rose from obscurity to found the National Socialist German Workers' Party. During political unrest in 1933, he was appointed chancellor.

THE GREAT DEPRESSION 1929–1939

After World War I the U.S. economy saw rapid growth. The Wall Street Crash of 1929 brought an abrupt end to this and led to worldwide depression.

During the Depression of the 1930s, thousands of poverty-stricken American families fled the East Coast and rural farming areas to search for work in the West, especially in California.

In October 1936, 200 men from Jarrow in northeast England marched to London with a petition. A major shipyard had closed down and caused unemployment to soar.

The Great Depression came at the end of a period of economic turbulence. In 1919, the Treaty of Versailles forced Germany to pay a lot of compensation to the Allies. Many Germans lost all their savings as the value of their money plummeted. In Britain, France, and the United States, industry struggled to adjust to peacetime trade. Millions of soldiers came home and looked for jobs, but there were none. Trade unions called on workers to strike against employers who imposed wage cuts. Food prices fell so low that many farmers were ruined and forced to give up their land.

During the 1920s, the U.S. economy grew at a tremendous rate. This was due to the continued development of industry and manufacturing. The growth was also encouraged by the economic policies of presidents Harding and Coolidge. Stock market share prices had been forced up beyond their real value by reckless speculators.

On October 29, 1929, the Wall Street Crash caused panic on the streets of New York. Share prices dropped so fast that many people lost all their money.

THE WALL STREET CRASH

In October 1929, people began to panic and sell their shares rapidly. On a single day, almost 13 million shares were sold on the New York Stock Exchange. This started the crisis known as the Wall Street Crash. It soon affected the whole world.

Many people lost all their money. Banks and businesses closed. Unemployment began to rise. By 1933, the worst year of the Depression, there were 12 million people unemployed in the United States alone. Those who still had jobs saw their salaries halved, and more than 85,000 businesses went under. President Hoover arranged for federal loans to banks and businesses, but refused to give anything directly to the unemployed. People lost all faith in him as a leader.

The situation was made worse by a drought on the Great Plains. The soil turned to dust in many places and blew away in the wind, leading to crop failure on a massive scale.

THE DUST BOWL

Because of a long drought in the 1930s, the soil in the southern Great Plains of the United States became very dry. A series of terrible dust storms swept across the area, which became known as the Dust Bowl. By 1933, hundreds of millions of tons of topsoil had been carried off by the winds, destroying the land. Faced with ruin, thousands of families fled the Dust Bowl looking for work in California and elsewhere.

Franklin D. Roosevelt (1882–1945) was elected governor of New York in 1928. In 1932, he was elected president, and in 1933, he introduced the New Deal to combat the problems caused by the Depression.

Under Roosevelt's New Deal many unemployed people were given work on government projects. Here, young members of the Civilian Conservation Corps (CCC) lift seedlings from the ground in Oregon for the Forest Service.

ROOSEVELT'S NEW DEAL

For the first two years of the Depression, President Hoover and the federal government took little direct action, believing that the economy would recover naturally. Franklin D. Roosevelt was elected president in 1932, and in 1933, he introduced the New Deal to combat the problems caused by the Depression. This was a set of laws designed to ease the worst of the poverty, provide support for the banks, and protect people's savings. Farm prices were subsidized, a minimum wage was introduced, and a huge construction program was started to create employment. The New Deal helped considerably, but it was not until 1939, when the outbreak of World War II gave an enormous boost to heavy industry, that the Depression came to an end.

GLOBAL DEPRESSION

The Wall Street Crash led to the collapse of the system of international loans that handled war reparations. This affected Europe and North America directly. Other regions were also badly hit since much of their economies relied on selling food and raw materials to Europe and North America. As these markets collapsed, many people around the world lost their jobs. As a result, unrest increased, and nationalism grew in many countries.

▶ Although the U.S.S.R. escaped the worst effects of the Depression, Stalin's five-year plan caused other problems. Announced in 1928, the plan included a program to introduce collective farms. To put this into action, the richest peasant farmers were either executed or banished to Siberia. The rest of the peasants were forced to work on collective farms. This action severely disrupted agricultural production and led to a famine in 1933.

WEIMAR AND HITLER 1919–1939

Adolf Hitler took advantage of the economic and social turmoil in Germany in the 1920s to promote fascism. He seized power in 1933.

Field Marshal von Hindenburg (1847–1934) was president of the German Republic. At his death, the chancellor Adolf Hitler became Führer of Germany.

Adolf Hitler (1889–1945) was born in Austria. In World War I, he served in the German army and won the Iron Cross. Hitler became leader of the Nazi Party in 1920.

Following Germany's defeat in 1918, Kaiser Wilhelm II abdicated and fled to the Netherlands. Germany became a republic, and its new government ruled from Weimar, instead of Berlin. From 1919 to 1933, Germany was known as the Weimar Republic. Following elections in January 1919, Friedrich Ebert, a socialist, became its first president. Under his leadership, the Weimar Republic accepted the harsh terms of the Treaty of Versailles. In 1922–1923, the Republic survived several attempts to bring it down, first by the Bolsheviks, then by financial pressure, and finally through an attempted political revolution led by an unknown Austrian fascist named Adolf Hitler.

Ebert died in 1925 and was succeeded by Field Marshal Paul von Hindenburg, who was by then 78 years old. Germany joined the League of Nations in 1926. However, the worldwide Depression of the early 1930s led to massive social and financial problems in Germany.

THE RISE OF ADOLF HITLER

The next presidential election was in 1932, when Germany was in economic crisis, with sky-high inflation and unemployment. Hindenburg was elected as president again, with Adolf Hitler, by then the leader of the National Socialist German Workers' (Nazi) Party, in second place. By using intimidation and violence started by Hitler's followers, the Nazi Party won a majority of seats in the Reichstag (German parliament). Hindenburg reluctantly appointed Hitler as chancellor in January 1933.

When the Reichstag was burned down in February, Hitler brought in emergency powers and called for new elections. By April 1933, he had gained absolute power in Germany, and established a single-party government. As a result, Germany withdrew from the League of Nations.

On the "Night of the Long Knives" in June 1934, Hitler had many of his rivals killed. When Hindenburg died in August, Hitler was appointed *Führer* (leader) of the Third Reich (German Empire). He set out to avenge the humiliation brought on Germany by the Treaty of Versailles and to make Germany a powerful empire.

THE NUREMBERG RALLIES

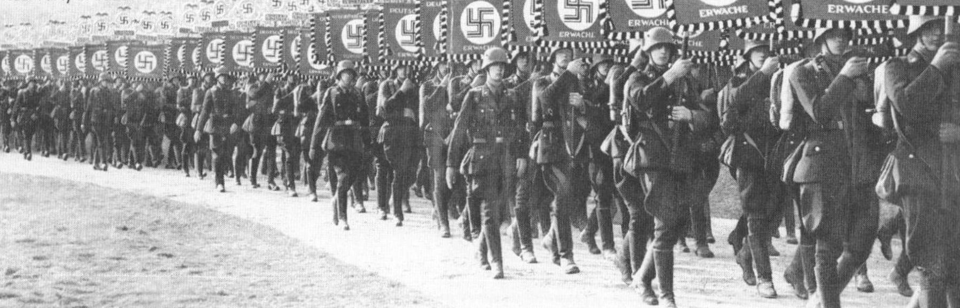

German soldiers parade with the Standards of Victory at a Nazi Party rally at Nuremberg in 1933. The Nazi propaganda techniques of the 1930s were successfully used to create enormous public support for Hitler. His policies were popular because they promised to make Germany powerful.

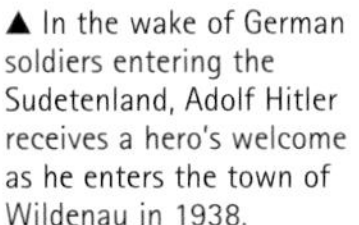
▲ In the wake of German soldiers entering the Sudetenland, Adolf Hitler receives a hero's welcome as he enters the town of Wildenau in 1938.

The deliberate burning of the Reichstag building in Berlin on February 27, 1933, was an excuse for Adolf Hitler to bring in emergency powers and call for new elections.

THE RISE OF ANTI-SEMITISM

Hitler blamed the Jews for Germany's problems. In 1935, the Nuremberg Laws took away their citizenship and banned them from marrying non-Jews. Other laws stopped them being able to work and allowed their property to be taken. The Nazis forbade Jews from being educated, using public transportation, or even the telephone. Most Jews had to wear a yellow star, and they were eventually all forced to live in ghettos.

On *Kristallnacht* ("Night of Broken Glass"), in November 1938, Nazis attacked Jewish property all over Germany, and 30,000 Jews were arrested. This was just the beginning—it seemed that nothing could stop the Nazis now.

GERMAN MILITARY EXPANSION

In 1935, Germany abolished its agreement to the armament restrictions imposed by the 1919 Treaty of Versailles. In 1936, its forces entered the Rhineland, an area of Germany that had been demilitarized at the end of World War I. Germany entered alliances with fascist Italy and the military rulers of Japan. German forces also became involved in the Spanish Civil War, where they supported the fascists, led by General Francisco Franco.

▲ In Hitler's Germany, most Jews were forced to wear a yellow star to show their race.

KEY DATES

1919	Friedrich Ebert becomes first president of German Republic
1920	Adolf Hitler becomes leader of Nazi Party
1925	Ebert dies; Hindenburg becomes president
1933	Hitler is appointed chancellor
1934	Hindenburg dies and Hitler becomes Führer; The "Night of the Long Knives" takes place
1935	Jews deprived of German citizenship
1936	German forces enter demilitarized Rhineland; Germany forms alliances with Italy and Japan
1938	Germany annexes Austria and the Sudetenland
1939	Germany annexes Czechoslovakia and invades Poland—World War II starts

▶ When Hitler came to power, he used every means to destroy opposition. This included the imposition of state censorship of newspapers, books, and radio. In support of this, students and members of the Nazi Party threw banned literature into a bonfire in Berlin in May 1933.

THE SPANISH CIVIL WAR 1936–1939

The Spanish Civil War was a battle between two opposing ideologies—fascism and socialism. Fascism won—to be followed by 36 years of dictatorial rule.

Francisco Franco (1892–1975) led the rebellion against the republican government in 1936. From 1939 until his death, he ruled Spain as dictator.

Before World War I, Spain sent military expeditions to strengthen its position in northern Morocco. In 1921, the Spanish forces were defeated by the Berber leader, Abd el-Krim, and it was not until 1927 that Spain was able to subdue the Berbers. In 1923, a military defeat in Morocco led to a fascist military dictatorship in Spain, headed by General Primo de Rivera.

Primo de Rivera ruled Spain until he fell from power in 1930. In the following year, King Alfonso XIII gave in to the demand for elections. The Republican Party won, and the monarchy was overthrown. During the following years, the government survived revolts in Asturias and Catalonia, and a new Popular Front government was elected in February 1936.

The new government under the presidency of Manuel Azana included members of the Socialist Workers' Party and the Communist Party. With their support, it opposed the power of the Roman Catholic Church in Spanish affairs. The Church was supported by the army and by the fascists.

Both men and women fought in the civil war. These republican women are defending a barricade on a Barcelona street in 1936. The U.S.S.R. and the International Brigade of volunteers helped the republicans.

FASCISM VERSUS SOCIALISM

On July 17, 1936, army generals in Spanish Morocco, in North Africa, began a rebellion. Led by General Francisco Franco, and supported by the nationalists, or Falange Party, they invaded Spain. They had the support of the fascist governments of Italy and Germany. The rebellion led to a bitter civil war. By the end of 1936, the nationalists controlled most of western and southern Spain.

▲ During the Spanish Civil War, people from many countries volunteered to fight in support of their political ideals. This British poster was designed by the artist Roland Penrose to help raise funds for the republican side.

▶ The Nationalists were supported by the fascist governments of Italy and Germany. This photograph, by war photographer Robert Capa, shows nationalist militia in action against republicans on the Córdoba Front in September 1936.

BATTLEGROUND OF BELIEFS

The republicans, supported by the Soviet Union, held the urban areas in the north and east, including the cities of Barcelona, Bilbao, Madrid, and Valencia. The nationalists captured Bilbao in 1937. In support of the nationalists, German dive-bombers attacked the Basque town of Guernica on April 27 of that year and killed hundreds of civilians. This was the first time that unrestricted aerial bombing was used in wartime against civilians, and marked a turning point in modern warfare.

The Spanish Civil War was a battleground between the beliefs of fascism and socialism. People from many countries, supporting one side or the other, volunteered to travel to Spain to fight because of their political ideals.

Some 750,000 people were killed in the war before government forces surrendered Barcelona in January 1939, and Madrid in March, to the nationalists. General Franco was declared "Caudillo of the Realm and Head of State."

Franco banned any opposition to the Falange Party, restored power to the Roman Catholic Church and took Spain out of the League of Nations. Although sympathetic to Hitler, he kept Spain neutral during World War II. Franco ruled Spain until his death in 1975, when the monarchy and democracy were restored.

▲ General Franco's troops are shown in battle with the republicans in the streets of Madrid during 1936. The surrender of Madrid by the republicans in March 1939 marked the end of the civil war.

▼ A turning point in modern warfare was the unrestricted aerial bombing of civilians in the town of Guernica by German aircraft in 1937. The event is recorded in one of Pablo Picasso's most famous paintings.

GERMAN EXPANSION 1938–1939

Hoping to avoid another war, Britain and France tolerated Hitler's expanionist policies, and allowed Germany to annex Austria and Czechoslovakia.

After the signing of the Munich Agreement in September 1938, Britain's prime minister, Neville Chamberlain, declared, "I believe it is peace for our time."

One of Adolf Hitler's ambitions was to unite Germany and Austria. This union had been forbidden by the Treaty of Versailles in 1919, because France and other countries thought it would make Germany too powerful. By the early 1930s, however, many people in Germany and Austria wanted their countries to unite. In 1934, an attempted Nazi coup in Austria failed. In 1938, Hitler met with the Austrian chancellor, Kurt von Schuschnigg, and made new demands. With chaos and German troops threatening his country, Schuschnigg resigned in favor of Artur von Seyss-Inquart, leader of the Austrian Nazis. He invited German troops to occupy Austria, and the union, or *Anschluss*, of the two countries was formally announced on March 13, 1938.

Hitler also wanted to reclaim areas of Europe given to other states by the Treaty of Versailles. One of these was areas was Czechoslovakia's Sudetenland. The Munich Agreement of 1938 was signed as an attempt to keep peace in Europe.

German troops marched into Vienna in 1938. Hitler wanted to unite all German-speaking peoples into a Greater Germany, an important part of his vision of the third German Empire, or Third Reich.

This agreement gave the Sudetenland to Germany. This was seen as a reasonable concession to Hitler—a policy known as appeasement. But it was not enough for Hitler. He broke the agreement, and seized all of Czechoslovakia in March 1939.

▲ Artur von Seyss-Inquart (1892–1946), the leader of the Austrian Nazis, was a member of the Austrian government. He invited the Germans to occupy his country and make it a part of the Third Reich. The annnexation of Austria in March 1938 brought little criticism from Britain or France.

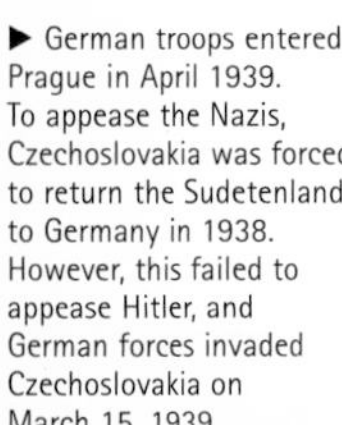

► German troops entered Prague in April 1939. To appease the Nazis, Czechoslovakia was forced to return the Sudetenland to Germany in 1938. However, this failed to appease Hitler, and German forces invaded Czechoslovakia on March 15, 1939.

THE START OF WORLD WAR II 1939

Hitler's confidence grew after years of appeasement by the rest of Europe. But his invasion of Poland led Britain and France to declare war on Germany.

Winston Churchill (1874–1965) became British prime minister in 1940 and led Britain during World War II.

The three Axis Powers, German, Italy, and Japan, all wanted more territory. After his invasion of Czechoslovakia, Hitler did not expect any international military action against his plans to expand farther. To counter any military threat to the east of Germany, he signed a non-agression pact, the Molotov–Ribbentrop Pact, with the Soviet Union in August 1939. The two countries secretly agreed to divide eastern Europe. Despite appeals from the United States, Britain and the Vatican, and feeling secure from any military threat, Hitler invaded Poland on September 1, 1939. Britain and France declared war on Germany two days later. Troops from the Soviet Union, which had signed the nonaggression pact with Germany, then invaded Poland from the east. Poland was divided between Germany and the U.S.S.R. In April 1940, German troops invaded Denmark and Norway, and in May, they invaded Belgium, the Netherlands, and France.

Messerschmitt Me 109

Supermarine Spitfire

▲ Between July and October 1940, the German air force (*Luftwaffe*) bombed British cities and attacked Britain's Royal Air Force (RAF). During these attacks, the RAF destroyed 1,733 Luftwaffe planes, while the RAF lost 915. By October 31, the British had won the Battle of Britain.

German forces attack the poorly equipped Polish army near the Vistula River in September 1939. Much of western Poland was taken into the Third Reich and many of its people were deported to Germany as forced labor.

In June, Italy declared war on the Allies. British troops sent to France were forced to retreat to Dunkirk, where hundreds of thousands of them were evacuated to Britain. With most of Europe under fascist control, Hitler planned to invade Britain. In July 1940, the *Luftwaffe* (German air force) started to attack targets in Britain. The United States remained in isolation.

▶ On May 10, 1940, German forces invaded Holland and Belgium. British troops were sent to France in an unsuccessful attempt to halt the German advance. They were forced to retreat to the French port of Dunkirk. Between May 29 and June 4, 335,000 British and Allied troops were evacuated safely back to England from the beaches around Dunkirk.

WAR IN THE WEST 1939–1945

After German successes in Europe and North Africa, Allied victories at El Alamein and Stalingrad were a turning point in the war, and led to Germany's defeat.

Erwin Rommel (1891–1944) was a brilliant leader of German armored units. In North Africa, his tanks showed their superiority over the aging British machines.

Bernard Law Montgomery (1887–1976) led the British forces in North Africa and Europe. The victory of his Eighth Army at El Alamein was a major turning point in the war.

Georgy Zhukov (1896–1974) commanded the Soviet Red Army in their struggle against the German invaders.

Dwight D. Eisenhower (1890–1969) was Supreme Allied Commander during the war and was elected president in 1952.

The Battle of Britain lasted until October 31, 1940, and forced Hitler to abandon his plan to invade Britain. Instead, he turned his attention to bombing Britain's industry, cities, and shipyards. This lasted until May 1941, but failed to break the morale of Britain, which received substantial supplies and equipment from the United States.

GERMAN ADVANCES

Meanwhile, the Italians had invaded Greece and North Africa. British forces defeated the Italians in North Africa, but in April 1941, Hitler's troops occupied Greece and Yugoslavia to assist Mussolini's army. The Germans drove the British out of Greece and sent a large force, under General Rommel, to North Africa. His superior forces succeeded in driving the British back to Egypt.

In June 1941, encouraged by military successes in the West, and to capture oil supplies, Hitler's armies launched a massive attack on Russia. The Germans drove the Russian army back as far as Leningrad, Moscow, and Kiev. However, during the harsh Soviet winter they lost a large part of their recently gained territory.

British RAF pilots rest beside a Spitfire fighter plane during a lull in the Battle of Britain. Completely outnumbered, but with superior aircraft, British pilots halted the German air force's bombing of Britain.

THE TIDE TURNS AGAINST GERMANY

In August 1941, British prime minister Winston Churchill, and U.S. president Franklin D. Roosevelt, signed the Atlantic Charter—a declaration of freedom for all people. In December, the United States entered the war after the Japanese attack on Pearl Harbor. Meanwhile, Allied troops were sent to Africa to fend off Rommel's advance on Egypt. In November 1942, the Allies won the decisive battle of El Alamein against the Germans and the Italians. To the east, the Russians launched a counterattack against German forces at Stalingrad, forcing them to retreat. These two Allied victories marked the turning point of the war in the West.

A German mortar detachment moves off in support of the infantry during the Battle of Stalingrad. In November 1942, the Russians launched a surprise counterattack on the German forces attacking the city, and forced them to retreat.

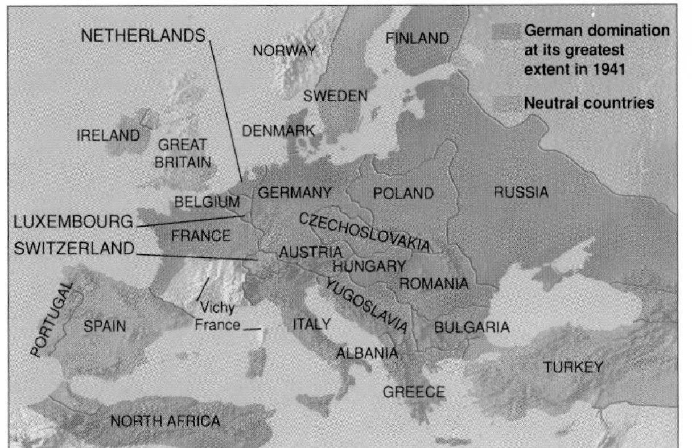

By 1941, Germany had conquered most of Europe apart from Britain, and was expanding into North Africa. From June 1940, Vichy France was ruled from the town of Vichy by Marshal Pétain as a puppet of the Germans.

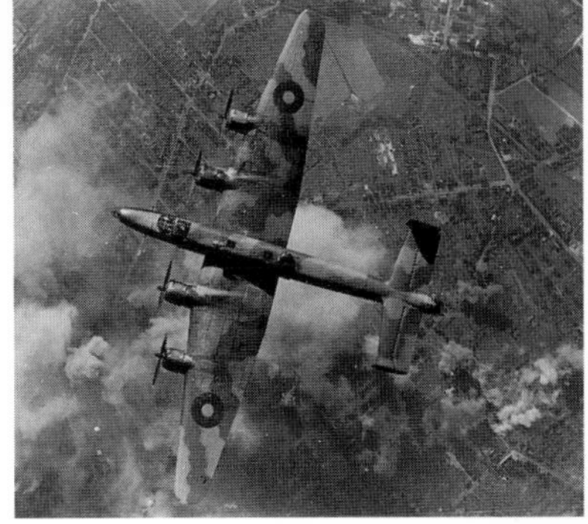

A British Halifax bomber flies over the target during a daylight bombing raid on the oil plant at Wanne-Eickel in the Ruhr in 1944. The heavy bombing of German industry and cities by Allied air forces was a significant factor in the final defeat of Germany.

Throughout 1942 and 1943, German U-boats attacked convoys of ships carrying supplies and equipment to Britain. This threat was countered by protection from ships and aircraft. In 1943, Britain and the United States started bombing German industrial centers and cities. In July, British and American forces landed in Sicily, and by September they had invaded Italy. This brought about the downfall of Mussolini and the surrender of Italy.

When France fell in 1940, General Charles de Gaulle became the leader of the Free French. He served as president of France in 1945 and 1959–1969.

FINAL DEFEAT OF GERMANY

On the Eastern front, Russian troops were slowly driving the Germans back. A second front was opened on D-Day, June 6, 1944, with the Allied invasion of Normandy. The Germans launched a counteroffensive. The Soviets began to march toward Berlin, while the Allies liberated Paris in August and reached the German border by December. By March 1945, they had crossed the Rhine and the Soviets had reached Berlin. Hitler killed himself on April 30, and Germany surrendered unconditionally on May 7.

THE HOLOCAUST

The Allies soon discovered the greatest case of genocide in history. Twelve million Jews, gypsies, homosexuals, and other victims of Hitler's persecution had been exterminated, mostly in concentration camps. Around half were Jewish.

On D-Day (June 6, 1944), Allied forces landed on the coast of Normandy: 1,200 warships and 4,100 landing craft put 132,500 men ashore, and 10,000 aircraft attacked German positions. The D-Day landings allowed Allied troops to drive the Germans out of France.

WAR IN THE PACIFIC 1941–1945

The Japanese attack on Pearl Harbor catapulted the United States into World War II. After initial success, the Japanese were slowly driven back to their country.

Admiral Yamamoto Isoroku (1884–1943) planned Japan's attack on Pearl Harbor. In April 1943, while flying to inspect Japanese forces in the Solomon Islands, his route was located by Allied codebreakers who were listening to Japanese radio signals. He was killed when American fighters shot his plane down.

Since September 1940, Japan had allied itself with Germany and Italy, but had not been involved in the fighting. After Japan's invasion of China in 1937, it had come under increasing pressure from the United States to withdraw its forces from that country. The war in the Pacific began on December 7, 1941, when Japanese aircraft from six aircraft carriers launched an unprovoked attack on the U.S. naval base at Pearl Harbor, Hawaii. More than 2,400 U.S. soldiers and sailors were killed and 18 major naval vessels were destroyed or severely damaged. The Japanese lost fewer than 100 men. Japanese forces invaded Thailand on the same day. On the following day, Congress declared war on Japan. Germany and Italy then declared war on the United States.

The U.S. battleships *Tennessee* and *West Virginia* on fire after the Japanese attack on Pearl Harbor on December 7, 1941. In the attack, 18 major U.S. ships, including eight battleships, were destroyed or severely damaged.

JAPANESE KAMIKAZE PILOTS

Kamikaze means "divine wind," a reference to a heaven-sent gale that scattered the ships of a Mongol invasion fleet in 1281. Toward the end of the war in the Pacific, there was no shortage of Japanese pilots who volunteered to die for their emperor by diving their aircraft, laden with bombs, straight into an Allied ship. More than half of the 2,900 kamikaze attacks were launched during the defense of the island of Okinawa. The plane used most often in kamikaze attacks was the Zero fighter, because large numbers of them were available.

▲ Kamikaze pilots often performed rituals before takeoff, and wore a special scarf.

▼ Kamikaze attacks were first mounted by the Japanese Imperial Navy on October 25, 1944, during the Battle of Leyte Gulf. During the war, around 300 Allied ships were hit by kamikaze attacks.

On December 10, 1941, the British battleship *Prince of Wales* and the battle cruiser *Repulse* were sunk in the Gulf of Siam by Japanese aircraft. With American and British fleets severely damaged, the Japanese now thought that they had complete control of the Pacific. Within five months, their forces had overrun Burma, Hong Kong, Singapore, Malaya, the Dutch East Indies (Indonesia), Thailand, and the Philippines. They also invaded New Guinea and threatened the north coast of Australia. With most of its own troops and equipment helping the Allies in Europe, Australia had to turn to the United States for protection.

▲ After their victory at Midway, U.S. forces took the island of Guadalcanal in August 1942. Following in their footsteps, New Zealand troops come ashore at Guadalcanal Bay in November 1943.

JAPANESE LOSSES AT SEA

Not all of the U.S. fleet had been sunk at Pearl Harbor. Three American aircraft carriers were at sea at the time of the attack and they were soon joined by two new carriers. Japanese hopes of further expansion were stopped in 1942 in two major sea battles.

The Battle of the Coral Sea (May 4–8) was the first in naval history in which opposing ships were out of each other's sight during the fighting. It was fought by aircraft launched from aircraft carriers. There was no clear winner, but the battle did halt Japanese plans to invade Australia. In June, the Japanese planned to invade the small but strategic island of Midway and the Aleutian Islands. But first they had to destroy American aircraft based on Midway. However, the United States had cracked the Japanese radio codes and were prepared for the attack.

In the Battle of Midway (June 4–6) the Japanese navy was so severely damaged by U.S. carrier-borne aircraft that it retreated. Midway was a decisive victory for the United States and a turning point in the war. With the Japanese advance halted, the task of recapturing territory began.

Over the following three years, U.S. forces regained the Gilbert, Marshall, Caroline, and Mariana islands. From there, they could bomb Japanese cities and industry. In September 1944, U.S. forces began to retake the Philippines, while the British Fourth Army began to reconquer Burma. After fierce fighting, U.S. forces took the Japanese islands of Okinawa and Iwo Jima in early 1945.

▼ Dislodging the Japanese from the jungles of Burma was a difficult task. In the early stages of the war, a small British force under General Wingate, known as the Chindits, operated many miles behind Japanese lines.

KEY DATES

- **1941** December 7—Japan attacks American Pacific Fleet in Pearl Harbor, Hawaii; United States declares war on Japan; Japanese sink British warships in Gulf of Siam
- **1942** Japanese overrun Hong Kong, Burma, Thailand, Singapore, Malaya, Dutch East Indies, and the Philippines; Battles of Coral Sea, Midway, and Guadalcanal
- **1944** Battle of Leyte Gulf; U.S. forces recapture the Philippines
- **1945** U.S. Air Force takes Okinawa and Iwo Jima; American air force drops atomic bombs on Hiroshima and Nagasaki; Japan surrenders on August 14

PEACE IN THE PACIFIC 1945–1948

With U.S. forces on their doorstep, the Japanese were prepared to fight to the bitter end. The dropping of atomic bombs forced them into surrender.

Japanese representatives wait to sign the formal statement of surrender with General Douglas MacArthur (1880–1964) on the deck of the U.S. battleship *Missouri* on September 2, 1945.

In the taking of the island of Okinawa, more than 100,000 Japanese and 12,000 American soldiers were killed. After these enormous losses, Allied commanders were fearful of the deaths that might result if they invaded the Japanese mainland. They knew that the Japanese would fight to their last drop of blood to defend their country, and estimated that up to a million Allied soldiers would die in the invasion.

In the United States, Roosevelt had been elected to his third term of office as president in 1944. Meanwhile, amid great secrecy, American scientists had been developing a new and terrible weapon—the atomic bomb. Roosevelt died in office on April 12, 1945, and his successor, Harry S. Truman, made the decision to drop the new atomic bomb on Japan.

JAPANESE SURRENDER

Truman argued that the use of atomic bombs would quickly end the war and possibly save millions of Allied soldiers' lives. At the end of July 1945, the Allies gave Japan an ultimatum, threatening complete destruction if Japan did not surrender. Japan gave no signs of surrendering, so an atomic bomb was dropped on Hiroshima on August 6, 1945. It killed about 130,000 people. Three days later a second atomic bomb was dropped on the city of Nagasaki and caused up to 750,000 deaths. Thousands more died later from injuries and radiation sickness. The use of the bombs finally forced the Japanese to surrender on August 14.

World War II ended when the Japanese formally surrendered on September 2, 1945. More than two million Japanese had been killed in World War II, 100 of their cities were destroyed by bombing, and industrial production had practically ceased. It took ten years for Japanese industry to regain its prewar levels.

THE BOMBING OF HIROSHIMA

The development of the atomic bomb by American scientists had been kept secret. Two atomic bombs were used in war. The five-ton "Little Boy" was dropped on Hiroshima (below) by an American B-29 Superfortress, the *Enola Gay* on August 6, 1945. Three days later a second atomic bomb, "Fat Man" was dropped from another Superfortress, the *Bockstar*, to destroy the city of Nagasaki.

The Boeing B-29 Superfortress was the largest bomber used in World War II.

THE UNITED NATIONS 1945–1948

At the end of World War II, the victorious Allied powers divided Germany into four zones. The United Nations was created to keep international peace.

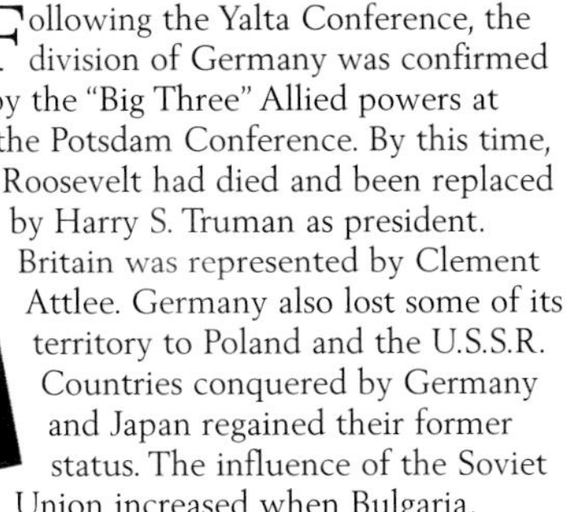

On April 25, 1945, the United Nations was formally set up at a conference in San Francisco. It was meant to keep world peace and solve problems by international cooperation.

Following the Yalta Conference, the division of Germany was confirmed by the "Big Three" Allied powers at the Potsdam Conference. By this time, Roosevelt had died and been replaced by Harry S. Truman as president. Britain was represented by Clement Attlee. Germany also lost some of its territory to Poland and the U.S.S.R. Countries conquered by Germany and Japan regained their former status. The influence of the Soviet Union increased when Bulgaria, Hungary, Poland, Romania, Czechoslovakia, Yugoslavia, and eastern Germany became communist states. The Truman Doctrine promised American aid to all free peoples that were threatened by communism, while the Marshall Plan provided help for economic recovery.

At the Yalta Conference in February 1945, the "Big Three" Allied powers, represented by their leaders, Churchill (Britain), Roosevelt (U.S.), and Stalin (U.S.S.R.), decided to divide Germany into four zones after the war.

THE UNITED NATIONS

The term "United Nations" (UN) was first used in January 1942 when the Atlantic Charter was signed by the Allies. In the Charter, they agreed to fight the Axis countries and not make any separate peace agreements. The UN was planned to be stronger than the League of Nations had been. It had a powerful Security Council to decide what should be done if disputes broke out. Members were to contribute arms and personnel to UN peacekeeping missions. In 1948, the UN issued a Universal Declaration of Human Rights.

▲ The Potsdam Declaration of 1945 made it possible to bring Nazi war criminals to justice. War trials were held in the German city of Nuremburg. Here, former Nazi leaders Hermann Goering, Rudolf Hess, and Joachim von Ribbentrop await cross-examination at the trials. All three were found guilty. Goering committed suicide hours before his execution; Hess received a life sentence and died in 1987 in Spandau Prison; von Ribbentrop was hanged along with nine other high-ranking Nazis on October 16, 1946.

▶ On June 25, 1948, the Soviet Union set up a blockade around Berlin to try to force France, Britain, and the United States to give up their rights to the western part of Berlin. To feed the population, Britain and the United States flew supplies into the city for 15 months until the blockade was lifted.

ISRAEL 1948–1949

Growing demands for a separate Jewish state and the flood of refugees from Europe forced the British to withdraw from Palestine. Israel became a reality.

David Ben-Gurion (1886–1973) was born in Poland. As a young man he went to live in Palestine and in 1930 became leader of the Mapai Party. In 1948, he declared the State of Israel and became its first prime minister.

Until the end of World War I, Palestine was part of the Ottoman Empire. It was inhabited by Arabs and a growing number of Jews, some of whom wanted a Jewish homeland. When the Ottoman Empire collapsed, Palestine was ruled by Britain under a 1922 League of Nations' mandate. In 1917, the Balfour Declaration had promised British support for a Jewish homeland in Palestine, with specific protection for the rights of non-Jewish Palestinians. As problems grew in Europe, Jewish immigration increased.

Between 1922 and 1939, the Jewish population in Palestine had risen from 83,000 to 445,000. Tel Aviv had become a Jewish city with a population of 150,000. The Arabs resented this and fighting often broke out between the two groups. After 1945, Jewish immigration increased again. Under pressure from the Arabs, Britain restricted the number of new settlers allowed. Jewish terrorists then began to attack both the Arabs and the British.

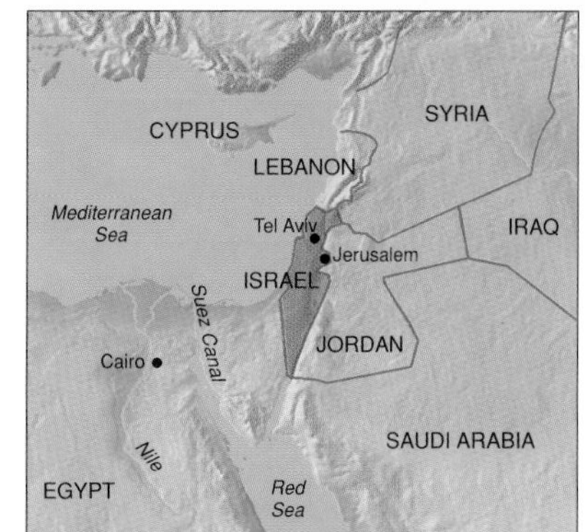

The new State of Israel was surrounded by Arab states. On May 14, 1948, the Arab League of Lebanon, Syria, Iraq, Jordan, and Egypt declared war on Israel and attacked it. They were defeated and Israel increased its territory.

A secret Jewish army called *Haganah* (self-defense) was formed in 1920. More extreme groups were later formed, notably Irgun and the Stern Gang. Both groups thought that Britain had betrayed the Zionist cause—to establish a Jewish state in Palestine—and took part in a violent terrorist campaign against the Arabs and the British. Jewish leaders such as Chaim Weizmann and David Ben-Gurion took a more peaceful approach.

▲ One result of the hostility between the Arabs and Jews in 1948 was the migration of nearly one million Arabs from Palestine. They left their homes and became refugees because they were afraid of the action Israel might take after the war with the Arab League.

▶ After World War II, the number of Jewish refugees from Europe trying to enter Palestine became a problem for the British. In October 1947, the ship *Jewish State* arrived at the port of Haifa with 2,000 illegal Jewish immigrants aboard.

By June 1945, an enormous number of Jewish refugees, displaced by the war in Europe, were clamoring to live in Palestine. Despite British efforts to stop them, the number of refugees entering the country continued to increase. The United States put pressure on Britain to allow the admission of 100,000 refugees, but Britain refused. It soon found itself involved in a full-scale war with Jewish terrorist organizations.

THE NEW STATE OF ISRAEL

Unwilling to be caught up in another bloody and costly war, Britain took the matter to the United Nations. In 1947, the UN voted to divide Palestine into two states. One would be Jewish and the other one Arab. Jerusalem, which was sacred to Jews, Muslims, and Christians, would be international. The Jews agreed to this, but the Arabs did not.

On May 14, 1948, Britain gave up its mandate to rule Palestine and withdrew its troops. On the same day, the Jews, led by Mapai Party leader David Ben-Gurion, proclaimed the State of Israel, and its legitimacy was immediately recognized by the governments of the United States and the Soviet Union.

During the War of Independence, Jewish Haganah militiamen watch over the road to Jaffa. They captured this important position on April 17, 1948, after stiff Arab resistance.

Israel was immediately attacked by the surrounding Arab League states of Lebanon, Syria, Iraq, Jordan, and Egypt. Israel defeated them and increased its territory by a quarter. Nearly one million Palestinian refugees, afraid of Jewish rule, fled to neighboring Arab countries. The United Nations negotiated a cease-fire in 1949, but conflicts between Israel and its Arab neighbors continue to this day.

Members of Haganah, the Jewish defense force, keep a sharp lookout for possible Arab looters in the destroyed Jewish border area between Jaffa and Tel Aviv, the scene of constant disorder.

The Israeli flag was raised at Eilat on the Gulf of Aqaba in 1949. It is the southernmost point in Israel, and its only port on the Red Sea.

BRITISH COMMONWEALTH 1914–1949

In 1931, the countries that formed the British Empire joined together to form the Commonwealth. Over the next 60 years they were given their independence.

During both World Wars, soldiers from all corners of the British Empire and Commonwealth fought on the British side. Here, members of the Rhodesian Air Askari Corps practice square drill in 1943.

The relationship between Britain and parts of its empire had begun to change by the beginning of the 1900s. Some of the larger countries were made independent as dominions. They were completely self-governing, but they maintained strong links with Britain—the "mother country." Dominions retained the British Crown (king or queen) as the symbolic head of state. Each dominion had a lieutenant governor, a native resident of that country, who represented the Crown.

In the 1920s, the dominions asked for a clear definition of their status. In the 1931 Statute of Westminster dominions were defined as "autonomous (self-ruling) communities within the British Empire, equal in status... united by a common allegiance to the Crown and freely associated as members of the British Commonwealth of Nations." After this, the name British Commonwealth of Nations was used instead of British Empire. Many colonies started to clamor for independence.

INDEPENDENT MEMBERS OF THE COMMONWEALTH

Antigua and Barbuda 1981
Australia 1901
Bahamas 1973
Bangladesh 1972
Barbados 1966
Belize 1981
Botswana 1966
Brunei 1984
Canada 1867
Cyprus 1960
Dominica 1978
Gambia 1965
Ghana 1957
Great Britain, Founder 1931
Grenada 1974
Guyana 1966
India 1947
Jamaica 1962
Kenya 1963
Kiribati 1979
Lesotho 1966
Malawi 1964
Malaysia 1957
Maldives 1965
Malta 1964
Mauritius 1968
Namibia 1990
Nauru 1968
New Zealand 1907
Nigeria 1960
Pakistan 1947
Papua New Guinea 1975
St. Kitts-Nevis 1983
St. Lucia 1979
St. Vincent and the Grenadines 1979
Seychelles 1976
Sierra Leone 1961
Singapore 1965
Solomon Islands 1978
South Africa 1994
Sri Lanka (Ceylon) 1948
Swaziland 1968
Tanzania 1961
Tonga 1970
Trinidad and Tobago 1962
Tuvalu 1978
Uganda 1962
Vanuatu 1980
Western Samoa 1962
Zambia 1964
Zimbabwe 1980

In 1932, the dominions received better terms for trading with Britain than countries outside the Commonwealth. Canada, Australia, New Zealand, and South Africa had all become dominions before World War I. The Irish Free State also became a dominion in 1921. The first three colonies to gain independence after World War II were India (1947), Ceylon (1948), and Burma (1948). India and Ceylon (now Sri Lanka) stayed in the Commonwealth, but Burma did not join, and the Republic of Ireland left in 1949.

▼ Here, Commonwealth premiers pose with King George VI at Buckingham Palace while attending the Conference of Commonwealth Prime Ministers in London in April 1949.

COMMUNIST CHINA 1945–1949

After the defeat of Japan in 1945, the Chinese nationalists and communists resumed their civil war. In 1949, the People's Republic of China was declared.

The communists introduced collective farming to China. This meant that all the land, buildings, and machinery belonged to the community. Committees in each village decided what to grow. One improvement was that they replaced their oxen with tractors, which they called "Iron Oxen."

In 1936, the Chinese nationalist leader, Chiang Kai-shek, was forced to make an alliance with the Communist Party to fight against the Japanese in Manchuria. This alliance lasted until 1945 and brought China into World War II on the Allies' side. While the Chinese were fighting the Japanese, Britain and the United States gave them aid. After the defeat of Japan in 1945, the alliance collapsed and civil war broke out in 1946. The nationalists were weak and divided, but Mao Zedong's communists had the support of the people. The communists also had a large army, and by January 1949 they had taken Tianjin and Beijing (Peking). From there they moved southward, where they defeated Chiang Kai-shek and the nationalists and took control of the whole country. The People's Republic of China was declared on October 1, 1949, but many countries refused to recognize it.

The People's Republic of China came into being on October 1, 1949. In the following years, the Chinese communist leader Mao Zedong introduced reforms in the countryside in order to gain the support of the people. This 1949 poster for the Chinese Communist Party shows farmers and soldiers working together.

Large posters of Communist Party leaders formed the backdrop to speeches at a meeting of the Communist Party in Shanghai. When they took power in 1949, the communists soon moved to control the press and nationalized industries.

USA
NASA
Discovery

THE MODERN WORLD

1950–2000

The years between 1950 and the present day are recent history. Some of the events have occurred during our lifetime, or we have seen reports of them on television. The latter half of the 1900s has seen social, technological, and environmental changes on a scale never witnessed before. Politicians and policy-makers, as well as historians, have identified several important trends that will continue to transform our world: environmental pollution, ever-increasing population, changing family structures, and a growing gap between rich and poor.

▲ Aircraft carriers from Britain and the United States played an important peacekeeping role in the 1990s in various world trouble spots, such as the Middle East and Yugoslavia.

◀ The space shuttle *Discovery* blasts off from the Kennedy Space Center at the beginning of its twenty-first spaceflight in July 1995.

THE WORLD AT A GLANCE 1950–2000

This period was dominated by the Cold War between the communist East and the capitalist West. The United States and the U.S.S.R. played the leading roles. These two were also involved in the space race. The U.S.S.R. was the first to send a man into space, and the United States the first to put a man on the moon. Changes in the U.S.S.R. led to the end of the Cold War, but created uncertainty about the future as nationalists demanded independence.

In western Europe, the European Union encouraged economic growth and worked toward political unity. In Africa, many nations became independent, but faced severe economic problems, as well as droughts and famines. In Southeast Asia, technology and industry developed, and Japanese business became the most successful in the world. China experienced a cultural revolution, and Indochina was devastated by a series of wars.

NORTH AMERICA

This half-century was the high point in the development of the United States, which led the way materially and culturally. By now, the West Coast was as much a center for the movie and aircraft industries as the East Coast, and home to many futuristic ideas. The United States led the way in the nuclear arms race and equaled the U.S.S.R. in the space race. The 1950s saw growing prosperity, although the 1960s saw conflict over civil rights and social issues. American culture reached its high point in music, movies, inventions, and new ideas in the 1970s, despite the war in Vietnam and the exposure of government corruption. In the 1980s, computer technology and free-market economics brought an economic boom, the space shuttle, and the end of the Cold War. In the 1990s, Asia made great strides toward catching up, and the United States became more multicultural. The United States acted as a global policeman in a complex world, though its internal politics have never been settled. Yet this was its greatest time in history. American culture spread to every corner of the world.

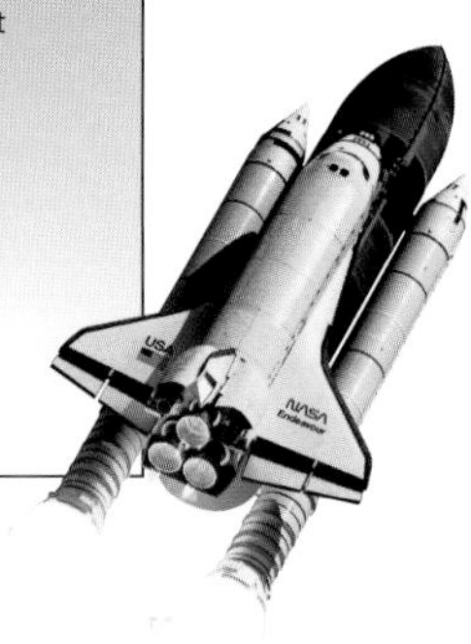

NORTH AMERICA

LATIN AMERICA

LATIN AMERICA

Until the 1970s, there was a battle between right-wing dictators and left-wing revolutionaries in Latin America. Poverty, power, and guerrilla wars were the issues facing the area. As the continent grew richer and more liberal governments came to power, these pressures eased. The Catholic Church also lost ground, and the destruction of the rain forest, government corruption, human rights, and the drug trade became the pressing issues. Civil wars were resolved, and in the 1990s, Latin America, now industrialized, played an increasing role in global affairs.

EUROPE

Ruined by World War II, and overshadowed by the Cold War, Europe made a dramatic recovery between the 1950s and the 1970s, beginning a long process of cooperation through the founding of the European Community. Europe worked with a "social market" model of economics, with ample welfare and social systems that, by the 1990s, became a burden. Despite crises such as the Hungarian uprising of 1956 and the "Prague Spring" of 1968, Europe remained at peace. The greatest breakthrough was the ending of the Cold War, which reunited Germany and brought reconciliation between East and West, though ugly scenes such as the Yugoslavian civil wars of the 1990s hindered progress. Environmental and social concerns were important, especially after the Russian nuclear disaster at Chernobyl in 1986. Europe began to play a more equal role in the world community than in previous centuries.

ASIA

During this period, the fortunes of Asia rose again. The Maoist era in China brought mixed results, some impressive, some disastrous. They led to reforms in the 1980s, and to China's reentry into the world's market economy. Japan became the economic and technological powerhouse of Asia, and fueled great economic growth in Southeast Asia from the early 1970s. India modernized in the 1970s, though conflicts continued with Pakistan. The withdrawal of colonial powers, the Vietnam War, the rise of Islamic and Confucian values, the fall of the U.S.S.R. in central Asia and the globalization of the world economy all had a great effect on Asia.

EUROPE

ASIA

MIDDLE EAST

AFRICA

AUSTRALASIA

AUSTRALASIA

Australia and New Zealand became leading countries, although they had to get used to being neighbors to Asia. Australia became one of the world's wealthiest countries. Polynesia became a tourist destination, but also a place for nuclear weapon testing.

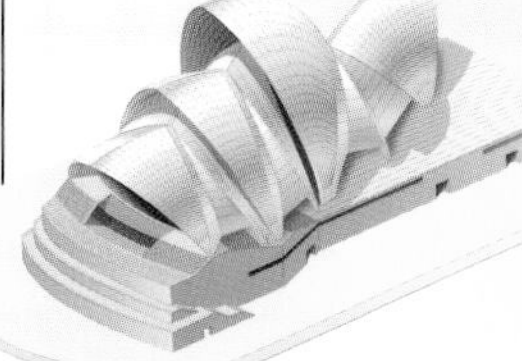

AFRICA

After a promising start in the 1960s, when most states gained independence, Africa was troubled by wars, corruption, famine, and social crises. Foreign interference and exploitation were common. In South Africa, torn by apartheid, reform came in 1990, and brought the dawn of a new, multiracial society. Africa remains troubled, but the lessons learned may lead to improvements in the future.

MIDDLE EAST

Oil rich, the Middle East witnessed extremes of wealth and suffering during this period. Rising Islamic fundamentalism had a mixed outcome, disturbing the peace, yet helping the less affluent. Caught between different world powers, war and interference by foreign powers were common.

THE COLD WAR 1945–1989

After the end of World War II, tensions between East and West and the buildup of nuclear weapons almost brought the world to the brink of war.

This 1962 cartoon, produced at the time of the Cuban missile crisis, shows the two superpower leaders arm-wrestling for power. The U.S.S.R.'s Nikita Khrushchev (1894–1971), on the left, is facing the U.S. president, John F. Kennedy (1917–1963). They are both sitting on nuclear weapons.

The U.S.S.R. and the United States fought as allies in World War II. But in 1945, these two superpowers became rivals and then enemies. This division became known as the Cold War, a conflict largely without any actual fighting. Both countries made threats and built up their armed forces and weapons. Each side also accumulated an enormous stockpile of nuclear weapons. The idea was to hold a kind of balance in which neither side would want to start a real war.

Friendly contacts ceased. The U.S.S.R. became shut off from the world. The great British statesman Sir Winston Churchill described the frontier between East and West as the "Iron Curtain" in a speech at Fulton, Missouri on March 5, 1946.

The Cold War dominated world politics for many years. On one side, the United States became the leader of NATO (North Atlantic Treaty Organization), a military alliance of Western nations providing collective defense against the communist powers. On the other side, the U.S.S.R. led the Warsaw Pact, a military alliance of East European states that backed communism.

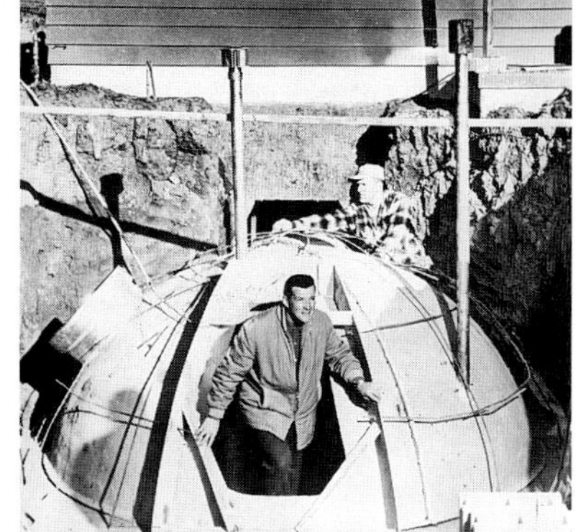

Because of the serious threat of nuclear war between East and West during the 1960s, many Americans built fallout shelters in their backyards.

BERLIN: A DIVIDED CITY

In 1945, the United States, France, and Britain took control of West Germany. The U.S.S.R. controlled East Germany. The capital, Berlin, inside East Germany, was also divided. In 1948, the Soviets closed all access to West Berlin. The Western powers brought in supplies by air, until the blockade was lifted in 1949. From 1949 to 1958, three million people escaped from East to West Berlin. In 1961, East Germany closed off this escape route by building the Berlin Wall across the city. It crossed tram lines and roads and created an area on either side known as No Man's Land.

▲ The Berlin Wall, built in 1961 to divide East and West Berlin, finally "fell" in November 1989.

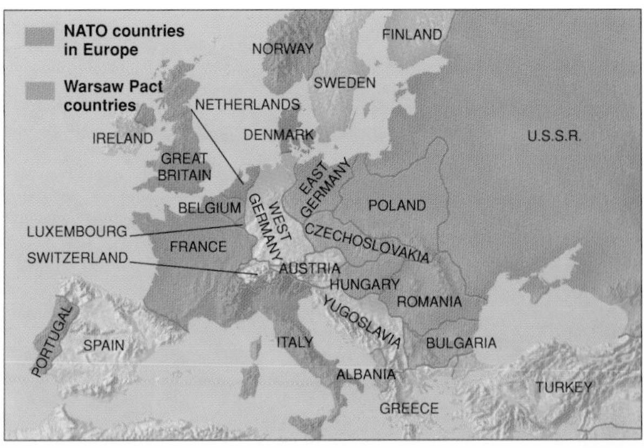

▶ By 1949, most European states had joined rival alliances. Warsaw Pact countries supported the U.S.S.R. Members of NATO backed the U.S.A.

CUBAN MISSILE CRISIS

Although the United States and the U.S.S.R. never fought, they came close. The world held its breath for a week in October 1962. President John F. Kennedy received Air Force photographs showing that the Soviet Union was building missile launch sites in Cuba. From there, the nuclear missiles could reach and destroy many U.S. cities. On October 22, the president ordered a naval blockade of Cuba. The United States made plans to invade Cuba, and the world braced itself for nuclear war. Finally, on October 28, Nikita Khrushchev, the Soviet leader, backed down and agreed to remove the missiles and destroy the Cuban launch sites. The crisis was over.

◀ Francis Gary Powers (1929–1977) was the pilot of an American U-2 spy plane that was shot down over Russian territory in 1960. He was released in exchange for the imprisoned Soviet spymaster Rudolf Abel (1903–1971).

THE END OF THE COLD WAR

The friendly relationship between the American president Ronald Reagan and the Soviet leader Mikhail Gorbachev helped reduce Cold War tensions. By 1987, they had agreed to abolish medium-range nuclear missiles. In 1989, Gorbachev allowed the communist countries of Eastern Europe to elect democratic governments. And in 1991, the Soviet Union broke up into 15 republics. The Cold War was over. On March 12, 1999, Hungary, Poland, and the Czech Republic joined NATO. The joining ceremony was held at the Harry S. Truman Library in Independence, Missouri.

▼ Czech students tried to stop Soviet tanks in Prague, in August 1968. The U.S.S.R. feared that independent actions by Warsaw Pact members might weaken its power, so it moved into Czechoslovakia.

▶ During the Cold War many groups of people, such as the Peace Pledge Union, were formed to try and influence governments and stop the spread of nuclear weapons.

◀ Here, supporters of the Campaign for Nuclear Disarmament (CND) march through London in 1983 to demonstrate against the deployment of Cruise and Trident nuclear missiles on British soil.

IN SPACE 1957–2000

Space exploration began in 1957 when the U.S.S.R. launched Sputnik I, the first artificial satellite to orbit the Earth. Twelve years later, a man stood on the moon.

The development of missile technology during World War II helped scientists to believe that one day space travel might be possible. Cold War rivalry between the United States and the U.S.S.R. triggered the space race. Both sides felt that being the first nation in space would increase their prestige. They also hoped that space science would help them develop new, more powerful weapons.

The Soviets achieved the key "space first" when they sent a satellite into orbit around the Earth in 1957. Soon, both sides were investing enormous amounts of time and money in space science. The U.S.S.R. achieved another first in 1961, when Yuri Gagarin became the first person in space. Other notable achievements by both countries included probes sent to the moon and past Venus, further manned flights, spacewalks, and the launch of communications satellites.

The Apollo spaceflight program saw the United States land people on the moon. Between July 1969 and December 1972, there were six successful Apollo missions, the last three involving the use of a lunar roving vehicle, or lunar rover.

Sputnik 1 was launched by Russia on October 4, 1957. The satellite orbited the Earth for six months and was used to broadcast scientific data.

This picture shows Russian cosmonaut Yuri Gagarin (1934–1968) in the cabin of *Vostok 1*, the spacecraft in which he became the first person to orbit the Earth on April 12, 1961.

In the run-up to the Apollo flights, the American Gemini program was designed to teach astronauts how to cope with space travel. In November 1966, "Buzz" Aldrin carried out three spacewalks high over the Earth.

The ending of the Cold War and the economic crisis of the 1970s led the two superpowers to scale down their space programs. However, the Soviets gained valuable experience with long-endurance flights on permanent space stations. Cooperation between the two countries is important for the construction of the international space station.

MAN ON THE MOON

In 1961, President John F. Kennedy said that his scientists would send a man to the moon by 1970. In fact, the first manned moon landing took place on July 20, 1969. The crew of the *Apollo 11* mission consisted of Neil Armstrong, the first man to set foot on the moon, Edwin "Buzz" Aldrin, who was the second man to walk on the lunar surface, and Michael Collins, who remained in orbit in the command and service module. Armstrong described his first step on the moon as "one small step for a man, one giant leap for mankind."

◀ *Apollo 11* was launched from Cape Canaveral, Florida, on July 16, 1969. The first manned landing on the moon was just four days later.

SPACE SHUTTLES

The U.S. National Aeronautics and Space Administration (NASA) required a reusable space vehicle to construct and serve planned space stations. The shuttles could take off like a rocket—with a large payload—and return to Earth like a plane. The launch of the first space shuttle, in 1981, marked a new phase in space exploration. Since that first flight, space shuttles have carried a variety of payloads (cargo), and retrieved and repaired satellites. In 1995, the space shuttle *Atlantis* docked with the Russian *Mir* space station, marking an important step forward in international cooperation.

▲ This view of the dusty, rock-strewn surface of Mars was taken by one of the two U.S. Viking landers in 1976. Part of the spacecraft is visible in the foreground.

The Soviet space station *Mir* was launched in 1986. It was designed to stay in orbit for a long time, so that complicated scientific experiments could be carried out on board. It has now far exceeded its planned life span. Although requiring fairly constant repair and maintenance, the station is still manned after 13 years of service.

THE EXPLORATION OF DEEP SPACE

Unmanned space probes have flown by, or landed on, every planet in the solar system except Pluto. Soviet probes landed on Venus in 1975 and sent back pictures. In 1976, two U.S. Viking craft landed on Mars and began observations that lasted six years. In 1977, the United States launched the two Voyager missions. These craft traveled around the solar system using the slingshot technique—the spacecraft used each planet's gravitational field to propel them onward. Before they disappeared into deeper space, they transmitted valuable data and color photographs of Jupiter, Saturn, Uranus, and Neptune.

The Hubble Space Telescope, launched in 1990, enabled scientists to produce high-resolution images of objects billions of light years away, providing valuable information about the universe.

► Here, the U.S. space shuttle *Endeavour* climbs away from the launch site on June 21, 1993. The first reusable space shuttle, *Columbia*, was launched in April 1981.

WORLD ECONOMY 1950–2000

The industrialized countries of the world had improved their standard of living since 1950, but many poorer countries saw little or no improvement.

This is the flag of the European Union (EU), the successor to the European Economic Community, first formed after the two Treaties of Rome, in March 1957. The EU currently includes 15 member states.

After the end of World War II, countries such as the United States and those in Western Europe enjoyed rapid growth in their economies. After the war, there was an enormous amount of rebuilding to be done, particularly in Europe. There was full employment; and the amount people were paid, compared to what things cost to buy, steadily climbed. In other words, their standard of living rose. To a slightly lesser extent, this also applied to countries such as Australia and New Zealand, as well as Southeast Asian countries, such as Hong Kong, Singapore, and Taiwan.

All this came to a sudden halt in 1973 when the price of crude oil started to increase. The Organization of Petroleum (oil) Exporting Countries (OPEC) was founded in 1960 to get the best price on world markets for its member states' oil. OPEC members include many Middle Eastern Arab states as well as Venezuela, Algeria, Indonesia, Nigeria, and Gabon.

The OECD (Organization for Economic Cooperation and Development) was created to protect weak nations from powerful market forces and aid economic development.

Between 1973 and 1974, OPEC quadrupled the price of oil, which led to a worldwide energy crisis. Poorer nations were badly hit by the rise in oil prices (by 1981, they had increased by almost twenty times) and their economies had to be supported by Western loans. In advanced nations, the energy crisis caused inflation, because the rise in oil prices was passed on in the price of goods, and unemployment rose as fewer goods were exported.

▼ Panic trading on the floor of the New York Stock Exchange in October 1987. In that year, world stock markets all suffered a dramatic fall in share prices.

COMMON MARKETS

Throughout the world, neighboring countries, or countries with shared economic interests, have joined to form powerful associations. Some groups have also set up economic communities, known as common markets. Within them, members buy and sell at favorable rates. They also agree to protect one another from outside economic competition.

In Asia, there are the Asia-Pacific Economic Cooperation Group (APEC) and the Association of Southeast Asian Nations (ASEAN). The North American Free Trade Agreement (NAFTA), originally the United States and Canada, now also includes Mexico. The Group of Seven, or G-7, is a group of countries that meets to monitor the world economic situation. The European Union (EU) is the successor to the European Economic Community (EEC) of the 1950s. It has 15 members and forms a significant world trading bloc. There are plans for common European taxation and legal systems, and by 2002, a common currency, the euro.

The collapse of the Soviet Union in the early 1990s meant that the former communist countries had to compete with third world countries. The richer Western nations had provided aid to poorer countries in the past, but they remained reluctant to share a substantial part of their wealth or expertise.

By the 1990s, it was estimated that the world's oil reserves amounted to around 700 billion barrels. Of these, 360 billion barrels were to be found in the Middle East.

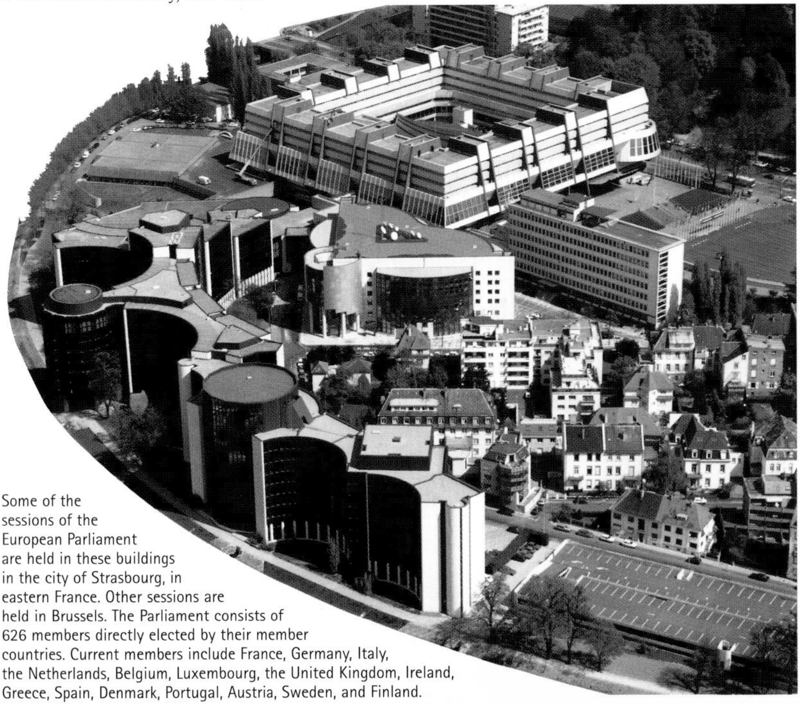

▲ On January 1, 1999, the euro became the common currency that, by 2002, will be used by all members of the European Union. It will replace individual currencies, such as the French franc, Italian lira, Spanish peseta, or German mark.

Some of the sessions of the European Parliament are held in these buildings in the city of Strasbourg, in eastern France. Other sessions are held in Brussels. The Parliament consists of 626 members directly elected by their member countries. Current members include France, Germany, Italy, the Netherlands, Belgium, Luxembourg, the United Kingdom, Ireland, Greece, Spain, Denmark, Portugal, Austria, Sweden, and Finland.

WARS IN ASIA 1950–1988

Japan's defeat and the collapse of colonial rule led to fighting among political rivals. The superpowers took sides, based on economic interest or Cold War strategy.

Australian soldiers were part of the United Nations forces that, by the end of 1950, had pushed the North Koreans back as far as the border with China.

In 1950, many nations in the East had not yet recovered from Japanese invasions during World War II. People needed peace and stability, but many countries were soon at war. These wars caused further damage to people, cities, and land. Eastern countries wanted to be free of distant European powers. The old colonial masters (France, Britain, and the Netherlands) wanted to hold on to these potentially rich lands.

Fighting broke out in Vietnam and its neighbors Laos, Thailand, and Cambodia, and in Indonesia, Malaysia, Burma, and the Philippines. These wars were often complicated by political differences between rival groups seeking independence. The situation became even more dangerous when the Soviet Union, China, and America joined in, offering money, weapons, or technical advice to these rival groups.

▼ Fighting between rival political groups flared up in many parts of Asia between 1946 and 1988. After Japan's defeat in World War II and the collapse of European colonial power, Asia became very unstable.

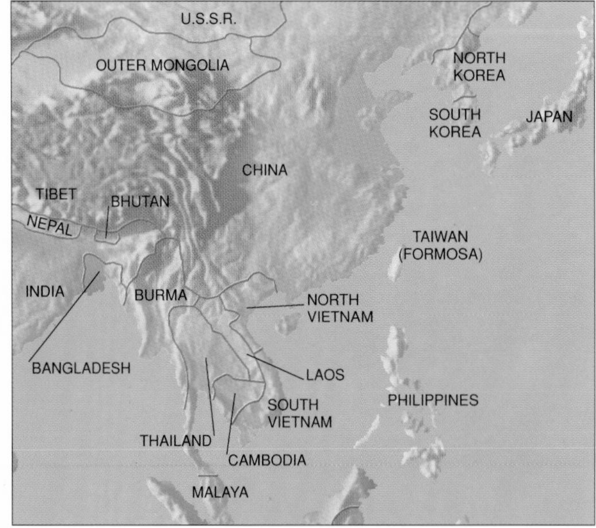

In 1945, French colonial rule was restored to Vietnam. French Foreign Legion troops were sent to North Vietnam in 1953 to try to suppress a communist uprising.

THE KOREAN WAR

The Korean War began when communist North Korea attacked South Korea in June 1950. The United Nations quickly authorized its members to aid South Korea. The United States, along with 16 other countries, began sending troops. Within two months, North Korean troops had captured most of South Korea. In September, UN forces mounted a massive land, sea, and air assault at Inchon, near Seoul. The UN troops recaptured most of South Korea and advanced into the North. By November 1950, they had reached the North Korean border with China. Chinese troops then entered the fighting and forced the UN forces to retreat south. A cease-fire ended the war in July 1953.

Between 1948 and 1960, British troops were sent to Malaya to fight a communist guerrilla offensive. Here, soldiers of a jungle patrol rest beneath a "basha" shelter.

During the war in Vietnam (1964–1975), large areas of the country were devastated. Many civilians were killed and injured. Others were made homeless, and fled as refugees to neighboring lands. Peace finally came in 1976 when Vietnam was united.

Ho-Chi Minh (1892–1969) was a founder member of the French Communist Party. As a revolutionary Vietnamese leader, he led the struggle against French colonial rule and American-supported South Vietnam

WAR IN VIETNAM

After the French were defeated by Vietnamese communists in 1954, the country was temporarily divided into North and South. Planned elections for the country did not take place, and the communists in the North started giving aid to South Vietnamese communists, the Viet Cong, to help them overthrow the government of Ngo Dinh Diem.

In 1965, the United States sent the first troops to help the South—by 1969, there were over half a million U.S. troops in Vietnam. After Richard Nixon became president in 1969, he began to withdraw troops. A cease-fire was signed in 1973, and the remaining American soldiers returned home. During the war more than 57,000 Americans were killed or missing in action.

KEY DATES

1950	North Korean forces invade South Korea
1953	Cease-fire in Korea
1954	Vietnamese communists defeat the French and Vietnam is divided
1963	Civil war starts in Cambodia
1965	First U.S. troops land in Vietnam
1969	Richard Nixon becomes president
1973	All U.S. troops withdrawn from Vietnam
1975	Pol Pot takes over Cambodia
1979	Pol Pot deposed by Vietnamese forces
1993	First free elections in Cambodia for 20 years

CIVIL WAR IN CAMBODIA

In Cambodia, a guerrilla army, the Khmer Rouge, was led by Pol Pot. They sought to overthrow the government of Lon Nol. The Khmer Rouge took over Cambodia in 1975 and Pol Pot became Prime Minister. His regime of terror was overthrown in 1979 by Vietnamese troops.

▲ After Richard Nixon (1913–1994) became president in 1969, he began to withdraw U.S. troops from Vietnam. In 1973, a cease-fire was signed and all U.S. troops were withdrawn.

◀ In Cambodia, Pol Pot (1926–1998) was the leader of the Khmer Rouge guerrillas. They fought a long civil war, beginning in 1963, and took over the country in 1975. Over the following three years, it is estimated that between two and four million people were executed or died of famine and disease.

TERRORISM 1952–2000

During the latter half of the 1900s, people increasingly began to use spectacular acts of violence to promote their particular political causes.

During 1981, some members of the Irish Republican Army (IRA) who were serving prison sentences in Northern Ireland for terrorist offences went on hunger strike. When one of them died, there was rioting.

Some groups of people use violence (terrorism) to gain publicity and win support for a political cause. They are often called freedom fighters by their supporters. Terrorists murder and kidnap people, set off bombs, and hijack aircraft. The reasons behind terrorism are not always the same. Some terrorists want to spread their own political beliefs, while others (nationalists or liberationists) want to establish a separate state for peoples who do not have a country of their own. For example, in the Middle East, terrorists have kidnapped people and carried out bombing campaigns to draw attention to the cause of the Palestinian people, who do not have a homeland.

In Spain, the *Euzkada Ta Askatasuna* (ETA) began a terrorist campaign in the 1960s to pressurize the government into creating a separate state for the Basque people. Similarly, in Northern Ireland from the 1970s, nationalist groups such as the Irish Republican Army (IRA) escalated their terrorist campaign against British rule in the province.

In April 1995, a bomb destroyed the Murrah Federal Building in Oklahoma City, and killed 168 people. The bomber, Timothy McVeigh, thought the federal government had too much control over people's lives.

During the 1970s, the Red Army Faction in West Germany robbed banks, and in 1977, kidnapped and murdered a businessman called Hans-Martin Schleyer. They were also involved with acts of terrorism carried out by Palestinians, including the murder of Israeli athletes at the 1972 Olympic Games in Munich. In Italy, in 1978, terrorists called the Red Brigade kidnapped and murdered the former Italian prime minister, Aldo Moro.

Most governments around the world fight terrorist demands, because they feel that to give in would only encourage other terrorists to commit acts of violence.

▼ In 1988, an American jumbo jet was blown up by a bomb in midair over the Scottish town of Lockerbie, killing 270 people. Terrorists were suspected of being responsible for this act.

FAMINE IN AFRICA 1967–2000

Africa has suffered periodic drought and famine since ancient times. More recently, civil war in newly independent states has only added to the misery.

In 1985, musician Bob Geldof organized the Live Aid rock concert. They raised $70 million to help the victims of the famine in Ethiopia.

Widespread famines have occurred periodically in most parts of sub-Saharan Africa since ancient times. Factors such as a failure of the annual rains, poor soil conditions, and low food reserves have all played a part in these tragedies. Following independence in the latter half of the 1900s, civil wars have added to the misery.

CIVIL UNREST AND FAMINE

Most of the worst famines during this period happened in countries that suffered civil unrest. In Nigeria, the people who lived in the east of the country were the Christian Ibo tribe. They were oppressed by the majority Islamic Hausa and Fulani peoples. When tens of thousands of Ibos were massacred, the Eastern Region declared its independence as the Republic of Biafra in May 1967. War continued between the two sides until January 1970. It is believed that over a million Biafrans died of starvation because the Nigerians stopped food getting through to them.

Civil strife in Mozambique in the 1980s led to the almost total collapse of health care, education, and food production. By the beginning of the 1990s, nearly a million people had been killed. Another one-and-a-half million had fled the country and were refugees.

During the 1991–1993 civil war in Somalia, around 300,000 people starved to death because the war made foreign food aid too dangerous to deliver.

▼ Zaire has had periods of military uprising and civil strife that have made life dangerous for foreign aid workers. In 1994, the arrival of hundreds of thousands of refugees from neighboring Rwanda prompted massive aid from international relief agencies.

Ethiopia suffered from drought and famine for many years. Between 1977 and 1991, the combination of civil war and famine killed millions of Ethiopians.

In Ethiopia, the combination of the withdrawal of aid from the U.S.S.R., drought, and a civil war in the 1970s and 1980s led to millions of people dying from famine. Through the Western media, people all around the world became aware of the catastrophe. International relief charities, such as the Red Cross, the Live Aid rock concert of 1985, and individual governments all provided vast amounts of aid for the victims.

▲ Foreign aid does more than supply food in emergencies or crises. Here, we see the results of a project to provide clean water for a community in Kenya. Projects like this help to improve the health of local people.

WARS IN THE MIDDLE EAST 1956–2000

Following the formation of the State of Israel in 1948, there have been many tensions in the Middle East that have led to bitter disputes and even war.

The Six-Day War took place between June 5–10, 1967. In a surprise attack. Israeli bombers destroyed Egyptian planes, and then sent in troops to capture the Egyptian soldiers left in Sinai.

The lands around Jerusalem have long been held by the Jewish people to be their traditional home. After World War II, many Jewish refugees settled in Palestine, although the area was occupied by Arab peoples. The State of Israel was formed in 1948, and fighting broke out with neighboring Arab countries and continued on and off for many years.

In 1956, Egypt took over control of the Suez Canal, which was owned by Britain and France. Because it felt threatened, Israel invaded Egyptian territory in the Sinai, and Britain and France attacked the canal area. There was international disapproval, and the United States and U.S.S.R. both called for a cease-fire. UN troops moved in to keep the peace after the withdrawal of Israeli, British, and French troops.

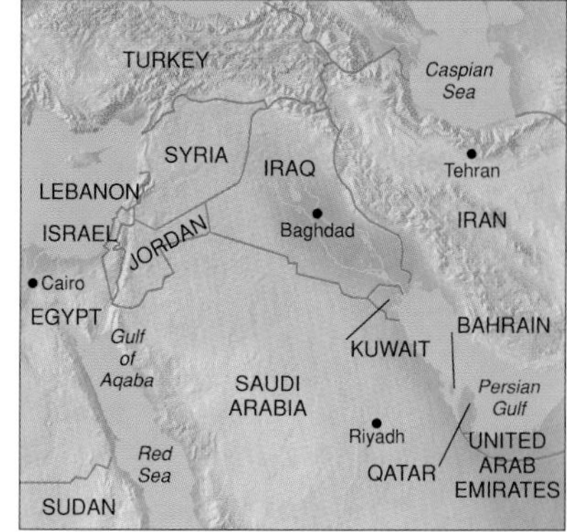

There have been many conflicts in the Middle East between Israeli, Palestinian, and Arab peoples, especially since 1948. Some areas of territory are still in dispute.

Tensions continued to grow in the 1960s between Israel and the Arab countries of Egypt, Jordan, and Syria. They were aided by several other Arab countries including Iraq, Kuwait, Saudi Arabia, Algeria, and Sudan. Both sides were hostile and unwilling to negotiate their differences. Both sides were also busy getting their troops ready for a possible armed conflict. In May 1967, Egypt closed the Gulf of Aqaba to Israeli shipping.

▼ The Yom Kippur War started in 1973 when Egypt and Syria launched a surprise attack on Israel after it refused to give up land captured during the Six-Day War.

In 1980, Iraq invaded Iraq. The two countries fought a long and bitter war. It did not end until August 1988, and cost the lives of over a million soldiers, and almost two million wounded.

Saddam Hussein (1937–) is the leader of Iraq. He fought a costly war against Iran (1980–1988) and invaded Kuwait in August 1990. U.S., British, and other Middle East forces drove him out in February 1991.

SIX-DAY WAR

In June 1967, the Israeli air force launched a surprise air attack on the Arab forces' air bases, which took them completely out of action. They then swiftly moved their army to occupy the Gaza Strip and parts of the Sinai. They also pushed their border with Jordan back and captured the Golan Heights from Syria.

IRAQI AGRESSION

In 1979, the Shah of Iran was deposed and replaced by Islamic fundamentalist Shiite Muslims led by the Ayatollah Khomeini. Tension between Iran and Iraq finally resulted in Iraq's invasion of the oil-rich Iranian territory of Khuzistan in 1980. Iraq feared the power of the new Iranian government set up by the Ayatollah Khomeini. When the war ended in 1988, neither country had made any gains but the cost was enormous—over a million dead, and nearly two million injured.

Rivalries within the Arab world have often been caused by the region's rich oil deposits. In 1990, Iraq invaded Kuwait to improve its sea access. The UN Security Council passed several resolutions demanding that Iraq withdraw its troops immediately. When Saddam Hussein refused, a multinational force led by the United States forced him to withdraw. Kuwait City was liberated within five days and thousands of Iraq's soldiers were captured. Retreating Iraqis caused huge ecological damage because they set fire to most of Kuwait's oil wells.

Other tensions in the region are caused by religious differences. There are two main divisions of Islam: Sunni and Shiite. Sunnis follow "the practice of the Prophet." Shiites follow the teachings of the Prophet Muhammad's son-in-law, Ali.

KEY DATES	
1948	Independent State of Israel declared; fighting with Arab neighbors erupts
1956	Suez Crisis
1964	Palestinian Liberation Organization (PLO) founded in Lebanon
1967	Six-Day War between Israel and Egypt
1973	Yom Kippur War in Israel
1979	Saddam Hussein becomes president of Iraq; Shah of Iran deposed
1980	Iraq invades Iran
1988	Iran-Iraq War ends
1990	Iraq invades Kuwait
1991	Iraq forced out of Kuwait

▼ U.S. forces mounted a massive international military campaign to liberate their ally Kuwait, when Iraq invaded in 1990. Preparation for the war was extensive, but actual fighting was fairly short lived.

THE SCIENTIFIC REVOLUTION 1950–2000

The second half of the 1900s was a period of rapid development in science and technology. The arrival of the computer age revolutionized people's lives.

Since lasers were invented in the early 1960s, they have been used for a wide range of tasks, including eye surgery, construction work, mapping, and weapon guidance systems.

Scientists and business people were able to develop the discoveries made earlier in the century and put them to practical use. Industry and business realized that there were enormous financial benefits to be made by working with universities and other academic centers and a great deal of important research was done in partnership between the two.

ELECTRONICS

The most important breakthrough was the silicon chip, a tiny electronic component that could be cheaply mass-produced. It replaced old, bulky, and fragile pieces of equipment, and allowed much smaller, but more powerful, electronic machines to be built. Microprocessors—complex circuits fitted on a single chip—became widely used in all electrical devices ranging from computers and space rockets to robots and telephones. The silicon chip changed life radically in the late 1900s.

The silicon chip microprocessor, developed in the United States in 1971, caused a technological revolution. The chips were printed with tiny electronic circuits so that computers could process and store information.

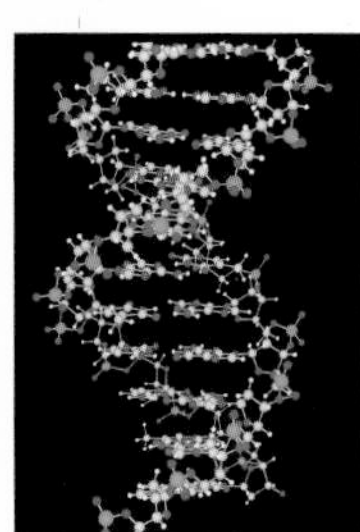

▲ The double helix of DNA was discovered by Crick and Watson in 1953. It carries the blueprint for all of an organism's cells, along with all the instructions that control their activities. This discovery helped scientists understand the cause of many diseases.

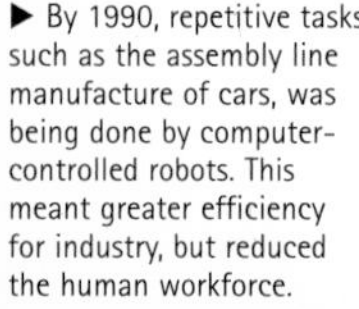

► By 1990, repetitive tasks, such as the assembly line manufacture of cars, was being done by computer-controlled robots. This meant greater efficiency for industry, but reduced the human workforce.

THE COMPUTER AGE

The developments in electronics also led to a revolution in communications. Copy and fax machines meant that office workers could handle vast amounts of information more quickly than ever before. They could also communicate rapidly with other people around the world. As the means of communications improved, information became more freely available. By the end of the 1900s, anyone with a personal computer and a telephone line could contact millions of other people around the world in an instant using the Internet.

In industry, electronics also brought about a new industrial revolution. By the 1990s, most aspects of the manufacturing process in a wide range of industries were computer controlled. Repetitive tasks on assembly lines were carried out by electronic machines or robots. Stock control, distribution, and administrative systems also came under the control of computer technology

MEDICAL BREAKTHROUGHS

First developed in the 1960s, lasers were used in surgery to burn away diseased tissue and perform delicate eye operations. In the 1950s, American and British scientists discovered the structure of DNA, the basic building blocks from which living cells are made. This knowledge led eventually to the production of new drugs by genetic engineering, which helped cure serious diseases. The discovery of DNA means that many genetic illnesses, passed down through families, will be curable.

Genetic engineering also raised the possibility of creating new or improved strains of plants and animals, resistant to disease. This technology has helped to feed people in poorer countries by increasing the amount that the land can support.

◀ The Hubble Space Telescope was launched into orbit by the U.S. space shuttle *Discovery* in April 1990. It allowed scientists to capture images of objects billions of light years away in space.

▲ The first communication satellite was launced in 1960. The introduction, in 1964, of geosynchronous satellites, which remain over the same place on Earth, meant that any two places on Earth could be linked almost instantly.

THE WORLD WIDE WEB

The World Wide Web (WWW) was invented in 1990, to allow users to "surf" the Internet quickly and easily. By clicking on the screen with a mouse, users can move between pages of information located on a vast network of computers around the world. Each page has "hot spots," or links, connecting it to related pages.

▼ Search engines greatly speed up the process of finding Web pages and specific pieces of information on the Web.

▼ The Web allows people to watch live video clips of a current U.S. space mission.

▲ Many goods and services can be ordered and paid for over the Internet.

▶ Using e-mail, people can send letters and pictures to each other across the world within minutes.

◀ Information on sports, movies, museums, and many other types of entertainment can be found on the Internet.

THE ENVIRONMENT 1950–2000

Unlike any other species on Earth, humankind has the power to destroy the world. People only recently grasped that their environment was being threatened.

In the latter half of the 1900s, people began to realize that the Earth was in danger, threatened with pollution and overexploitation from ignorance and greed. At first, only a few naturalists, like Rachel Carson, dared to speak up. Her book *Silent Spring* caused a sensation when it was published in 1962. It showed how widespread the damage was when pesticides were overused, and led to the banning of DDT (an insecticide) in the United States and many other countries.

On the night of March 24, 1989, the *Exxon Valdez*, a 985-ft. (300-m) oil tanker, ran aground in Prince William Sound, Alaska. The ship leaked over 35,000 tons of toxic petroleum over the next two days and was the biggest oil spill in American history. It destroyed much wildlife and required a major cleanup operation.

Then, pressure groups such as Greenpeace and Friends of the Earth also began to campaign. It slowly became clear that the environment had been seriously damaged.

The oceans in many parts of the world have been overfished, and in many cases scientists believe that for stocks to return to their previous levels, fishing would have to stop completely for between five and ten years. Car exhausts and factories pump fumes into the air. Some of these gases mix with clouds to form acid rain, which kills plants. In many cities, like Los Angeles, the air quality is so poor that smog forms over them. Continual exposure to smog causes serious breathing problems and premature death.

▼ Cities such as São Paulo in Brazil suffer from dangerous levels of air pollution from motor vehicles and industry.

Hundreds of oil-well fires were lit by Iraqi troops retreating from Kuwait in 1991, causing widespread pollution in the desert. It took a year to extinguish them.

PROTECTING THE ENVIRONMENT

In the 1970s, British scientists working in Antarctica discovered that the ozone layer above them was becoming thinner. The ozone layer is vital to all life on Earth because it blocks much of the sun's harmful ultraviolet radiation. It was discovered that the protective barrier was being seriously damaged by the release of chemicals called CFCs. They were used in refrigeration and as a propellant for aerosols. These chemicals have now been banned in many countries.

By the 1980s, some governments had passed laws to protect the environment, but some scientists believed that these attempts to protect our planet were too little and too late. Change was slow to take effect, because at first people did not believe that the Earth was really in danger. New information was collected by scientists that proved that the threat was real. Clean (nonpolluting) products started to appear, but they proved expensive to buy and less profitable to produce.

▲ Huge tracts of the tropical rain forests in South America were being destroyed so that local farmers could graze cattle.

▲ In 1900, the world's population was around one billion. By 1990, it had risen to almost six billion. By 2050, almost ten billion people are expected to live on Earth.

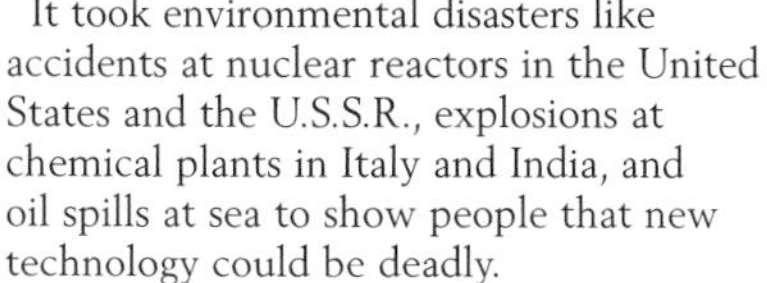

It took environmental disasters like accidents at nuclear reactors in the United States and the U.S.S.R., explosions at chemical plants in Italy and India, and oil spills at sea to show people that new technology could be deadly.

Public opinion gradually forced many governments to take action and to reduce pollution. Laws were passed to protect the environment and encourage conservation and recycling.

In the poorer countries of the world, however, people's only income still comes from farming or forestry, which often damage the land. Their governments do not like being told by the developed world to slow their growth to reduce pollution.

RENEWABLE ENERGY

Most of the world's electricity is produced in power plants by burning coal, oil, or gas. These fuels are known as fossil fuels, and there is a limited supply of them to be taken from the Earth. Electricity made from rivers (hydroelectric), the sun (solar), and from the wind, is a nonpolluting "renewable resource," because it will not run out.

▼ Nonpolluting wind turbines are built on exposed sites where wind power is used to generate electricity. They are not perfect and can cause significant noise pollution.

▶ Solar power uses the sun's heat to provide a clean, nonpolluting source of energy. Solar panels can be relatively inexpensive, and yet are very efficient.

ASIAN "TIGER" ECONOMIES 1970–2000

With the help of Western aid, economic growth in the countries of Southeast Asia was very rapid. It soon outstripped that of the Europe and the United States.

Manufacturing is the single most important economic activity in Japan. Japanese factories uses the most advanced equipment and processes available, and they produce high quality goods for export to the rest of the world.

In Japan, government and business had to rebuild their economy after World War II. They took a different approach than China, and planned a complete industrial redevelopment of their country, and rapid capitalist growth. The United States had occupied Japan and encouraged it to move toward a democracy. They also helped Japan financially, and after the war, the United States was providing money at the rate of more than ten million dollars a week. The Japanese brought in industrial and land reforms and greatly improved the education system for their children. Free elections were held, and women were not only allowed to vote for the first time, but some were also elected to the Japanese parliament. In the 1970s and 1980s, Japan's economic growth was one of the most rapid in the world.

Along with other stock markets around the world, the Tokyo Stock Market saw panic selling in October 1987. In one day it traded over one billion shares.

OTHER ECONOMIES

Although it took longer to get started, by the late 1970s and 1980s, South Korea's industrialization was growing by nearly ten percent every year, far more than Western countries. The United States provided a large amount of support, as did Japan. Hong Kong also became a major Southeast Asian financial trading center, attracting much outside investment.

Malaysia became a major exporter of both raw materials—oil and natural gas, rubber, palm oil, timber, and metals such as tin—and manufactured goods such as electrical machinery and semiconductors.

Singapore soon became one of the countries with the highest standards of living when it started to build up its industry in the 1960s. Shipping played a growing part in the economy along with the building of extensive oil refineries. It became a major exporter of petroleum products, rubber, and electrical goods.

By the beginning of the 1990s, however, these once-booming economies began to suffer because of the downturn in world markets. Japan's export-led economy, worth more than half of the region's total, had been in poor shape since 1989 and over the next ten years its stock-market value fell by two thirds. This inevitably had a knock-on effect on the other countries in the region, which slowed their growth dramatically.

Built as a symbol of Malaysia's once-booming economy, the twin Petronas Towers in Kuala Lumpur are the world's tallest buildings, at a height of 1,483 ft. (452m).

PEACEKEEPING 1950–2000

In 1945, the United Nations was formed by the international community to guarantee civil liberties and to work for peace and stability on a global scale.

Fifty countries formed the United Nations after World War II. By the end of the century, membership was up to over 180 countries.

The United Nations was formed after World War II with the intention of trying to make sure that such a war could not happen again. It was established to maintain international peace and security; to develop friendly relations among nations; to achieve international cooperation in solving economic, social, and cultural problems; and to encourage respect for basic human rights and fundamental freedoms.

Delegates from 50 nations attended what was known as the United Nations Conference on International Organization in San Francisco, in April 1945. The United Nations Charter was approved in June and permanent headquarters for the organization were built in New York City.

During the 1990s, Britain used its significant naval presence to support UN peacekeeping and humanitarian missions in many parts of the world.

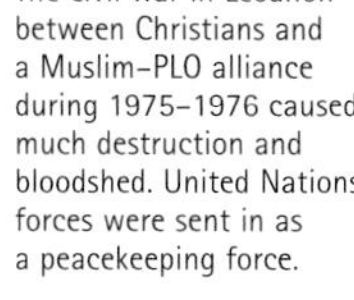

The civil war in Lebanon between Christians and a Muslim-PLO alliance during 1975–1976 caused much destruction and bloodshed. United Nations forces were sent in as a peacekeeping force.

THE SECURITY COUNCIL

Keeping international peace is the job of the UN Security Council. The permanent members are China, France, Great Britain, the United States, and Russia, plus ten other members elected for two-year terms.

WORLD PEACEKEEPING

The first use of a United Nations peacekeeping force was during the Korean War in 1950. They remained there until 1953, when an armistice was signed. Further deployment happened in Egypt during the Suez Crisis in 1956—UN forces supervised the withdrawal of invading British, French, and Israeli forces.

The first large-scale UN operation in Africa went into action in 1960. Belgium had granted independence to the Republic of the Congo, now known as Zaire, but civil unrest threatened the new country. UN troops were able to provide aid as well as security. In the following years, UN peacekeeping forces were involved in many troubled areas of the world, including Cyprus, Lebanon, Somalia, and Rwanda.

▶ During conflicts in the former Yugoslavia in the 1990s, UN peacekeeping troops were fired on by more than one side. Here, French UN troops keep a watchful eye out for snipers in Sarajevo's notorious sniper alley.

SOUTH AFRICA 1990–2000

South Africa was the last bastion of imperialist, white minority rule in Africa. The release of Nelson Mandela from prison in 1990 signaled the end of apartheid.

Frederick W. de Klerk (1936–) became president of South Africa in 1989, after P. W. Botha resigned because of his health. He worked toward ending apartheid.

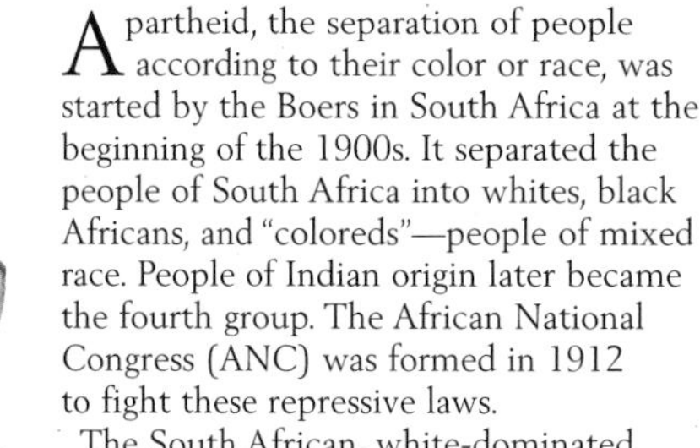

Apartheid, the separation of people according to their color or race, was started by the Boers in South Africa at the beginning of the 1900s. It separated the people of South Africa into whites, black Africans, and "coloreds"—people of mixed race. People of Indian origin later became the fourth group. The African National Congress (ANC) was formed in 1912 to fight these repressive laws.

The South African, white-dominated government passed a series of harsh laws to try to suppress opposition. In 1960, it made all black political parties illegal after the violent antiapartheid riots at Sharpeville. In the mid-1970s, the government relaxed its controls a little and started to allow some unions. In the mid-1980s, the government allowed coloreds into Parliament, but not black people.

The ANC and other political parties wanted a true democracy in which everyone had a vote, regardless of their color or race. P. W. Botha, president of South Africa from 1978, was the first white leader to want reform.

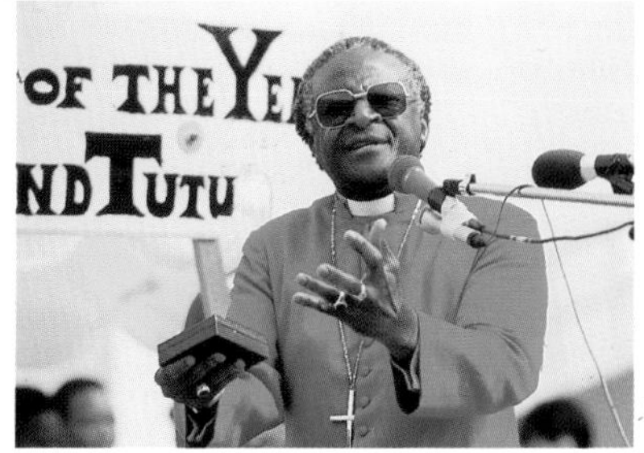

As Archbishop of Cape Town and head of the Anglican Church in South Africa, Desmond Tutu won the Nobel Peace Prize for his fight against apartheid in 1984.

THE REFORMER: F. W. DE KLERK

Although Botha had made some changes to make life fairer for blacks, these did not made any radical difference. His health failed him, and he resigned in 1989. A reformer, F. W. de Klerk, then became president, and in 1990, ended the ban on black people's political parties, including the ANC. In order to show he really wanted change, he also had many black political prisoners released from prison. One of these was Nelson Mandela, who had been in prison since 1964. De Klerk had regular meetings with him, both while he was in prison, and after his release.

▲ Nelson Rolihlahla Mandela (1918–) shared the Nobel Peace Prize with F. W. de Klerk in 1993 for their work in ending apartheid. Following free elections in 1994, he became the first black president of South Africa in 1994.

▶ Under apartheid, many black South Africans were moved out of cities and forced to live in shabby and crowded conditions in shantytowns on the outskirts. Their movement was severely restricted.

THE END OF APARTHEID

Nelson Mandela became the leader of the ANC. He campaigned for the civil rights of his people, but he also argued strongly for a peaceful settlement. By working closely with de Klerk, it was possible for both white and black people to work for change. In 1992, de Klerk organized a whites-only referendum, asking them whether they would like to end apartheid. Two thirds of the voters were in favor of ending apartheid.

After a great deal of negotiation, the first free election, in which black people could also vote, was held in South Africa, in April 1994. The ANC won a decisive victory, and Nelson Mandela became the first black president of South Africa when de Klerk handed over power to him in May. Although the ANC now formed a government, de Klerk stayed on as one of two vice presidents.

Although a great victory for equality had been won, the new democracy still faced enormous problems. By the end of the century there were two million children who were receiving no schooling at all. Over half the people still lived in homes without electricity. Twelve million people had no access to a steady supply of clean drinking water. A third of the adult population was unemployed. The huge gap between rich and poor led to street crime becoming a major problem.

The modern city of Johannesburg is the financial center of South Africa and lies in the area known as Witwatersrand, at the heart of the gold-mining area.

▲ Supporters of Nelson Mandela celebrate the triumph of the African National Congress after the first free elections in South Africa, in 1994. The ANC were clear winners and Nelson Mandela became president.

◀ Following the end of apartheid, some white South African farmers were concerned about their property. They thought that the huge farms that they lived on would be taken away from them by the government and given to black farmers in land redistribution.

YEAR 2000 AND BEYOND

The 1900s ended with a technological revolution, yet our world is still threatened by war, poverty, and human rights abuses. What does the future hold for us?

Racial harmony, tolerance, equal opportunity, and individual freedom will be important factors for achieving world peace and prosperity in the future.

The 1900s saw more change in the world than any previous century. Most of the household objects that we now use every day and take for granted did not exist a hundred years ago. The automobile was in its infancy, and telephone and radio were still in the early stages of development. Televison, VCRs, credit cards, computers, and jet airplanes were unheard of.

At the end of the century, the ability to communicate instantly with people all over the world—thanks to modern satellite telecommunications and the Internet—brought about an explosion of information exchange. It also made it difficult for governments to keep their people ignorant of what was happening in the rest of the world.

PREDICTIONS AND CONCERNS

It would have been very hard for someone living in 1900 to foretell these changes, and equally, we can only guess at our future in the coming century.

There are some things that seem very likely, such as doctors and scientists inventing new ways of preventing and curing diseases. Other predictions are more speculative. We would like to think that major wars will be a thing of the past, but there is no guarantee of this.

The growing population of the world is a major concern for the future. Although as a planet we grow enough food to feed everyone, millions go without because it is not distributed evenly. Most of the children in poorer countries still receive little or no education, which makes self-improvement impossible.

The environmental concerns of the latter half of the 1900s will continue to perplex governments and scientists. The Earth has finite resources that need to be carefully managed and shared among all of its peoples.

International cooperation will be an important factor in the exploration of our resource-rich solar system. This artist's impression of a manned base on Mars shows what many people, including the men and women at NASA, believe will be the next great space adventure. It will take an enormous amount of money and resources to accomplish, but there is good reason to believe it may happen by the year 2050.

INDEX

J

K

L

ACKNOWLEDGMENTS

The publishers wish to thank the following for their contributions to this book:

Photographs
(*t* = top; *b* = bottom; *m* = middle; *l* = left; *r* = right)
Page 1 *bl* ET Archive, *ml* Bridgeman Art Library; 2 *mtl* Werner Forman Archive, *m* ET Archive; 6–7 Gavin Hellier/Robert Harding Picture Library; 8 Robert Harding Picture Library; 16 ET Archive; 17 Ancient Art & Architecture Collection Ltd; 18 AKG; 19 *t* ET Archive, *ml* AKG; 20 ET Archive; 21 ET Archive; 22 *tl* ET Archive, *bl* ET Archive, *br* ET Archive; 23 ET Archive; 27 Ancient Art & Architecture Collection Ltd; 28 ET Archive; 30 ET Archive; 32 AKG; 33 ET Archive; 34 ET Archive; 36 *t* ET Archive, *b* ET Archive; 38 Roy Rainford/Robert Harding Picture Library; 47 *t* Ronald Sheridan/Ancient Art & Architecture Collection Ltd, *b* Ronald Sheridan/Ancient Art & Architecture Collection Ltd; 57 Robert Harding Picture Library; 58 Richard Ashworth/Robert Harding Picture Library; 59 Richard Ashworth/Robert Harding Picture Library; 61 ET Archive; 63 *t* ET Archive, *b* ET Archive; 65 Ancient Art & Architecture Collection Ltd; 68 Robert Frerck/Robert Harding Picture Library; 69 Bridgeman Art Library; 72 Bridgeman Art Library; 73 *t* ET Archive, *b* ET Archive; 77 ET Archive; 78 *tl* Ancient Art & Architecture Collection, *tr* Bridgeman Art Library, *b* Bridgeman Art Library; 80 ET Archive; 81 The Bridgeman Art Library; 87 AKG; 89 *t* Robert Harding Picture Library, *b* Robert Harding Picture Library; 92 Bridgeman Art Library; 95 *t* R. Sheridan/Ancient Art & Architecture Collection, *m* Ancient Art & Architecture Collection; 96 *t* ET Archive, *b* ET Archive; 97 *tl* ET Archive, *tr* ET Archive; 98 ET Archive; 104 ET Archive; 106 ET Archive; 107 ET Archive; 112 ET Archive; 113 ET Archive; 115 Robert Harding Picture Library/Geoff Renner; 120 ET Archive; 124 ET Archive; 125 *m* ET Archive, *b* ET Archive; 126 Robert Harding Picture Library; 127 A. Barrington/Ancient Art & Architecture Collection; 128 ET Archive; 137 *tl* ET Archive, *tr* ET Archive, *b* ET Archive; 138 Bridgeman Art Library; 139 ET Archive; 144 *tl* Werner Forman Archive, *tr* Werner Forman Archive, *bl* Werner Forman Archive; 145 Bridgeman Art Library; 147 ET Archive; 150 Bridgeman Art Library; 155 *t* Ancient Art & Architecture Collection Ltd, *b* Bridgeman Art Library; 156 Bridgeman Art Library; 157 *t* AKG, *b* AKG; 160 Margaret Collier/Robert Harding Picture Library; 163 *mr* ET Archive, *br* ET Archive; 164 Werner Forman Archive; 165 Werner Forman Archive; 167 Bridgeman Art Library; 168 *tl* ET Archive, *ml* AKG; 169 *t* AKG, *m* AKG, *b* AKG; 171 *t* ET Archive, *b* Ancient Art & Architecture Collection Ltd; 173 Bridgeman Art Library; 175 ET Archive; 176 Bridgeman Art Library; 177 *t* Bridgeman Art Library, *m* Werner Forman Archive; 178 *t* ET Archive, *b* ET Archive; 179 *t* ET Archive, *b* ET Archive; 182 Bridgeman Art Library; 183 *t* AKG, *m* ET Archive; 184 *t* Bridgeman Art Library, *b* Bridgeman Art Library; 185 Bridgeman Art Library; 186 *tl* ET Archive, *ml* Bridgeman Art Library; 190 ET Archive; 194 ET Archive; 195 ET Archive; 196 *l* Bridgeman Art Library, *b* Bridgeman Art Library; 197 *t* ET Archive, *m* ET Archive; 198 ET Archive; 199 ET Archive; 201 ET Archive; 203 *t* Bridgeman Art Library, *b* Bridgeman Art Library; 205 *t* ET Archive, *b* ET Archive; 206 *tl* ET Archive, *tr* ET Archive; 207 ET Archive; 208 *tl* ET Archive, *ml* ET Archive; 209 ET Archive; 217 Peter Newark's American Pictures; 218 ET Archive; 219 ET Archive; 220 ET Archive; 223 ET Archive; 226 *tl* ET Archive, *b* ET Archive; 227 *t* ET Archive, *b* ET Archive; 228 ET Archive; 229 *t* ET Archive, *b* ET Archive; 230 ET Archive; 231 *t* ET Archive, *b* ET Archive; 233 Hulton Getty Picture Library; 234 Hulton Getty Picture Library; 235 AKG; 236 ET Archive; 237 ET Archive; 238 ET Archive; 239 ET Archive; 241 ET Archive; 242 *tr* Hulton Getty Picture Library, *ml* Hulton Getty Picture Library, *b* ET Archive; 243 ET Archive; 244 *t* Hulton Getty Picture Library, *b* ET Archive; 245 ET Archive; 246 ET Archive; 247 ET Archive; 248 *ml* Peter Newark's American Pictures, *bl* Peter Newark's American Pictures; 249 Mary Evans Picture Library; 250 ET Archive; 251 ET Archive; 252 ET Archive; 254 ET Archive; 255 Imperial War Museum; 256 ILN; 257 *t* Hulton Deutsch Collection, *b* Hulton Getty Picture Library; 258 ET Archive; 259 *b* ET Archive; 260 Hulton Getty Picture Library; 261 Hulton Getty Picture Library; 262 *tl* ILN, *ml* ILN, *tr* ILN; 263 *tl* ET Archive, *tr* ILN, *mr* ILN; 264 *tl* Imperial War Musem, *tr* ET Archive, *b* ET Archive; 265 *tr* ET Archive, *mr* ILN; 266 *tl* ILN, *b* Hulton Deutsch Collection; 267 *t* Hulton Getty Picture Library, *mr* ET Archive, *br* ILN, *bl* ET Archive; 268 *tl* Hulton Getty Picture Library, *tr* Hulton Getty Picture Library, *bl* Hulton Getty Picture Library; 269 *mr* Corbis, *b Novosti*; 270 *tl* AKG, *ml* ILN, *b* ET Archive; 271 *t* ILN, *tr* AKG, *br* AKG; 272 *tl* ILN, *ml* ET Archive, *tr* Magnum Photos, *b* Magnum Photos; 273 *tr* ET Archive, *b* ET Archive; 274 *tl* AKG, *ml* AKG, *tr* ET Archive, *b* AKG; 275 *tl* ILN, *tr* ET Archive, *b* ET Archive; 276 *tr* ILN, *b* ET Archive; 277 *tr* Imperial War Museum, *m* ILN; 278 ET Archive; 279 *tr* Imperial War Museum, *b* ET Archive; 280 *tl* ET Archive, *b* ET Archive; 281 *tl* ET Archive, *tr* ET Archive, *ml* ILN, *br* Hulton Getty Picture Library; 282 Hulton Deutsch Collection; 283 *tr* Hulton Getty Picture Library, *bl* Hulton Getty Picture Library; 284 *tl* Imperial War Museum, *b* Hulton Getty Picture Library; 285 ET Archive; 286 Science & Society Picture Library; 288 NASA/Science Photo Library; 289 *tl* Rex Features, *tr* Rob Francis/Robert Harding Picture Library, *br* Stuart Franklin/Magnum Photos, *bl* G.Mendel/Magnum Photos; 290 *tr* Popperfoto, *bl* Rex Features; 291 *t* Hulton Getty Picture Library, *m* Magnum Photos, *br* ET Archive, *bl* Hulton Getty Picture Library; 292 *ml* Novosti/Science Photo Library, *bl* NASA/Science Photo Library, *tr* NASA/Science Photo Library; 293 *t* NASA/Science Photo Library, *b* NASA/Science Photo Library; 294 *tr* OECD, *b* Elliot Erwitt/Magnum Photos; 295 *t* Abbas/Magnum Photos, *mr* Popperfoto/Reuters, *b* European Parliament/Airdiasol; 296 *tl* Hulton Getty Picture Library, *tr* Roger-Viollet, *bl* Corbis; 297 *t* Magnum Photos, *b* Griffiths/Magnum Photos; 298 *tl* James Natchwey/Magnum Photos, *tr* Rex Features, *b* Rex Features; 299 *tr* F. Scianna/Magnum Photos, *bl* Liba Taylor/Robert Harding Picture Library, *br* Robert Harding Picture Library; 300 *tl* Burt Glinn/Magnum Photos, *b* Jones-Griffiths/Magnum Photos; 301 *t* Jean Gaumy/Magnum Photos, *mr* Stuart Franklin/Magnum, *br* Steve McCurry/Magnum Photos; 302 *tl* Hank Morgan/University of Massachusetts at Amherst/Science Photo Library, *ml* Alfred Pasieka/Science Photo Library, *b* Brian Brake/Science Photo Library, *t* Tim Davis/Science Photo Library, *tr* Dr Jeremy Burgess/Science Photo Library; 303 *t* NASA/Science Photo Library, *mr* NASA/Science Photo Library; 304 *tr* Steve McCurry/Magnum Photos, *b* Bruno Barbey/Magnum Photos; 305 *tl* G.Peress/Magnum Photos, *tr* Thomas Hopker/Magnum Photos, *bl* Russell D. Curtis/Science Photo Library, *br* Martin Bond/Science Photo Library; 306 *tl* Robert Harding Picture Library, *bl* Rob Francis/Robert Harding Picture Library, *tr* Rene Burri/Magnum Photos; 307 *ml* Micha Bar-Am/Magnum Photos, *br* Paul Lowe/Magnum Photos; 308 *tl* G.Mendel/Magnum Photos, *ml* G.Mendel/Magnum Photos, *b* Frank Spooner Pictures/Gamma, *tr* Gideon Mendel/Magnum Photos; 309 *t* Frank Spooner Pictures/Gamma, *m* Frank Spooner Pictures/Gamma, *b* Frank Spooner Pictures/Gamma; 310 *tl* Eli Reed/Magnum Photos, *b* Detlev Van Ravenwaay/Science Photo Library.

Artwork archivists Wendy Allison, Steve Robinson

Editorial and design Aimee Johnson, Sheila Clewley, Julie Ferris, Emma Wild, Dileri Johnston, Giles Sparrow, Joanne Brown

Artists Jonathan Adams, Hemesh Alles, Marion Appleton, Sue Barclay, R. Barnett, Noel Bateman, Simon Bishop, Richard Bonson, Nick Cannan, Vanessa Card, Tony Chance, Harry Clow, Stephen Conlin, Peter Dennis, Dave Etchell, Jeff Farrow, James Field, Ian Fish, Michael Fisher, Eugene Fleury, Chris Forsey, Dewey Franklin, Terry Gabbey, Fred Gambino, John Gillatt, Matthew Gore, Jeremy Gower, Neil Gower, Ray Grinaway, Allan Hardcastle, Nick Harris, Nicholas Hewetson, Bruce Hogarth, Christian Hook, Richard Hook, Simon Huson, John James, Peter Jarvis, John Kelly, Deborah Kindred, Adrian Lascombe, Chris Lenthall, Jason Lewis, Chris Lyon, Kevin Maddison, Shirley Mallinson, Shane Marsh, David MacAllister, Angus McBride, Stefan Morris, Jackie Moore, Teresa Morris, Frank Nichols, Chris D. Orr, Sharon Pallent, R. Payne, R. Philips, Jayne Pickering, Melvyn Pickering, Malcolm Porter, Mike Posen, Mike Roffe, Chris Rothero, David Salarya, Mike Saunders, Rodney Shackell, Rob Shone, Mark Stacey, Paul Stangroom, Branca Surla, Smiljka Surla, Stephen Sweet, Mike Taylor, George Thompson, Martin Wilson, David Wright, Paul Wright